NON-BORING TEST PREP S

Tutor Ted's SAT* practice tests

Ted Dorsey, M.A.

Martha Marion

Linda Stowe

Than Rossoff

Claudine Quadrat

For more information, visit our website: **www.tutorted.com**

Book Design: Sherri Nielsen
Book Layout: Anita Johnson

ISBN: 978-0-9834471-6-0

STAY CONNECTED!

We love to connect with our students!
Follow us on Twitter, add us on Facebook, or just send us an old-fashioned email!

 TWITTER @tutorted

 FACEBOOK /tutorted

 INSTAGRAM @tutorted

YOUTUBE /tutorted

 EMAIL sayhello@tutorted.com

Special Thanks!

Special Thanks to:
Matt Casper
Maryann Dorsey
Nathan Fox
Wes Carroll
Uma Incrocci

Table of Contents

A Note from Ted 5

PREPARE FOR LIFTOFF 6

Practice in the Style of the Test 6
Find Out What You Know...and What You Don't 6
Track Your Success And Aim for Improvement 6
An Overview Of The SAT 7
The Myth Of The Bad Test Taker 8
Before The Test 10
During The Test 11
After The Test 12
Score Choice To The Rescue 13
Superscore! 14
Official Stuff 14

PRACTICE TEST 1 17

Answer Sheet 17
Reading 24
Writing and Language 39
Math — No Calculator 52
Math — Calculator 58
Essay 68
Answers & Solutions 71

PRACTICE TEST 2 91

Answer Sheet 91
Reading 98
Writing and Language 114
Math — No Calculator 127
Math — Calculator 133
Essay 144
Answers & Solutions 147

PRACTICE TEST 3 165

Answer Sheet 165
Reading 172
Writing and Language 188
Math — No Calculator 201
Math — Calculator 207
Essay 218
Answers & Solutions 221

PRACTICE TEST 4 239

Answer Sheet 239
Reading 246
Writing and Language 261
Math — No Calculator 273
Math — Calculator 279
Essay 290
Answers & Solutions 293

SCORE TABLE 311

Another Note from Ted 313

Tutor Ted®

A Note from Ted

A young fella walking down a Manhattan sidewalk asks an older guy with a violin case, "excuse me...how do you get to Carnegie Hall?"

The older guy replies, "practice, practice, practice!"

How do you improve your SAT score? Practice, practice, practice.
Included in this book are four realistic SAT practice tests. We worked hard to make them the most SAT-like tests available anywhere. If you're going to take a practice test, shouldn't it be just like the real one?

Use this book alongside our companion book, "Tutor Ted's Guide to the SAT" and you'll have the strategies and knowledge needed to master the SAT plus the chance to put your strategies and knowledge into practice.

Get crackin'! Take a test and see how you do. Use the solutions in the back to figure out what you know and what you need to study. Learn that stuff, then come back and take another test. Repeat.

Go get 'em, tiger.

TED

How to Use This Book

LIFTOFF

Check it out:

PRACTICE IN THE STYLE OF THE TEST.

Our goal is to make you as comfortable and confident as you possibly can be when you take the SAT.

To make that happen, you want to simulate the experience of taking the test before the test ever happens. That means sitting down on a Saturday morning at a table in a quiet room, with no phone or computer within reach. Do that, and you'll be more prepared for the test—we promise.

FIND OUT WHAT YOU KNOW...AND WHAT YOU DON'T.

From one SAT to the next, the content of the test does not change. This is a huge advantage for students who are prepping. Take advantage by figuring out what you know and what you don't. Then work on the stuff you don't know. You can use our companion book, "Tutor Ted's Guide to the SAT," to study the specific areas that you need to improve.

TRACK YOUR SUCCESS AND AIM FOR IMPROVEMENT.

At the back of this book we provide an approximate score conversion table. You can use it to measure your progress. As you learn more concepts and become comfortable with the test, the number of questions you get right will go up. Guess what happens then? Your score goes up.

Practice will boost your score. Simple as that.

Now let's get into some details.

Your job on the SAT is to answer 154 multiple-choice questions and write one essay.

Yes, the essay is technically optional, but like everything else in the college admissions process that's optional, it's mandatory.

Are you ready for the world's shortest, simplest, most effective SAT advice?

You should always answer all of the questions. You do not get penalized for wrong answers, so even if you have to guess you should answer all of the questions.

Hot Tip: You should even guess on free-response math questions if you have to. Read the question to see what it's asking you to find. If it's an angle measure in degrees, guess something reasonable, like 40, or 75. If it's a fraction, well, guess a fraction. Totally stuck? Guess 0.

Every correct answer is right for a reason. Read the questions carefully. Don't overcomplicate or overthink these questions. Always have a specific, justified reason for choosing what you did.

The SAT really is a simple, straightforward test. It's boring, but it's predictable. Let's talk about that.

AN OVERVIEW OF THE SAT

The Reading Test asks 52 questions in 65 minutes. By the standards of standardized testing, that is a luxurious amount of time! It's also a clue that you actually *need* that amount of time to find the answers. Keep this in mind: the name of the section includes the adjective "Evidence-Based." They were not joking around when they did that. You want to find evidence in the passages to justify every answer you pick—literally, every single one.

The Writing and Language Test asks 44 questions in 35 minutes. This section is about two things: the technical aspects of grammar and the editorial expertise you need to make an essay better. With a little practice, you can know ***exactly*** what to expect on this section, and score significantly better here as a result. In other words: do not sleep on the Writing and Language Test.

The Math Test includes two sections: one on which you don't get to use your calculator, and one on which you do. The No Calculator section asks 20 questions in 25 minutes, and the Calculator Allowed section asks 38 questions in 55 minutes. Hot SAT math topics include algebra, more algebra, and yet a little bit more algebra. Just kidding. Well, kind of. The section focuses on linear and quadratic equations, algebraic simplification, chart and graph reading, and a few advanced topics. The limited focus of the SAT Math Test makes it an easier to test to prep.

The (optional-but-not-really-optional) Essay is a 50-minute analytical task with the same question every time. You'll be given a persuasive essay or speech, and your job is to understand it and analyze its rhetorical techniques.

THE MYTH OF THE BAD TEST TAKER

Before I go any further, I've got something important to say. Ready? OK. There is no such thing as a Bad Test Taker. There is no chromosome that predisposes you to perform poorly on tests. There is such a thing as an *unprepared* test taker, but that's different. Students get labeled as Bad Test Takers when they don't perform up to a certain level during a timed test. But the name does not fit the individual.

Some people point to anxiety as the explanation for poor test performance. Let's talk about anxiety for a minute. Take a look at this graph:

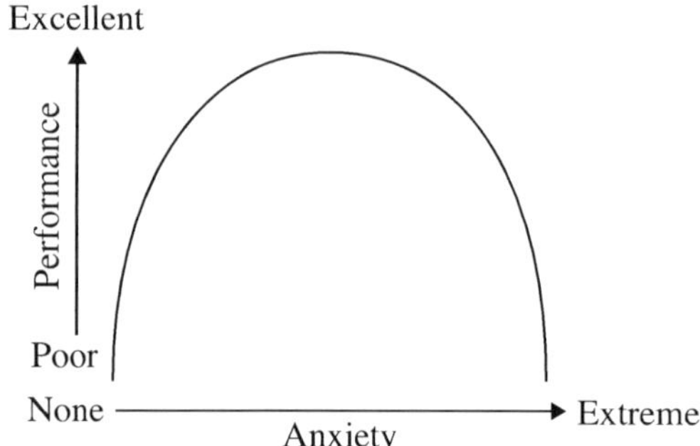

What this shows is a classic finding of psychology across every discipline from academics to athletics to music. The graph shows that at either extremely high or extremely low levels of anxiety, performance is poor. However, at moderate levels of anxiety, performance is at its peak!

In other words, anxiety is actually your friend. You WANT to be a little anxious and/or nervous. It is not a lot of fun to feel anxious or nervous...but it is actually beneficial to you if you are.

What I think students need to perform at their best is a reasonable amount of anxiety PLUS a healthy dose of confidence. When will you perform your best on the SAT, or on any other test you ever take? When you know the content of the test, right?

Let's put it another way.

If you learn the material and concepts on the test, and familiarize yourself with the strategies and techniques necessary to do well, you will come out on the other side confident, with just the right amount of anxiety, ready to face the test. And when you're in that position, you'll score higher.

There is no such thing as a Bad Test Taker, just test takers who are unprepared. And you're not going to be one of those people.

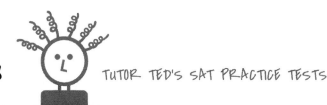

PRACTICE, PRACTICE, PRACTICE... PRACTICE?

How many practice tests should you take? We recommend that ALL students take a minimum of four practice tests before their actual exam. You've got four tests in this book, and the College Board has released eight official tests at this link—

collegereadiness.collegeboard.org/sat/practice/full-length-practice-tests
—so you're pretty well covered!

When should you take those practice tests? Take one at the very beginning of your prep. That will help you establish a baseline score and show you where you need to focus your energy during prep. Take the other tests as you study. Our rule of thumb is that you shouldn't take another practice test until you think you'll do better on the next test than on the previous one.

Also, don't wait till just before your actual SAT to take all of your practice tests—you'll get a lot more benefit when you have some time between practice tests.

DO I NEED A TUTOR?

The decision to work with a tutor is a personal one for each student. It is a matter of how you study and learn best. Some students are independent and can manage their time and practice diligently until they understand a concept or problem. Others can use guidance and encouragement along the way, and might better understand a problem by talking it through with a tutor. You can always start with self-study and work with a tutor later on.

If you decide you would like to work with someone, Tutor Ted is here to help. Our expert tutors are equipped with the best technology and will work with you face-to-face via the computer, just like they would in person. The difference? You can connect from anywhere, at any time, on any device, to get the support you need. Visit our website (www.tutorted.com) for additional information about our services.

THE NEED FOR SPEED

With 154 multiple choice questions to complete in three hours, you don't want to waste any time trying to figure out how many minutes you have remaining in a section. The SAT proctors are instructed to warn you when each section is approximately halfway complete, and when five minutes remain.

That's helpful, but it's not as much info as you would like to have.

One really bad option is to rely on the clock in the classroom. Sure, you COULD use it to figure out that if it is 9:18 am now and the section ends at 9:55am, you have 37 minutes remaining. But when you're frazzled and anxious and racing against the clock do you really want to? Silent digital watches are a great option to help you keep an eye on the clock, and they are allowed in the test room.

Bring a watch with you into the test room, one with no beep. That'll help you keep a close eye on how much time you have left on any section of the test.

BEFORE THE TEST

What should you do in the days leading up to the test? Hopefully you've completed at least four practice tests and feel confident that you know what to expect on the real exam. The heavy studying should be out of the way by now, but we do recommend you look back at your practice tests to review the problems you've learned how to solve. Remind yourself of the strategies that have worked for you. If you feel like you have to, you could do a timed section or two, but in those last couple of days, focus on reviewing—and sleeping!

WALK IN YOUR OWN SHOES

A great way to ease your nerves before the test is to visualize what you will do on the actual test day. This might sound silly but it really does help!

Picture yourself arriving at the test center a little early. You are certain that you have your admission ticket, ID card, pencils, digital watch, and calculator because you packed them the night before. You sign in and find a seat. You take out your pencils and calculator, put your watch on your wrist, and put everything else under your seat. Everyone settles in and the proctor reads the long list of instructions. Later, he/she starts the timer or writes the end time for the first section. You are working at a good pace as you move through each section. You might have a moment of panic here and there, but overall you can feel that the work you put into preparing for the test is paying off now. Before you know it the test is over and you breathe a huge sigh of relief.

Give this visualization a try! It can help calm you during the week of the test and boost your performance on test day too.

THE SAT DIET

What is the magical meal you can eat that will give you a 1600 on the test? Yeah... unfortunately, that meal does not exist. However, you can eat in a way that will put you in the best possible performance shape for the test. Here are the rules:

- ***Eat a well-balanced dinner the night before the test.***
- ***Eat a breakfast the morning of the test that includes protein. You need long-term fuel!***
- ***Don't eat a sugary breakfast that will make you crash.***
- ***Bring a snack or two with you to the test—something healthy and substantial, like a Clif bar.***

It's going to be a long morning: make sure you are fueled up!

GET SOME SLEEP!

Is this the most obvious advice ever given? Well, maybe...but there is a twist. You want to get not just ONE good night of sleep before the test but TWO. If you're testing on a Saturday, that means getting good sleep on Thursday and Friday nights.

One more piece of sleep advice: don't try to go to bed at 6:30pm or anything crazy. Go to bed at a time that will let you get eight solid hours of sleep.

DURING THE TEST

Remember that anxiety, though not fun at all to experience, is not your enemy. That said, you want to have a strategy to calm yourself down if you feel overly anxious. Feel free to use this tip or find another that works for you. Ready?

Okay, here it is:

Put your pencil down. Go on. It's okay. Now close your eyes and visualize your favorite beach. Here are a few suggestions: Waikiki. Paradise Beach. Bora Bora. Can you picture it? Good. Now, with that image in mind, count to five. Take deep, slow breaths as you listen to sound of the waves crashing, smell the salty air, and dig your toes into the warm, grainy salt. Feels good, right? Now open your eyes, pick up your pencil, and keep plugging along.

Repeat as necessary.

WHAT TO DO WHEN YOU'RE STUCK

Here are some great ways to get un-stuck:

Read the question one more time, slowly and carefully.

Write down all of the given information in a Math problem.

Refer back to the passage on a Reading question

Underline all the big words in the answer choices, and evaluate based on those.

If after a minute goes by you still can't solve it, follow the next step:

KNOW WHEN TO FOLD 'EM

The SAT used to penalize you for guessing incorrectly. It does not do that anymore. Take advantage!

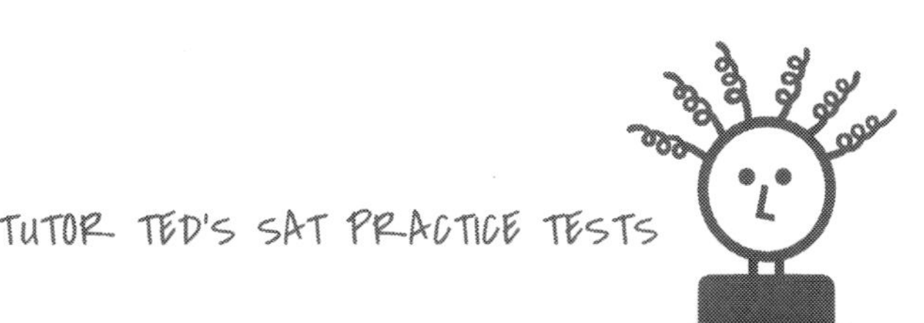

Do NOT spend 2-3 minutes on a hard question on your first pass—even if you get it right, it may cost you the time you need to answer several easier questions later in the section. When you feel like you can't find the right answer, try to eliminate answer choices and make a good guess. Do not hesitate to skip and come back. Circle the question number in your test booklet and return to it if you have time at the end of the section.

WHEREVER YOU GO, THERE YOU ARE

Keep this in mind: you can only answer one question at a time. That means that it is not beneficial to stress about a question that came before or one that will come next. Focus on the question that you're on and remember: you are allowed to make mistakes. Your job is to do your best, not to be perfect.

TAKE A BREAK

The Gods of the SAT, in a rare act of kindness, have granted you a 10-minute break after the Reading Tests. How should you spend that time? Use it to refuel. Eat the snack bar or sandwich you brought with you. Walk around a bit. Get some water. Use the restroom. Get up and move around a bit—you want to get your blood flowing.

Oh, and stay away from the people who are obsessively discussing the test. You will have plenty of time to talk about the test later.

Clear your mind so you can come back to the test focused and calm.

AFTER THE TEST

You'll get your SAT score about two weeks after you take the test. During the wait, it's your job to chill and not think about the SAT. You've already done your part.

IF AT FIRST YOU DON'T SUCCEED...

...try, try again! One of the best things about this test is that you can take it multiple times. People typically do better on something when they've done it once before. The experience of taking the test the first time, spending time doing some additional practice work, focusing on your schoolwork to get even smarter than you were—these factors will most likely lead you to a higher score on your second attempt at the SAT.

If you didn't reach your target score by the spring of junior year, we highly recommend re-testing in the fall of your senior year. 90% of our students earn their highest score in the fall of senior year. Join that group by taking the SAT then.

How many times can you re-test? College admissions officers we have spoken to say that seeing three or fewer test dates on a student's record is totally normal, and that four or more test scores starts to look fishy. You don't really want to take the SAT more than three times, right? If you do the prep—you take the practice tests from this book and study the lessons from learn.tutorted.com or from our companion book, "Tutor Ted's Guide to the SAT"—you won't need more than three shots at the test.

UNHAPPY WITH YOUR SCORE? SCORE CHOICE TO THE RESCUE!

Things get a little awkward when you ask this specific question:

Do I have to submit all of my SAT scores to the colleges on my list?

I'll explain.

First things first, I strongly recommend you wait until you have finished the testing process and have your list of schools finalized before you submit any scores at all. Sure, when you sign up for the test, you can submit your scores for free to four colleges. What if the scores you get does not represent you well?

Here's where Score Choice comes in. Score Choice is a College Board program that allows you to submit scores from whichever test dates you choose. Suppose you took the SAT twice, and on your second try you scored much higher than you did on your first. You would rather submit only that second, better test score, which would make you look better on paper.

Here's the trick, though: some schools say that you are required to submit ALL of your test scores. Some will even make you sign an affidavit stating that you did so.

Where it gets awkward is that they don't know whether you did or did not submit all of your test scores. Here's what College Board says:

> ***"Colleges cannot opt out of or reject Score Choice. Score Choice is a feature available to students. However, some colleges require students to submit all SAT scores. Be sure to check college websites to learn more about their score send policies.***
>
> ***"Colleges set their own policies and practices regarding the use of test scores. The College Board does not release SAT test scores without student consent. Colleges and scholarship programs receive only the scores applicants send them."***

You see what I mean? You're required by some schools to submit all your SAT scores, but because of Score Choice they don't know if you've taken the SAT once or fifteen times.

Trust your sense of ethics to help you make a decision on how to submit your scores.

Even with Score Choice available, by the way, we still recommend you take the test a maximum of three times. If you do thoughtful prep, you won't need more than three chances to take the SAT!

MIXED RESULTS? SUPERSCORE!

Many colleges superscore the SAT. That means that they will cherry-pick your highest section scores from multiple test dates and consider your application based on those.

Here's an example:

	Reading and Writing	Math	Total
March SAT	680	710	1390
October SAT	740	650	1390
Superscore	740	710	1450

This student got a 1390 on both her first and second test... but her superscore is a 1450! Sweet!

To find out whether the schools you are applying to look at SAT superscores, search the web for "Which colleges superscore the SAT?"

OFFICIAL STUFF

Sign up for the actual exam at collegeboard.org. That's also where you'll go to check your scores and send score reports to colleges.

To study with us for the SAT, visit learn.tutorted.com. If you're thinking about tutoring with us, reach out by calling 310-600-9595 or emailing contact@tutorted.com.

For printable answer sheets to use when you complete practice tests or sections, visit tutorted.com/resources.

SAT Practice Test 1

Multiple Choice Answer Sheet

SAT

TEST 1: READING

1 ⒶⒷⒸⒹ	9 ⒶⒷⒸⒹ	17 ⒶⒷⒸⒹ	25 ⒶⒷⒸⒹ	33 ⒶⒷⒸⒹ	41 ⒶⒷⒸⒹ	49 ⒶⒷⒸⒹ
2 ⒶⒷⒸⒹ	10 ⒶⒷⒸⒹ	18 ⒶⒷⒸⒹ	26 ⒶⒷⒸⒹ	34 ⒶⒷⒸⒹ	42 ⒶⒷⒸⒹ	50 ⒶⒷⒸⒹ
3 ⒶⒷⒸⒹ	11 ⒶⒷⒸⒹ	19 ⒶⒷⒸⒹ	27 ⒶⒷⒸⒹ	35 ⒶⒷⒸⒹ	43 ⒶⒷⒸⒹ	51 ⒶⒷⒸⒹ
4 ⒶⒷⒸⒹ	12 ⒶⒷⒸⒹ	20 ⒶⒷⒸⒹ	28 ⒶⒷⒸⒹ	36 ⒶⒷⒸⒹ	44 ⒶⒷⒸⒹ	52 ⒶⒷⒸⒹ
5 ⒶⒷⒸⒹ	13 ⒶⒷⒸⒹ	21 ⒶⒷⒸⒹ	29 ⒶⒷⒸⒹ	37 ⒶⒷⒸⒹ	45 ⒶⒷⒸⒹ	
6 ⒶⒷⒸⒹ	14 ⒶⒷⒸⒹ	22 ⒶⒷⒸⒹ	30 ⒶⒷⒸⒹ	38 ⒶⒷⒸⒹ	46 ⒶⒷⒸⒹ	
7 ⒶⒷⒸⒹ	15 ⒶⒷⒸⒹ	23 ⒶⒷⒸⒹ	31 ⒶⒷⒸⒹ	39 ⒶⒷⒸⒹ	47 ⒶⒷⒸⒹ	
8 ⒶⒷⒸⒹ	16 ⒶⒷⒸⒹ	24 ⒶⒷⒸⒹ	32 ⒶⒷⒸⒹ	40 ⒶⒷⒸⒹ	48 ⒶⒷⒸⒹ	

TEST 2: WRITING AND LANGUAGE

1 ⒶⒷⒸⒹ	8 ⒶⒷⒸⒹ	15 ⒶⒷⒸⒹ	22 ⒶⒷⒸⒹ	29 ⒶⒷⒸⒹ	36 ⒶⒷⒸⒹ	43 ⒶⒷⒸⒹ
2 ⒶⒷⒸⒹ	9 ⒶⒷⒸⒹ	16 ⒶⒷⒸⒹ	23 ⒶⒷⒸⒹ	30 ⒶⒷⒸⒹ	37 ⒶⒷⒸⒹ	44 ⒶⒷⒸⒹ
3 ⒶⒷⒸⒹ	10 ⒶⒷⒸⒹ	17 ⒶⒷⒸⒹ	24 ⒶⒷⒸⒹ	31 ⒶⒷⒸⒹ	38 ⒶⒷⒸⒹ	
4 ⒶⒷⒸⒹ	11 ⒶⒷⒸⒹ	18 ⒶⒷⒸⒹ	25 ⒶⒷⒸⒹ	32 ⒶⒷⒸⒹ	39 ⒶⒷⒸⒹ	
5 ⒶⒷⒸⒹ	12 ⒶⒷⒸⒹ	19 ⒶⒷⒸⒹ	26 ⒶⒷⒸⒹ	33 ⒶⒷⒸⒹ	40 ⒶⒷⒸⒹ	
6 ⒶⒷⒸⒹ	13 ⒶⒷⒸⒹ	20 ⒶⒷⒸⒹ	27 ⒶⒷⒸⒹ	34 ⒶⒷⒸⒹ	41 ⒶⒷⒸⒹ	
7 ⒶⒷⒸⒹ	14 ⒶⒷⒸⒹ	21 ⒶⒷⒸⒹ	28 ⒶⒷⒸⒹ	35 ⒶⒷⒸⒹ	42 ⒶⒷⒸⒹ	

TEST 3: MATHEMATICS - NO CALCULATOR

1 ⒶⒷⒸⒹ	9 ⒶⒷⒸⒹ	16 ☐☐☐☐	17 ☐☐☐☐	18 ☐☐☐☐	19 ☐☐☐☐	20 ☐☐☐☐
2 ⒶⒷⒸⒹ	10 ⒶⒷⒸⒹ	/ (/)(/)(/)(/)	/ (/)(/)(/)(/)	/ (/)(/)(/)(/)	/ (/)(/)(/)(/)	/ (/)(/)(/)(/)
3 ⒶⒷⒸⒹ	11 ⒶⒷⒸⒹ	. (.)(.)(.)(.)	. (.)(.)(.)(.)	. (.)(.)(.)(.)	. (.)(.)(.)(.)	. (.)(.)(.)(.)
4 ⒶⒷⒸⒹ	12 ⒶⒷⒸⒹ	0 ⓪⓪⓪⓪	0 ⓪⓪⓪⓪	0 ⓪⓪⓪⓪	0 ⓪⓪⓪⓪	0 ⓪⓪⓪⓪
5 ⒶⒷⒸⒹ	13 ⒶⒷⒸⒹ	1 ①①①①	1 ①①①①	1 ①①①①	1 ①①①①	1 ①①①①
6 ⒶⒷⒸⒹ	14 ⒶⒷⒸⒹ	2 ②②②②	2 ②②②②	2 ②②②②	2 ②②②②	2 ②②②②
7 ⒶⒷⒸⒹ	15 ⒶⒷⒸⒹ	3 ③③③③	3 ③③③③	3 ③③③③	3 ③③③③	3 ③③③③
8 ⒶⒷⒸⒹ		4 ④④④④	4 ④④④④	4 ④④④④	4 ④④④④	4 ④④④④
		5 ⑤⑤⑤⑤	5 ⑤⑤⑤⑤	5 ⑤⑤⑤⑤	5 ⑤⑤⑤⑤	5 ⑤⑤⑤⑤
		6 ⑥⑥⑥⑥	6 ⑥⑥⑥⑥	6 ⑥⑥⑥⑥	6 ⑥⑥⑥⑥	6 ⑥⑥⑥⑥
		7 ⑦⑦⑦⑦	7 ⑦⑦⑦⑦	7 ⑦⑦⑦⑦	7 ⑦⑦⑦⑦	7 ⑦⑦⑦⑦
		8 ⑧⑧⑧⑧	8 ⑧⑧⑧⑧	8 ⑧⑧⑧⑧	8 ⑧⑧⑧⑧	8 ⑧⑧⑧⑧
		9 ⑨⑨⑨⑨	9 ⑨⑨⑨⑨	9 ⑨⑨⑨⑨	9 ⑨⑨⑨⑨	9 ⑨⑨⑨⑨

TEST 4: MATHEMATICS - CALCULATOR ALLOWED

1 ⒶⒷⒸⒹ	6 ⒶⒷⒸⒹ	11 ⒶⒷⒸⒹ	16 ⒶⒷⒸⒹ	21 ⒶⒷⒸⒹ	26 ⒶⒷⒸⒹ	31 ☐☐☐☐
2 ⒶⒷⒸⒹ	7 ⒶⒷⒸⒹ	12 ⒶⒷⒸⒹ	17 ⒶⒷⒸⒹ	22 ⒶⒷⒸⒹ	27 ⒶⒷⒸⒹ	/ (/)(/)(/)(/)
3 ⒶⒷⒸⒹ	8 ⒶⒷⒸⒹ	13 ⒶⒷⒸⒹ	18 ⒶⒷⒸⒹ	23 ⒶⒷⒸⒹ	28 ⒶⒷⒸⒹ	. (.)(.)(.)(.)
4 ⒶⒷⒸⒹ	9 ⒶⒷⒸⒹ	14 ⒶⒷⒸⒹ	19 ⒶⒷⒸⒹ	24 ⒶⒷⒸⒹ	29 ⒶⒷⒸⒹ	0 ⓪⓪⓪⓪
5 ⒶⒷⒸⒹ	10 ⒶⒷⒸⒹ	15 ⒶⒷⒸⒹ	20 ⒶⒷⒸⒹ	25 ⒶⒷⒸⒹ	30 ⒶⒷⒸⒹ	1 ①①①①
						2 ②②②②
						3 ③③③③
						4 ④④④④
						5 ⑤⑤⑤⑤
						6 ⑥⑥⑥⑥
						7 ⑦⑦⑦⑦
						8 ⑧⑧⑧⑧
						9 ⑨⑨⑨⑨

CONTINUE

SAT Practice Test 1

Multiple Choice Answer Sheet

TEST 4: MATHEMATICS - CALCULATOR ALLOWED *(continued)*

	32	33	34	35	36	37	38
/	(/)(/)(/)(/)	(/)(/)(/)(/)	(/)(/)(/)(/)	(/)(/)(/)(/)	(/)(/)(/)(/)	(/)(/)(/)(/)	(/)(/)(/)(/)
.	(.)(.)(.)(.)	(.)(.)(.)(.)	(.)(.)(.)(.)	(.)(.)(.)(.)	(.)(.)(.)(.)	(.)(.)(.)(.)	(.)(.)(.)(.)
0	(0)(0)(0)(0)	(0)(0)(0)(0)	(0)(0)(0)(0)	(0)(0)(0)(0)	(0)(0)(0)(0)	(0)(0)(0)(0)	(0)(0)(0)(0)
1	(1)(1)(1)(1)	(1)(1)(1)(1)	(1)(1)(1)(1)	(1)(1)(1)(1)	(1)(1)(1)(1)	(1)(1)(1)(1)	(1)(1)(1)(1)
2	(2)(2)(2)(2)	(2)(2)(2)(2)	(2)(2)(2)(2)	(2)(2)(2)(2)	(2)(2)(2)(2)	(2)(2)(2)(2)	(2)(2)(2)(2)
3	(3)(3)(3)(3)	(3)(3)(3)(3)	(3)(3)(3)(3)	(3)(3)(3)(3)	(3)(3)(3)(3)	(3)(3)(3)(3)	(3)(3)(3)(3)
4	(4)(4)(4)(4)	(4)(4)(4)(4)	(4)(4)(4)(4)	(4)(4)(4)(4)	(4)(4)(4)(4)	(4)(4)(4)(4)	(4)(4)(4)(4)
5	(5)(5)(5)(5)	(5)(5)(5)(5)	(5)(5)(5)(5)	(5)(5)(5)(5)	(5)(5)(5)(5)	(5)(5)(5)(5)	(5)(5)(5)(5)
6	(6)(6)(6)(6)	(6)(6)(6)(6)	(6)(6)(6)(6)	(6)(6)(6)(6)	(6)(6)(6)(6)	(6)(6)(6)(6)	(6)(6)(6)(6)
7	(7)(7)(7)(7)	(7)(7)(7)(7)	(7)(7)(7)(7)	(7)(7)(7)(7)	(7)(7)(7)(7)	(7)(7)(7)(7)	(7)(7)(7)(7)
8	(8)(8)(8)(8)	(8)(8)(8)(8)	(8)(8)(8)(8)	(8)(8)(8)(8)	(8)(8)(8)(8)	(8)(8)(8)(8)	(8)(8)(8)(8)
9	(9)(9)(9)(9)	(9)(9)(9)(9)	(9)(9)(9)(9)	(9)(9)(9)(9)	(9)(9)(9)(9)	(9)(9)(9)(9)	(9)(9)(9)(9)

TEST 5: ESSAY - OPTIONAL

If you are writing the essay, you may use the space below to plan and outline your work. Be sure to write the essay itself on the lined pages that follow.

SAT

SAT Practice Test 1

Essay Answer Sheet

BEGIN YOUR ESSAY HERE.

You may continue on the next page.

SAT Practice Test 1

Essay Answer Sheet

DO NOT WRITE OUTSIDE THE BOX.

You may continue on the next page.

SAT Practice Test 1

Essay Answer Sheet

BEGIN YOUR ESSAY HERE.

You may continue on the next page.

SAT Practice Test 1

Essay Answer Sheet

DO NOT WRITE OUTSIDE THE BOX.

SAT® Practice Test #1

IMPORTANT REMINDERS

A No. 2 pencil is required for the test. Do not use a mechanical pencil or pen.

Sharing any questions with anyone is a violation of Test Security and Fairness policies and may result in your scores being canceled.

This cover is representative of what you'll see on test day.

Reading Test

65 MINUTES, 52 QUESTIONS

Turn to Section 1 of your answer sheet to answer the questions in this section.

DIRECTIONS

Each passage or pair of passages below is followed by a number of questions. After reading each passage or pair, choose the best answer to each question based on what is stated or implied in the passage or passages and in any accompanying graphics (such as a table or graph).

Questions 1-10 are based on the following passage.

This passage is adapted from Nathaniel Hawthorne, *The Minister's Black Veil,* originally published in 1836.

With this gloomy shade before him, good Mr. Hooper walked onward, at a slow and quiet pace, stopping somewhat and looking on the ground, as is customary with abstracted men, yet nodding kindly to those of his parishioners who still waited on the meeting-house steps. But so wonder-struck were they, that his greeting hardly met with a return.

"I can't really feel as if good Mr. Hooper's face was behind that piece of crape," said the sexton.

"Our parson has gone mad!" cried Goodman Gray, following him across the threshold.

A rumor of some unaccountable phenomenon had preceded Mr. Hooper into the meetinghouse and set all the congregation astir. Few could refrain from twisting their heads toward the door; many stood upright and turned directly about; while several little boys clambered upon the seats, and came down again with a terrible racket. There was a general bustle, a rustling of the women's gowns and shuffling of the men's feet, greatly at variance with that hushed repose which should attend the entrance of the minister. But Mr. Hooper appeared not to notice the perturbation of his people. He entered with an almost noiseless step, bent his head mildly to the pews on each side and bowed as he passed his oldest parishioner, a white-haired great-grandsire, who occupied an armchair in the centre of the aisle. It was strange to observe how slowly this venerable man became conscious of something singular in the appearance of his pastor. He seemed not fully to partake of the prevailing wonder till Mr. Hooper had ascended the stairs and showed himself in the pulpit, face to face with his congregation except for the black veil. That mysterious emblem was never once withdrawn. It shook with his measured breath as he gave out the psalm, it threw its obscurity between him and the holy page as he read the Scriptures, and while he prayed the veil lay heavily on his uplifted countenance. Did he seek to hide it from the dread Being whom he was addressing?

Perhaps the pale-faced congregation was almost as fearful a sight to the minister as his black veil to them.

Mr. Hooper had the reputation of a good preacher, but not an energetic one: he strove to win his people heavenward by mild, persuasive influences rather than to drive them thither by the thunders of the word. The sermon which he now delivered was marked by the same characteristics of style and manner as the general series of his pulpit oratory, but there was something either in the sentiment of the discourse itself or in the imagination of the auditors which made it greatly the most powerful effort that they had ever heard from their pastor's lips. It was tinged rather more darkly than usual with the gentle gloom of Mr. Hooper's temperament. The subject had reference to secret sin and those sad mysteries which we hide from our nearest and dearest, and would fain conceal from our own consciousness, even forgetting that the Omniscient can detect them. A subtle power was breathed into his words. Each member of the congregation, the most innocent girl and the man of hardened breast, felt as if the preacher had crept upon them behind his awful

veil and discovered their hoarded iniquity of deed or thought. Many spread their clasped hands on their bosoms. There was nothing terrible in what Mr. Hooper said—at least, no violence; and yet with every tremor of his melancholy voice the hearers quaked. An unsought pathos came hand in hand with awe. So sensible were the audience of some unwonted attribute in their minister that they longed for a breath of wind to blow aside the veil, almost believing that a stranger's visage would be discovered, though the form, gesture, and voice were those of Mr. Hooper.

1

Which choice best summarizes the passage?

A) Parishioners believe Mr. Hooper has fallen ill and fear for the future of their church.

B) Mr. Hooper's wearing of a black veil creates feelings of unease and guilt among his parishioners.

C) During his sermon, Mr. Hooper wears a black veil to coerce his followers into confessing their worst sins in church.

D) Parishioners believe a stranger in a veil has taken over the pulpit and worry about what has become of Mr. Hooper.

2

Which choice provides the best evidence for the answer to the previous question?

A) Lines 12-14 ("A…astir")

B) Lines 34-38 ("It…countenance")

C) Lines 45-52 ("The…lips")

D) Lines 59-63 ("Each…thought")

3

Over the course of the passage, the parishioners' attitudes shift from

A) apathetic to agitated.

B) confused to inquisitive.

C) fearful to indignant.

D) inquisitive to concerned.

4

In line 21, the word "attend" most nearly means

A) visit.

B) manage.

C) assist.

D) accompany.

5

Which choice best describes the parishioners?

A) unnerved.

B) skeptical.

C) distrustful.

D) hopeful.

6

The passage indicates that Mr. Hooper is typically regarded as

A) arrogant.

B) terrifying.

C) histrionic.

D) reserved.

7

Which choice provides the best evidence for the answer to the previous question?

A) Lines 21-23 ("But...people")

B) Lines 40-41 ("Perhaps...them")

C) Lines 42-45 ("Mr. Hooper...word")

D) Lines 59-63 ("Each...thought")

8

The narrator uses the phrase "tinged rather more darkly than usual" (line 52) to describe

A) the veil worn by Mr. Hooper.

B) Mr. Hooper's pulpit oratory.

C) the congregation's reception of Mr. Hooper.

D) the sermon as received by the congregation.

9

What function does the fifth paragraph (lines 40-41) serve in the passage as a whole?

A) It gives the reader a brief speculation of Mr. Hooper's feelings.

B) It expresses Mr. Hooper's dismay towards the congregation's improprieties.

C) It demonstrates Mr. Hooper's lack of awareness towards the effect of his veil on others.

D) It characterizes Mr. Hooper as a frightful man.

10

Which choice best describes why Mr. Hooper wears the veil?

A) To deceive his congregation.

B) An undisclosed reason.

C) To impersonate a fellow pastor.

D) Because he is ill.

Questions 11-20 are based on the following passage and supplementary material.

This passage is adapted from Rohini Ruhil, "Is Population Really a Problem?" ©2017 by Centre for Social Medicine and Community Health, Jawaharlal Nehru University, India.

In 1968, American demographer Kingsley Davis attracted the world's attention to the population situation of India and Pakistan. He argued that the decline in death rate was not followed by a decline in birth rate in these countries and posed it as a problem. After that stance, the trend of blaming India's population growth for its poverty began. The first family planning clinic of India was started in 1925, which later led to the formulation of the official family planning policy. The developed world was convinced that the increasing population growth in developing countries was a threat to survival and should be addressed through the implementation of policies and funding received from the Ford and Rockefeller Foundations. It is important to mention that the scars of the family planning program during this emergency period led to 1,774 reported deaths and about 7 million forced sterilizations involving bachelors, hospital patients, old persons, persons with no children, jail inmates, pavement dwellers, and inmates in night shelters. As a consequence, people started avoiding hospitals and health services, including vaccination, due to fear of being nabbed for sterilization.

Held in Cairo in 1994, the International Conference on Population and Development (ICPD) involved a paradigm shift discussing and promoting the reproductive rights and reproductive health of women. Article 16 of the UN Convention also talked about the rights of reproductive choice for women. In particular, the Cairo Conference discussed the right to legal abortions because the religious fundamentalists in the USA, Vatican, and conservative Islamic countries were against abortion-influenced policy decisions to support their stance.

The ICPD was revolutionary in the way the population problem was understood. The focus then shifted to women's empowerment and reproductive health. There was criticism of the 'Cairo Consensus' by some organizations that termed it an 'old wine in a new bottle' and associated it with neo-liberal globalization. National and international organizations realized that education and employment were equally important in reducing birth rate, along with modern contraception. It was also realized that the role of women could not be confined to reproduction and that increased status of women in society would automatically help with population stabilization.

However, opposition to the shift and the ICPD's resolutions emerged. At the time of the Cairo Conference, India had a strong anti-natalist* family planning program guided by the principle that the Net Reproductive Ratio (NRR) equals one as explained in the National Health Policy of 1983. Another committee recommended abandoning incentive programs for those who used contraceptives. The ICPD faced widespread criticism for proposing disincentives such as debarring those with more than two living children from candidacy for and voting in village councils, and for adopting a mandatory 'two children' norm for recruitment and promotion in government jobs.

Yet research kept showing a different story. One 1984 study showed that population growth has a rather positive effect on economic growth in the long run. Another argued that poverty was not a consequence of overpopulation, but rather overpopulation a consequence of poverty. Public opinion increasingly believed each couple should be responsible for planning a family, not tradition, religion, church, law, or state. In the beginning of the 21st century, India's Millennium Development Goals included investing in sexual and reproductive health. Through public policy and advocacy, the country shifted its concern from population control to reproductive health, specifically focusing on reducing maternal mortality and infant/child mortality. By 2015, policymakers formulated the Sustainable Development Goals, targeted to comprehensively eradicate hunger, poverty, maternal and child deaths, and ensuring healthy lives and well-being.

**Anti-natalism is the belief that population density should be controlled by reducing birthrate.*

The following graph details the world's population growth rate between the years 1950-2050.

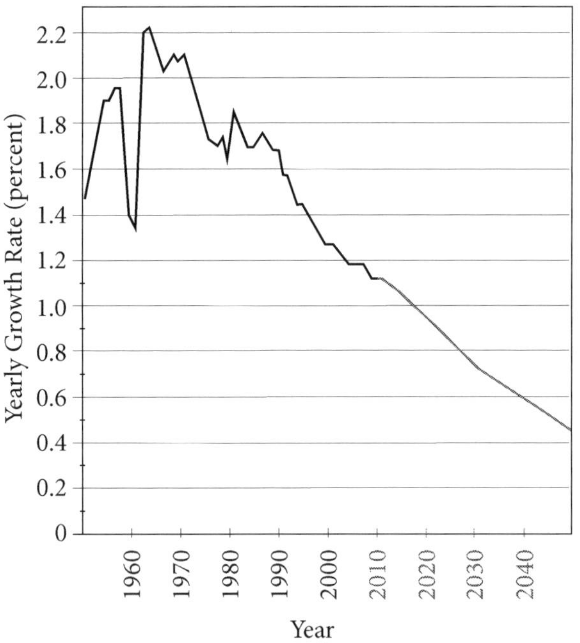

11

The main purpose of the passage is to

A) shed light on the horrors caused by early family planning measures, including the sterilization of about 7 million people.

B) discuss the Cairo Conference's struggle to appease countries with strong anti-abortion and anti-birth control religious followings.

C) provide support for government regulations which dictate family planning.

D) explore the root causes of overpopulation with regards to women's empowerment and reproductive rights.

12

Over the course of the passage, the central argument for population control shifts from

A) the rejection of the Cairo Conference to the acceptance of the ICPD's resolutions.

B) the idea that overpopulation causes poverty to the realization that poverty causes overpopulation.

C) the notion that poverty causes overpopulation to the acceptance that overpopulation causes poverty.

D) Kingsley Davis' beliefs to the ICPD's resolutions.

13

Which choice provides the best evidence for the answer to the previous question?

A) Lines 44-47 ("It...stabilization")

B) Lines 61-63 ("One...run")

C) Lines 64-66 ("Another...poverty")

D) Lines 71-75 ("Through...mortality")

14

As used in line 6, "trend" most nearly means

A) movement.

B) tendency.

C) development.

D) shift.

15

It can reasonably be inferred that the author views overpopulation as

A) dangerous.

B) uncontrollable.

C) misunderstood.

D) ultimately inconsequential.

16

Data in the graph indicate that the yearly growth rate percentages are most similar in which of the following years?

A) 1950 and 1995.
B) 1955 and 1970.
C) 1960 and 2010.
D) 1980 and 2000.

17

Based on the passage, Indian citizens' feelings on population control policies before the Cairo Convention can best be described as

A) timid.
B) fearful.
C) incensed.
D) shocked.

18

The main purpose of the fourth paragraph (lines 48-60) is to

A) provide ideas contradictory to those previously discussed as the basis for eventual compromise.
B) pit religious beliefs against scientific research in an increasingly religious society.
C) support the findings of the previous paragraph with additional policy measures.
D) introduce alternative viewpoints that were once potentially popular.

19

As used in line 57, "debarring" most nearly means

A) expelling.
B) condemning.
C) prohibiting.
D) refusing.

20

Which of the following statements is supported by the graph?

A) Increased enrollment in higher education led to the pre-1960 decrease in population growth rate.
B) The population growth rate since 1960 has consistently been trending downward.
C) The population growth rate will most likely surge upward in 2050 as it did in 1950.
D) The population growth rate has had an overall downward trend since 1980.

Questions 21-30 are based on the following passage and supplementary material.

This passage is adapted from Rui Li, et al., "Mercury Pollution in Vegetables, Grains, and Soils from Areas Surrounding Coal-Fired Power Plants." ©2017 by Scientific Reports.

Rapid industrial development in China is highly dependent on coal energy. This has had severe environmental consequences in China, including thick smog in Beijing and many other cities, exacerbating the greenhouse effect, and widespread heavy metal pollution in the air, water, soil, and agricultural products. Mercury is a particularly important heavy metal to consider when examining the environmental consequences of coal burning. In 1995, the total mercury emissions from coal-fired boilers in China based on mercury emission factors was 302.87 tons. In fact, between 1978 and 1995, about 2,493.8 tons of mercury were released into the environment from coal combustion. Mercury can be harmful at very low concentrations because of its high toxicity and ability to bioaccumulate. Mercury can build up and accumulate in the human body and cause severe neurological disorders in children and adults. In 1955, inhabitants of Minamata Bay, Japan who consumed mercury-contaminated fish and seafood suffered from mercury poisoning, which particularly damaged patients' nervous systems. As a result, at least 439 people died of Minamata disease. Although mercury is released into the environment from natural and anthropogenic sources, coal-fired power plants have been identified as the largest source of mercury emissions. What effects do these mercury-emitting power plants have on local food sources and their neighboring communities?

We investigated the mercury content of the edible parts of ten types of vegetable and grain crops from selected locations. The samples collected from a grocery store, which is far from any power plants (greater than 55km), were used as the uncontaminated to compare with samples from the coal-fired power plant areas. The mercury contents in 79% of vegetable samples and 67% of grain samples from the sites near coal-fired power plants exceeded the maximum allowed mercury levels defined by the Food Safety Standards in China. The highest mercury concentrations measured in the vegetable and grain samples were 8.6 and 6.3 times higher than the allowed levels, respectively. Meanwhile, none of the vegetable and grain samples purchased from a grocery store greater than 55km away from any coal-fired power plant exceeded the maximum levels allowed.

Comparing the mercury concentrations in different types of vegetables and grains, we found that the mercury contents in the edible parts of lettuce, amaranth, water spinach, tomato, eggplant, pepper, cucumber, and cowpea were 2.1, 2.9, 5.4, 7.6, 4.3, 6.2, 1.8, and 5.7 fold greater than the maximum allowed mercury levels, respectively. In addition, the mercury concentrations in the rice and maize seed samples were 3.0 and 2.1 fold higher than the maximum allowed mercury level in grains, respectively. The mercury content differed significantly among different vegetable and grain crops, and the differences in mercury concentration among different plants may be due to species-specific metal absorption and accumulation properties. This type of information can help farmers to choose crop plant species that accumulate relatively low amounts of mercury.

Mercury concentrations were much higher in leaves than in fruits, and the mercury concentrations in the aboveground organs were higher than those in roots.

Previous studies have demonstrated that plants can absorb mercury from both air and soil. When plants absorb mercury mainly from the soil, the mercury content should be higher in roots, while the mercury contents should be higher in leaves' tissues if air mercury is the main source of mercury. In our studies, the mercury contents were much greater in leaves than in roots, indicating that the source of the mercury in the plant samples collected near Power Plant A and Power Plant B should be mainly from the air.

In China, there are thousands of coal-fired power plants and most of them are located in densely populated eastern regions, particularly in suburbs where vegetables for residents in cities are produced. Thus, mercury generated from coal-fired power plants may cause potential health risks for the people living surrounding coal-fired power plants.

The following graph details the maximum acceptance levels of mercury for vegetables and the measured levels of mercury found in sample vegetables.

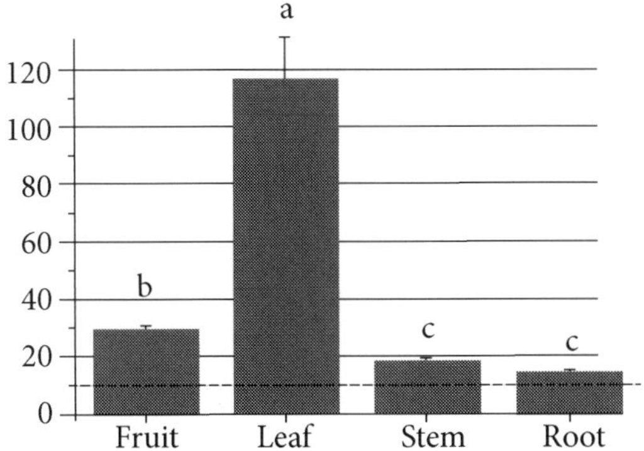

Dashed line: Maximum allowed mercury level in vegetable (10μg/kg FW) (Food Safety Standard China, GB 2762-2012)
Tomato tissue samples were collected from Location B3 located 5km from Power Plant B. The level of significance was defined at $P < 0.05$ using T-test.

21

The primary purpose of the passage is to

A) detail the neurological effects mercury can have on people.
B) warn against Japan's mercury-contaminated seafood industry.
C) discuss how coal-fired power plants affect local produce.
D) show that certain levels of mercury are acceptable in vegetation.

22

In the first paragraph, the authors' anecdote set in Minamata Bay, Japan serves to

A) compare the effectiveness of Chinese versus Japanese regulations regarding contamination.
B) illustrate the destructive effects of overfishing in Japan.
C) explain the rise in Chinese vegetation production in conjunction with its declining fishing industry.
D) provide evidence of the dangers of mercury contamination.

23

As used in line 8, "consider" most nearly means

A) contemplate.
B) study.
C) judge.
D) respect.

24

The authors' attitude toward coal-fired power plants is best described as one of

A) understanding.
B) disdain.
C) apprehension.
D) ambivalence.

25

Which choice provides the best evidence for the answer to the previous question?

A) Lines 2-7 (This...products)
B) Lines 9-14 (In...combustion)
C) Lines 41-45 (Meanwhile...allowed)
D) Lines 80-82 (Thus...plants)

26

According to the passage, which of the following is true of plants' mercury absorption?

A) If mercury is absorbed mainly from soil, the plants' fruits will have higher concentration than their roots.
B) If mercury is absorbed mainly from the air, the plants' roots will have higher concentration than their fruits.
C) Cowpeas had the highest concentration of mercury contamination of the vegetables tested.
D) Grains tended to have lower concentrations of mercury contamination than vegetables.

CONTINUE

27

Which choice provides the best evidence for the answer to the previous question?

A) Lines 39-41 (The…respectively)
B) Lines 52-55 (In…respectively)
C) Lines 63-65 (Mercury…roots)
D) Lines 67-71 (When…mercury)

28

Which of the following statements is supported by the graph?

A) Plants grown underground had lower measured levels of mercury contamination.
B) Leaves have the highest maximum acceptance level of mercury contamination.
C) Mercury contamination occurred more frequently in fruits than in roots.
D) All sample vegetables had the same measured level of mercury contamination.

29

It can reasonably be inferred that, when choosing what to plant, farmers should

A) research species-specific metal absorption and accumulation properties before planting.
B) investigate the proximity of potential contaminates.
C) plant grains instead of vegetables because mercury contamination was lower in grains.
D) know whether the mercury concentration is higher in the air or in the soil.

30

Which statement is best supported by the data presented in the graph and information in the passage?

A) The mercury concentration found in the roots is at the acceptable level, according to China's Food Safety Standards.
B) Mercury concentration in fruits is triple the roots' level of concentration.
C) Mercury contamination in the plants tested was most likely spread through the soil.
D) Mercury contamination in the plants tested was most likely spread through the air.

Questions 31-41 are based on the following passages.

Passage 1 is adapted from John Jay, "Concerning Dangers from Foreign Force and Influence," originally published in 1787. Passage 2 is adapted from Robert Yates, "Antifederalist Paper #17," originally published in 1788.

Passage 1

Nothing is more certain than the indispensable necessity of government, and it is equally undeniable that, whenever and however it is instituted, the people must cede to it some of their natural rights in order to vest it with requisite powers. It is well worthy of consideration therefore, whether it would conduce more to the interest of the people of America that they should, to all general purposes, be one nation, under one federal government, or that they should divide themselves into separate confederacies, and give the head of each the same kind of powers which they are advised to place in one national government.

A strong sense of the value and blessings of union induced the people, at a very early period, to institute a federal government to preserve and perpetuate it. They formed it almost as soon as they had a political existence; nay, at a time when their habitations were in flames, when many of their citizens were bleeding, and when the progress of hostility and desolation left little room for those calm and mature inquiries and reflections which must ever precede the formation of a wise and well-balanced government for a free people.

It is worthy of remark that not only the first, but every succeeding Congress, as well as the late convention, have invariably joined with the people in thinking that the prosperity of America depended on its Union. To preserve and perpetuate it was the great object of the people in forming that Constitutional convention, and is also the great object of the plan which the convention has advised them to adopt. With what propriety, therefore, or for what good purposes, are attempts at this particular period made by some men to depreciate the importance of the Union? Or why is it suggested that three or four confederacies would be better than one? They who promote the idea of substituting a number of distinct confederacies in the room of the plan of the convention, seem clearly to foresee that the rejection of it would put the continuance of the Union in the utmost jeopardy.

Passage 2

This new government is to possess absolute and uncontrollable powers, legislative, executive, and judicial, with respect to every object to which it extends, that the Congress shall have power "to make all laws which shall be necessary and proper for carrying into execution the foregoing powers, and all other powers vested by this Constitution in the government of the United States, or in any department or office thereof." And by the sixth article, it is declared, "that this Constitution, and the laws of the United States, which shall be made in pursuance thereof, and the treaties made, or which shall be made, under the authority of the United States, shall be the supreme law of the land; and the judges in every State shall be bound thereby, any thing in the Constitution or law of any State to the contrary notwithstanding."

It is as much one complete government as that of New York or Massachusetts; it has absolute and perfect powers to make and execute all laws, to appoint officers, institute courts, declare offenses, and annex penalties, with respect to every object to which it extends, as any other in the world. So far, therefore, as its powers reach, all ideas of confederation are given up and lost.

The powers of the general legislature extend to every case that is of the least importance—there is nothing valuable to human nature, nothing dear to freemen, but what is within its power. It has the authority to make laws which will affect the lives, liberty, and property of every man in the United States; nor can the Constitution or laws of any State, in any way prevent or impede the full and complete execution of every power given.

This clause invested with the power of making all laws, proper and necessary, for carrying all these into execution; and they may so exercise this power as entirely to annihilate all the State governments, and reduce this country to one single government. And if they may do it, it is pretty certain they will; for it will be found that the power retained by individual States, small as it is, will be a clog upon the wheels of the government of the United States; the latter, therefore, will be naturally inclined to remove it out of the way.

31

As used in line 5, "vest" most nearly means

A) furnish.
B) entrust.
C) invest.
D) dress.

32

The author of Passage 1 would most likely agree that

A) confederacies are more vulnerable to foreign influence.
B) leaders should govern their regions separately from others.
C) a strong, centralized government will best preserve the Union.
D) the people must give the government complete authority to construct and enforce laws.

33

Which choice provides the best evidence for the answer to the previous question?

A) Lines 1-5 ("Nothing…powers")
B) Lines 16-22 ("They…people")
C) Lines 27-30 ("To…adopt")
D) Lines 35-39 ("They…jeopardy")

34

As used in line 74, "exercise" most nearly means

A) train.
B) employ.
C) rehearse.
D) observe.

35

The central claim of Passage 2 is that

A) A centralized government will eventually cast states' rights aside in favor of its own power.
B) The country's strength depends on the strength of each confederate state.
C) A country of separate confederacies is more susceptible to attacks.
D) Other states should regard New York and Massachusetts as model confederacies.

36

Which choice provides the best evidence for the answer to the previous question?

A) Lines 40-48 ("This…thereof")
B) Lines 61-62 ("So…lost")
C) Lines 66-71 ("It…given")
D) Lines 76-81 ("And…way")

37

In lines 43-48, the author of Passage 2 quotes Article Six of the US Constitution primarily to

A) express support for the Constitution as it was written then.
B) show the centralized government's power to enter into any treaty.
C) expose the states' lack of control with respect to the federal government's absolute authority.
D) demonstrate the hypocrisy of taxation without representation in the new country.

38

Which statement best describes the relationship between the passages?

A) Passage 2 refutes the central claim advanced in Passage 1.

B) Passage 2 draws alternative conclusions from the evidence presented in Passage 1.

C) Passage 2 elaborates on the proposal presented in Passage 1.

D) Passage 2 validates some conclusions in Passage 1 but opposes others.

39

On which of the following points would the authors of both passages most likely agree?

A) No freedom should ever be yielded for any cause.

B) Citizens should be actively involved in the governance of a country.

C) Freedoms should be infringed upon for the purpose of security.

D) Each state should enforce laws specific to its needs, regardless of its adherence to federal law.

40

The author of Passage 1 would most likely respond to the discussion of the dangers of a centralized government's authority in lines 63-81, Passage 2, by countering that

A) the new country's success will depend on its ability to pacify each state in the laws passed by the federal government.

B) each state must prove its merit before the federal government will consider protecting it.

C) a centralized way of thinking about law and society will enrich the shared culture amongst the states.

D) a centralized government that streamlines important decision-making more effectively balances the needs of the entire country, making it better equipped to preserve the Union.

41

The main purpose of each passage is to

A) determine what a government's power should be in the new country.

B) propose further amendments to a new constitution.

C) argue for more transparency in government operations and decision-making.

D) describe the government's responsibilities to its citizens.

Questions 42-52 are based on the following passage and supplementary material.

This passage is adapted from Manoj Kumar Behera, "Assessment of the State of Millet Farming in India." ©2017 by MedCrave Online Journal Ecology & Environmental Science, Odisha, India.

Millets are among the oldest cultivated crops in India and the rest of the world. Nearly 60 million acres of land in India are under millet cultivation. India is the largest producer of sorghum and millet, accounting for over 80% of Asia's production. In the last few decades, India has evinced a sharp decline in the area under millet cultivation due to several factors. However, in India and other parts of the world, a growing number of farmers are switching to millet cultivation. The Consultative Group on International Agricultural Research (CGIAR) has estimated that the global production of wheat, rice, and maize could decrease by 13 to 20 percent in the coming decades because of climate change. Global agricultural production will have to battle against this loss, even as production needs to rise by an estimated 70 percent in order to feed 9 billion people by 2050. Millet may be the answer to this dire need.

The father of the Green Revolution in India has opined that state policies related to crop loan, subsidies, favorable conditions for commercial agriculture, and the supply of food items like rice, wheat, maida, and rava at a reasonable cost through the public distribution system (PDS), have shaped the minds of people to neglect minor millet. The food policies pursued over the years have pushed many people away from millet despite it being more nutritious than rice and wheat. The approach of selective utilization of crops and varieties have reportedly threatened agro-biodiversity leading to rapid erosion of natural resources and consequently affecting the nutritional security of people. Though generally unrecognized, millet's impact on climate change has received fair recognition. Global bodies are pushing millet farming with the idea that it reduces agriculture's carbon footprint while ensuring food and nutritional security.

As India's agriculture suffers hugely from the vagaries of monsoons, millets, which are also known as "famine reserves" for their prolonged and easy storability under ordinary circumstances, are of great relevance. They are most suitable for mixed and intercropping, thus offering sustainable resource use, food, and livelihood stability to farmers. Additionally, given the fact that millets are very good sources of nutrients, developing countries like India which report dramatic rates of malnutrition (about one fifth of the population), particularly among children and women, promotion of millet farming can help fight malnutrition.

The 2014 National Council of Applied Economic Research (NCAER) report has revealed the exponential drop in the consumption of hardy millet from 32.9 kg in 1960 to 4.2 kg in 2010 since urbanization made Indians switch to wheat and rice. Yet from a farming perspective, millets probably provide the best option for achieving the triple objective of farming: profitability, adaptability, and sustainability. Millets are highly tolerant of increased temperatures, droughts, and floods. Millets can be cultivated well in dry zones and rain-fed areas under marginal conditions of soil fertility and moisture. Storage life is comparatively high (two years or beyond) and millet farming requires low investment. From a human nutrition perspective, millets are a rich source of nutrients. Millets are richer in calcium, iron, and beta-carotene than are rice and wheat. Millets are also rich in dietary fiber, which is negligible in rice, improve the digestive system, reduce cancer risk, and strengthen the immune system. It seems that millet could be the answer to fighting climate change, poverty, and malnutrition.

The following figure details the amount of water required for the cultivation of different crops.

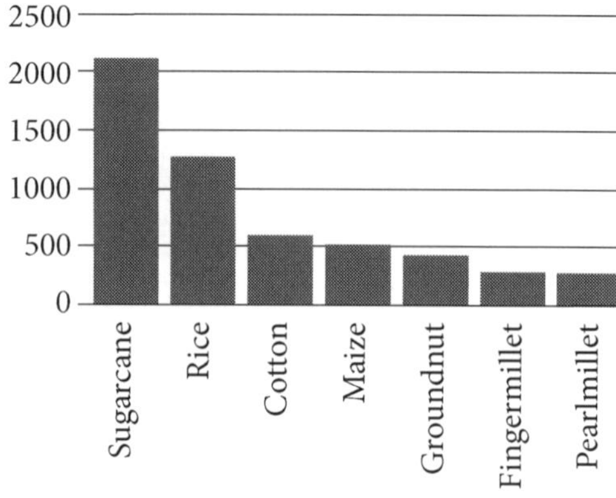

CONTINUE

42

The primary purpose of the passage is to

A) point to millet as an underutilized solution to climate, agricultural, and population issues.
B) expose the shortcomings of cultivating wheat, rice, and grains.
C) understand why India's legislative policies on food have neglected millet.
D) detail the nutritional value of millet as compared to other grains.

43

As used in line 32, "impact" most nearly means

A) collision.
B) significance.
C) authority.
D) effect.

44

According to the second paragraph (lines 19-36), the author most likely believes India's food policies promoting wheat production are

A) astonishing.
B) ambitious.
C) neglectful.
D) productive.

45

Which choice provides the best evidence for the answer to the previous question?

A) Lines 14-17 ("Global…2050")
B) Lines 25-27 ("The…wheat")
C) Lines 28-32 ("The…people")
D) Lines 32-33 ("Though…recognition")

46

Based on information in the passage, it can reasonably be inferred that millet

A) is perceived by farmers as one-dimensional and less cost-efficient than other grains.
B) farmers prioritize profitability over adaptability and sustainability.
C) became an underutilized resource after state policies caused consumers to favor rice and wheat, among other grains.
D) is now widely viewed as the resource which will help solve malnutrition and foot shortage issues.

47

With which of the following statements about grain production would the author most likely agree?

A) Farmers will rally behind the NCAER's 2014 report to influence others to advocate for increased millet cultivation.
B) The CGIAR will endorse millet cultivation as a solution for an impending food crisis.
C) The impact of climate change should lead countries to seek alternatives grains to wheat, rice, and maize.
D) Neighboring Asian countries will follow India's lead to compel farmers to cease the production of any grain but millet.

48

Which choice provides the best evidence for the answer to the previous question?

A) Lines 10-14 ("The…change")
B) Lines 14-17 ("Global…2050")
C) Lines 43-49 ("Additionally…malnutrition")
D) Lines 50-54 ("The…rice")

49

As used in line 40, "ordinary" is closest in meaning to

A) plain.
B) pedestrian.
C) typical.
D) customary.

50

Data in the graph indicate that finger millet and pearl millet require about

A) 475mm of water
B) 600mm of water
C) 300mm of water
D) 200mm of water

51

Which of the following statements is supported by the graph?

A) Compared to other grains, at least two types of millet can be considered less demanding resources.
B) Sugarcane may use more water than other crops, but are much more monetarily valuable to farmers.
C) Groundnut requires the same amount of water as pearl and finger millet.
D) Rice should be grown in favor of cotton and millet due to its durability.

52

Based on the passage and the graph, which of the following is the most logical next step for India's agriculture industry?

A) India should implement a family planning policy limiting the number of children born to counteract resource deprivation.
B) India should use current research on grain sustainability and resourcefulness to justify implementing more millet-friendly farming policies.
C) India should seek the help of other Asian nations to be as productive as their higher volumes to help the economy and the environment.
D) India should continue its trend of growing more wheat, rice, and maize in order to contribute to the rapidly increasing population of 9 billion people by 2050.

STOP

If you finish before time is called, you may check your work on this section only.
Do not turn to any other section.

Writing and Language Test

28/44

35 MINUTES, 44 QUESTIONS

Turn to Section 2 of your answer sheet to answer the questions in this section.

DIRECTIONS

Each passage below is accompanied by a number of questions. For some questions, you will consider how the passage might be revised to improve the expression of ideas. For other questions, you will consider how the passage might be edited to correct errors in sentence structure, usage, or punctuation. A passage or a question may be accompanied by one or more graphics (such as a table or graph) that you will consider as you make revising and editing decisions.

Some questions will direct you to an underlined portion of a passage. Other questions will direct you to a location in a passage or ask you to think about the passage as a whole.

After reading each passage, choose the answer to each question that most effectively improves the quality of writing in the passage or that makes the passage conform to the conventions of standard written English. Many questions include a "NO CHANGE" option. Choose that option if you think the best choice is to leave the relevant portion of the passage as it is.

The Lowell Mill Girls' Place in the History of the Industrial Revolution

When people imagine the face of a typical factory worker during the Industrial Revolution, that of a 12-year-old farmer's daughter rarely comes to mind. But it is just these kinds of people—**1** women and girls, as young as twelve, in Lowell, Massachusetts in the 1830s and '40s who left farms to become textile workers—who would serve at the vanguard of the world's most transformative structural change since the advent of agriculture.

1

A) NO CHANGE
B) women and girls as young as twelve who left farms to become textile workers in Lowell, Massachusetts in the 1830s and '40s
C) women, and girls who left farms as young as twelve to become textile workers, in the 1830s and '40s in Lowell, Massachusetts
D) women as young as twelve and girls who became textile workers after farms in the 1830s and '40s in Lowell, Massachusetts

CONTINUE

2 Born in Newbury, Massachusetts to John Lowell II and Susanna Cabot, Francis Cabot Lowell realized that the path toward American economic independence lay in manufacturing. After a trip to Scotland convinced him that the textile trade would be the most lucrative industry to introduce to his native New England, Lowell and his partners established the Boston Manufacturing Company, which built **3** its first mill beside the Charles River.

Lowell died before the industrial town named after him was created, but it is for this town, its factories, and the system of labor that he is best known. **4** The Lowell System is notable not only for the wage-factory model it created **5** but it also employed women and girls who left life on the farm to become factory workers. Some of the

2

Which of the following provides the most logical introduction to the sentence?

A) NO CHANGE
B) Having used his father's inheritance, upon his death, to purchase merchant ships,
C) Already an established merchant by the time of the Embargo of 1807 that disrupted trade between the United States and Europe,
D) A first-hand witness to the grisly turns taken by the French Revolution,

3

A) NO CHANGE
B) his
C) there
D) one's

4

The writer is considering deleting the previous sentence. Should the sentence be kept or deleted?

A) Deleted, because it introduces unnecessary information into the passage.
B) Deleted, because it provides an illogical transition from the previous paragraph.
C) Kept, because it provides a relevant transition from paragraphs two to three.
D) Kept, because it provides autobiographical information that corrects a misconception described elsewhere in the passage.

5

A) NO CHANGE

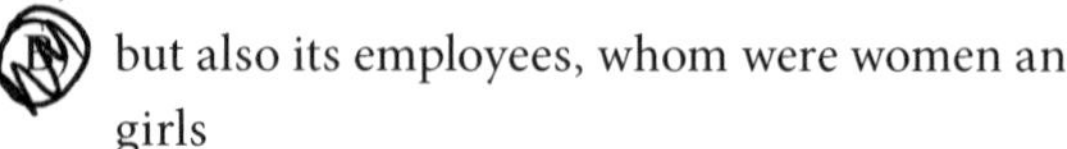

B) but also its employees, whom were women and girls
C) employing namely women and girls
D) but also for whom it employed, namely women and girls

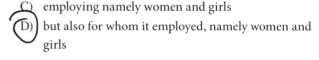

first women in the history of the U.S. to work outside the home, "Mill Girls" came to Lowell for a variety of reasons, and though life included **6** murderous hours and highly regimented days even outside the **7** factory all at half the pay of male workers: many women saw it as an opportunity for more independence than **8** she could have otherwise found. One Mill Girl, Harriet Farley, wrote in a newsletter published by mill employees that despite working 11-13 hours a day, she felt a sense of freedom to "read, think, and write without restraint."

The Mill Girls experienced both the conflicts **9** who would catalyze labor movements half a century later and the gender discrimination that would give birth

6

Which choice best maintains the tone established in the essay?

A) NO CHANGE
B) back-breaking
C) grueling
D) annoying

7

A) NO CHANGE
B) factory all at half the pay of male workers,
C) factory; all at half the pay of male workers,
D) factory—all at half the pay of male workers—

8

A) NO CHANGE
B) they could have otherwise found.
C) she could otherwise find.
D) they could otherwise found.

9

A) NO CHANGE
B) they

C) which

D) that

to the struggle for women's rights in the late Nineteenth century and beyond. When confronted with these injustices, they did not fail to act. Mill Girls organized strikes in both 1834 and 1836 when management threatened to cut 10 wages. 11 However their actions were largely unsuccessful in their time, these women were pioneers in the fields of workers' and women's rights who would help to change the face the American workforce for centuries to come.

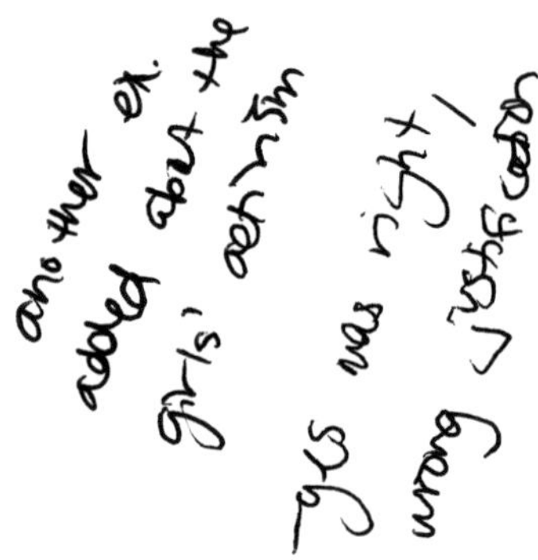

10

The writer is considering revising the underlined portion of the sentence to read:

> wages and they created the first union of working women in U.S. history—the Lowell Female Labor Reform Association—to press for a 10-hour work day.

Should the writer make this addition here?

A) Yes, because it provides an additional example of the Mill Girls' activism.
B) Yes, because it provides a logical transition to the ideas in the final sentence of the essay.
C) No, because it should be placed earlier in the paragraph.
D) No, because this information has already been conveyed elsewhere in the passage .

11

A) However
B) Since
C) Though
D) Insomuch as

The Sleepy Teenage Brain at School

Research on circadian rhythms—those invisible clocks that regulate so many of the [12] bodies most important functions—has proven what anyone who has lived through their teens can attest: [13] sleeping late is a right of passage. This trend is pervasive across cultures and even across mammalian species, making it impossible that social factors alone can account for it. In addition, scientists have found proof that the period of secondary sex development we call puberty coincides with a delay in the melatonin secretion that [14] allows animals to fall asleep. Put more simply, adolescent mammals [15] stay up later and sleep later than either their younger or older counterparts.

12

A) NO CHANGE
B) bodies' most important function's
C) body's most important functions
D) body's most important functions'

13

Which choice provides the most appropriate introduction to the passage?

A) NO CHANGE
B) adolescents want to sleep late.
C) sleep is more about attitude than biology.
D) teenagers' sleep patterns are culturally regulated.

14

A) NO CHANGE
B) allow
C) have allowed
D) is allowing

15

A) NO CHANGE
B) stay up later, and sleep later, than do either
C) stay up later and sleep later than either does
D) stay up later, and they sleep later than either

16 This tendency is one of biology rather than attitude. However, it seems that our social structures have yet to catch up to the science. Most misguided of all, perhaps, is our resistance to delay the start of school for high school students. Scientists agree that the most natural time for an adolescent to wake up lies somewhere between 8-9am. However, most high schools in the United States start by 8:30 or earlier, nearly guaranteeing that the entire student body of a given high school will arrive both chronically sleep-deprived 17 in a habitual way.

18 Through the effects of sleep on human health, here too the science is conclusive. Sleep deprivation can have serious negative consequences on humans both physically and mentally. 19 Regardless, it can also lead to decreased academic performance. It is also linked to a host of other personal and social ills. Studies have shown that sleep

16

Which choice most effectively combines the underlined sentences?

A) That this tendency is one of biology rather than attitude is fact, but it seems that our social structures have yet to catch up to the science.
B) This is a tendency that is not attitude but rather factual biology, so it seems, and our social structures have yet to catch up to the science.
C) Social structures have yet to catch up, but the science of biology rather than attitude is fact regarding this tendency.
D) Biology, not attitude, is the science; however, this tendency is a fact that social structures have yet to catch up to.

17

A) NO CHANGE
B) habitually.
C) over the long-term.
D) DELETE the underlined portion and end the sentence with a period.

18

A) NO CHANGE
B) On
C) With
D) DELETE the underlined portion.

19

A) NO CHANGE
B) Finally,
C) Obviously,
D) Alternatively,

deprivation in teenagers can exacerbate depression, lead to higher rates of drug abuse, and cause automobile accidents. This last correlation is so direct that a district in Wyoming that adopted a later start time for its high schools in 2013 saw **20** a significant increase in attendance over all grades in just the first year of implementation.

So why then, if the science is definitive and the potential benefit to both students and public safety so dramatic, do most schools continue to drag sleep-deprived teenagers out of their beds way too early to do them any good? Much of the problem is logistical. Despite the increasing diversity in the ways in which adults work in the 21st century, society is still very much modeled around the "9 to 5" workweek. In addition, adolescence is a relatively short period of life, **21** that means at any given moment the majority of the population is actually served quite well by the "early to rise" philosophy. **22** Yet an increasing number of schools are finding ways to make it work, much to the delight of sleep researchers, doctors, and yes…teens.

20

Which choice most specifically supports the main idea of the sentence?

A) NO CHANGE

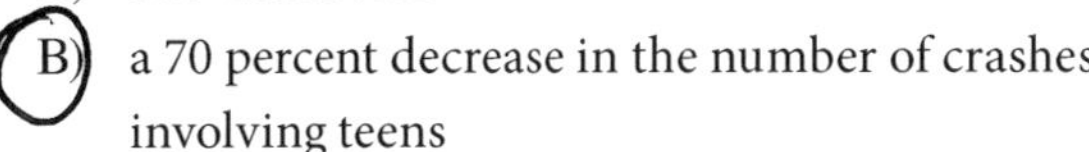

B) a 70 percent decrease in the number of crashes involving teens

C) rates of teen alcohol and cigarette use decrease by 20 percent

D) a sharp decline in accidents involving drunk or distracted driving

21

A) NO CHANGE

B) they are

C) meaning that

D) so that

22

At this point, the writer is considering adding the following sentence.

Today's adolescents make up only 13.2% of the population, and their participation in the workforce is at an all time low.

Should the writer make this addition here?

A) Yes, because it is quantitative data that supports the idea being presented.

B) Yes, because it clarifies a point that was previously unclear.

C) No, because it interrupts the flow of ideas as written.

D) No, because it undermines the writer's point by trivializing a problem.

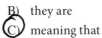

Are We Engineering the Smell out of Flowers?

People have been tinkering with plants since the beginning of agriculture. Flowers, especially, have been bred and rebred across the world by botanists and hobby gardeners alike for millennia. However, due to the ways in which the global economy has changed the flower **23** industry we now must confront a difficult reality. We seem to be engineering the smell out of flowers.

[1] According to Darwinian theory, all of an organism's primary traits **24** had an evolutionary purpose. [2] The scent of flowers is no different, as it is this trait that attracts pollinators like bees. [3] However, scent has no reproductive function in cultivated flowers other than the pleasure it provides, and since any organism has finite energetic resources, flowers (or their human caretakers) must choose where to allocate those resources. [4] Without the ability to create scent, flowers in the wild are unable to reproduce—**25** that is an evolutionary death-sentence not just for an organism itself but its entire species. [5] For flower producers—**26** which now work in an international marketplace where crops must be shipped sometimes thousands of miles before being sold—traits like longevity, resistance to disease, and aesthetic perfection are more important to the success of their businesses than fragrance. [6] Thus, fragrance has become a casualty of globalization much like the flavor of a tomato has become secondary to its **27** stimulating color on a grocery store's shelf. **28**

23

A) NO CHANGE

B) industry, we must now confront a difficult reality: we
C) industry we must now confront a difficult reality; we
D) industry, we must now confront a difficult reality, we

24

A) NO CHANGE

B) have
C) has
D) would have

25

A) NO CHANGE

B) it is

C) being

D) DELETE the underlined portion.

26

A) NO CHANGE
B) that
C) whom

D) who

27

A) NO CHANGE
B) vibrant
C) spirited
D) animated

28

To make this paragraph most logical, Sentence 4 should be placed

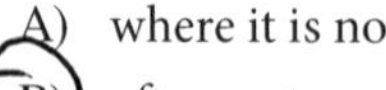
A) where it is now.
B) after sentence 2.
C) after sentence 5.
D) after sentence 6.

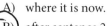

Scientists are now trying to reverse the trend and put the aroma back in commercial flowers using biogenetics. By comparing two type of rose, the strongly-scented Papa Meilland and the relatively odorless Rouge Meilland, Jean-Louis Magnard and his team have been able to pinpoint the gene that "switches on" a flower's power of scent. **29** This gene is found on Chromosome 10 and turns on an enzyme known as RhNUDX1. It acts in the cytoplasm of the cells in the petals thus creating a sweet fragrance.

Now that we understand the mechanism that drives the process, many believe we will be better positioned to harness it. This, of course, is not a solution without controversy, as it would involve genetic modification, a process that many believe to be a threat to both human health and biodiversity. Therefore, unless a solution is found that pleases everyone, we must continue to ask ourselves which sensory experience we value more in our flowers: sight or smell? We must consider whether it is worth it to be able to purchase a lily hundreds of miles from **30** its origin in the middle of winter. Already, when

29

Which choice most effectively combines the underlined sentences?

A) This gene, found on Chromosome 10, turns on an enzyme known as RhNUDX1 which, acting in the cytoplasm of the cells in the petals, creates a sweet fragrance.

B) This gene is found on Chromosome 10, turning on an enzyme, RhNUDX1, which acts in the cytoplasm of the cells in the petals, creating a sweet fragrance.

C) This gene turns on RhNUDX1, an enzyme found on Chromosome 10; it acts in the cytoplasm of the cells that creates a sweet fragrance.

D) This gene, RhNUDX1, is an enzyme that acts in the cytoplasm of the cells of the petals in Chromosome 10, which then produce the sweet fragrance-creater.

30

A) NO CHANGE
B) it's
C) their
D) there

consumers are asked to rate certain characteristics, **31** a majority values look above all else. **32** However, science may yet make it so that we don't have to choose. **33**

Survey of 300 flower consumers asked to rank their top 3 criteria in selecting flowers.

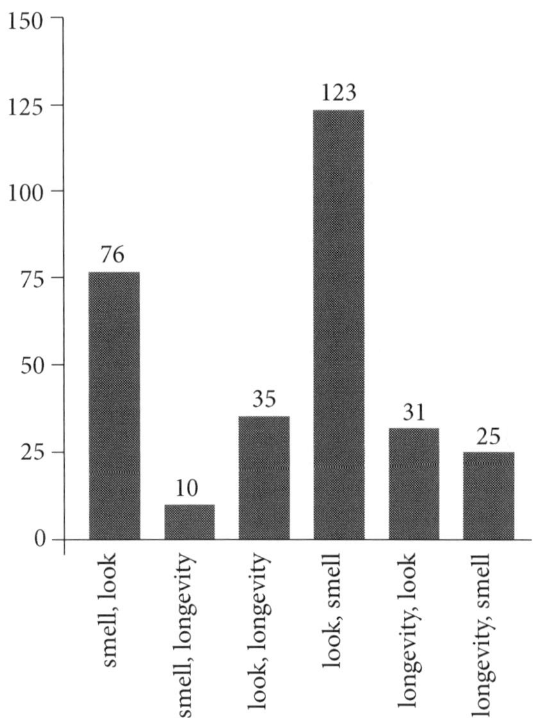

31

Which choice offers the most accurate and relevant interpretation of the data in the graph?

A) NO CHANGE
B) there is much disagreement as to which traits matter most.
C) smell is their top priority, followed by longevity.
D) a majority of respondents cite smell as a priority.

32

The writer wants a conclusion that considers the trade-offs involved in modifying living things. Which choice best accomplishes this goal?

A) NO CHANGE
B) And if so, we will have beautiful, long-lasting flowers for centuries to come.
C) But what simple pleasures might we lose in the bargain?

D) Unfortunately, we can't have it all.

33

Which choice, if added at an appropriate place in the passage, would best connect the information in the graph to the relationship between the flower producers and consumers?

A) In exclusively breeding for look and longevity, producers ignore the needs of their customers.
B) Since there is no consensus regarding what consumers want, producers must take their best guess.
C) In relation to "longevity," flower producers and consumers may have a different level of understanding regarding what it takes to bring a flower to market.
D) Producers are largely right to ignore aroma, as smell and longevity are consumers' least prized qualities.

Songs About Cars

From "My Merry Oldsmobile" to "Mustang Sally," as long as cars have existed, Americans have been singing about them. These songs often say less about the cars than they do about **34** themselves, and the broader American culture, especially as it relates to the "American Dream."

From the beginning of the 20th century through the 1920s, only wealthy consumers could afford to own an automobile, and thus car songs—and the drivers portrayed in **35** them, projected prosperity and glamor. It was an aspirational American Dream, the rags-to-riches tale of Andrew Carnegie, who worked his way from humble beginnings **36** becoming one of the richest industrialists in the world. **37** The automobile was a shining symbol of the kind of upward mobility that people believed they could achieve through American ingenuity and a bit of daring.

34

A) NO CHANGE
B) itself
C) themself
D) ourselves

35

A) NO CHANGE
B) them—
C) them;
D) them

Okas

36

A) NO CHANGE
B) became
C) to become ← right ahswer
D) had become

37

At this point, the writer is considering adding the following sentence.

The son of a working class weaver, Carnegie would make $480 million when he sold his Carnegie Steel Company to JP Morgan in 1901.

Should the writer make this addition here?

A) Yes, because it provides specific details on the claim that has just been made.
B) Yes, because it makes clear that the writer is an expert on the subject.
C) No, because it fails to indicate how Carnegie went from "rags to riches."
D) No, because it provides information that is irrelevant to the paragraph.

[1] It was not until the 1950s that the American dream became democratized. [2] After **38** WWII, no longer tasked with producing war-related, supplies American Industry was free to produce consumer goods once more. [3] This consumer boom, coinciding with suburbanization, the establishment of the Interstate Highway System, and a growing middle class that now had the money to buy cars en masse, meant millions more cars on the road. [4] Cars were for everyone because the American Dream now meant not just the accumulation of massive wealth but the kind of comfortable, middle class life that was available to a larger share of the population than ever before. [5] Not surprisingly, car ownership and songs about cars reflect this shift. [6] This optimistic **39** outlook can be heard in the car songs of the day, where care-free couples grab milkshakes at the Drive-In Diner before parking somewhere more private and "Greasers" race hot rods as their pony-tailed girlfriends cheer on. **40**

41 This economic boom time would fade as the fabric of society was tested by social upheaval, war, and finally a **42** halted economy in the 1960s and '70s. There is perhaps no songwriter more reflective of Americans' disappointments and increasingly conflicted relationship with the promise of the American Dream than Bruce

38

A) NO CHANGE
B) WWII no longer tasked, with producing war-related supplies,
C) WWII no longer tasked with producing war-related supplies
D) WWII, no longer tasked with producing war-related supplies,

39

A) NO CHANGE
B) way
C) circumstance
D) panorama

40

To make this paragraph the most logical, sentence 5 should be placed

A) where it is now
B) after sentence 1
C) after sentence 2
D) after sentence 3

41

The writer wants to link the fourth paragraph to the central idea of the passage. Which choice best accomplishes this goal?

A) NO CHANGE
B) The rate of consumerism would fall
C) Car songs would go out of fashion
D) That optimism would take a hit

42

A) NO CHANGE
B) stagnating
C) withering
D) inactive

CONTINUE

Springsteen. Paradoxically, Springsteen depicts the car both as evidence of the failure of that dream and as the way for his characters to escape broken towns in search of something better. As the characters in his classic "Thunder Road" "roll down the window and let the wind blow back" their hair, these no-longer-youthful dreamers **43** conveys a simultaneous **44** desire to stay together and a wish to break-up. The chips may be down, but they still have choices. One could argue that this belief lies at the very heart of The American Dream itself.

43

A) NO CHANGE
B) conveying
C) convey
D) conveyed

44

A) NO CHANGE
B) love of home and desperate longing to leave it.
C) need to cling to the past and yet embrace the future.
D) sense of futility and a wild, defiant hope.

STOP

If you finish before time is called, you may check your work on this section only.
Do not turn to any other section.

Math Test – No Calculator

25 MINUTES, 20 QUESTIONS

Turn to Section 3 of your answer sheet to answer the questions in this section.

DIRECTIONS

For questions 1-15, solve each problem, choose the best answer from the choices provided, and fill in the corresponding circle on your answer sheet. **For questions 16-20,** solve the problem and enter your answer in the grid on the answer sheet. Please refer to the directions before question 16 on how to enter your answers in the grid. You may use any available space in your test booklet for scratch work.

NOTES

1. The use of a calculator **is not permitted**.
2. All variables and expressions used represent real numbers unless otherwise indicated.
3. Figures provided in this test are drawn to scale unless otherwise indicated.
4. All figures lie in a plane unless otherwise indicated.
5. Unless otherwise indicated, the domain of a given function *f* is the set of all real numbers *x* for which *f* (*x*) is a real number.

REFERENCE

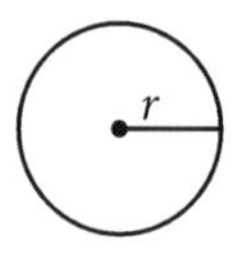

$A = \pi r^2$

$C = 2\pi r$

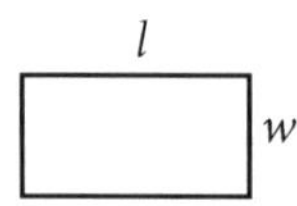

$A = lw$

h, b

$A = \frac{1}{2}bh$

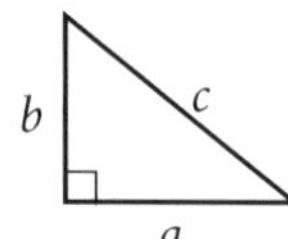

$c^2 = a^2 + b^2$

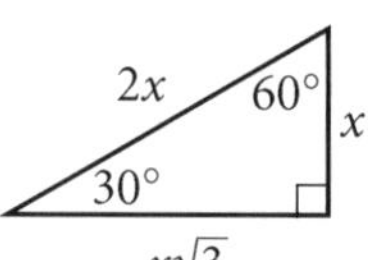

s, $45°$, $s\sqrt{2}$, $45°$, s

Special Right Triangles

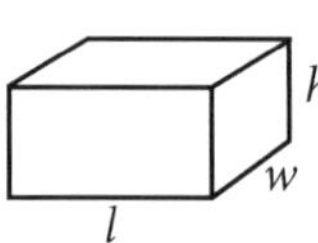

$V = lwh$

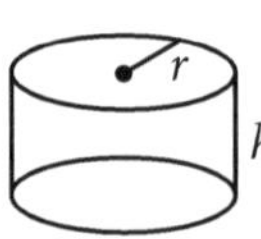

$V = \pi r^2 h$

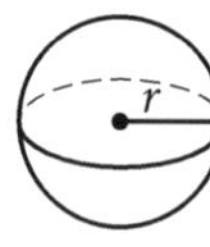

$V = \frac{4}{3}\pi r^3$

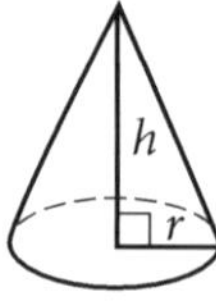

$V = \frac{1}{3}\pi r^2 h$

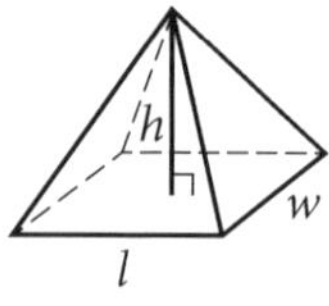

$V = \frac{1}{3}lwh$

The number of degrees of arc in a circle is 360.
The number of radians of arc in a circle is 2π.
The sum of the measures in degrees of the angles of a triangle is 180.

1

If $3(x - 7) = t$ and $t = 9$, what is the value of x?

A) -10

B) -4

C) 3

D) 10

2

For $i = \sqrt{-1}$, what is the value of the expression below?

$(4 + 3i)(-5 + 7i)$?

A) $1 + 13i$

B) $1 - 13i$

C) $-41 + 13i$

D) $-41 - 13i$

3

Amy and Oscar recorded the number of miles each of them walked. Amy walked n miles each day for 12 days. Oscar walked 4 miles more each day than Amy walked each day. If Oscar walked for t days, which of the following represents the total number of miles that Oscar walked?

A) $n + 4t$

B) $t(n + 4)$

C) $n(t + 4)$

D) $4n + 16t$

4

April decorates cakes for the Sunshine Bakery. Each week she is responsible for decorating the same number of cakes. The number of cakes that she has left to decorate at the end of each day can be estimated with the equation, $C = 72 - 15d$, where C is the number of cakes left to decorate and d is the number of days she has worked that week. What is the meaning of the value 15 in this equation?

A) April decorates the cakes at a rate of 15 per day.

B) April decorates the cakes at a rate of 15 per hour.

C) April has a total of 15 days to decorate all the cakes.

D) April is responsible for decorating 15 cakes each week.

5

$$\frac{15x^2y - 3y^2 - 12xy^2}{3y}$$

Which of the following is equivalent to the expression above?

A) $5x^2 - y - 12xy^2$

B) $5x^2 - 4x - 1$

C) $5x^2 - y - 4xy$

D) $5x^2 - y - 4x$

6

$$V = 48m + 650$$

Juan uses the equation above to estimate the value, V, of his savings account, in terms of the number of months, m, after he opened the account. What does the number 650 represent in this equation?

A) the value of the account after 1 year
B) the value of the account after 1 month
C) the dollar amount that the account increased by each month
D) the dollar amount that Juan deposited in the account when he opened the account

7

$$S = \pi rl + \pi r^2$$

The formula above gives the total surface area, S, of a cone whose base has a radius of r and a slant height of l. Which of the following gives l in terms of r and s?

A) $l = \frac{S}{\pi r} - r$
B) $l = \frac{S}{\pi r} + r$
C) $l = \frac{rS}{\pi} - r^3$
D) $l = \frac{S}{\pi} - r^2$

8

If $\frac{t}{r} = 5$ and $\frac{r}{t} + m = 9.2$ what is the value of m?

A) 4.2
B) 9
C) 9.2
D) 14

9

$$4y - 2x = -24$$
$$5x + y = 5$$

What is the solution to the system of equations above?

A) (0, – 6)
B) (1, 0)
C) (2, – 5)
D) (3, – 10)

10

If the value of the discriminant of equation $y = ax^2 + bx + c$ is equal to 0, which of the following graphs could be the graph of the equation?

A)

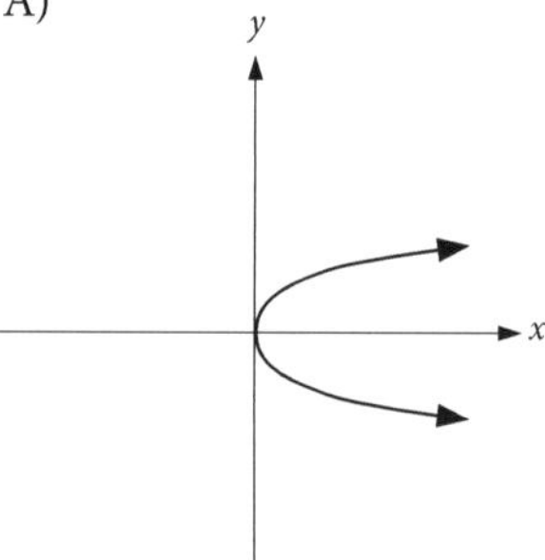

B)

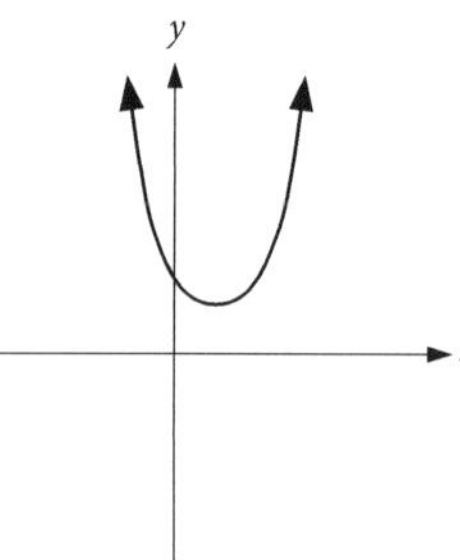

C)

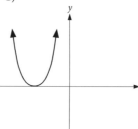

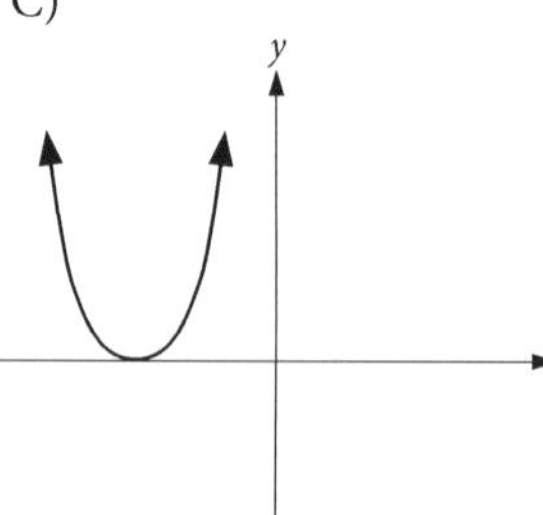

D)

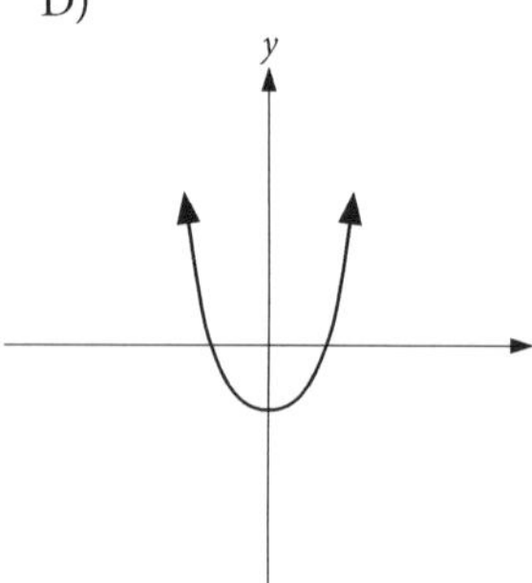

11

$$W = 3.15x + 60$$

$$B = 4.55x + 46$$

In the equations above, W and B represent the cumulative number of miles biked by William and Ben, respectively, x days after May 1. What was the total number of miles each of them had biked when they had accumulated the same number of miles?

A) 63.15

B) 50.55

C) 91.5

D) 113.7

12

Hailstones are formed when frozen raindrops are carried into the high clouds. The radius (in inches) of the hailstone varies directly with the time (in seconds) that the hailstone is in the high cloud. After a hailstone has been in a high cloud for 60 seconds, its radius is $\frac{1}{4}$ inch. Which equation gives the radius r as a function of time t?

A) $r = \frac{1}{240}t$

B) $r = \frac{1}{15}t$

C) $r = 15t$

D) $r = 240t$

13

What is the inverse of the function $f(x) = 3x - 2$?

A) $f^{-1}(x) = \frac{x+2}{3}$

B) $f^{-1}(x) = \frac{x-2}{3}$

C) $f^{-1}(x) = 2x - 3$

D) $f^{-1}(x) = -3x + 2$

14

If $2x + 5y = 20$, what is the value of $\frac{8^x}{2^y}$?

A) 2^5

B) 4^3

C) 8^2

D) The value cannot be determined from the information given.

15

$$f(x) = (7x + 1)(2x - 5)$$

Which of the following is also an equation for function $f(x)$?

A) $f(x) = 14x^2 + 37x + 5$

B) $f(x) = 14x^2 - 37x - 5$

C) $f(x) = 14x^2 + 33x + 5$

D) $f(x) = 14x^2 - 33x - 5$

DIRECTIONS

For questions 16 – 20, solve each problem, enter your answer in the grid, as described below on the answer sheet.

1. Although not required, it is suggested that you write your answer in the boxes at the top of the columns to help you fill in the circles accurately. You will receive credit only if the circles are filled in correctly.
2. Mark no more than one circle in any column.
3. No question has a negative answer.
4. Some problems may have more than one correct answer. In such cases, grid only one answer.
5. **Mixed numbers** such as $3\frac{1}{2}$ must be gridded as 3.5 or $\frac{7}{2}$. (If 3 1 / 2 is entered into the grid, it will be interpreted as $\frac{31}{2}$, not $3\frac{1}{2}$.)
6. **Decimal answers:** If you obtain a decimal answer with more digits than the grid can accommodate, it may be either rounded or truncated, but it must fill the entire grid.

Write answer in boxes.

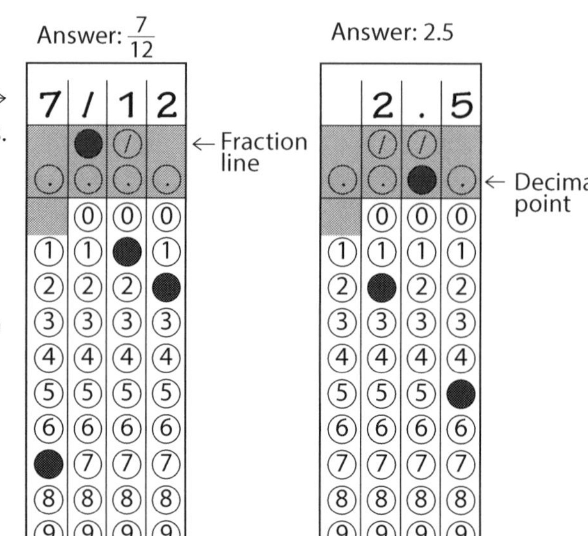

Acceptable ways to grid $\frac{2}{3}$ are:

2 / 3 | . 6 6 6 | . 6 6 7

Answer: 201 – either position is correct

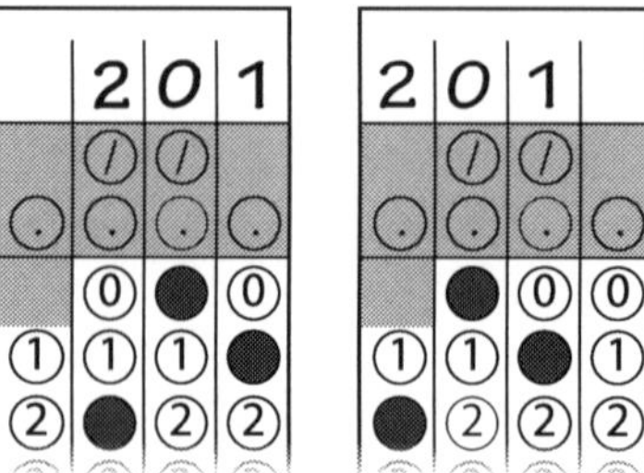

NOTE: You may start your answers in any column, space permitting. Columns you don't need to use should be left blank.

16

If $k > 0$ and $k^2 - 36 = 0$, what is the value of k?

17

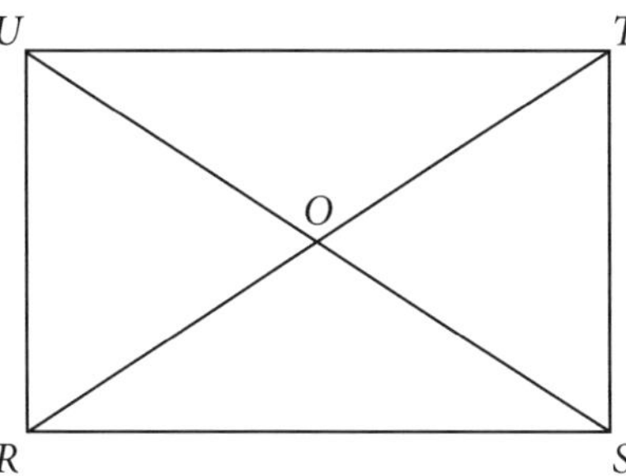

In the diagram above, the rectangle has diagonals $\overline{RT}$ and $\overline{SU}$ which intersect at point O. If $RT = 6x + 4$ and $SO = 7x - 6$, what is the length of $\overline{SU}$?

18

$$x + y = -4$$

$$2x + y = 9$$

Using the system of equations shown above, what is the value of x?

19

In a right triangle, the measure of one angle, in degrees, is x. If $\cos(90 - x) = \frac{7}{8}$, what is the value of $\sin(x)$?

20

If the function $h(n) = 0.5n$, what is the value of $h(2) + h(3) + h(4) + h(5) + h(6)$?

Math Test – Calculator

55 MINUTES, 38 QUESTIONS

Turn to Section 4 of your answer sheet to answer the questions in this section.

DIRECTIONS

For questions 1-30, solve each problem, choose the best answer from the choices provided, and fill in the corresponding circle on your answer sheet. **For questions 31-38,** solve the problem and enter your answer in the grid on the answer sheet. Please refer to the directions before question 16 on how to enter your answers in the grid. You may use any available space in your test booklet for scratch work.

NOTES

1. The use of a calculator **is not permitted**.
2. All variables and expressions used represent real numbers unless otherwise indicated.
3. Figures provided in this test are drawn to scale unless otherwise indicated.
4. All figures lie in a plane unless otherwise indicated.
5. Unless otherwise indicated, the domain of a given function *f* is the set of all real numbers *x* for which *f* (*x*) is a real number.

REFERENCE

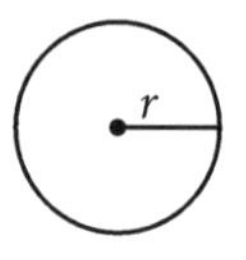

$A = \pi r^2$
$C = 2\pi r$

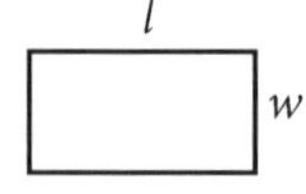

$A = lw$

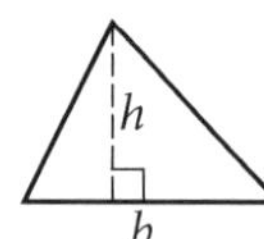

$A = \frac{1}{2}bh$

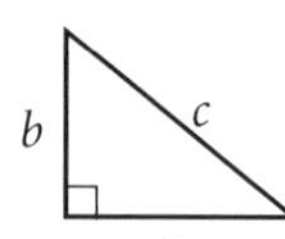

$c^2 = a^2 + b^2$

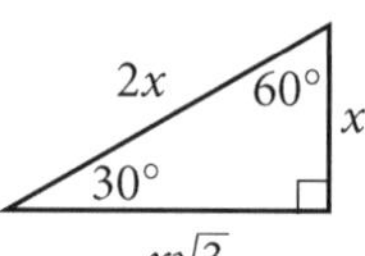

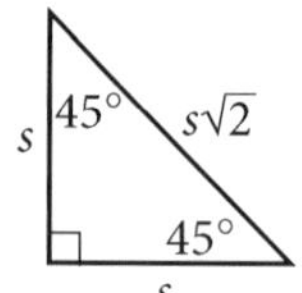

Special Right Triangles

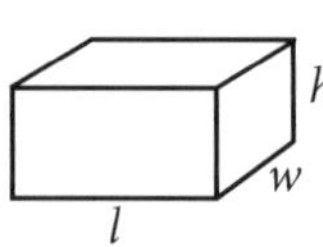

$V = lwh$

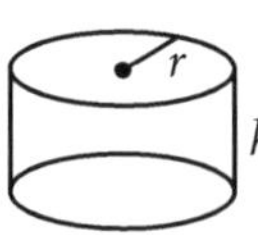

$V = \pi r^2 h$

$V = \frac{4}{3}\pi r^3$

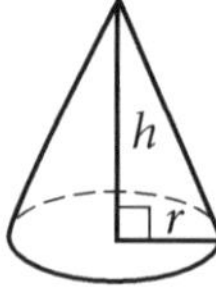

$V = \frac{1}{3}\pi r^2 h$

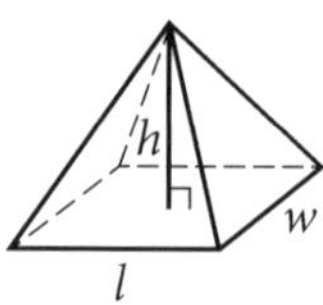

$V = \frac{1}{3}lwh$

The number of degrees of arc in a circle is 360.
The number of radians of arc in a circle is 2π.
The sum of the measures in degrees of the angles of a triangle is 180.

1

Consider the graph of the function, $f(x) = x^2 + 6x + 4$. For which of the following intervals is function $f(x)$ always increasing?

A) $-10 \le x \le 0$
B) $-7 \le x \le 0$
C) $-5 \le x \le 0$
D) $-3 \le x \le 0$

2

Given the linear function with the equation, $y = 7x - 5$, what is the y-intercept of the graph of the function?

A) -7
B) -5
C) 5
D) 7

3

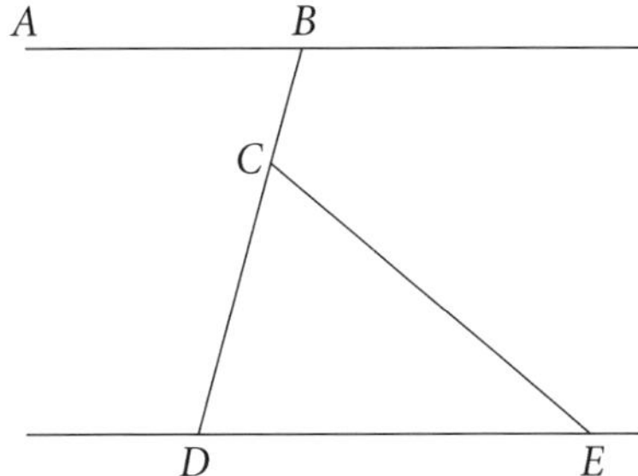

In the diagram above, $\overline{AB}$ and $\overline{DE}$ are parallel, the measure of $\angle DCE$ is 70°, and the measure of $\angle CED$ is 36°. What is the measure of $\angle ABC$?

A) 37°
B) 53°
C) 74°
D) 106°

4

If $\frac{a}{2} - 3 = 11$, what is the value of a?

A) 14
B) 17
C) 25
D) 28

5

A survey of Americans shows that 78% get to work by driving alone, 9% use a carpool, 5% use mass transportation, and 8% use other methods such as walking or biking. To make a circle graph of this data, what would be the measure, rounded to the nearest degrees, of the central angle representing the people who get to work using a carpool?

A) 16°
B) 32°
C) 90°
D) 328°

6

The warehouse building of a major food distribution company has a sidewalk near the outer edges of the building. The base of the building is a rectangle with a length of 425 meters and a width of 100 meters. The team leader for the dairy division walked the entire perimeter of the building 5 times during the week of May 1. How many kilometers did she walk that week?

A) 1.05
B) 2.625
C) 5.25
D) 5,250

7

Level of Time (minutes)	Frequency
17	3
18	7
19	7
20	4
21	6

Students in a physical education class ran 2 miles and each of their times were rounded to the nearest minute and recorded. The frequency table above gives this information. To the nearest 0.1 minute, what is the mean of this data?

A) 19.1
B) 19.2
C) 19.3
D) 19.4

8

$$\left|\frac{1}{2}p + 20\right| = 28$$

Which list of value(s) contains all the values of p that satisfy the equation above?

A) 16
B) -96
C) -16 and 96
D) -96 and 16

Questions 9 and 10 refer to the following information.

$$d = 40.5\pi r$$

The formula above can be used to determine the distance (d), in feet, that Ben's new bicycle will travel based on the number of revolutions (r) of the pedal.

9

For this bicycle, which formula can be used to find the number of revolutions of the pedal is needed to travel a certain distance?

A) $r = \frac{40.5\pi}{d}$
B) $r = \frac{d}{40.5\pi}$
C) $r = \frac{d}{40.5}$
D) $r = \frac{\pi d}{40.5}$

10

How many revolutions of the pedal, rounded to a whole number, are needed for the rider of this bike to travel 1 mile? (1 mile = 5,280 feet)

A) 41
B) 100
C) 130
D) 409

11

$$4x + 1 \leq 7x - 14$$

Which expression represents the set of all solutions to the above inequality?

A) $x \leq \frac{13}{3}$
B) $x \geq \frac{13}{3}$
C) $x \leq 5$
D) $x \geq 5$

12

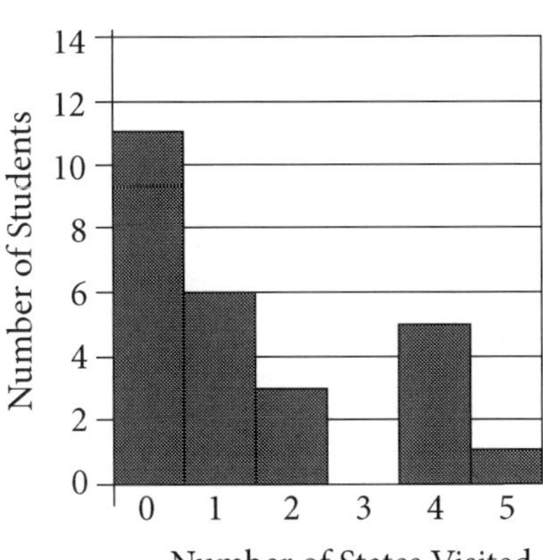

The histogram above displays the results of asking 26 second grade students how many states each of them had visited not including the state where they live. Based on the data in the histogram what is the median number of states visited?

A) 0
B) 1
C) 1.5
D) 2.5

13

The set of data in the table below shows the results of a survey on the number of text messages that people of different ages send on their cell phones each month.

Age Group	Number of Text Messages per Month		
	0-10	11-50	Over 50
15-22	4	37	68
23-39	6	25	87
40-60	25	47	157

If a person from this survey is selected at random, what is the probability that the person texts over 50 messages per month given that the person is between the ages of 40 and 60?

A) $\frac{157}{229}$
B) $\frac{157}{312}$
C) $\frac{157}{384}$
D) $\frac{157}{456}$

14

Juan has one more history test to take for the semester. The scores he received on the first five tests were 89, 92, 78, 83, and 83. Juan wants to have an average of 87 on all six history tests. Which equation can be used to find the score, x, that Juan will need on his last test?

A) $\frac{425}{x} = 87$
B) $\frac{425}{5} + x = 87$
C) $\frac{x + 425}{5} = 87$
D) $\frac{x + 425}{6} = 87$

Questions 15 and 16 refer to the following information.

Two hot air balloons are in the air. Balloon A is at an altitude of 900 feet and rising at a rate of 100 feet per minute. Balloon B is at an altitude of 2,300 feet and descending at a rate of 250 feet per minute.

15

Which of the following contains an equation for each balloon showing the relationship of the altitude, y, of the balloon to the number of minutes, x, that have passed?

A) $y = 900x + 100$
$y = 2{,}300x - 250$

B) $y = 100x + 900$
$y = -250x + 2{,}300$

C) $y = 100x + 900$
$y = 250x + 2{,}300$

D) $y = -100x + 900$
$y = 250x + 2{,}300$

16

Which of the following statements about the point (4, 1300) is true?

A) After 4 minutes have passed, only balloon A will be at an altitude of 1300 feet.

B) After 4 minutes have passed, only balloon B will be at an altitude of 1300 feet.

C) After 4 minutes have passed, both balloons will be at an altitude of 1,300 feet.

D) After 4 minutes have passed, neither balloon will be at an altitude of 1,300 feet.

17

What is the maximum of the function $f(x) = -2\,(x + 3)^2 - 7$?

A) -7

B) -3

C) -2

D) There is no maximum value.

18

$$y < -x + 5$$

$$y < x - 5$$

The point $(0, a)$ is a solution for the system of inequalities defined above. What must be true about the value of a?

A) $a \le -5$

B) $a \ge -5$

C) $a < -5$

D) $a > -5$

19

A toll bridge in Florida charges \$0.75 for each car and \$1.10 for each truck crossing the bridge. During a 24-hour period, a total of \$326.55 was collected for tolls. The total number of vehicles that paid a toll was 399. How many trucks crossed the bridge that day?

A) 78

B) 148

C) 176

D) 297

20

The value of a new car depreciates at a rate of 15% per year. If C represents the cost of the car when it was new, which expression represents the value of the car t years after it was purchased?

A) $0.15Ct$

B) $1.15Ct$

C) $C(0.85)^t$

D) $C(1.15)^t$

21

The student council wanted to showcase the music talent of their students by featuring two students at their next school assembly. Two drum players and three piano players volunteered. It was decided that their names would be put in a hat and drawn. One name was drawn and not replaced. Then a second name was drawn. What is the probability that the two drummers were chosen?

A) 0.8
B) 0.2
C) 0.16
D) 0.1

Questions 22 and 23 refer to the following information.

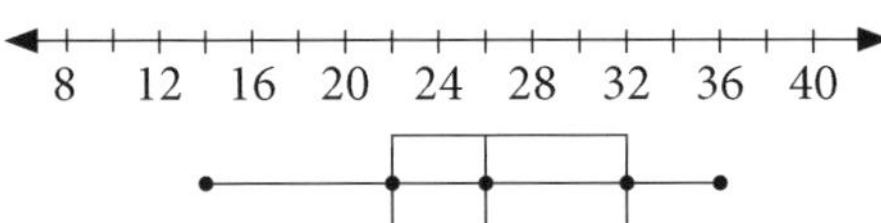

The box-and-whisker plot above summarizes data collected dring a survey about the ages of a piano teacher's students.

22

What is the median age of the piano teacher's students?

A) 32
B) 26
C) 25
D) 22

23

What are the lower and upper quartiles for this data?

A) 14 and 36
B) 18 and 34
C) 22 and 32
D) 32 and 36

24

Given a circle with equation $(x - 5)^2 + (y + 2)^2 = \frac{121}{9}$. Which of the following points lies on the circle?

A) $\left(\frac{26}{3}, -2\right)$
B) $\left(\frac{11}{3}, -2\right)$
C) $\left(5, \frac{10}{3}\right)$
D) $\left(-5, \frac{10}{3}\right)$

25

What is the solution set for the equation $|3 - 2x| = 5$?

A) {-1, 4}
B) {1, -4}
C) {-1}
D) {4}

26

Years (x)	Value of Investment (y)
1	\$5,500
2	\$6,050
3	\$6,655
4	\$7,321

Amanda made an investmet of \$5,000 in a clothing company. The table above shows the value of her investment at the end of each year for 4 years after her initial investment. What equation can be used to model this data, using x for the number of years and y for the value of the investment?

A) $y = 1.1x^2$
B) $y = 5000(0.1)^x$
C) $y = 5000(1.1)^x$
D) $y = 500x + 5000$

27

A right circular cone has a diameter of $10\sqrt{2}$ and a height of 12. What is the volume of the cone in terms of π?

A) 200π
B) 600π
C) 800π
D) 2400π

28

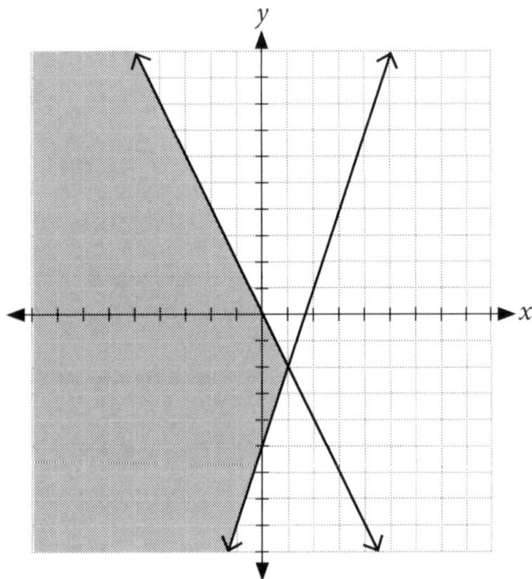

What is the system of inequalities that is graphed above?

A) $y > -2x$
$y < 3x - 5$
B) $y < -2x$
$y < 3x - 5$
C) $y \geq -2x$
$y \geq 3x - 5$
D) $y \leq -2x$
$y \geq 3x - 5$

29

$$p(x) = x^3 + 5x^2 + 5x - 2$$

Use the function $p(x)$ defined above and the fact that $p(-2) = 0$, what is the factored form of $p(x)$?

A) $p(x) = (x + 2)(x^2 - 3x + 1)$
B) $p(x) = (x + 2)(x^2 + 3x - 1)$
C) $p(x) = (x - 2)(x^2 - 5x + 1)$
D) $p(x) = (x - 2)(x^2 + 5x - 1)$

30

The function $f(x) = 2x^2$ is translated 5 units to the left and 8 units down to create function $g(x)$. Which of the following is the equation for $g(x)$, in the form that reveals its x-intercepts?

A) $g(x) = 2(x + 5)^2 - 8$
B) $g(x) = 2(x + 3)(x + 7)$
C) $g(x) = 2x^2 + 20x + 42$
D) $g(x) = 2(x^2 + 10x + 21)$

DIRECTIONS

For questions 31 – 38, solve each problem, enter your answer in the grid, as described below on the answer sheet.

1. Although not required, it is suggested that you write your answer in the boxes at the top of the columns to help you fill in the circles accurately. You will receive credit only if the circles are filled in correctly.
2. Mark no more than one circle in any column.
3. No question has a negative answer.
4. Some problems may have more than one correct answer. In such cases, grid only one answer.
5. **Mixed numbers** such as $3\frac{1}{2}$ must be gridded as 3.5 or $\frac{7}{2}$. (If 3 1 / 2 is entered into the grid, it will be interpreted as $\frac{31}{2}$, not $3\frac{1}{2}$.)
6. **Decimal answers:** If you obtain a decimal answer with more digits than the grid can accommodate, it may be either rounded or truncated, but it must fill the entire grid.

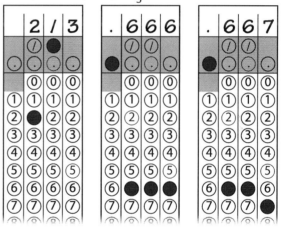

Answer: $\frac{7}{12}$

Write answer in boxes. → 7 / 1 2 ← Fraction line

Grid in result.

Answer: 2.5

2 . 5 ← Decimal point

Acceptable ways to grid $\frac{2}{3}$ are:

2 / 3   . 6 6 6   . 6 6 7

Answer: 201 – either position is correct

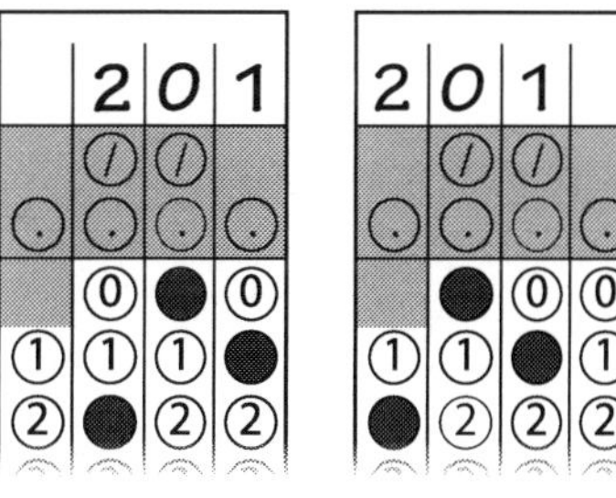

NOTE: You may start your answers in any column, space permitting. Columns you don't need to use should be left blank.

31

Evaluate the expression below for $m = -35$ and $n = -17$.

$$6mn - n^2 + 48$$

32

Addie and Lyla went to a book sale where all the books either cost x dollars or y dollars. Addie bought 5 books costing x dollars each and 3 books costing y dollars each. She spent $21.55 for all 8 books. Lyla bought 2 books costing x dollars each and 6 books costing y dollars each for a total of $23.74. What is the value of y?

33

Frequency of Ages of Members of History Club

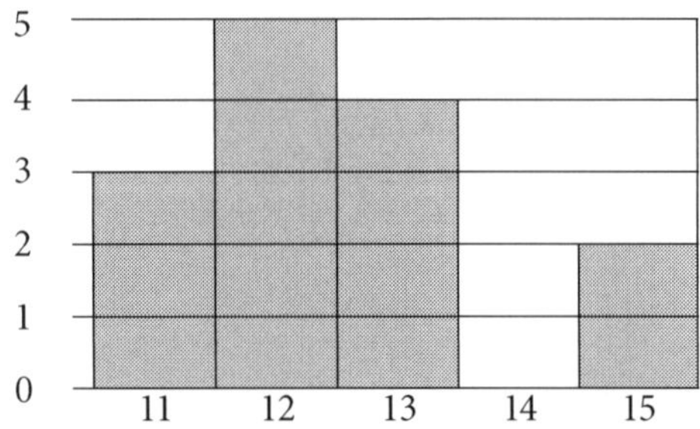

The histogram above contains data showing the number of students of each age that belong to the History Club. What is the range of the data?

34

Samar is buying a sweater that had a pricetag of $22.00, and was on sale for 20% off. When he went to pay for the sweater, he also had a coupon for $10 off which was applied after the sale price. Finally, 7% sales tax was added to his cost. How much did Samar pay for the sweater, rounded to the nearest cent?

(Note: disregard the $ when gridding your answer.)

35

A central angle of a circle has a measure of $\frac{4\pi}{15}$ radians. What is the measure of the angle, in degrees?

36

What is the result of the problem shown below?

$$(10 + 3i)(10 - 3i)$$

Questions 37 and 38 refer to the following information.

A scientist has 6 cells in Lab A. The number of cells increase according to the formula shown below, where is the number of cells and is the number of weeks that have passed.

$$y = 6(3)^x$$

37

How many cells are in Lab A at the end of 4 weeks?

38

A second scientist has 12 cells being used in an experiment in Lab B. The number of these cells increase at the same rate as those in Lab A. How many cells are in Lab B after 6 weeks?

STOP

If you finish before time is called, you may check your work on this section only. Do not turn to any other section.

Tutor Ted®

SAT® Practice Essay #1

ESSAY BOOK

DIRECTIONS

The essay gives you an opportunity to show how effectively you can read and comprehend a passage and write an essay analyzing the passage. In your essay, you should demonstrate that you have read the passage carefully, present a clear and logical analysis, and use language precisely.

Your essay must be written on the lines provided in your answer booklet; except for the Planning Page of the answer booklet, you will receive no other paper on which to write. You will have enough space if you write on every line, avoid wide margins, and keep your handwriting to a reasonable size. Remember that people who are not familiar with your handwriting will read what you write. Try to write or print so that what you are writing is legible to those readers.

You have 50 minutes to read the passage and write an essay in response to the prompt provided inside this booklet.

REMINDERS:

— Do not write your essay in this booklet. Only what you write on the lined pages of your answer booklet will be evaluated.

— An off-topic essay will not be evaluated.

This cover is representative of what you'll see on test day.

THIS TEST BOOKLET MUST NOT BE TAKEN FROM THE ROOM. UNAUTHORIZED REPRODUCTION OR USE OF ANY PART OF THIS TEST BOOKLET IS PROHIBITED.

As you read the passage below, consider how President Lyndon Johnson uses

- evidence, such as facts or examples, to support claims.
- reasoning to develop ideas and to connect claims and evidence.
- stylistic or persuasive elements, such as word choice or appeals to emotion, to add power to the ideas expressed.

Adapted from President Lyndon Johnson's address to the nation delivered March 15, 1965, Washington D.C. Johnson speech was given in support of the Voting Rights Act of 1965, a law to protect the rights of minorities to vote.

1 I speak tonight for the dignity of man and the destiny of democracy.

2 I urge every member of both parties—Americans of all religions and of all colors—from every section of this country—to join me in that cause.

3 At times history and fate meet at a single time in a single place to shape a turning point in man's unending search for freedom. So it was at Lexington and Concord. So it was a century ago at Appomattox. So it was last week in Selma, Alabama.

4 There is no Negro problem. There is no southern problem. There is no northern problem. There is only an American problem.

5 And we are met here tonight as Americans—not as Democrats or Republicans—we are met here as Americans to solve that problem.

6 This was the first nation in the history of the world to be founded with a purpose. The great phrases of that purpose still sound in every American heart, north and south: "All men are created equal" — "Government by consent of the governed" — "Give me liberty or give me death."

7 Those words are a promise to every citizen that he shall share in the dignity of man. This dignity cannot be found in man's possessions. It cannot be found in his power or in his position. It really rests on his right to be treated as a man equal in opportunity to all others. It says that he shall share in freedom, he shall choose his leaders, educate his children, provide for his family according to his ability and his merits as a human being....

8 Many of the issues of civil rights are very complex and most difficult. But about this there can and should be no argument. Every American citizen must have an equal right to vote. There is no reason which can excuse the denial of that right. There is no duty which weighs more heavily on us than the duty we have to ensure that right.

9 Yet the harsh fact is that in many places in this country, men and women are kept from voting simply because they are Negroes....

10 Experience has clearly shown that the existing process of law cannot overcome systematic and ingenious discrimination. No law that we now have on the books—and I have helped to put three of them there—can ensure the right to vote when local officials are determined to deny it.

11 In such a case our duty must be clear to all of us. The Constitution says that no person shall be kept from voting because of his race or his color. We have all sworn an oath before God to support and to defend that Constitution.

12 We must now act in obedience to that oath.

13 Wednesday I will send to Congress a law designed to eliminate illegal barriers to the right to vote....

14 To those who seek to avoid action by their National Government in their home communities—who want to and who seek to maintain purely local control over elections—the answer is simple. Open your polling places to all your people. Allow men and women to register and vote whatever the color of their skin. Extend the rights of citizenship to every citizen of this land. There is no constitutional issue here. The command of the Constitution is plain. There is no moral issue. It is wrong—deadly wrong—to deny any of your fellow Americans the right to vote in this country. There is no issue of States rights or National rights. There is only the struggle for human rights.

15 I have not the slightest doubt what will be your answer....

16 But even if we pass this bill, the battle will not be over. What happened in Selma is part of a far larger movement which reaches into every section and State of America. It is the effort of American Negroes to secure for themselves the full blessings of American life.

17 Their cause must be our cause too, because it is not just Negroes but really it is all of us, who must overcome the crippling legacy of bigotry and injustice. And we shall overcome.

> Write an essay in which you explain how President Lyndon Johnson builds an argument to persuade his audience of the importance of the passage of the Voting Rights Act. In your essay, analyze how Johnson uses one or more of the features listed in the box above (or features of your own choice) to strengthen the logic and persuasiveness of his argument. Be sure that your analysis focuses on the most relevant features of the passage.
>
> Your essay should not explain whether you agree with Johnson's claims, but rather explain how Johnson builds an argument to persuade his audience.

Practice Test 1 ANSWERS

READING

#	Answer	#	Answer
1	B	27	A
2	D	28	A
3	D	29	A
4	D	30	D
5	A	31	B
6	D	32	C
7	C	33	C
8	D	34	B
9	A	35	A
10	B	36	D
11	D	37	C
12	B	38	A
13	C	39	B
14	B	40	D
15	C	41	A
16	A	42	A
17	B	43	D
18	D	44	C
19	C	45	B
20	D	46	C
21	C	47	C
22	D	48	A
23	B	49	C
24	C	50	C
25	D	51	A
26	D	52	B

WRITING & LANGUAGE

#	Answer	#	Answer
1	B	23	B
2	C	24	B
3	A	25	D
4	C	26	D
5	D	27	B
6	C	28	B
7	D	29	A
8	B	30	A
9	D	31	D
10	A	32	C
11	C	33	C
12	C	34	D
13	B	35	B
14	A	36	C
15	A	37	D
16	A	38	D
17	D	39	A
18	B	40	B
19	C	41	D
20	B	42	B
21	C	43	C
22	C	44	D

MATH (No Calculator)

#	Answer
1	D
2	C
3	B
4	A
5	C
6	D
7	A
8	B
9	C
10	C
11	C
12	A
13	A
14	D
15	D
16	6
17	16
18	13
19	7/8 or .875
20	10

MATH (Calculator)

#	Answer
1	D
2	B
3	C
4	D
5	B
6	C
7	A
8	D
9	B
10	A
11	D
12	B
13	A
14	D
15	B
16	C
17	A
18	C
19	A
20	C
21	D
22	B
23	C
24	A
25	A
26	C
27	A
28	D
29	B
30	B
31	3329
32	3.15
33	4
34	8.13
35	48
36	109
37	486
38	8748

PRACTICE TEST 1: SOLUTIONS

Practice Test 1 SOLUTIONS

SECTION 1: READING

PASSAGE: THE MINISTER'S BLACK VEIL

1) B
Main idea questions are great to answer first while the passage is fresh in your mind. No one sincerely believes that a stranger has taken Mr. Hooper's place as minister and there is no evidence that he wears the veil in order to coerce confessions from his parishioners, so we can eliminate C and D. His wearing of the veil motivates the passage's events as the parishioners react with unease, so B is the best choice.

2) D
The parishioners' feelings of "unease and guilt" brought about by the minister's black veil are expressed when the author states, "Each member of the congregation... felt as if the preacher had crept upon them behind his awful veil and discovered their hoarded iniquity of deed or thought."

3) D
The parishioners are never "apathetic," always expressing some sort of sentiment toward the minister's veil. Initially they are curious as to why he wears a veil. D best fits because by the end of the passage, the parishioners feel concerned, quaking and longing to see who is truly beneath the veil.

4) D
The context describes the "hushed repose" that meets, or accompanies, a minister's entrance. Vocabulary questions are easy money—grab them first!

5) A
While the parishioners may be described as "skeptical" of why the minister wears a veil or "distrustful" of who is behind the veil, the general sentiment is "unnerved," as the whole congregation is in some way perturbed by the veil.

6) D
Mr. Hooper is described as more mild than energetic, so we can eliminate "arrogant," "terrifying," and "histrionic," all very extreme descriptions. "Reserved" most aptly fits the minister.

7) C
C describes Mr. Hooper as a good, reserved preacher who avoids driving his congregation "thither by the thunders of the word," which someone more bold and theatrical would likely do.

8) D
The phrase describes Mr. Hooper's sermon that day, which was "marked by the same characteristics of style and manner as the general series of his pulpit oratory," but due to his unnerving veil, was received by the congregation as something much darker.

9) A
Questions which tell you exactly where to look (i.e. fifth paragraph) are easy money as there's no need to scan the passage and your caveman notes to find the location of the answer. Tackle these first if you're low on time! The fifth paragraph enlightens the reader on the minister's point of view. It neither characterizes him nor shows his dismay, but it does signify his awareness of his auditors, giving the reader a "brief speculation of Mr. Hooper's feelings."

10) B
While A, C, and D are all expressed as possibilities by the parishioners, the reason for Mr. Hooper's veil is never disclosed.

PASSAGE: IS POPULATION REALLY A PROBLEM?

11) D
A and B are points specific to certain paragraphs, not the passage as a whole. The author never supports government regulations as mentioned in C. The passage explores the causes of overpopulation, discussing reproductive rights and women's empowerment in paragraphs 2 and 3, respectively. Always answer main idea questions first while the passage is fresh in your mind!

12) B
The passage begins with Davis' research on India's birth and death rates, which gave rise to the stance that overpopulation begets poverty. By the conclusion, research on the effects of modern contraception, education, and employment points to the reverse: poverty begets overpopulation.

13) C
Evidence for the shift mentioned in the previous question is in the conclusion when the author discusses a study which points to the reverse of the trend with which the passage opened. Overpopulation is actually a result of poverty.

14) B
There was a "tendency" to blame India's poverty for its overpopulation. Easy money!

15) C
The author certainly doesn't view overpopulation as "inconsequential," nor does she discuss it as "dangerous" or "uncontrollable." The author seeks to correct opinions on India's poverty and overpopulation, so "misunderstood" best fits.

16) A
Graph questions are easy money as you know exactly where to find the answer: the graph! Use your pencil to line up each year with its respective growth rate percentage. While all the year pairs are relatively close, 1950 and 1995 are the closest.

17) B
Prior to the Cairo Conference, forced sterilizations were common practice in order to combat overpopulation. "As a consequence, people started avoiding hospitals and health services, including vaccination, due to fear of being nabbed for sterilization." Therefore, B is the correct answer.

18) D
Questions with line or paragraph numbers are great questions to knock out early as you know exactly where to go. After discussing the ICPD's "paradigm shift," the author discusses the conference's opposition, presenting alternate viewpoints. A is false as compromise was never reached, B is incorrect as religion is never discussed in the fourth paragraph, and C is out as the fourth paragraph does not support previous findings.

19) C
To debar one from candidacy means to prevent, not to expel or to condemn. "Prohibiting" most nearly means to prevent. Another easy money!

20) D
The graph shows no support for A or C. The trend in the world's population growth rate actually rose after 1960. The downward trend began in 1980, so D is your answer.

PASSAGE: MERCURY POLLUTION IN VEGETABLES, GRAINS, AND SOILS

21) C
"Reading the Intro" is a great strategy to use for main idea questions, especially on scientific passages. The title, "Mercury Pollution in Vegetables, Grains, and Soil," enlightens us to the fact that mercury pollution affects the health of surrounding crops and soil, or "local produce." According to the passage, this mercury pollution is caused by coal-fired power plants, so C is the best answer.

22) D
Residents of Minamata Bay, Japan suffered from mercury poisoning as a result of consuming mercury-contaminated fish and seafood, resulting in at least 439 deaths. This anecdote serves to show the severe danger of mercury contamination.

23) B
The authors write, "when examining the environmental consequences of coal burning," mercury is an important metal to "consider," or "study." Vocabulary questions are easy money—you have the line number so you just need to read the context of the word! Start with these if you're short on time.

24) C
We can eliminate A and D, as the authors are neither "understanding" nor "ambivalent" towards the dangers of coal-fired power plants. "Apprehension" accurately describes the authors' attitude; "disdain" does not fit the tone of the passage.

25) D
The authors reveal the "potential health risks for the people living surrounding coal-fired power plants," demonstrating their "apprehension."

26) D
A and B are both reversed. Mercury concentration is higher in roots when absorbed from the soil, and higher in leaves and fruits when absorbed from the air. C is incorrect because tomato and pepper both had higher concentrations of mercury contamination. The second paragraph provides evidence for D.

27) A
A evidences that mercury concentrations in vegetable samples were higher than those in grain samples.

28) A
B is incorrect because the maximum acceptance level of mercury contamination is the same for all vegetables. C is false because the graph does not depict mercury contamination frequency. D is incorrect because the measured levels of mercury contamination differed for each vegetable. A is correct because plants grown underground (i.e. roots) had the lowest measured level of mercury contamination.

29) A
A best answers this question as metal absorption and accumulation differ for all species of plants. The proximity of potential contaminates may not matter for certain species. Mercury contamination may not be the specific culprit for a farmer so grains are not necessarily better than vegetables, and air versus soil may not be relevant.

30) D
All measured mercury concentrations exceeded the maximum acceptance level. Mercury concentration in fruits was double, not triple, that of roots. Mercury contamination was most likely spread through the air because the measured levels of mercury concentration in fruits, leaves, and stems were all greater than the level in roots.

PASSAGE: "CONCERNING DANGERS FROM FOREIGN FORCE AND INFLUENCE" AND "ANTIFEDERALIST PAPER #17"

31) B
Easy money vocabulary questions are a great place to start! According to Passage 1, in order for the government to function, the people must cede some of their rights and "entrust" it with its necessary powers. While "furnish" could technically work, it doesn't fit the tone of the sentence.

32) C
The author of Passage 1 argues that the prosperity of the country depends on the preservation and prosperity of the Union. He doesn't defend giving the government complete authority, so C best describes this view.

33) C
C notes that "to preserve and perpetuate [the Union] was the great object of the people in forming that Constitutional convention," evidence that the author of Passage 1 defends having a "strong, centralized government."

34) B
An effective strategy with paired passages is to complete all Passage 1 questions before reading Passage 2. Another easy money vocabulary question—knock these out first! One single government may "exercise," or use, the power to make laws; "employ" best fits this sentence.

35) A

The author of Passage 2 argues against a centralized government, in favor of individual states' rights. We can eliminate any answer choices that oppose this thesis, like C. D inaccurately mentions New York and Massachusetts and is too specific to be a central claim. B is also inaccurate as the author argues that there should be a check on the centralized authority of one government, not that there should be strength in each confederate state. A best encapsulates Passage 2's central claim: be weary of one national government as it will eventually eliminate state governments.

36) D

Passage 2 suspects the federal government's ambition to cast aside individual states' rights as they "will be a clog upon the wheels of the government of the United States," as mentioned in D.

37) C

Questions that give you the line numbers are great questions to tackle if you're short on time—you know exactly where to find the answer! Article Six asserts the Constitution as the "supreme law of the land" to which all states are bound. The author chooses to quote this article in order to demonstrate the federal government's control and the state governments' lack thereof.

38) A

Passage 1 maintains that a centralized government is necessary for the country to survive and prosper. Passage 2 directly refutes this claim, arguing that a centralized government violates states' rights in pursuit of a self-serving ambition of total authority. A reflects this relationship.

39) B

The author of Passage 1 would disagree with A and D, while the author of Passage 2 would disagree with C. By writing their respective arguments, both authors support the belief that citizens should be actively involved in the country's governance.

40) D

Wordier questions are usually best to save for last—don't spend too much time getting one right answer versus several right answers! The author of Passage 1 argues that a centralized government would "conduce more to the interest of the people of America." The danger lies with distinct confederacies, which would put the Union's preservation and prosperity in jeopardy.

41) A

Passage 1 supports a centralized federal government to which states cede some of their natural rights in order to preserve the Union. Passage 2 defends states' rights, cautioning against a centralized government with too much power. Both passages form an opinion on the extent of the government's power in the new country, so A is your answer.

PASSAGE: ASSESSMENT OF THE STATE OF MILLET FARMING IN INDIA

42) A

Always remember to read the intro first! Intros give you an idea of the passage's subject and/or tone. In this case, we know the passage is about millet, so we can eliminate B. C and D are specific points in the passage, not the main purpose. Throughout the passage, the author presents the many benefits of millet in "fighting climate change, poverty, and malnutrition," so it's A.

43) D

Millet "reduces agriculture's carbon footprint." This "impact" could also be called an "effect." Vocabulary questions are easy money—knock 'em out first!

44) C

In the second paragraph, the author notes that, "The food policies pursued over the years have pushed many people away from millet despite it being more nutritious than rice and wheat." "Neglectful" best describes this practice.

45) B

We know the evidence for the previous question has to be in the second paragraph, so we can eliminate A. B describes "neglectful" food policies which push people towards less nutritious grains.

46) C

In the second paragraph, the author blames state policies which have "shaped the minds of people to neglect minor millet." The passage directly negates A, and D extrapolates beyond what the passage asserts. B makes an assumption about all farmers which is not supported by the passage. We can reasonably infer that C is true.

47) C

The CGIAR estimated that global agricultural production of wheat, rice, and maize will face considerable loss due to climate change. The author states, "Millet may be the answer to this dire need," so he would most likely agree with C.

48) A

A provides evidence of a 13 to 20 percent decrease in global production of wheat, rice, and maize in the coming decades as a result of climate change, supporting the author's belief that countries should seek alternative grains because of this.

49) C

Millets are known for their "prolonged and easy storability under ordinary circumstances." Therefore, if circumstances are normal, or "typical," millets are easily stored. Never leave a vocabulary question unanswered—they're easy money!

50) C

Graph questions are generally easy money as you know exactly where to look for the answer. We know finger millet and pearl millet require under 500mm, but over 250mm of water, which leaves A and C. The bars are not close enough to 500mm to be 475mm, so C is your answer.

51) A

Finger millet and pearl millet both require the least amount of water of all the crops studied. The graph does not tell us the crops' monetary value nor their durability, so we can eliminate B and D. Groundnut requires more water than do finger millet and pearl millet, so C is incorrect as well.

52) 52 B

Wordier questions are best saved for last if you're low on time—they take longer to answer! The passage directly addresses the problems associated with D, and A and C are not supported by the passage. Throughout the passage, the author asserts the widespread benefits of millet farming, so the answer is B.

SECTION 2: WRITING AND LANGUAGE

PASSAGE: THE LOWELL MILL GIRLS' PLACE IN THE HISTORY OF THE INDUSTRIAL REVOLUTION

1) B

Jumping right in on a wordy clause you need to simplify...welcome to the SAT Writing and Language Test! The key on this one is to make sure all of the modifying, adjective clauses are in the right place. Answer choice A is wrong because of where the phrase "in Lowell, Massachusetts" is located. What happened in Lowell? The girls and women became textile workers, so that adjective clause needs to be right next door to that. Answer choice B puts that (and the other adjective phrases) in the right place so that everything is being described sensibly.

2) C

Give the SAT what it wants! This question asks you to provide a logical introduction to the sentence. Figuring out what that will be will definitely require reading at LEAST the whole sentence, if not the paragraph above and below too. Once you read, you should see that this paragraph introduces Francis Lowell and his business interests. C provides the most useful and relevant information to set up his Lowell in the passage.

3) A

Possessive pronoun question. Whose "first mill" are we talking about? The one belonging to the Boston Manufacturing Company, right? That's a singular, collective noun, so the singular possessive "its" is the right call.

4) C

The correct answer describes pretty perfectly what this sentence's function is in the paragraph.

5) D

Parallelism question. "Not only for the wage model it created" followed by "but also for who it employed" is the closest match.

6) C

We are looking for a word that means *really hard,* which eliminates A as too extreme and D as not extreme enough. Between B and C, C is the more academic choice. Give 'em what they want!

7) D

The clause in question, though informative (and pretty infuriating), is a grammatically inessential "appositive" clause. Therefore, we can either punctuate it with two commas or two dashes, making D the only valid option.

8) B

The plural noun "women" earlier in the sentence should leave you deciding between B and D. Grammatically, we need the word "have" to complete the sentence.

9) D

If you remembered the "that v. which" lesson in Chapter 1, you got this right. If not, go back and check it out.

10) A

This example is both new information and relevant to the claim that the Mill Girls "did not fail to act when confronted with injustice." That's a pretty perfect recipe for adding or including something.

11) C

The ideas in the two clauses of this sentence definitely contrast, which should leave you deciding between answer choices A and C. Your ears may help you with this one, but if you're still having trouble, "however" usually begins an independent clause (However, the band decided not to play any of its classic songs) while "though" usually begins a dependent one (Though Rhode Island is the smallest state by area).

PASSAGE: THE SLEEPY TEENAGE BRAIN AT SCHOOL

12) C

Let's fight this apostrophe battle first. We're talking about one body possessing functions, so C and D are the only answer choices in contention. What's the only difference between these answer choices? The additional apostrophe after functions in answer choice D. Since these functions are not possessing anything, the answer must be C.

13) B

If "social factors alone" cannot account for it, any answer choice that suggest that teenagers' sleep needs are dependent on culture or socialization can be eliminated. That pretty much leaves us with answer choice B.

14) A

These answer choices make us consider a combination of verb tense and singular/plural. What allows animals to fall asleep? Melanin secretion, which is singular. That leaves us with A and D, and I think we can all agree that D sounds very very stupid in the sentence.

15) A

What's rule #1 on the SAT Writing and Language Test? Keep it short and simple! All of the wrong answer choices complicate the sentence by adding unnecessary words or punctuation.

16) A
The right answer here is no one's first choice, so let's work through process of elimination. C and D are both jumbled hot messes. The fact that the correct answer begins with the word "that" has a tendency to freak people out, so let's look at B. This sentence is fundamentally about the contrast between ideas: teenagers have a biological need to sleep late *but* society doesn't seem to give a crap. You may not love the structure of A, but B simply can't work because of the "and." A grammatically correct sentence that means makes no sense, after all, defeats a zombie apocalypse in a yellow but watermelon helicopter. (Case in point.)

17) D
Redundancy question. "Habitual," "habitually" and "over the long-term" are all ways of saying "chronically."

18) B
This is an idiom question, so you've just got to ask yourself, "do we say it that way?"

19) C
We are looking for a transition word that indicates agreement. This paragraph is all about the negative effects of sleep deprivation; in other words, all of these ideas *agree.* A and D indicate contrast, so they're out. B is about chronology/time, and that's not what we want either.

20) B
If sleep deprivation causes an increase in automobile accidents, and a school district in Wyoming instituted a later start time to address this problem, the answer that supports this idea most directly will be one that shows a correlation between the later start time and a decrease in automobile accidents involving teenagers.

21) C
A brief review of "that v. which" in Chapter 1 of this book should help you eliminate A. Punctuation rules tell us that B is a comma splice and, well, D just sounds bad in the sentence.

22) C
Classic relevance question. Sure, the sentence references adolescents, but the information presented in the sentence is not only irrelevant to the point being made but interrupts the flow of thought that's flowin' quite nicely as it is.

PASSAGE: ARE WE ENGINEERING THE SMELL OUT OF FLOWERS?

23) B
Two battles here, both related to punctuation. If you read the entire sentence (and you always should), you should see that "due to the...industry" is an appositive clause setting aside grammatically inessential information. Therefore, we need the comma after the word "industry" to bookend the clause. That leaves us with B and D. Look at what's on either side of the suggested punctuation. Could these both be standalone sentences? Yes, they could. Therefore, we have three punctuation options: period, semicolon, and colon. Do you see comma on that list? No, you do not. So even if the idea of picking an answer with a colon still strikes fear into your heart, the comma just ain't gonna cut it.

24) B
All about the verb. Darwin may be long dead, but his theory is alive and well in the present, and according to his theory- "traits" (plural) *have* an evolutionary purpose.

25) D
Remember, the SAT loves to eliminate extraneous words from a sentence or passage, so DELETE is very often the right move. This sentence is grammatically correct and clear without any of the additional words in A, B, or C. Additionally, answer choices A and B create independent clauses that, if inserted, would need to be punctuated

differently. The word "being" is probably the word the SAT hates the more than any other word in the English language. Maybe "being" once stole the SAT's boyfriend. Point is: if you see this word as any part of an answer choice, eliminate it without a second thought.

26) D
Knowing that flower producers are people and people must be referred to using either "who" or "whom" should help you get it down to C and D. And then? Ah, the old who v. whom debate! Are flower producers a subject (are they in charge of the action), or are they an object on the receiving end? The flower producers are "working," which is pretty active, so we want to use the subject pronoun "who" to describe them. You can also remember the tip that "whom" will almost always follow a preposition (to whom/for whom/from whom/by whom/etc.) and we don't see one here.

27) B
For this diction question, remember that the adjective has to be something we use to describe "color." If you got creative, you could probably make a case for A, C, or D, but does the SAT want you to get creative? NO IT DOES NOT. We are looking for the least creative, most academic choice, and of these options, "vibrant" is most common choice for describing color.

28) B
Let's flow, baby! This question usually comes down to A and B, as this sentence about how scent relates to reproduction is off topic once we move on to the ways in which flower producers have come to prioritize traits other than scent. Sentence 4 does not sound terrible where it is, but notice that we are still talking about flowers *in the wild.* Sentence 2 is also about the evolutionary benefit of scent for flowers in the wild; however, sentence 3 contrasts wild with "cultivated" flowers, and at this point the paragraph transitions to a discussion about these flowers only. Therefore, we must move sentence 4 so as to complete our discussion about wild flowers before moving on.

29) A
Is this sentence the exception to basically all of our tried-and-true SAT strategies? Yes. It's wordy. It's chock full of commas. It is, however, the only sentence that accurately and directly describes the RhNUDX1 as the thing that creates the sweet fragrance.

30) A
This pronoun refers to the singular noun "lily," so C and D are out. Now it's time for the it's/its game! Ooh, look at my "it's" in the previous sentence. That could also read: "it is time." It's = it is. Its = possessive, as in "its origin."

31) D
Because "valuing look above all else" would only include the columns where look is the highest priority, the data does not support answer choice A. B is out because, while preferences are not unanimous, the majority of people seem to prioritize look and smell in some combination. C is wrong because longevity is definitely not #2, and that leaves us with D. If you add the totals in every column where smell is a priority (not necessarily #1), you do arrive at a majority of respondents.

32) C
The key word in this question stem is "trade-offs." Trade-offs = some good, some bad, right?

33) C
The word "exclusively" eliminates A as too extreme, B is irrelevant to the point both the passage and the graph are making, and D is definitely disproven by the graph.

PASSAGE: SONGS ABOUT CARS

34) D
It should be pretty easy to get this down to A and D. The subject "songs" eliminates the singular "itself" in answer choice B. Answer

choice C is not a thing- how can a "them" have one "self"? Okay, maybe conjoined twins, but I still say that's two "selves" connected...you know what? Let's just move on. D is correct because we are introducing the idea that car songs are really about *us.* If this is not yet clear, keep reading a sentence or two and it should be.

35) B
Do you see that lonely first dash earlier in the sentence, sitting all by herself with no like-minded punctuation to talk to? On the SAT, dashes are used to create appositive clauses, and therefore will almost always come in pairs. Don't let that first dash stay lonely! Give her a friend!

36) C
If you're reading the entire sentence (and you should be), your ear should be able to do most of the heavy lifting on this one, as B and D sound very very stupid in this sentence. C is correct because Carnegie "worked" (past tense) "to become" (further down the road of his own life) mega-rich; however, you can also end up with C if you recognize that the –ing verb "becoming" would require a comma before it in order to work at all.

37) D
Yes, the passage brought up the brief example of Andrew Carnegie, but it was only to provide context for the *real* focus of the paragraph: cars.

38) D
Comma question. C is tempting because we know the SAT *loves* to eliminate commas, but this sentence without any pauses feels like a train with no breaks. D provides us with a nice, easy ride- setting off the grammatically inessential appositive clause "no longer tasked with producing war-related supplies" with two commas.

39) A
This is a diction question, so the SAT wants you to choose the most conventional word for the intended meaning.

40) B
The clue "this shift" in sentence 5 tells us that the sentence before must refer explicitly to a "shift," which in this case is the democratization of the American Dream. In addition, sentence 5 introduces that both car songs and car *ownership* reflected this shift, which means that all sentences (including sentences 2, 3, and 4) that further discuss car ownership need to come after this introductory thought. Yes, we don't get to car *songs* until later in the paragraph, but sentence 5 introduces both ownership and songs and thus must precede both discussions.

41) D
A good transition builds a full bridge between paragraphs- a little of what just happened combined with a little of what we're about to get into. "That optimism" in answer choice D is our harkening back, and "would take a hit" is what drives us forward into the next idea. Full bridge! If you chose either A or B, remember that the central idea of the passage relates more to *our* perception of the times rather than the economic realities of the times themselves.

42) B
Which of these choices do we most conventionally use to describe the "economy"? If you keep it academic, you'll ace these questions every time.

43) C
Who or what is the subject? Dreamers! Plural! And dreamers "convey." If you chose D, look at the tenses of the other verbs in the sentence. They're all present tense! Sure, the song was written in the past, but the story itself is not constrained by time. (So I guess the real lesson from this question is that the only way to live forever is to have someone write a song about you.)

44) D
All of these choices are grammatically correct, so the SAT must be testing you on *meaning.* Where's a good place to find the main idea of

a passage? In the conclusion, and look- we're right there! The following sentence describes a combination of despair and defiance, and that's a perfect match for D.

SECTION 3: MATH - NO CALCULATOR

1) D

As usual, the SAT wants to test your Algebra skills; start here by substituting 9 for t. Distribute the 3 to both the x and the -7 (forgetting to do that might be the most common error students make), and combine like terms! You should get that $3x = 30$, and $x = 10$.

2) C

Kind of a tougher type of question for #2. Start by doing what we do with two binomial terms that are being multiplied together: FOIL. You'll get $-20 + 28i - 15i + 21i^2$. Combine the two like terms, and then substitute -1 in for i^2. Be careful with your negative signs—that $21i^2$ will turn into -21. Once you do all that, you'll be left with $-41 + 13i$.

3) B

Story problem in terms of variables...shoot, I wish we had a strategy for those. Oh wait, we do! Plugging in numbers! On this one, I chose $n = 2$, which means that Oscar walked 6 miles (four more than two) per day. I used $t = 10$ as the number of days because 10 is a fun and easy number to use. That means that Oscar walked a total of $6 \times 10 = 60$ miles. Go Oscar! Now, which answer choice gives us the same result of 60? Only B, the right answer.

4) A

Classic SAT question that asks you to *understand* the linear equation. Think about slope and intercept. 72 is the y-intercept—aka the "starting point," as we've learned to think of it, and -15 is the slope because it's being multiplied by the x (or in this case, the d) variable. We're being asked about the -15, or the slope. The question asks about it as positive 15, so I'll switch to that. Slope represents what's changing in an equation. What's *changing* here? The number of cakes that April has left to decorate. How much is it going down by? The number of cakes she can decorate each day. That's what the 15 is—it's how many cakes she can frost in one day.

5) C

Just a bunch of algebra (which, come to think of it, would be a really good name for the SAT Math test.) You want to carefully divide each term in the numerator by that $3y$ in the denominator. USE YOUR PENCIL. This is a question that is 100% about working carefully. When you divide by $3y$, you'll wind up with the three terms in answer choice C.

6) D

Again, a question about what a linear equation *means. These aren't the worst questions, really. Once you do a few of them and start to get it, they become pretty easy. 650 is the y-intercept, aka the "starting point." What's Juan's starting point? In this case, the amount of money he had in his account to begin with. That's D.*

7) A

Can I interest you in an algebra problem? Whether you replied "yes" or "no," this is another one for you. We need to solve for l in this equation. To do that, we've got to bring our algebraic fundamentals. First, move the πr^2 term to the left by subtracting it from both sides. Next, divide by πr to get l by itself. You might think you're done now, but what you have does not yet match any of the answer choices. That's because you can reduce the $\frac{\pi r^2}{\pi r}$ term down to just r. Once you do, you'll have answer choice A.

8) B

Good ol' fashioned algebra, plus some arithmetic! Remember when math was JUST arithmetic? Ah, fourth grade. Good times. Anyway, notice here that you're given $\frac{t}{r}$, then asked for $\frac{r}{t}$. What's the relationship there? They are reciprocals! OK, so if $\frac{t}{r} = 5$, then $\frac{r}{t} = \frac{1}{5}$. Substitute that into the second equation. Here's the fun arithmetic part: subtracting $\frac{1}{5}$ from 9.2...*without a calculator!!!* You may know that $\frac{1}{5}$ is the same thing as 0.2. Wow, does that make this question pretty simple. Subtract that 0.2 from 9.2 and *voila*: you are left with the answer, 9.

9) C

Solving systems on the SAT is pretty much a matter of picking the best approach. *Any* approach *can* work...but frequently, the *best* approach can save you time and pain. I think substitution is the best approach here—you can't readily combine these equations, and there is single, solitary y in the second equation just begging to be left alone on one side of the equation. When you move that equation around, you'll get $y = 5 - 5x$. Substitute that in for y in the first equation and you'll be off to the races!

Special bonus thought: on this one, you're solving for a coordinate pair—an (x, y) solution. You don't need both. Once you find $x = 2$, you are already down to one answer choice. Use that value to confirm that both equations give you a -5 as your y to confirm. If you've worked carefully you should have the answer at the ready.

10) C

What's the discriminant? It's the thing under the radical in the quadratic equation. Go back to that chapter and refresh it if you weren't sure. What does the discriminant tell us? How many roots we have. When it's equal to 0, we have one "double-root," aka two roots at one single point. Pick the answer choice with the upward facing parabola (it can't be sideways because this is $y = x^2$, not $x = y^2$) with its vertex right on the x-axis. Boom.

11) C

More systems to solve manually (since we don't have a calculator on this section). Here, we want to find the point when the total miles biked are equal for both guys. Set the two equations equal to each other, do some careful arithmetic, and you'll get a good clean value of $x = 10$. Plug that value into BOTH equations—to make sure you get the same output from each one—and you'll be sure that 91.5 is the answer.

12) A

Varying directly means that to get from one variable to another, we need to multiply by some constant value. Here, we're trying to get from radius, r, to time, t, in minutes. What could you multiply 60 minutes by to get to a radius of $\frac{1}{4}$? The answer is in the arithmetic: it's $\frac{1}{240}$, since $\frac{60}{240}$ reduces to $\frac{1}{4}$.

13) A

What's an inverse function? Check out the chapter called "Advanced Stuff" in our book to find out. What you want to do is switch x and y and re-solve for y. It's really pretty easy once you know the rules! Add the 2, divide by 3, and you're there.

14) D

This one is GNARLY...by which I mean that I like it. You want to use your exponent properties. Actually, before you do that, you want to rewrite 8 as 2^3. Why? Because all of our exponent properties depend on starting with the same base. Once you do that, you'll be left with $\frac{(2^3)^x}{2^y}$. You can simplify that (using the first exponent property) to $\frac{2^{3x}}{2^y}$. And you can simplify THAT, using the second exponent property, to 2^{3x-y}. Now: what does that equal, if $2x + 5y = 20$? Bad news: those two expressions—$(3x - y)$ and $(2x - 5y)$—have pretty much nothing in common. The second one does not help you to find the first one. If we have two missing variables, we need two equations to find them. Here, we only have one, so we don't have enough information, and the answer is the somehow-always-slightly-dissatisfying "Cannot be determined" answer choice.

15) D
By comparison, 15 is hella easier than 14. You just have to FOIL carefully. So let's do it. You should get $14x^2 - 35x + 2x - 5$. Combine like terms (and watch your negative signs) and you should wind up with D.

16) 6
I find that domain restrictions (like $k > 0$ on this question) tend to be more confusing than helpful. You can't grid a negative sign on these questions anyway, so why would we be tempted to do so? Anyway, you should pretty much disregard these on the SAT—I literally cannot remember a single time when a domain restriction was helpful. Just solve. $k^2 = 36$, and $k = 6$. No sweat.

17) 16
Here's a combo pack of geometry and algebra. Mind those letters carefully: RT is the WHOLE diagonal, while SO is just HALF a diagonal. The diagonals of a rectangle are congruent, which, looking at the thing, I am willing to bet you would have figured out just based on the diagram. Set $6x + 4$ equal to TWICE $7x - 6$. When you get that $x = 2$, avoid the temptation to answer that since you want the length of the diagonal, not x. Plug it into $6x + 4$ to get 16, your answer.

18) 13
Another system of equations, so again, we're deciding what the right approach is. It's substitution or combination since we don't have our calculators. I recommend combination since the y values can be eliminated, and I recommend you stack the 2nd equation on top of the first. Do that, then subtract the second equation from the first. You'll quickly get that $x = 13$.

19) 7/8 or .875
Trig identity question. Good news! If you know the identity, this question is mad easy. Bad news! If you don't know that identity, you're out of luck, pal. The rule is that the sine of any angle is equal to the cosine of its complementary angle. Review our chapter on trig to make sure you know this one so that you are on the "good news" side of the battle.

20) 10
First off, don't be thrown off by the choice of the letters "h" and "n" here...they work just the same way as "f" and "x." Second, don't be too concerned about the seemingly extensive amount of work required...once you jump in, you'll realize it won't actually be that tedious. Find $h(2)$. OK, that's equal to 1. Now find $h(3)$. That's 1.5. Keep on going. Eventually you'll have $1 + 1.5 + 2 + 2.5 + 3$. Add that REALLY CAREFULLY to get 10, the right answer.

SECTION 4: MATH - CALCULATOR

1) D
Hooray for the calculator! There is no better way to start this section than with a question most easily solved with the ol' graphing calculator. Try this: graph the equation exactly as written. Press TRACE, then start typing the values in the answers. You'll see that at -3, the function bottoms out, and as it moves to the right, it is indeed increasing.

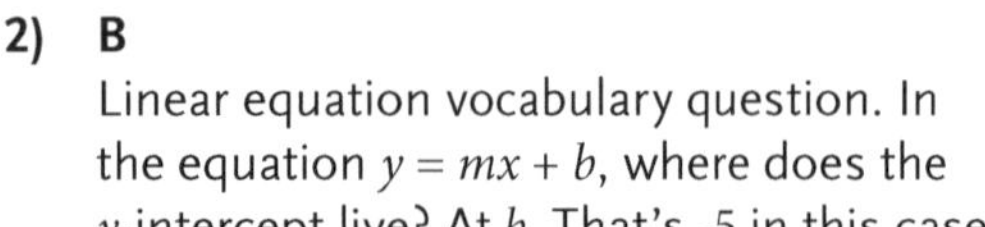

2) B
Linear equation vocabulary question. In the equation $y = mx + b$, where does the y-intercept live? At b. That's -5 in this case.

3) C
Use your angle knowledge here: the fact that the angles in triangle CED have to add up to 180. Then remember the trick about numbering the angles around parallel lines cut by a transversal. That angle we're trying to find will have the same measure as angle EDC, 74 degrees.

4) D
Hope you like algebra! That's what it says on the welcome mat at SAT headquarters. Add the three, multiply by 2, and hopefully you get 28.

5) B
Circle graphs are all about setting a proportion out of 360 degrees. Here's the one you want on this problem: $\frac{9\%}{100\%} = \frac{x \text{ degrees}}{360 \text{ degrees}}$. Cross multiply to solve, and you'll get x approximately equals 32.

6) C
A geometry problem AND a word problem... ooh la la! Not sure why that should be exciting at all, actually. OK, what you want to do is find the perimeter of the building. The formula for rectangle perimeter is $2l + 2w$, but I think it's easier just to draw a rectangle and realize that you've got two pairs of equal sides and you need to add them together. Here, that'll be $2(425) + 2(100)=1,050$ meters. Then, the team leader marches around five times: $5 \times 1,050 = 5,250$. Notice that 5,250 is a WRONG answer here...that's because the question asks for the answer in kilometers. 1 kilometer = 1,000 meters, so 5,250 meters converts into 5.25 kilometers.

7) A
One tricky thing about this problem: you might be tempted to average 17, 18, 19, 20, and 21. The reason you can't do it that way is that different numbers of students got each of these times. We need to include the frequency when we make the calculation. We have to add up everybody's times. Easiest way is to multiply each time by the number of students who got that time, then add the results, so $17 \times 3 + 18 \times 7 + 19 \times 7 + 20 \times 4 + 21 \times 6 = 516$. Then divide that by the total number of students $(3 + 7 + 7 + 4 + 6 = 27)$, and $\frac{516}{27} = 19.1111$ etc.

8) D
Even though there are absolute value brackets involved here, this is still just basic algebra. You want to break this equation into two: one where it is equal to positive 28, and another where it is equal to -28. That's all you gotta do. Solve those two equations and you'll get 16 and -96.

9) B
SAT loves these formula questions. Key thing for you: don't panic. Just move stuff around the way you know how. In this case, divide by 40.5π and you'll have r all by itself. Voila.

10) A
Another usage of the formula, and another case when we're happy we have a calculator. Plug 5280 in for the distance and divide by 40.5π. One thing: be careful to put the40.5π in parentheses if you divide it in one step. If you don't divide by (40.5π), the calculator will divide by 40.5, then MULTIPLY by π. You don't want that.

11) D
Keep it real chill and solve for x. Remember, inequalities only mess with you when have to multiply or divide by a negative. When that happens, you have to switch the direction the inequality sign is pointing. But we don't have to worry about that on this question if we subtract the $4x$ to the right side and simplify from there.

12) B
What is median? The middle value. In this classroom, who represents the middle value? There are 26 students, an even number, so the two middle students are the 13th and 14th

students. Where are they located? In the group of students who have visited one other state. (For the record, as of this moment I have visited 46 states. Wow, am I competing with the hypothetical first-graders from the question? That is sad.)

13) A

Table and graph questions are frequently really reading questions. You have to make sure you read the question carefully so you can give them what they asked for. When the question says "given that the person is between 40 and 60," that means we ONLY want to include that group as our total number. That's $25 + 47 + 157 = 229$. Then, we want to put the selected group, the "winners," on top. Here, that's the 157 who send over 50 messages. And that's it: $\frac{157}{229}$.

14) D

Use your average formula. Add all of Juan's tests thus far, plus his unknown final score. Divide that by the total number of tests once he's taken the last test (that's 6), and set it equal to Juan's goal of 87. Boom. Don't even need to solve it.

15) B

Paying attention to plus and minus signs is the most important factor here. Balloon A is rising, so it's slope, or gain, should be positive. Balloon B is descending, so it's slope should be negative. Add in their "starting point" values and you'll have a right answer pretty quickly.

16) C

Fun, weirdly phrased question. You want to throw four in as your x-value in both equations from the previous problem and see what happens. They'll both return 1300 as the altitude, so the answer is C. Tricky: this reminds me of Evidence Buddies on the Reading test, where if you get the first one right, you're a lot more likely to get the second one too.

17) A

Graph this thing, baby! Unless you know just from looking what the maximum is, in which case, pick the answer right away, baby! When you graph it, you'll see that -7 is the maximum. Any questions?

18) C

Kind of a tough inequality. Plug in 0 for both x values to simplify a bit. You'll get $y < 5$ and $y < -5$. If a has to be a solution to the SYSTEM of inequalities, then it needs to make both of them true. The only way it can do that in this case is if it is less than -5.

19) A

Get used to these questions, guys, because you are going to see a LOT of them on the SAT. Start by writing a system of equations. First one: $c + t = 399$. (In case it wasn't clear, c = cars and t = trucks.) Second one: $0.75c + 1.1t = 326.55$. Then pick your approach. In this case, I'm between using the answer choices to see what works and substituting. I used the answers myself and it worked pretty quickly. Not a slam dunk, but this is kind of a pain-in-the-ass question anyway.

20) C

Great percent trick: if you want to quickly apply a discount (or an increase, like a tax), multiply by 1 minus (or plus) the change in percent. In this case, we want a 15% decrease each year. That means we want to have 85% left over once the decrease happens, since $1 - 0.15 = 0.85$. You can keep multiplying by .85 to make subsequent 15% reductions of the value.

21) D

Ahhh...my fave, probability. Find the probability of each outcome happening first. In the first drawing, we have 2 winners out of 5 possible musicians. In the second drawing, since we did NOT put that first person's name back in the mix, we have 1 winner out

of 4 possible musicians. Since both things need to happen for us to win, multiply $\frac{2}{5}$ by $\frac{1}{4}$ to get $\frac{2}{20} = \frac{1}{10} = 0.1$.

22) B
This is about knowing how to read a box-and-whisker plot. Funny name, boring concept. The median is the one in the middle of the box. That's 26. See, boring.

23) C
Quartiles are the values on the left and right edges of the box in the ol' box-and-whisker plot. Here, that's 22 and 32. I just had the thought that the weirdest name you could give a child is Box-and-Whisker Plot, as in Box-and-Whisker Plot Dorsey. Is that the name I should give to my first child? Share your thoughts on our Facebook page or don't.

24) A
Probably the ugliest question on Test 1. The pain-in-the-ass way to do it is to test the values in the answers. It works; it's just not fun. I don't make the SAT, so don't blame me!

25) A
Again, don't be afraid of absolute value (or inequalities, or absolute value inequalities). Two separate equations: $3 - 2x = 5$ and $3 - 2x = -5$. Solve. Answer. Fun.

26) C
You could try plugging the values from the table into the equations; that's the slow way. The faster way is to look for a pattern. How is this \$5,000 investment increasing? Well, it went to \$5,500 in the first year, an increase of 10%. What about the next year? Yep, another 10% increase. How do we represent that? By multiplying by 1 plus the percent increase, so $1 + 0.1 = 1.1$. Then we multiply that by the principal investment and raise it to the power of the number of years. Hooray C!

27) A
The reference information comes in handy for THE FIRST TIME ON TEST 1. It's about time! We've got a cone and we want to find its volume. We need radius and height. They gave us diameter (SO SNEAKY SAT.... OOOOOOOHHH!!!) so we need to cut it in half and use $5\sqrt{2}$ as our radius. Then do some careful arithmetic using the formula for the volume of a cone, $V = \frac{1}{3}\pi r^{2h}$. When you do, you'll get 200π as the result.

28) D
See if you can find any shortcuts by looking at the graph. My favorite is that the lines are solid, not dotted, which means that we need a "greater than or equal to" sign rather than just a "greater than" sign. That alone gets us down to C and D. To decide whether you want $\leq$ or $\geq$, ask yourself whether we're shading above or below the line. On the line with the negative slope (the one that passes through the origin, $(0, 0)$), notice how we're shaded to the left? Yeah, that's mostly to the left, but it's also below the line rather than above, so we want $\leq$ as our sign, and D is the answer.

29) B
Fancy math! Polynomial division. If I like this stuff, does that make me lame? Because I... uh, totally like this stuff? I mean, I don't like it? Anyway, we know that -2 is a root, which means that $(x + 2)$ is a factor. So it's A or B. Next step: divide the original polynomial by that factor. I recommend synthetic division—it's SO much prettier and easier than long division. Either way, though. When you do (carefully), you'll get the quotient $(x^2 + 3x - 1)$. The answer then is B.

30) B
Kind of a LONG algebra question. Start by translating the equation. It should become $y = 2(x + 5)^2 - 8$. Remember, that change in the x-direction goes the opposite way that you'd expect! Next, FOIL that out, distribute the 2, and combine like terms. You'll get $2x^2 + 20x + 42$. Factor out the 2, then factor again so you can see the roots, or x-intercepts. That is answer B. Warning: this question is not for everybody. Wear your algebra hard hat on this one because it does get a little messy!

31) 3329

Great question on which to store values on your calculator... it just makes it really hard to make a mistake! Store -35 as m and -17 as n (if you forget how to do this, hit up the chapter/section How to Use your Calculator... it's in the unit on Strategies). Then write the expression JUST like they wrote it, press enter and you have the answer.

32) 3.15

Another system of equations. Creative, SAT... very creative. Here are your two equations: $5x + 3y = 21.55$ and $2x + 6y = 23.74$. My approach to solving was to double the first equation, then use combination to eliminate the y values and go from there. Take whatever approach makes you happy, though! The numbers are kind of ugly, so work carefully and check your work.

33) 4

Ahhh... this one is a breather after the last question. Range is simply the difference between the biggest and the smallest value in a data set. Here, that's $15 - 11 = 4$. A great reason to know your statistical vocabulary, friends...

34) 8.13

Let's use our fun percent trick! Start with \$22. To take a 20% discount, multiply that \$22 by $1 - 0.20$, or 0.80. $\$22 \times 0.80 = \$17.60$. Then take a \$10 discount: $\$17.60 - \$10 = \$7.60$. Finally, multiply by 1 plus the tax amount, or 1.07. $\$7.60 \times 1.07 = \$8.132$, which rounds to \$8.13.

35) 48

You need to know the conversion between degrees and radians on this question. The most common conversion is 180 degrees = π radians. If you know that, you can set up a quick proportion: $\frac{180 \text{ degrees}}{\pi \text{ radians}} = \frac{x \text{ degrees}}{\frac{4\pi}{15} \text{ radians}}$.

I love proportions: you just cross multiply and you get your answer!

36) 109

Just a careful i question. If you recognize "difference of squares," you can speed up this question a bit (It'll be $10^2 - (3i)^2$ if you do). Otherwise, just FOIL it out and simplify carefully. You'll wind up at $100 - 9i^2$, which is $100 - (-9)$, which equals 109. Work carefully on this question! With no answer choices to pick, you have no safety net!

37) 486

Fun with formulas. That's going to be title of my SAT tutoring memoir that I never plan to write. Plug the 4 in for x. Solve carefully. Use the calculator. 486.

38) 8748

This is just like question 37, just wordier. Swap the 6 out for a 12, plug in 6 for x, and use your calculator. You'll get 8748, which is a big number, but not too big to grid as your answer to this, the final question of Test #1.

Tutor Ted®

SAT Practice Test 2

Multiple Choice Answer Sheet

TEST 1: READING

1 ⒶⒷⒸⒹ	9 ⒶⒷⒸⒹ	17 ⒶⒷⒸⒹ	25 ⒶⒷⒸⒹ	33 ⒶⒷⒸⒹ	41 ⒶⒷⒸⒹ	49 ⒶⒷⒸⒹ
2 ⒶⒷⒸⒹ	10 ⒶⒷⒸⒹ	18 ⒶⒷⒸⒹ	26 ⒶⒷⒸⒹ	34 ⒶⒷⒸⒹ	42 ⒶⒷⒸⒹ	50 ⒶⒷⒸⒹ
3 ⒶⒷⒸⒹ	11 ⒶⒷⒸⒹ	19 ⒶⒷⒸⒹ	27 ⒶⒷⒸⒹ	35 ⒶⒷⒸⒹ	43 ⒶⒷⒸⒹ	51 ⒶⒷⒸⒹ
4 ⒶⒷⒸⒹ	12 ⒶⒷⒸⒹ	20 ⒶⒷⒸⒹ	28 ⒶⒷⒸⒹ	36 ⒶⒷⒸⒹ	44 ⒶⒷⒸⒹ	52 ⒶⒷⒸⒹ
5 ⒶⒷⒸⒹ	13 ⒶⒷⒸⒹ	21 ⒶⒷⒸⒹ	29 ⒶⒷⒸⒹ	37 ⒶⒷⒸⒹ	45 ⒶⒷⒸⒹ	
6 ⒶⒷⒸⒹ	14 ⒶⒷⒸⒹ	22 ⒶⒷⒸⒹ	30 ⒶⒷⒸⒹ	38 ⒶⒷⒸⒹ	46 ⒶⒷⒸⒹ	
7 ⒶⒷⒸⒹ	15 ⒶⒷⒸⒹ	23 ⒶⒷⒸⒹ	31 ⒶⒷⒸⒹ	39 ⒶⒷⒸⒹ	47 ⒶⒷⒸⒹ	
8 ⒶⒷⒸⒹ	16 ⒶⒷⒸⒹ	24 ⒶⒷⒸⒹ	32 ⒶⒷⒸⒹ	40 ⒶⒷⒸⒹ	48 ⒶⒷⒸⒹ	

TEST 2: WRITING AND LANGUAGE

1 ⒶⒷⒸⒹ	8 ⒶⒷⒸⒹ	15 ⒶⒷⒸⒹ	22 ⒶⒷⒸⒹ	29 ⒶⒷⒸⒹ	36 ⒶⒷⒸⒹ	43 ⒶⒷⒸⒹ
2 ⒶⒷⒸⒹ	9 ⒶⒷⒸⒹ	16 ⒶⒷⒸⒹ	23 ⒶⒷⒸⒹ	30 ⒶⒷⒸⒹ	37 ⒶⒷⒸⒹ	44 ⒶⒷⒸⒹ
3 ⒶⒷⒸⒹ	10 ⒶⒷⒸⒹ	17 ⒶⒷⒸⒹ	24 ⒶⒷⒸⒹ	31 ⒶⒷⒸⒹ	38 ⒶⒷⒸⒹ	
4 ⒶⒷⒸⒹ	11 ⒶⒷⒸⒹ	18 ⒶⒷⒸⒹ	25 ⒶⒷⒸⒹ	32 ⒶⒷⒸⒹ	39 ⒶⒷⒸⒹ	
5 ⒶⒷⒸⒹ	12 ⒶⒷⒸⒹ	19 ⒶⒷⒸⒹ	26 ⒶⒷⒸⒹ	33 ⒶⒷⒸⒹ	40 ⒶⒷⒸⒹ	
6 ⒶⒷⒸⒹ	13 ⒶⒷⒸⒹ	20 ⒶⒷⒸⒹ	27 ⒶⒷⒸⒹ	34 ⒶⒷⒸⒹ	41 ⒶⒷⒸⒹ	
7 ⒶⒷⒸⒹ	14 ⒶⒷⒸⒹ	21 ⒶⒷⒸⒹ	28 ⒶⒷⒸⒹ	35 ⒶⒷⒸⒹ	42 ⒶⒷⒸⒹ	

TEST 3: MATHEMATICS - NO CALCULATOR

1 ⒶⒷⒸⒹ	9 ⒶⒷⒸⒹ	16	17	18	19	20
2 ⒶⒷⒸⒹ	10 ⒶⒷⒸⒹ	/ ⊘⊘⊘⊘	/ ⊘⊘⊘⊘	/ ⊘⊘⊘⊘	/ ⊘⊘⊘⊘	/ ⊘⊘⊘⊘
3 ⒶⒷⒸⒹ	11 ⒶⒷⒸⒹ	. ○○○○	. ○○○○	. ○○○○	. ○○○○	. ○○○○
4 ⒶⒷⒸⒹ	12 ⒶⒷⒸⒹ	0 ⓪⓪⓪⓪	0 ⓪⓪⓪⓪	0 ⓪⓪⓪⓪	0 ⓪⓪⓪⓪	0 ⓪⓪⓪⓪
5 ⒶⒷⒸⒹ	13 ⒶⒷⒸⒹ	1 ①①①①	1 ①①①①	1 ①①①①	1 ①①①①	1 ①①①①
6 ⒶⒷⒸⒹ	14 ⒶⒷⒸⒹ	2 ②②②②	2 ②②②②	2 ②②②②	2 ②②②②	2 ②②②②
7 ⒶⒷⒸⒹ	15 ⒶⒷⒸⒹ	3 ③③③③	3 ③③③③	3 ③③③③	3 ③③③③	3 ③③③③
8 ⒶⒷⒸⒹ		4 ④④④④	4 ④④④④	4 ④④④④	4 ④④④④	4 ④④④④
		5 ⑤⑤⑤⑤	5 ⑤⑤⑤⑤	5 ⑤⑤⑤⑤	5 ⑤⑤⑤⑤	5 ⑤⑤⑤⑤
		6 ⑥⑥⑥⑥	6 ⑥⑥⑥⑥	6 ⑥⑥⑥⑥	6 ⑥⑥⑥⑥	6 ⑥⑥⑥⑥
		7 ⑦⑦⑦⑦	7 ⑦⑦⑦⑦	7 ⑦⑦⑦⑦	7 ⑦⑦⑦⑦	7 ⑦⑦⑦⑦
		8 ⑧⑧⑧⑧	8 ⑧⑧⑧⑧	8 ⑧⑧⑧⑧	8 ⑧⑧⑧⑧	8 ⑧⑧⑧⑧
		9 ⑨⑨⑨⑨	9 ⑨⑨⑨⑨	9 ⑨⑨⑨⑨	9 ⑨⑨⑨⑨	9 ⑨⑨⑨⑨

TEST 4: MATHEMATICS - CALCULATOR ALLOWED

1 ⒶⒷⒸⒹ	6 ⒶⒷⒸⒹ	11 ⒶⒷⒸⒹ	16 ⒶⒷⒸⒹ	21 ⒶⒷⒸⒹ	26 ⒶⒷⒸⒹ	31
2 ⒶⒷⒸⒹ	7 ⒶⒷⒸⒹ	12 ⒶⒷⒸⒹ	17 ⒶⒷⒸⒹ	22 ⒶⒷⒸⒹ	27 ⒶⒷⒸⒹ	/ ⊘⊘⊘⊘
3 ⒶⒷⒸⒹ	8 ⒶⒷⒸⒹ	13 ⒶⒷⒸⒹ	18 ⒶⒷⒸⒹ	23 ⒶⒷⒸⒹ	28 ⒶⒷⒸⒹ	. ○○○○
4 ⒶⒷⒸⒹ	9 ⒶⒷⒸⒹ	14 ⒶⒷⒸⒹ	19 ⒶⒷⒸⒹ	24 ⒶⒷⒸⒹ	29 ⒶⒷⒸⒹ	0 ⓪⓪⓪⓪
5 ⒶⒷⒸⒹ	10 ⒶⒷⒸⒹ	15 ⒶⒷⒸⒹ	20 ⒶⒷⒸⒹ	25 ⒶⒷⒸⒹ	30 ⒶⒷⒸⒹ	1 ①①①①
						2 ②②②②
						3 ③③③③
						4 ④④④④
						5 ⑤⑤⑤⑤
						6 ⑥⑥⑥⑥
						7 ⑦⑦⑦⑦
						8 ⑧⑧⑧⑧
						9 ⑨⑨⑨⑨

CONTINUE

SAT Practice Test 2

Multiple Choice Answer Sheet

TEST 4: MATHEMATICS - CALCULATOR ALLOWED *(continued)*

	32	33	34	35	36	37	38
/	/ / / /	/ / / /	/ / / /	/ / / /	/ / / /	/ / / /	/ / / /
.	. . . .	. . . .	. . . .	. . . .	. . . .	. . . .	. . . .
0	0 0 0 0	0 0 0 0	0 0 0 0	0 0 0 0	0 0 0 0	0 0 0 0	0 0 0 0
1	1 1 1 1	1 1 1 1	1 1 1 1	1 1 1 1	1 1 1 1	1 1 1 1	1 1 1 1
2	2 2 2 2	2 2 2 2	2 2 2 2	2 2 2 2	2 2 2 2	2 2 2 2	2 2 2 2
3	3 3 3 3	3 3 3 3	3 3 3 3	3 3 3 3	3 3 3 3	3 3 3 3	3 3 3 3
4	4 4 4 4	4 4 4 4	4 4 4 4	4 4 4 4	4 4 4 4	4 4 4 4	4 4 4 4
5	5 5 5 5	5 5 5 5	5 5 5 5	5 5 5 5	5 5 5 5	5 5 5 5	5 5 5 5
6	6 6 6 6	6 6 6 6	6 6 6 6	6 6 6 6	6 6 6 6	6 6 6 6	6 6 6 6
7	7 7 7 7	7 7 7 7	7 7 7 7	7 7 7 7	7 7 7 7	7 7 7 7	7 7 7 7
8	8 8 8 8	8 8 8 8	8 8 8 8	8 8 8 8	8 8 8 8	8 8 8 8	8 8 8 8
9	9 9 9 9	9 9 9 9	9 9 9 9	9 9 9 9	9 9 9 9	9 9 9 9	9 9 9 9

TEST 5: ESSAY - OPTIONAL

If you are writing the essay, you may use the space below to plan and outline your work. Be sure to write the essay itself on the lined pages that follow.

SAT Practice Test 2

Essay Answer Sheet

BEGIN YOUR ESSAY HERE.

You may continue on the next page.

SAT Practice Test 2

Essay Answer Sheet

DO NOT WRITE OUTSIDE THE BOX.

You may continue on the next page.

SAT Practice Test 2

Essay Answer Sheet

BEGIN YOUR ESSAY HERE.

You may continue on the next page.

SAT Practice Test 2

Essay Answer Sheet

DO NOT WRITE OUTSIDE THE BOX.

SAT® Practice Test #2

IMPORTANT REMINDERS

A No. 2 pencil is required for the test. Do not use a mechanical pencil or pen.

Sharing any questions with anyone is a violation of Test Security and Fairness policies and may result in your scores being canceled.

This cover is representative of what you'll see on test day.

Reading Test

65 MINUTES, 52 QUESTIONS

Turn to Section 1 of your answer sheet to answer the questions in this section.

DIRECTIONS

Each passage or pair of passages below is followed by a number of questions. After reading each passage or pair, choose the best answer to each question based on what is stated or implied in the passage or passages and in any accompanying graphics (such as a table or graph).

Questions 1-10 are based on the following passage.

This passage is adapted from Emile Zola, *Ladies' Paradise*, originally published in 1886.

In the silk department, Robineau's return had set off a whole revolution. The department had been hoping that he would be so sick of the trouble people made for him all the time that he would not come back; and, indeed, one at a time, as he was under constant pressure from Vinçard, who wanted to transfer his business to him, he had almost taken it. Hutin's underhand activities, the mine which, for many months, he had been digging out under the assist buyer's feet, was on the point of exploding at last. During Robineau's leave, Hutin, as senior salesman, had deputized for him, and had done his utmost to injure his reputation in the eyes of his superiors, and to install himself in his place by being over-zealous; he discovered and exposed small irregularities, he submitted plans for improvement, he thought out new designs. Moreover, everyone in the department, from the newcomer dreaming of becoming a salesman to the senior salesman coveting Robineau's job, had only one fixed idea - to dislodge their comrade senior to them in order to move up a grade, to devour him if he should become an obstacle; and it was as if this struggle of desires, this pressure of one against another, was the very thing which made the machine run smoothly, which whipped up sales and ignited that blaze of success which astounded Paris. After Hutin, there was Favier, and then after Favier there were others, in queue. The sound of people loudly licking their lips could be heard. Robineau was condemned, everyone was already carrying away a bone. Therefore, when the assistant buyer reappeared, there was general grousing. The question had to be settled once and for all, and the attitude of the salesmen had seemed so menacing to the head of the department that he had just sent Robineau to the stock-room in order to give the management time to come to a decision.

"If they keep him on we'd all rather leave," Hutin was declaring.

This business was upsetting Bouthemont, whose gayness was ill-adapted to an internal worry of this sort. It grieved him no longer to see anything but glum faces around him. Nevertheless, he wished to be fair.

"Come now, leave him alone, he's not doing you any harm."

But there was an outburst of protest.

"What d'you mean, he's not doing us any harm? He's an unbearable person, always nervy and so stuck-up that he'd run you over as soon as he'd look at you!"

This was the great grudge the department had against him. Robineau had an overbearing manner and was touchy in a way they could not bear. At least twenty anecdotes were told about him, from how he had made a poor young fellow ill, to how he had humiliated customers with his cutting remarks.

"Well, gentlemen," said Bouthemont, "I can't do anything myself... I've spoken to the management about it, and I'm going to discuss it with them in a moment or two."

1

Which choice best summarizes this passage?

A) A slew of salesmen are upset with their superior for granting a special favor to a colleague.

B) Hutin plots revenge on Robineau for humiliating him in front of customers by taking his business.

C) Parisian salesmen hoping to advance their careers lament the return of their superior, the assistant buyer.

D) Robineau's return to work causes a stir amongst colleagues as they believed his clients to be theirs already.

2

As used in line 32, "attitude" most nearly means

A) approach.

B) reaction.

C) posture.

D) hostility.

3

Hutin's actions against Robineau can best be described as

A) spiteful.

B) insubordinate.

C) admirable.

D) overbearing.

4

The author most likely uses the phrases "loudly licking their lips" and "carrying away a bone" in lines 27-29 to create

A) an animalistic tone that highlights the competitive nature of the sales industry.

B) a critical tone to show the author's disdain for the salesmen's actions.

C) an aggressive tone to show how angry Robineau's colleagues are with him for his absence.

D) an eerie tone that makes the reader unsure of what the jealous salesmen might actually do to harm Robineau.

5

In the passage, the other salesmen's feelings towards Robineau can best be described as

A) jealous.

B) intimidated.

C) exasperated.

D) nervous.

6

Which choice provides the best evidence for the answer to the previous question?

A) Lines 36-37 ("If…declaring")

B) Lines 46-47 ("He's…you")

C) Lines 49-50 ("Robineau…bear")

D) Lines 50-53 ("At…remarks")

7

As used in line 49, "manner" most nearly means

A) demeanor.

B) technique.

C) habit.

D) etiquette.

8

Does the author paint the characters of Hutin, Vinçard, and Favier as different?

A) Yes; he proves that Vinçard is the best and most worthy of the three salesmen to replace Robineau.

B) Yes; he demonstrates Favier's reluctance to engage in demonstrative behaviors against Robineau.

C) Yes; he establishes Hutin as the hardest working salesmen with the most at stake when Robineau returns, as Hutin substituted for him in his absence.

D) No; he presents each with similar character traits.

9

Which choice provides the best evidence for the answer to the previous question?

A) Lines 16-25 ("Moreover…Paris")

B) Lines 25-27 ("After…queue")

C) Lines 28-29 ("Robineau…bone")

D) Lines 36-37 ("If…declaring")

10

The author includes the description of Robineau in the seventh paragraph (lines 48-53) in order to

A) expose the hypocrisy of the other salesmen's gripes because, in his absence, they were acting just as he did.

B) justify the complaints of the other salesmen by exposing his frequent theft of company profits

C) build on the narrative's archetype of salesmen as no salesman has proven himself to have outstanding moral character.

D) create a sense of wonder about Robineau due to his ability to do awful things yet still succeed in sales.

Questions 11-20 are based on the following passage.

This passage is adapted from Jane Addams, "Why Women Should Vote," originally published in 1910.

This paper is an attempt to show that many women today are failing to discharge their duties to their own households properly simply because they do not perceive that as society grows more complicated, it is necessary that woman shall extend her sense of responsibility to many things outside of her own home if she would continue to preserve the home in its entirety. One could illustrate in many ways. A woman's simplest duty, one would say, is to keep her house clean and wholesome and to feed her children properly. Yet if she lives in a tenement house, as so many of my neighbors do, she cannot fulfill these simple obligations by her own efforts because she is utterly dependent upon the city administration for the conditions which render decent living possible.

If women follow only the lines of their traditional activities, there are certain primary duties which belong to even the most conservative women. The first is a woman's responsibility for the members of her own household that they may be properly fed and clothed and surrounded by hygienic conditions. The second is a responsibility for the education of children.

The duty of a woman toward the schools which her children attend cannot be effectively carried out without some form of social organization, as the mothers' school clubs and mothers' congresses testify, and to which the most conservative women belong because they feel the need of wider reading and discussion concerning the many problems of childhood. It is, therefore, natural that the public should have been more willing to accord a vote to women in school matters than in any other, and yet women have never been members of a Board of Education in sufficient numbers to influence largely actual school curricula.

As the education of her children has been more and more transferred to the school, the woman has been left in a household of constantly-narrowing interests because one industry after another is slipping from the household into the factory. If woman's sense of obligation had enlarged as the industrial conditions changed she might naturally and almost imperceptibly have inaugurated movements for social amelioration in the line of factory legislation and shop sanitation. If conscientious women were convinced that it was a civic duty to be informed in regard to these grave industrial affairs, and then to express the conclusions which they had reached by depositing a piece of paper in a ballot-box, one cannot imagine that they would shirk simply because the action ran counter to old traditions.

Perhaps, the attitude of many busy women would be glad to use the ballot to further public measures in which they are interested and for which they have been working for years. It offends the taste of such a woman to be obliged to use indirect "influence" when she is accustomed to well-bred, open action in other affairs, and she very much resents the time spent in persuading a voter to take her point of view, and possibly to give up his own, quite as honest and valuable as hers, although different because resulting from a totally different experience. Public-spirited women who wish to use the ballot, as I know them, do not wish to do the work of men nor to take over men's affairs. They simply want an opportunity to do their own work and to take care of those affairs which naturally and historically belong to women, but which are constantly being overlooked and slighted in our political institutions.

11

The central problem Addams addresses in this passage is that women

A) are active in many of the issues that affect their families but cannot take full responsibility because they lack the power to influence public policy to reflect their experiences.
B) shirk the responsibility of implementing policy, leaving it to those who have not immersed themselves in the issues.
C) avoid adapting their responsibilities to the times, which would mean taking public stances for those public issues that affect the household.
D) do not want to overthrow men's societal responsibilities, even it means they cannot help society make more educated decisions.

12

Which choice best provides evidence for the answer to the previous question?

A) Lines 1-8 ("This paper...entirety")
B) Lines 11-15 ("Yet if...possible")
C) Lines 40-44 ("If woman's...sanitation")
D) Lines 54-61 ("It offends...experience")

13

As used in line 2, "discharge" most nearly means

A) eject.
B) release.
C) expel.
D) execute.

14

According to the passage, as schooling moves outside the home, schooling and decision-making policy has shifted to

A) children's new teachers.
B) those who can vote.
C) city officials who make decisions on curricula.
D) anyone who attends mothers' school clubs and congress meetings.

15

The main purpose of the third paragraph (lines 23-25) is to

A) provide an example of a maternal responsibility that mothers now have little control of because voting would be their only form of influence.
B) introduce the idea of women, not needing to educate their own children anymore, should all take to factories to maintain their interests.
C) pacify men who believe that only men should be on the Board of Education.
D) convince women to join the mothers' social organizations so that they may have a voice in school matters.

16

According to the passage, the main obstacle to women's suffrage is

A) conservative women who do not believe it their place to cast a ballot.
B) men who want to maintain the status quo in ever-changing times.
C) the attitudes and policies of current political institutions.
D) women who continue to influence politics by changing their husbands' minds.

17

Which choice provides the best evidence for the answer to the previous question?

A) Lines 16-18 ("If...women")
B) Lines 40-44 ("If...sanitation")
C) Lines 61-63 ("Public...affairs")
D) Lines 63-67 ("They...institutions")

18

As used in line 31, "accord" most nearly means

A) settle.
B) withhold.
C) grant.
D) deal.

19

Addams includes lines 44-50 ("If conscientious women...traditions") in order to

A) dispose of the stereotype that women do not like to be involved in new traditions.
B) debunk the idea that if allowed to vote, well-educated women would choose not to just because they are not used to it.
C) demonize women who believed industrial work to be the zenith of their social status.
D) criticize those who believe women should only stay in the household.

20

What is a main idea of the last paragraph?

A) Public-spirited women are content with persuading voters to take their points of view.
B) Women's votes are valuable as they result from a totally different experience than do men's votes.
C) The right to vote naturally and historically belongs to women.
D) A woman's responsibilities are to ensure the members of her household are properly fed and clothed, and to take care of her children's education.

Questions 21-30 are based on the following passage.

This passage is adapted from Ann Eklund, et al., "Limited Evidence on the Effectiveness of Interventions to Reduce Livestock Predation by Large Carnivores." ©2017 by Grimsö Wildlife Research Station, Department of Ecology, Swedish University of Agricultural Sciences, Sweden.

Carnivore depredation (i.e. carnivores attacking, injuring, or killing domestic animals) on livestock has occurred for thousands of years, at least since the expansion of livestock husbandry after domestication. Predation on domestic animals is an important factor influencing the coexistence between large carnivores and humans. In order to mitigate the negative impact of large carnivores on livestock, modern societies (through governments), non-governmental organizations, and individuals invest logistical and budgetary efforts in a large number of interventions that are believed to reduce the risk or impact of depredation. Authorities, wildlife managers, and owners of domestic animals face a wide variety of potential interventions to protect domestic animals from large carnivores. Interventions range from lethal (culling) to non-lethal methods (fences), overarching policy goals (carnivore population caps), interventions funded by authorities or initiated and undertaken by the affected people (compensation systems and increased guarding, respectively), to information dissemination.

Due to the long and extensive use of various interventions, it could be expected that the best interventions to reduce the impact of large carnivore depredation are by now well-tested and identified. Yet scientific evaluations of interventions are still surprisingly scarce, and, in general, our understanding of their efficacy is based on narrative review. This review assesses what scientific evidence is currently available and where there might be room for improvements in large carnivore management science.

One focus study evaluated the effect of livestock breed on livestock depredation and found that the heavier breed, Dala sheep, suffered more losses to wolverine depredation than did the lighter Norwegian short-tailed sheep, Norwegian fur-bearing sheep, and Rygja sheep breeds. Another study found that a pole construction used for enclosure kept spotted hyenas out of sheep and goat enclosures better than a bush fence construction, but the enclosure of pole construction left livestock more susceptible to leopard depredation than bush fence enclosures. In a study focused on guarding methods, guarding dogs present in sheep herds reduced the risk of depredation of sheep, particularly where herds were fenced. The largest decrease found in a study on predator removal in risk of livestock depredation was shown in studies where adult or breeding canids were selectively removed. In another study using a fladry (i.e. a rope or line running around an enclosure and from which strips of fabric are suspended), a field trial observed that livestock depredation by wolves ceased in treatment pastures, whilst it continued in control fields and another trial found that wolves did not trespass into fladry pastures whereas they did trespass into control fields. However, coyotes continued trespassing into treatment fields.

Our review reveals a worrying result with substantial implications for large carnivore management: there are not many scientific publications with evidence of effectiveness for any intervention intended to prevent livestock depredation by large carnivores. Nevertheless, the final set of selected studies allows some discussion about the current state of knowledge of intervention effectiveness. Unsurprisingly, the effect of interventions is context dependent and appears to vary with how well the actual problem is targeted. However, identifying the problem locally is rarely easy – the problem could be carnivores of various species, all individuals of a certain species, or even certain individuals within a species. Other carnivore species, or individuals, may be completely unaffected by a specific intervention, or potentially even be attracted to it.

In the past, large-scale predator removal programs, supported by carnivore eradication policies, brought many carnivore species to regional or national extinction, at which point livestock depredation would cease. In this regard, complete carnivore removal could be considered effective at eliminating livestock depredation. However, carnivores are now more highly valued by society and most large carnivore populations currently benefit from some levels of legal protection that precludes their unregulated killing. We suggest that future large carnivore management adopts the basic principles of an adaptive approach and plan interventions to allow evaluations of effect and causality.

While in a long-term perspective it would be beneficial to know the effect of interventions before investing in them, the short term goals for farmers, managers and researchers may not be in favor for these kinds of studies being conducted in the near future. Attempts to increase the involvement of these actors,

CONTINUE

contributing together to evidence-based approaches, may be one way to alter the odds in a favorable direction.

21

The main purpose of this passage is to

A) outline the effective measures necessary for carnivore predation prevention.
B) highlight the lack of effective universal methods for carnivore predation prevention as a call for collaboration.
C) prove that there is no designated way to stop certain carnivore predation and to call for farmers to be more aggressive in defending their land.
D) caution future researchers that carnivore predation is an unsolvable problem due to the myriad of differing tendencies among carnivores across the country.

22

As used in line 79, "cease" most nearly means

A) pause.
B) draw to a close.
C) continue.
D) stop.

23

Which choice best describes the author's view of previous efforts to ascertain the most effective method for carnivore depredation prevention?

A) Disheartened yet determined.
B) Frustrated and dejected.
C) Discouraged but sanguine.
D) Dissatisfied yet confident.

24

Which choice provides the best evidence for the answer to the previous question?

A) Lines 23-26 ("Due to...identified")
B) Lines 29-32 ("This review...science")
C) Lines 66-68 ("Unsurprisingly...targeted")
D) Lines 85-88 ("We suggest...causality")

CONTINUE

25

The main purpose of the second paragraph (lines 22-23) is to

A) establish the author's main issue with established research in order to build upon her argument with examples in the next paragraph.
B) offer brief insight into the complexity of predation intervention, using the third paragraph to highlight the issues of specific techniques.
C) summarize the findings of existing research as they relate to large-scale prevention methods.
D) scathe previous attempts to prevent carnivore depredation and establish the grounds for further questioning of existing research.

26

According to the passage, the main issue with using fladry as a prevention technique is that

A) though it proved effective in preventing wolves from entering livestock areas, not all carnivores were deterred by it.
B) it prevented neither wolves nor coyotes from entering treated pastures.
C) it is an unsustainable model, as fladry is a very localized technique and has not been adapted for various climates.
D) there is not enough evidence to state whether fladry has proven effective, as there exists only one study that used it.

27

As used in line 84, "precludes" most nearly means

A) sanctions.
B) fetters.
C) prohibits.
D) warrants.

28

Based on the passage, the most effective method for preventing animal predation on a large scale is

A) yet to be discovered.
B) the removal of carnivores.
C) based on research done on the local level, specific to the livestock in the area.
D) the breeding of smaller livestock, those less attractive to carnivores.

29

Which choice provides evidence for the answer to the previous question?

A) Lines 27-29 ("Yet scientific…review")
B) Lines 33-38 ("One focus…breeds")
C) Lines 75-79 ("In the…cease")
D) Lines 79-81 ("In this…depredation")

30

Based on the passage, the author would most likely agree with which statement?

A) Farming and research communities should try short-term solutions as a result of the lack of proven long-term large-scale prevention techniques.
B) Farmers and researchers should work together to solve predation problems on a local level.
C) Collaborative, research-based approaches would most effectively prevent depredation.
D) Federal agencies should place more carnivores under watch programs to monitor their movement and feeding styles.

Questions 31-41 are based on the following passages and supplementary material.

Passage 1 is adapted from David Spence, Associate Professor at the University of Texas McCombs School of Business, "Fracking Bans Do More Harm Than Good," published in 2013. Passage 2 is adapted from Greg Harman, "Fracking Texas, Recycling 'Flowback,' & Water Contamination, "originally published in 2013 for Deceleration News.

Passage 1

The shale gas revolution, a revolution partly enabled by fracking, seems likely to produce enormous environmental benefits for Americans. Fracking involves the injection of water, sand, and chemicals deep into shale formations to fracture rock, freeing formerly inaccessible natural gas. To be sure, we are still learning about the environmental impacts of fracking, but there is no real support in the scientific literature for the notion that fracking poses greater pollution or health risks than those we regularly accept in connection with our reliance on the primary alternative electric generation fuel – coal.

Americans are still learning about fracking, but are cautiously optimistic about its promise. The University of Texas at Austin Energy Poll has revealed that a surprising 59 percent of Americans say they are "not familiar" with fracking. Among those familiar with fracking, a plurality (47.5 percent) supports its use (against 35.7 percent opposed). Support exceeds opposition in all the shale gas states except New York.

Some locals support shale gas production because of its economic benefits (royalty payments to landowners, jobs, local taxes, etc.); for others, opposing fracking makes sense.

When a natural gas well is being drilled and "fracked," the production area is a hive of truck traffic, power generators, and other action that can transform a quiet rural landscape into an industrial area. These mostly temporary, though significant, local impacts are mostly amenable to regulatory solutions, but it is little wonder some people don't want to endure them. Natural gas-fired power plants give us electricity that yields half the greenhouse gases (and much smaller fractions of the more deadly pollutants) that we get from coal combustion. That is good for the environment, for all of us.

A February 2011 study by health professionals published in the Annals of the New York Academy of Sciences concluded that our reliance on coal for energy costs hundreds of billions of dollars and causes tens of thousands of premature deaths per year, far more than any other energy source. An August 2011 analysis published in the American Economic Review suggested that substituting natural gas for coal in the electric generation mix would yield enormous health and environmental benefits.

Shale gas production can and should be regulated. But given that it seems likely to yield enormous benefits for Americans, banning hydraulic fracturing is a bad idea.

Passage 2

Billions of gallons of water are wasted each year to fracture shale formations around the country and free trapped oil and gas. After the water is shot down a well, it returns to the surface heavily contaminated with hydrocarbons, fracking chemicals, heavy metals, and radioactivity. After the oil and gas is separated out, the water typically can't be used safely for anything else. In Texas, that means it is usually shot down any of an increasing number of disposal wells.

In a state nestled deep in ongoing drought, that doesn't go unnoticed. Neither do the earthquakes linked to the disposal operations.

While none of the water used to frack in South Texas' Eagle Ford Shale Play was being recycled when University of Texas researchers surveyed fracking operations recently, about 90 percent was being recycled in Pennsylvania, where regulations are tighter.

Recently, operators across South Texas have begun to use less drinking-water-quality water for fracking, and have even begun to recycle some. However, recycling water does nothing to address the Big Fear about fracking: the contamination of freshwater aquifers.

While the U.S. EPA has vacillated on this point, a new report shows indications that water wells in Pennsylvania's Marcellus Shale, at least, have been contaminated by fracking. The following passage discusses its conclusions:

"Of the 141 water wells measured within one kilometer of drilling operations, 82% contained high levels of methane. Twelve of these wells showed "immediate action" hazard levels. About one third also had high levels of propane and ethane. Both are hazardous and flammable gases." -Stephen Leahy at DeSmog Canada

Faulty casings and poor well construction is something Texas has suffered from. However, new rules adopted by the Texas Railroad Commission (RRC)

CONTINUE

in May that require pressure-testing those casings at fracking-related pressures, among other things, are intended to address those issues.

While those are important rule changes, their implementation, effectiveness, and the ability of the RRC to enforce them remain to be seen.

The question remains whether these measures will stop ozone-forming air pollution that concerns San Antonio residents or whether the release of large quantities of methane, a potent greenhouse gas, will grow exponentially worldwide as fracking operations expand.

The following graph details natural gas production between the years 2000-2013.

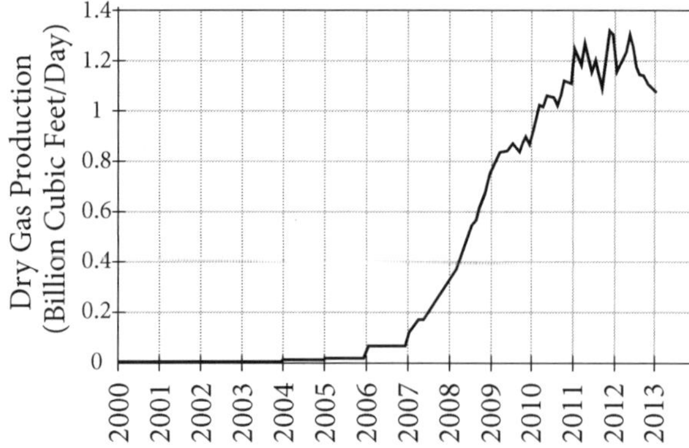

Source: Wikimedia Commons

31

The primary purpose of Passage 1 is to

A) challenge common perceptions by focusing on the positive outcomes of fracking.

B) cast doubt on the validity of fracking's opposition by presenting facts about the health and economic benefits of fracking.

C) suggest that though it may have inconvenient side effects, supporting fracking will yield an energy source more sustainable than many other alternative fuel sources, while also stimulating local economies.

D) discuss why fracking in Texas is different from fracking in Pennsylvania, among other states, and that, consequently, fracking regulation should look different in each state.

32

As used in line 8, "support" most nearly means

A) foundation.

B) maintenance.

C) substantiation.

D) strength.

33

In Passage 1, the main purpose of the fifth paragraph is to

A) compare the environmental impact of fracking to current methods for obtaining fuel agents, while building further on claims of other benefits.

B) establish the scientific relevance of the author's argument, while providing justifications for the disturbances discussed in the previous paragraph.

C) demonize the coal industry for overspending and spreading health issues.

D) suggest that America needs to reevaluate its dependency on natural gas in order to address issues of sustainability, public health, and the economy.

34

In Passage 2, the author's primary concern with fracking practices stems from

A) its effect on contamination of fresh water.
B) the inevitable increase of pollution's effect on the ozone layer.
C) the lack of enforcement of existing regulations.
D) the lack of uniform regulation across states, leading to great water waste in states that cannot afford it.

35

As used in line 54, "contaminated" most nearly means

A) dirty.
B) polluted.
C) diseased.
D) soiled.

36

According to the information in the graph, the highest increase in dry gas production occurred between

A) 2007 and 2008.
B) 2008 and 2009.
C) 2011 and 2012.
D) 2012 and 2013.

37

Which concern voiced in the passages is best supported by the data presented in the graph?

A) Lines 42-46 ("An August…benefits")
B) Lines 63-67 ("While none…tighter")
C) Lines 79-81 ("Of the…methane")
D) Lines 95-100 ("The question…expand")

38

The author of Passage 1 would most likely respond to the discussion of drilling operation hazard levels in lines 79-85, Passage 2, by

A) using the facts presented in the Annals of New York Academy of Sciences study to highlight the advantages of fracking.
B) stating that the side effects of fracking are better than those of mining coal.
C) arguing to implement policy that promotes the use of recycled water instead of drinking-quality water.
D) denying the validity of the evidence presented due to a lack of variety in sources.

39

Which choice provides the best evidence for the answer to the previous question?

A) Lines 17-19 ("Among…opposed")
B) Lines 47 ("Shale…regulated")
C) Lines 51-35 ("Billions…gas")
D) Lines 48-50 ("But given…idea")

40

Which choice best describes the relationship between the passages?

A) Passage 2 questions the authority of the author in Passage 1 and provides an alternative conclusion.
B) Passage 2 builds upon the argument presented in Passage 1 and presents other evidence to further their point.
C) Passage 1 argues against the practicality of the proposals put forth in Passage 2,
D) Passage 2 would agree with some arguments made in Passage 1 but would deny others in their entirety.

41

The primary purpose of both passages is to

A) provide evidence for why the use of fracking should be regulated.

B) introduce arguments and counterarguments for the effects of fracking on water supplies.

C) debate the prospective positive benefits of fracking from environmental, economic, and health perspectives.

D) discuss the perceived cost of fracking's effect on local, national, and global levels.

Questions 42-52 are based on the following passage and supplementary material.

This passage is adapted from Chan Tack, et al., "Making Friends in Violent Neighborhoods: Strategies Among Elementary School Children." ©2017 Chan Tack and Small for Sociological Science.

Friendships are essential to the socioemotional development of children. A large body of psychological literature has found that failure to form successful, enriching friendships during childhood can lead to maladjustment, low educational attainment, and criminal behavior in adulthood. In fact, researchers have argued that the friendship formation practices learned during childhood shape people's ability to maintain stable relationships as adults. Not surprisingly, understanding how children and adolescents form friendships has motivated a large body of work. However, there has been comparatively little research on how neighborhood violence affects how children make friends.

The question becomes particularly important given the persistently high levels of violence that some children experience. Violent crime rates in Chicago have been persistently high for some time. An earlier survey of more than 500 children in three elementary schools on Chicago's South Side found that 26 percent of elementary school children had witnessed a shooting, 30 percent had witnessed a stabbing, and 78 percent had witnessed a beating.

For our research, we interviewed 72 students, parents, and teachers in two elementary schools in violent Chicago neighborhoods to identify how children form friendships. While we confirm the finding in gang research that some children strategically befriend peers who can provide protection, we also find that many children do the opposite. In fact, many children adopt not one but multiple strategies, resulting in a heterogeneous stance toward friendship formation.

Many children cultivated friendships that provided physical protection in the event of a fight. The most common narratives about friendship revolved around the idea that friends should "stick up for" or "have [one's] back." Many students in the study described a similar idea, that friends "don't just hang with you. If somebody bother [sic] you, they don't let nothing [sic] happen to you; they always got your back." Because protection was tightly tied to friendship, children did not expect anyone beyond "real friends" to stand up for them in the face of conflict. While many children sought protection in response to violence, others avoided investing emotionally in friendships altogether. At some times, this avoidance manifested itself in total isolation; at other times, children cultivated many "associates" but no close friendships. Children also described how they used friendships to help them forge face-saving, nonviolent responses to reputational threats. Children selected friends who were skilled at neutralizing insults made about them in their absence, who informed them about others' insults, who publicly discouraged them from escalating arguments, and who publicly coaxed them away from physical fights. Many of the children turned to kin to buffer them from violence and to fulfill the emotional and companionship needs that friendships ordinarily provide. The idea that kin networks are one of the few reliable ways to secure one's safety in violent neighborhoods was strongly held among both adults and children in our field sites. Children related that their parents often chose to send them to particular schools because they already had cousins or fictive kin there.

These children adopted an instrumental approach to friendship, one explicitly governed by the need to manage the threat of violence. More than half of the children interviewed used several strategies to choose and form friendships. Their closest friends were those who not only protected them in the event of violence, but also helped them manage peer relations and their social status in ways that minimized the chances of violent escalation. We find that a consequence of exposure to neighborhood violence appears to be an approach to friendship formation that is unusually strategic, highly malleable, and notably heterogeneous.

The following graph details the homicide rates per 100,000 children and teens in 2011 in the United States.

Black Male Teens At Alarming Risk

Black males from the ages of 15 to 19 are far more likely to be killed by guns than other American children.

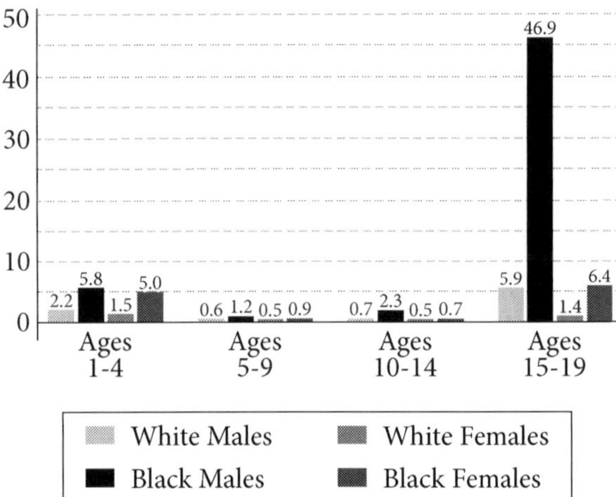

Source: Huffington Post via National Center for Health Statistics, National Vital Statistics Systems, Center for Disease Control and Prevention, U.S. Census Bureau

42

The main purpose of the passage is to

A) inform the public about the high rates of violence witnessed by young children in Chicago.

B) analyze the methods used by peer groups in order to avoid violence.

C) investigate the ways children form peer groups to protect themselves from potentially harmful incidents.

D) overview the difficulties faced by adolescents to manage relationships in highly volatile environments.

43

As used in line 43, "adopt" most nearly means

A) assume.

B) embrace.

C) approve.

D) manage.

44

The main purpose of the first and second paragraphs (lines 1-23) can best be described as to

A) introduce research relevant to the study discussed.

B) justify a study's necessity.

C) defend a deficit in research.

D) argue that previous conclusions were inconclusive.

45

The author suggests that friendship forming during childhood and adolescence is

A) necessary to stay safe when faced with enduring violence.

B) foundational for maintaining healthy relationships later in life.

C) critical solely to prevent maladjustment to adulthood and future financial demands.

D) not always necessary if a child knows how to stay out of trouble.

46

Which choice provides the best evidence for the answer to the previous question?

A) Lines 6-9 ("In fact...adults")

B) Lines 30-33 ("In fact...formation")

C) Lines 47-49 ("At some...friendships")

D) Lines 67-69 ("These children...violence")

47

Data in the graph indicate that black males between the ages of 15-19 are

A) eight times more likely to be killed by guns than white males of the same age.
B) only in danger of being killed by guns during this age range.
C) less likely to be killed by guns than white men and women of all age ranges shown.
D) eight times less likely to be killed by guns than black women.

48

According to the passage, the most successful friendship strategy is when children and adolescents

A) surround themselves with friends who are willing to step in during physical altercations on their behalf.
B) align themselves with friends who can successfully deescalate situations before they turn violent.
C) avoid others, keeping their head low so as to not rub anyone the wrong way.
D) adopt an assorted adaptation of interpersonal strategies.

49

Which choice provides the best evidence for the answer of the previous question?

A) Lines 67-69 ("These children…violence")
B) Lines 69-71 ("More than…friendships")
C) Lines 71-75 ("Their closest…escalation")
D) Lines 75-79 ("We find…heterogeneous")

50

As used in line 58, "buffer" most nearly means

A) insulate.
B) champion.
C) vindicate.
D) shield.

51

It is reasonable to infer that friendships formed in violent neighborhoods are

A) usually role-defined: each friend satisfies a specific need for the others.
B) based on merit: the more proven one is at handling violent situations, the more likely the person is to have many friends.
C) mutually beneficial: friends bond over their ability to be there for one another, potentially extending the relationship over generations.
D) short-lived: choosing one person for a certain period of time before finding another friend who satisfies a different need.

52

Which of the following statements is supported by the graph?

A) White males and white females have the same likelihood of being killed by a gun over all noted age ranges.
B) Black children, ages 1 to 4, are almost just as likely to be killed by guns as are white males, ages 15 to 19.
C) Black females are always second in death mortality rates behind black males.
D) White males, ages 5-9, have about the same likelihood of being killed by a gun as black males,

STOP

If you finish before time is called, you may check your work on this section only. Do not turn to any other section.

Writing and Language Test

35 MINUTES, 44 QUESTIONS

Turn to Section 2 of your answer sheet to answer the questions in this section.

DIRECTIONS

Each passage below is accompanied by a number of questions. For some questions, you will consider how the passage might be revised to improve the expression of ideas. For other questions, you will consider how the passage might be edited to correct errors in sentence structure, usage, or punctuation. A passage or a question may be accompanied by one or more graphics (such as a table or graph) that you will consider as you make revising and editing decisions.

Some questions will direct you to an underlined portion of a passage. Other questions will direct you to a location in a passage or ask you to think about the passage as a whole.

After reading each passage, choose the answer to each question that most effectively improves the quality of writing in the passage or that makes the passage conform to the conventions of standard written English. Many questions include a "NO CHANGE" option. Choose that option if you think the best choice is to leave the relevant portion of the passage as it is.

The Art of the East Side Gallery

On August 13, 1961, the ideological barriers separating a divided Germany [1] became all the more concrete. At midnight, authorities began closing the borders between West Germany and the GDR (German Democratic Republic) to the East, [2] sometimes it divided streets in the middle so that cross-"strasse" neighbors suddenly

1

Which choice effectively sets up the information that follows?

A) NO CHANGE
B) were replaced by chaos and confusion.
C) began to crumble as new laws were put into place.
D) created two separate nations.

2

A) NO CHANGE
B) sometimes dividing streets
C) that sometimes divided streets
D) which divided streets sometimes

CONTINUE

found themselves inhabitants of different countries. 3 The method of division was an imposing symbol of the struggle between Western Democracy and the Iron Curtain until its fall in 1989, and it was the Berlin Wall.

The Wall, a concrete barrier stretching 90 miles, immediately became a space of protest on the western side. 4 These depicted the oppression of the East German government and the pain of division in ways both humorous and sobering. However, the Eastern Wall 5 remains a desolate, white, blank space from the day it was erected until 6 when it was to be torn down. This contrast between the colorful display of public opinion on one side and its stark absence on the other symbolized, to many, the difference between life in the two nations.

3

Which choice most effectively combines the underlined sentences?

A) NO CHANGE
B) The method of division was The Berlin Wall, and it would remain an imposing symbol of the struggle between Western Democracy and the Iron Curtain until its fall in 1989.
C) The method of division, the Berlin Wall, was an imposing symbol of how Western Democracy and the Iron Curtain struggled until its fall in 1989.
D) The Berlin Wall, a method of division and an imposing symbol of the struggle between Western Democracy and the Iron Curtain, would remain until 1989, its fall.

4

A) NO CHANGE
B) This
C) It
D) Works of graffiti

5

A) NO CHANGE
B) remained
C) remain
D) has remained

6

A) NO CHANGE
B) that which it was torn
C) the day on which it was torn
D) that in which tearing it

Then, in December 1989, [7] a month after the Wall's fall, Scottish gallerist Christine MacLean had an [8] idea; paint the other side. Arriving first at a trickle and then in growing numbers, artists from all over the world came to create what became known as the East Side Gallery. Some paintings document the traumas of German history such as Kristallnacht, as well as the hardships of life in the former GDR. Russian artist Dmitri Vrubel's piece often referred to as "The Brother's Kiss" depicts Soviet leader Leonid Brezhnev and GDR General Secretary Erich Honecker locked in a kiss as a statement of disgust at how the Soviet regime manipulated its satellite states. [9] For example, many artists hoped to capture the euphoria of the transformation of the German state with images of hope and unity. One of the gallery's most famous images is that of one of the ubiquitous, Russian-made "Trabi" cars that East Germans held so dear bursting through the Wall. Titled "Test the Best," it symbolizes the countless escape attempts made by East German citizens as well as the eventual "bursting through" of all of its people as the Wall fell.

7

Which choice most effectively continues the timeline set by the previous paragraphs?

A) NO CHANGE
B) just over a year before the Soviet Union would begin its collapse
C) from the safe distance of the United Kingdom
D) though not an artist herself

8

A) NO CHANGE
B) idea:
C) idea,
D) idea

9

A) NO CHANGE
B) However,
C) Morever,
D) Although,

10

A) NO CHANGE
B) brags
C) showboats
D) boasts

All in all, the East Side Gallery **10** advertises 106 paintings from 118 artists on a near-mile stretch of wall, and as such is one of the largest canvases in the world. **11** It is a testament to the belief of one artist who contributed to the gallery with the painted statement that "may small people in many small places, who do many small steps, can change the face of the world."

11

At this point, the writer is considering adding the following sentence.

The project was able to turn a previously blank white wall into a form of free expression.

Should the writer make this addition here?

A) Yes, because it provides historical context for the transformation of Germany as described in the passage.
B) Yes, because it emphasizes the importance of free expression.
C) No, because it unnecessarily repeats information from earlier in the passage.
D) No, because there is still controversy surrounding whether the project counts as a true gallery.

Travel in the Age of the Sharing Economy

Twenty years ago, if a friend asked where you planned to stay on your upcoming vacation to Italy and you replied, "Oh, I'll be staying in a stranger's apartment," he or she likely would have looked at you as if you **12** went mad. However, in 2016, over 100 million people worldwide did just that—stayed with strangers. **13** The reason is the rise in collaborative consumption and "the sharing economy." Defined as the peer-to-peer based activity of obtaining, giving, or sharing access to goods and services, the sharing economy has changed how we live, work, communicate, and travel.

For travelers, especially, the sharing economy **14** has revolutionized, fundamentally changing, the way we see the world as well as the other people in it. From lodging to transportation to cultural exchange, there is something for everyone and every budget in the peer-to-peer marketplace. While Airbnb may be the best known, there are dozens of ways to rent, share, swap, or house-sit homes and apartments, from the website **15** Couchsurfing: where people around the world invite strangers into their homes at no charge whatsoever, to a company that connects affluent travelers who want to share multi-million dollar homes with one another. Want to get around? Try BlaBlaCar, which functions essentially as a way to put long-distance carpools **16** together, in addition, through the sharing economy travelers can find ways to eat a home-cooked meal with a local, take a class, rent a boat, get a private tour of a city, or camp in a vineyard.

12

A) NO CHANGE
B) are
C) had gone
D) are going

13

A) NO CHANGE
B) The reason is the rise of collaborative consumption, or
C) The reasons are the rise of collaborative consumption or
D) The reasons are the rise of collaborative consumption, and

14

A) NO CHANGE
B) made so great an alteration in the way
C) fundamentally revolutionized the way
D) revolutionized the way

15

A) NO CHANGE
B) Couchsurfing: where people around the world invite strangers into their homes at no charge whatsoever--
C) Couchsurfing—where people around the world invite strangers into their homes at no charge whatsoever—
D) Couchsurfing; where people around the world invite strangers into their homes at no charge whatsoever;

16

A) NO CHANGE
B) together. In addition, through
C) together; in addition
D) together, in addition. Through

CONTINUE

The benefits of participation in the sharing economy are, 17 subsequently, partly financial. 18 That's largely because the technology that has made collaborative consumption possible reduces transaction costs for those who offer their homes, vehicles, or expertise—all while allowing them to maximize use of underutilized resources. The traveler, too, 19 finds his or her travel costs reduced by booking a house swap instead of a hotel or working on an organic farm in exchange for free accommodation.

17

A) NO CHANGE
B) however
C) of course
D) therefore

18

At this point, the writer is considering adding the following sentence.

Travelers and those in local destinations who supply goods and services benefit from both the economic and cultural exchange.

Should the writer make this addition here?

A) Yes, because it supports the conclusion drawn in the following sentence.
B) Yes, because it expands upon the argument that is being made.
C) No, because it distracts from the focus of the paragraph by introducing irrelevant information.
D) No, because the idea of cultural enrichment is not introduced until the following paragraph.

19

A) NO CHANGE
B) can reduce their travel costs
C) reduces their travel costs
D) find that the cost of travel is reduced

[1] The sharing economy lets travelers and locals alike break down the barriers between them. [2] However, most travelers who engage in the sharing economy are looking not only for a cheaper tab but also for greater immersion in the culture and place they've chosen to visit. [3] As one travel writer who frequently stays with locals when she travels put it: 20 "I used to feel like a spectator in the life of the place I was visiting; now I feel like a participant." [4] Travelers and locals learn about one another in true cultural exchange, and it is perhaps this benefit that, though impossible to put a dollar value on, is the most exciting 21 eventuality of this growing economic trend. 22

20

Which choice best supports the point developed in this paragraph?

A) NO CHANGE
B) "by staying with locals, I have saved an enormous amount per trip."
C) "the sharing economy has allowed me to learn languages in an immersive environment."
D) "I come away from each adventure rejuvenated and refreshed by the culture I encounter."

21

A) NO CHANGE
B) repercussion
C) conclusion
D) effect

22

To make this paragraph most logical, sentence 1 should be

A) placed where it is now.
B) placed after sentence 2.
C) placed after sentence 3.
D) DELETED from the paragraph.

There's No Such Thing as a "Little White Lie"

According to Pamela Meyer, an expert on lying, the average human lies ten to two hundred times a day. People lie for a variety of [23] reasons—and lies can range from colossal to small and seemingly quite harmless. There is even a term for the kind of minor lie that is told out of politeness or a desire to lubricate social interaction: the "little white lie". Some of these "white lies" [24] achieved their purpose with little harm done to the speaker or the [25] recipient, in fact sometimes they can actually be [26] beneficial in a way that is helpful. No one would claim that lying to save oneself from personal danger is anything but necessary self-preservation. However, there is growing evidence that shows that lying, even in small ways, can have negative effects on both the brain and the body.

As it relates to brain function, a study published in Nature Neuroscience found that lying can desensitize the brain from the negative emotions associated with dishonest conduct or speech, and this desensitization can lead people to tell bigger and more frequent lies in the future. According to the scientists, lying activates the amygdala: the brain's emotional [27] middle. [28] Initially, the act of lying causes the amygdala to release negative feelings in the person who is being untruthful. However, in this study, as

23

A) NO CHANGE
B) reasons; and lies
C) reasons, and lies
D) reasons and lies,

24

A) NO CHANGE
B) achieve their
C) achieved there
D) achieve there

25

A) NO CHANGE
B) recipient, in fact,
C) recipient: while in fact
D) recipient; in fact,

26

A) NO CHANGE
B) beneficial.
C) beneficially good.
D) beneficial, which is good for both parties.

27

A) NO CHANGE
B) highlight.
C) nerve.
D) core.

28

A) NO CHANGE
B) In addition,
C) Consequently,
D) Unfortunately,

test subjects were asked to lie more frequently, the level of response in the amygdala decreased. 29 Thus, the study was able to conclude that the more a person lies, the easier it becomes not only to lie but to expand the scope and size of the lies they tell.

Now, perhaps there's an argument to be made that those findings could be looked at as positive. Couldn't an ability to lie easily and without consequence allow people to advance their own self- interests more effectively? There is certainly a school of thought 30 believing the idea of ethics to be more structure than nature. But then how would one deal with the negative effects lying, it seems, has on the body as well?

29

At this point, the writer is considering adding the following sentence.

The amygdala is also the center of the brain that lights up when one sees an image of an adorable kitten or terrifying crime scene.

Should the writer make this addition here?

A) Yes, because it adds a relevant detail that deepens the reader's knowledge of the subject.
B) Yes, because it provides support for the claim that the amygdala is an important center of the brain.
C) No, because it is irrelevant and interrupts the paragraph's natural flow of thought.
D) No, because it introduces information that has already been established by the passage.

30

A) NO CHANGE
B) that believes
C) from which people believe
D) the belief is that

Lying is an energetically taxing activity. When one **31** tells the truth, one simply recollects what one has experienced. Lying, **32** furthermore, requires effort. One must remember what one feels the need to hide, come up with a believable alternative, perform that alternative as if it is true, and then remember the lie in case one needs to repeat it. All of this creates stress on the **33** body. After considering the possible consequences, it makes one wonder: perhaps there's no such thing as the "little white lie."

31

A) NO CHANGE
B) tell
C) have told
D) telling

32

A) NO CHANGE
B) for example,
C) however,
D) therefore,

33

At this point, the writer wants to provide specific examples to elaborate on the claim made in the first part of the sentence. Which choice most effectively accomplishes this goal?

A) body, which requires oxygen from the respiratory and circulatory systems.
B) body which, in addition to the struggles of the brain, is simply too much for most people.
C) body, which has been found to cause maladies such as high blood pressure, heart disease, stroke, cancer, and depression.
D) body, which can present its own unique challenges.

Preserving Linguistic Diversity

If trends continue, nearly half of the world's 600 known languages are expected to disappear by the year 2100. Some are endangered because the populations themselves are dwindling, others because of demographic shifts in migration, and still others because [34] there uses were restricted. What worries linguists and anthropologists isn't that languages are fading— [35] though their concern is too little too late—but that they are doing so with such rapidity. Out of this worry has been born a movement, led not only by scientists [36] but even by members of the communities most directly impacted, to save the world's dying languages.

Among those at the vanguard of this movement are the members of various First Nations tribes in the United States. Among the 154 indigenous languages in the US, [37] 148 will likely become extinct within the next generation. The reasons are numerous, but this situation

34

A) NO CHANGE
B) their use is or has been
C) there use is or was
D) their use was

35

The writer wants to convey a recognition that not all language loss is bad without undermining the point being made. Which choice best accomplishes this goal?

A) NO CHANGE
B) for some languages are too backward for modern societies
C) that is part of the evolutionary process of life, much as it is in the natural world
D) since a universal language would certainly ease global conflict

36

A) NO CHANGE
B) and also by
C) but also by
D) also by

37

Which choice offers the most accurate and relevant interpretation of the data in the graph?

A) NO CHANGE
B) a majority are spoken by fewer than one hundred people.
C) there are as many ways of understanding the world as there are ways to communicate that understanding.
D) Navajo and Cree are the most widely-spoken.

38 results in part from policy that attempted to achieve cultural assimilation through linguistic annihilation. Now the descendants of those subjected to these policies are attempting to reclaim what was once taken from them, 39 who believe that perhaps a reversal is 40 possible a linguistic resuscitation that leads to cultural revitalization. Knowing they have limited time before the few who still speak these languages themselves die, activists from First Nations communities from Arizona to Hawaii are using everything from immersion programs to apps in an effort revive and pass on their native tongues.

[1] But why, one might ask, is language preservation important? [2] Let's start with the case for preservation. [3] When a language becomes extinct, practical knowledge can be lost. [4] Historical understanding, too, can fade, as it is difficult for a grandmother to truly convey what happened in her time or that of her own grandparents if she cannot speak fluently with her grandchild. [5] However, the death of a language can also mean the disappearance of more abstract concepts, for a language is more than a means of communication— 41 they are ways of understanding the world. [6] For example, one Aboriginal tribe in Australia makes clear just how egocentric the English language is. 42 [7] Most English speakers live in the industrialized

38

A) NO CHANGE
B) result
C) will result
D) resulting

39

A) NO CHANGE
B) they believe
C) and
D) believing

40

A) NO CHANGE
B) possible, a linguistic
C) possible; a linguistic
D) possible: a linguistic

41

A) NO CHANGE
B) it is a way
C) it is ways
D) they're a way

42

Which choice sets up the most relevant contrast?

A) NO CHANGE
B) We English speakers tend to think of direction in relation to themselves: to the left of me, behind me, etc.
C) This, perhaps, is why many people see Americans in particular as individualistic.
D) English speakers have a multitude of words to describe their appearance, feelings, and states of mind.

world, while members of this tribe live far from civilization. [8] The way the Aboriginals communicate direction is completely without relation to the speaker at all, so much so that if you asked a speaker where something is that is behind her, she would point right through herself. [9] That this vast a difference between oneself and one's relationship to space can be expressed linguistically is an argument for 43 striving to preserve linguistic diversity in a globalized world. 44

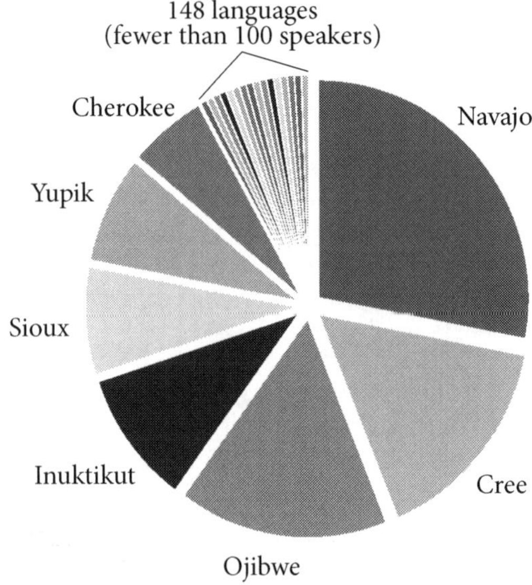

43

Which choice most effectively concludes the sentence and paragraph?

A) NO CHANGE
B) modifying the English language so that it is less self-centered.
C) funding further study of the linguistic variety found in our world.
D) bridging the linguistic divides that create global and regional conflict.

44

To improve cohesion and flow of the paragraph, the writer wants to add the following sentence.

Why does language diversity matter?

The sentence would most logically be placed after

A) sentence 1.
B) sentence 4.
C) sentence 5.
D) sentence 8.

STOP

If you finish before time is called, you may check your work on this section only. Do not turn to any other section.

Math Test – No Calculator

25 MINUTES, 20 QUESTIONS

Turn to Section 3 of your answer sheet to answer the questions in this section.

DIRECTIONS

For questions 1-15, solve each problem, choose the best answer from the choices provided, and fill in the corresponding circle on your answer sheet. **For questions 16-20,** solve the problem and enter your answer in the grid on the answer sheet. Please refer to the directions before question 16 on how to enter your answers in the grid. You may use any available space in your test booklet for scratch work.

NOTES

1. The use of a calculator **is not permitted**.
2. All variables and expressions used represent real numbers unless otherwise indicated.
3. Figures provided in this test are drawn to scale unless otherwise indicated.
4. All figures lie in a plane unless otherwise indicated.
5. Unless otherwise indicated, the domain of a given function *f* is the set of all real numbers *x* for which *f* (*x*) is a real number.

REFERENCE

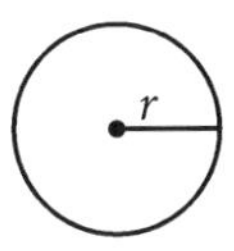

$A = \pi r^2$
$C = 2\pi r$

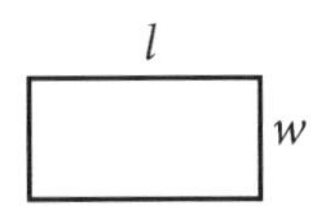

$A = lw$

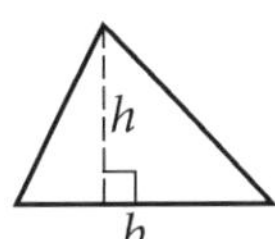

$A = \frac{1}{2}bh$

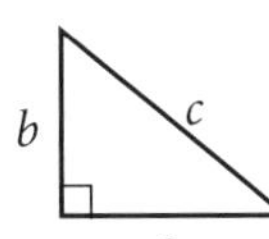

$c^2 = a^2 + b^2$

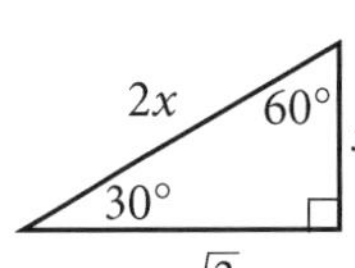

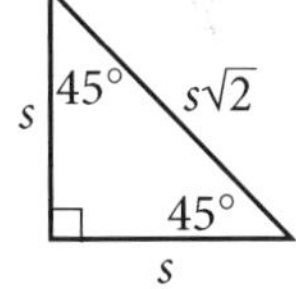

Special Right Triangles

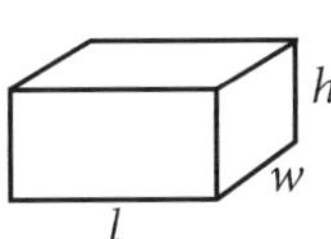

$V = lwh$

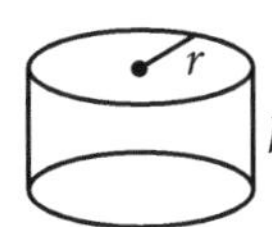

$V = \pi r^2 h$

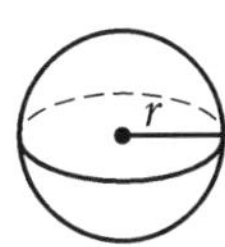

$V = \frac{4}{3}\pi r^3$

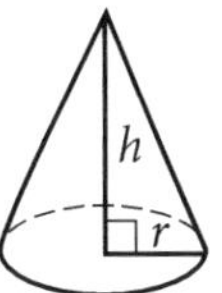

$V = \frac{1}{3}\pi r^2 h$

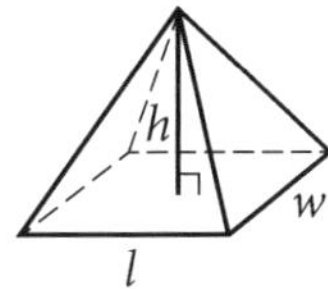

$V = \frac{1}{3}lwh$

The number of degrees of arc in a circle is 360.
The number of radians of arc in a circle is 2π.
The sum of the measures in degrees of the angles of a triangle is 180.

1

Which description of the graph having the equation, $5x - y = 2$, is accurate?

A) a parabola with a vertex of (5, -2)
B) a parabola with a vertex of (-2, 5)
C) a line with a slope of 5 and a y-intercept of -2
D) a line with a slope of -2 and a y-intercept of 5

2

Which system of equations has no solution?

A) $y = 5x$
$y = -\frac{1}{5}x$

B) $y = 3x + 2$
$y = -5x + 2$

C) $y = \frac{1}{2}x + 7$
$y = \frac{1}{2}x - 3$

D) $y = 4x + 3$
$y = -4x + 5$

3

Which expression has the greatest value when $b = 4$ and $c = 6$?

A) $\frac{b}{c}$
B) $\frac{c}{b}$
C) $\frac{b^2}{c^2}$
D) $\frac{c^2}{b^2}$

4

A polynomial function has x-intercepts of -3, 1, and 4 and a y–intercept of 24. The degree of the polynomial function is 3. What is the equation of function $f(x)$?

A) $f(x) = 2(x + 3)(x - 1)(x - 4)$
B) $f(x)= 2(x - 3)(x + 1)(x + 4)$
C) $f(x)= (x + 3)(x - 1)(x - 4)$
D) $f(x)= (x - 3)(x + 1)(x + 4)$

5

Which set of numbers contains only rational numbers?

A) $\left\{-2, 0, \sqrt{3}, \frac{4}{5}\right\}$
B) $\left\{\frac{1}{2}, -5, \frac{8}{3}, 9.8\right\}$
C) $\left\{-10, \pi, 0.75, \frac{8}{5}\right\}$
D) $\left\{2\sqrt{10}, \sqrt{16}, -17, \frac{1}{2}\right\}$

6

Line k is perpendicular to line l. The equation for line k is $y = \frac{2}{3}x + 5$. The equation for line l is $y = nx - 8$. What is the value of n?

A) $\frac{2}{3}$

B) $\frac{3}{2}$

C) $-\frac{2}{3}$

D) $-\frac{3}{2}$

7

If $m^5 = 8$, what is the value of m^{10}?

A) 16

B) 40

C) 64

D) 128

8

Triangle RST is an isosceles right triangle. The length of the hypotenuse is $36\sqrt{2}$. What is the length of each leg of the triangle?

A) 6

B) 12

C) 18

D) 36

9

A cubic (third power) polynomial written in the form $ax^3 + bx^2 + cx + d$ has x-intercepts at -5, -3, and 3, and $a = 1$. What is the value of d?

A) -45

B) -5

C) 5

D) 45

10

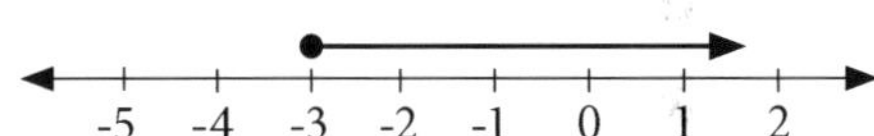

The graph above represents the solution set of an inequality. Which of the inequalities has this solution?

A) $-\frac{x}{3} < 1$

B) $-2y \leq 6$

C) $2 + w \leq -1$

D) $6z > 18$

11

Which of the following numbers is greater than 11 and less than 12?

A) $\sqrt{101}$

B) $\sqrt{120}$

C) $\sqrt{135}$

D) $\sqrt{145}$

12

A function is one-to-one if each x-value in the domain corresponds with exactly one y-value in the range, and each y-value in the range corresponds with exactly one x-value in the domain. Which function is not a one-to-one function?

A) $f(x) = 5x + 1$

B) $f(x) = x^3 - 5$

C) $f(x) = x^2 + 4$

D) $f(x) = 4x^3$

13

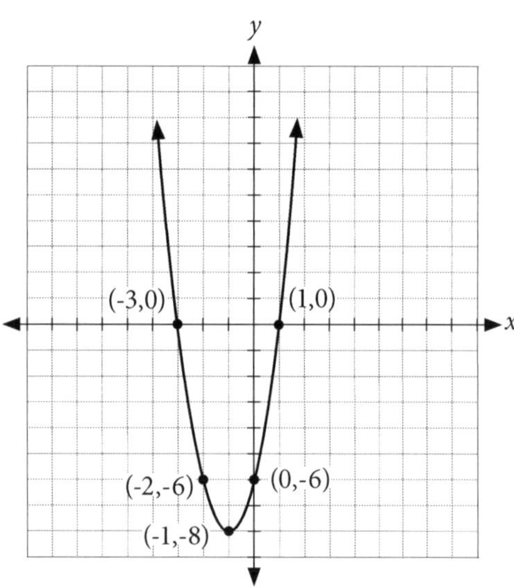

Use the graph of the parabola shown above. What is the equation for the parabola?

A) $f(x) = 2x^2 + 4x - 6$

B) $f(x) = 2x^2 - 4x - 6$

C) $f(x) = x^2 + 2x - 3$

D) $f(x) = 2x^2 - 6$

14

$$t_1 = 3$$

$$t_n = 2t_{n-1} + 1$$

The two terms above represent a recursive formula for a sequence. Which list contains the first 4 terms of the sequence?

A) 3, 5, 7, 9

B) 1, 4, 7, 10

C) 3, 6, 9, 12

D) 3, 7, 15, 31

15

$$f(x) = 3x^2 - 12x - 15$$

Function f is defined above. Which of the following is also an equation for function f and identifies the x-intercepts of the graph of the function?

A) $f(x) = (x + 1)(x - 5)$

B) $f(x) = (x - 1)(x + 5)$

C) $f(x) = 3(x + 1)(x - 5)$

D) $f(x) = 3(x - 1)(x + 5)$

DIRECTIONS

For questions 16 – 20, solve each problem, enter your answer in the grid, as described below on the answer sheet.

1. Although not required, it is suggested that you write your answer in the boxes at the top of the columns to help you fill in the circles accurately. You will receive credit only if the circles are filled in correctly.
2. Mark no more than one circle in any column.
3. No question has a negative answer.
4. Some problems may have more than one correct answer. In such cases, grid only one answer.
5. **Mixed numbers** such as $3\frac{1}{2}$ must be gridded as 3.5 or $\frac{7}{2}$. (If 3 1 / 2 is entered into the grid, it will be interpreted as $\frac{31}{2}$, not $3\frac{1}{2}$.)
6. **Decimal answers:** If you obtain a decimal answer with more digits than the grid can accommodate, it may be either rounded or truncated, but it must fill the entire grid.

Answer: $\frac{7}{12}$

Write answer in boxes. → 7 / 1 2

← Fraction line

Grid in result.

Answer: 2.5

2 . 5

← Decimal point

Acceptable ways to grid $\frac{2}{3}$ are:

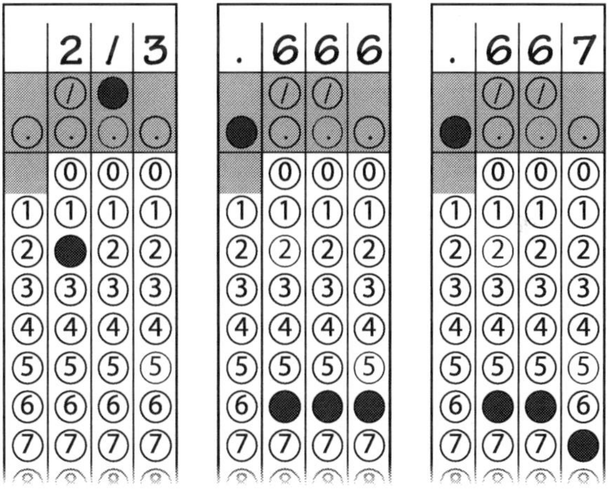

Answer: 201 – either position is correct

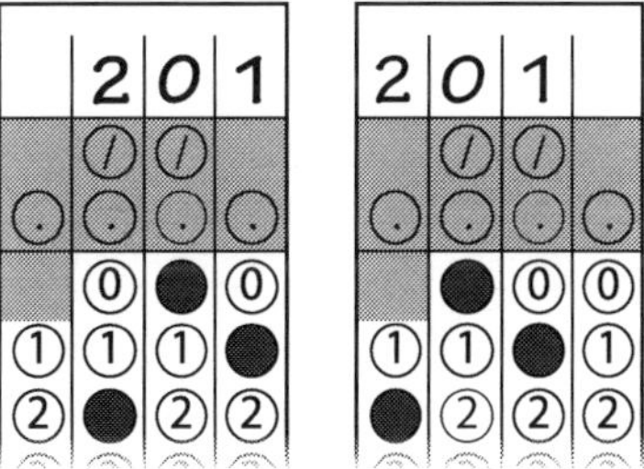

NOTE: You may start your answers in any column, space permitting. Columns you don't need to use should be left blank.

16

Erika was in charge of ordering supplies for the sixth grade art class. Regular pencils cost 10 cents each and colored pencils cost 50 cents each. The total number of pencils she ordered was 140 and the total cost of the order was $46.00. How many regular pencils were ordered?

17

What is the number of degrees in an angle whose radian measure is $\frac{11\pi}{12}$?

18

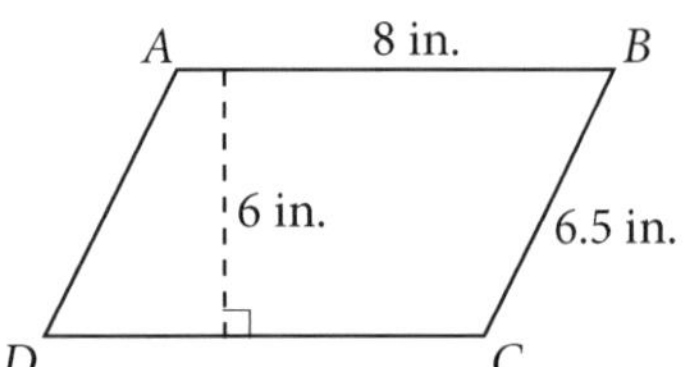

Parallelogram ABCD is shown above. What is the area, in square inches, of the parallelogram?

19

x	-1	0	1	2	3
$g(x)$	0	1	0	-2	0

If $g(x)$ is a polynomial function with a highest power of a and $a < 4$, what is the value of a?

20

If R is inversely proportional to A, and $R = 4$ when $A = 100$, what is the value of R when $A = 5$?

STOP

If you finish before time is called, you may check your work on this section only. Do not turn to any other section.

Math Test – Calculator

55 MINUTES, 38 QUESTIONS

Turn to Section 4 of your answer sheet to answer the questions in this section.

DIRECTIONS

For questions 1-30, solve each problem, choose the best answer from the choices provided, and fill in the corresponding circle on your answer sheet. **For questions 31-38,** solve the problem and enter your answer in the grid on the answer sheet. Please refer to the directions before question 16 on how to enter your answers in the grid. You may use any available space in your test booklet for scratch work.

NOTES

1. The use of a calculator **is not permitted**.
2. All variables and expressions used represent real numbers unless otherwise indicated.
3. Figures provided in this test are drawn to scale unless otherwise indicated.
4. All figures lie in a plane unless otherwise indicated.
5. Unless otherwise indicated, the domain of a given function f is the set of all real numbers x for which $f(x)$ is a real number.

REFERENCE

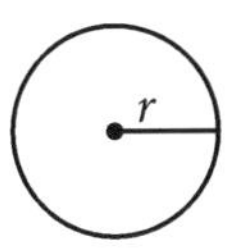

$A = \pi r^2$
$C = 2\pi r$

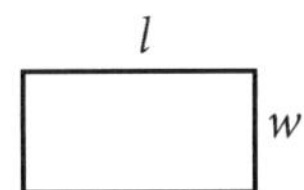

$A = lw$

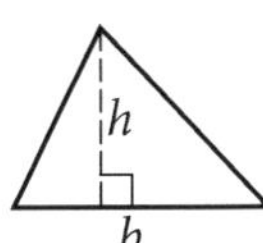

$A = \frac{1}{2}bh$

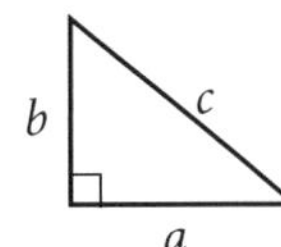

$c^2 = a^2 + b^2$

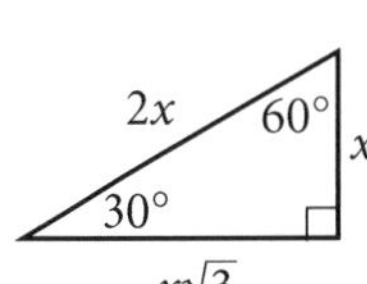

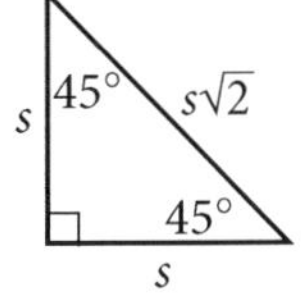

Special Right Triangles

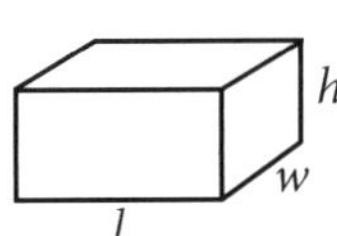

$V = lwh$

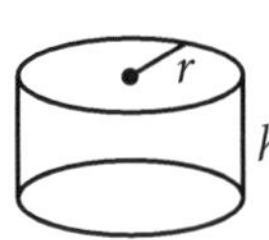

$V = \pi r^2 h$

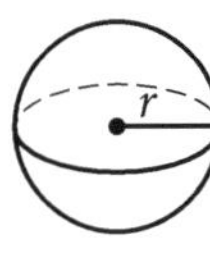

$V = \frac{4}{3}\pi r^3$

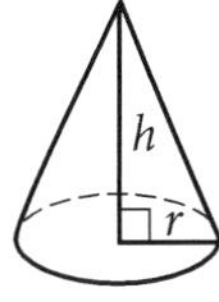

$V = \frac{1}{3}\pi r^2 h$

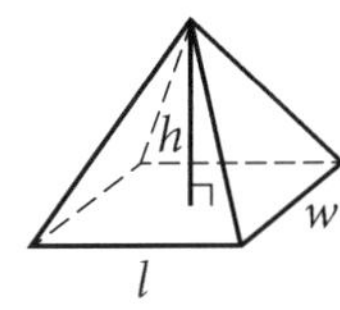

$V = \frac{1}{3}lwh$

The number of degrees of arc in a circle is 360.
The number of radians of arc in a circle is 2π.
The sum of the measures in degrees of the angles of a triangle is 180.

1

The president of a company is 3 years older than the vice president. The product of their ages is 3,190. Which of the following equations could be use to find their ages?

A) $4x = 3{,}190$
B) $2x + 3 = 3190$
C) $2(x + 3) = 3{,}190$
D) $x(x + 3) = 3{,}190$

2

On a science quiz with a normal distribution, the mean is 8. If the standard deviation is 0.5, which of the following scores deviates the most from the mean?

A) 10
B) 9
C) 8
D) 7

3

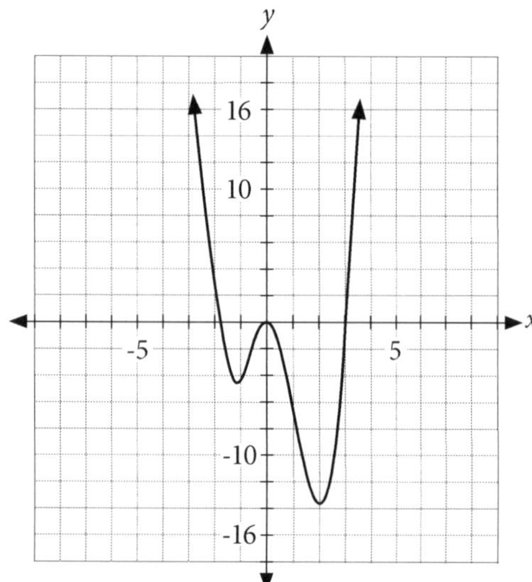

The graph of $f(x)$ is shown above. Which set of numbers lists ALL the real solutions of $f(x)$?

A) $\{-3, 2\}$
B) $\{-2, 3\}$
C) $\{-2, 0, 3\}$
D) $\{-3, 0, 2\}$

Questions 4 and 5 refer to the following information.

It takes Jerome 3.5 hours to climb his favorite mountain, which has an elevation of 2,100 feet.

4

If Addie can climb a mountain at the same rate as Jerome, how long will it take Addie to climb a mountain that has an elevation of 3,000 feet?

A) 4 hours
B) 4.5 hours
C) 5 hours
D) 6 hours

5

Jerome finds that his rate of climbing a mountain decreases by 50 feet/hour once he reaches an elevation above 5,000 feet. How long, to the nearest hour, will it take Jerome to climb a mountain with an elevation of 6,000 feet?

A) 8
B) 9
C) 10
D) 11

6

What is the product of $i^7 i^5$?

A) -1
B) 1
C) $-i$
D) i

7

$$\sqrt{x+3} = 3 - x$$

What is the solution set for the above equation?

A) {0}
B) {1}
C) {1, 6}
D) {2, 3}

8

	Watches basketball	Does not watch basketball	Total
Plays basketball	40	3	43
Does not play basketball	36	21	57
Total	76	24	100

A gym class instructor asked 100 students a two-question survey: do you play basketball, and do you watch basketball. The table above summarizes the results. Based on the data, what is the probability that a student selected at random plays basketball but does not watch basketball?

A) $\frac{3}{100}$
B) $\frac{3}{43}$
C) $\frac{40}{43}$
D) $\frac{43}{100}$

9

Shona wants to order copies of a picture of her son. The cost for each large photo is $9.49 and the cost for each wallet-size photo is 55 cents. She wants to purchase one large photo and she wants to spend $20 at most. Which of the following mathematical statements can be used to find the number of wallet-size photos, x, Shona can purchase?

A) $0.55x \le 20$
B) $9.49 + x < 20$
C) $9.49 + 0.55x \le 20$
D) $9.49 + 0.55x < 20$

10

If $a = 3$ and $b = 2$, what is the value of the expression $\frac{a^{-2}}{b^{-3}}$?

A) $-\frac{8}{9}$
B) $\frac{8}{9}$
C) -1
D) 1

11

Rahul works for a company that delivers packages. Each driver averages 52 deliveries every 8 hours. If Rahul works a 6 hour shift, about how many deliveries can he expect to make?

A) 42
B) 39
C) 36
D) 30

12

$$\begin{cases} y \leq 3 \\ y > 1 \\ y \geq -x + 1 \end{cases}$$

Which ordered pair is <u>not</u> a solution to the system of inequalities above?

A) (5, 3)
B) (2, 3)
C) (5, -2)
D) (2, 2)

13

A bag contains slips of paper numbered 1 through 9. Two slips of paper are drawn, one after the other, and without replacement. What is the probability that both numbers drawn are even?

A) $\frac{1}{18}$
B) $\frac{1}{6}$
C) $\frac{16}{81}$
D) $\frac{12}{81}$

14

The table below gives a car owner's average annual expenditure, y, in dollars, for gasoline for x years after 1900.

Number of years after 1900 (x)	35	45	55	65	75	85
Annual expenditure on gasoline in dollars (y)	35	57	93	152	247	400

Which function best represents the data shown in the table?

A) $y = x^2 + 6$
B) $y = 0.014x^2$
C) $y = 2.6x + 8.15$
D) $y = 6.36(1.05)^x$

15

A faulty faucet leaks rate at a rate of 100 milliliters every 10 minutes. How much water, in milliliters is wasted in a day?

A) 2,400
B) 12,000
C) 14,400
D) 144,000

16

Which statement about statistical studies is correct?

A) A survey of 100 randomly selected students in a high school would be a good sample to determine the number of hours students spend studying.

B) A survey of all ninth graders in a high school would be a good sample to determine the number of student parking spaces needed.

C) A survey of all students in one lunch period in a high school would be a good sample to determine the number of hours adults spend on social media websites.

D) A survey of all Calculus students in a high school would be a good sample to determine the number of students who don't like math.

17

Which expression has the greatest value?

A) $|-9|$

B) $-|-9|$

C) $|4-5|$

D) $-|4+5|$

18

Stem	Leaf
6	8 9 9
7	2 2 2 2 3 4 5 7
8	0 1 2 3 5 6 8 9
9	1 2 3 4 4 4

Using the data displayed in the stem-and-leaf-plot above, what is the mode of the data?

A) 2

B) 4

C) 72

D) 94

Questions 19 and 20 refer to the following information.

A survey asked users of online banking for their ages. The results are shown in the table below.

Users of Online Banking

Age, in years	Number of Users
Under 21	1,636
21-40	6,617
41-60	3,693
61-80	491
Over 80	6

19

What is the probability that a randomly selected user of online banking is at most 20 years old?

A) 0.25

B) 0.20

C) 0.17

D) 0.13

20

What is the probability that a randomly selected user of online banking is at least 41 years old, given that the user is at least 21?

A) 0.34

B) 0.39

C) 0.42

D) 0.60

21

The graph of the quadratic function f in the xy-plane intercepts the x-axis at $(c, 0)$ and $(d, 0)$. Which of the following could define the function f?

A) $x^2 - x(c - d) + cd$
B) $x^2 + x(c - d) + cd$
C) $x^2 - x(c + d) + cd$
D) $x^2 + x(c + d) + cd$

Questions 22 and 23 refer to the following information.

Two objects A and B are on a seesaw. The seesaw is balanced when the ratio of the weight (a) of Object A to the distance (y) of Object A from the fulcrum is equal to the ratio of the weight (b) of Object B to the distance (x) of Object B from the fulcrum. The equation representing this situation is below:

$$\frac{\text{Weight of Object A}}{\text{Distance of Object A from Fulcrum}} = \frac{\text{Weight of Object B}}{\text{Distance of Object B from Fulcrum}}$$

Using variables, the above equation can be written as shown below.

$$\frac{a}{y} = \frac{b}{x}$$

22

What is another way to write the relationship between the variables?

A) $ay = bx$
B) $ax = by$
C) $a + x = b + y$
D) $a + y = b + x$

23

If Object A weighs 50 pounds and is 29 inches from the fulcrum. Object B weighs 30 pounds. In order for the seesaw to be balanced, what is the distance Object B must be from the fulcrum?

A) 9 inches
B) 15 inches
C) 17.4 inches
D) 51.72 inches

24

$$f(x) = x^3 + 6x^2 + 11x + 6$$

One factor of the polynomial defined above is $x + 1$. What is the complete factorization of the polynomial?

A) $(x + 1)(x + 2)(x + 3)$
B) $(x + 1)(x + 1)(x + 6)$
C) $(x + 1)(x^2 + 5x + 6)$
D) $(x + 1)(x^2 + 6x + 1)$

25

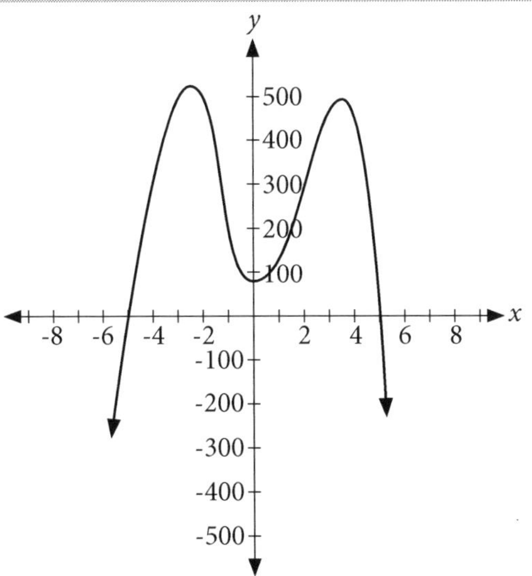

A sketch of the graph of a polynomial of 4th degree is shown above. Using the fact that the x-intercepts of the function are -5 and 5 and that the y-intercept is 75, what is the equation for the function?

A) $f(x) = 3(x^2 + 1)(x + 5)(x - 5)$
B) $f(x) = (3x^2 + 1)(x + 5)(x - 5)$
C) $f(x) = -3(x^2 + 1)(x + 5)(x - 5)$
D) $f(x) = -3(x^2 - 1)(x + 5)(x - 5)$

26

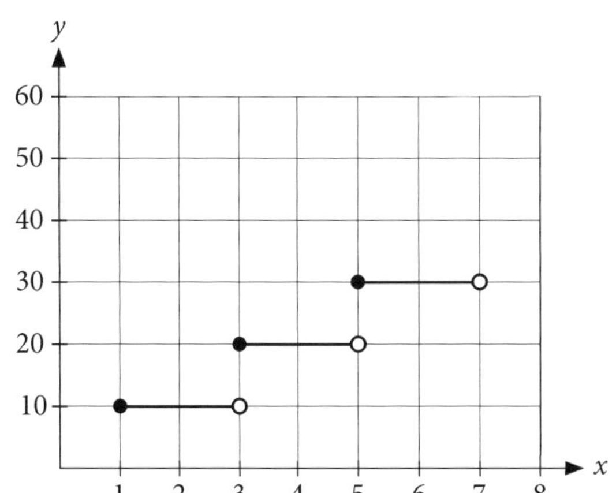

The graph above shows function $f(x)$. Which of the following statements is true for this function?

A) $f(1) = 10$ and $f(7) = 30$
B) $f(3) = 10$ and $f(3) = 30$
C) $f(3) = 20$ and $f(5) = 30$
D) $f(5) = 20$ and $f(7) = 30$

27

For function $g(x)$, y approaches 0 as x approaches ∞. Which equation could be the equation for function $g(x)$?

A) $g(x) = 14.5x - 80$
B) $g(x) = 2.8x^2$
C) $g(x) = 6.4(3.75)^x$
D) $g(x) = 6.4(0.58)^x$

28

Which expression is equivalent to the expression, $\frac{\sqrt{3} + 5}{\sqrt{3} - 5}$?

A) $-\frac{14 + 5\sqrt{3}}{11}$
B) $-\frac{17 + 5\sqrt{3}}{11}$
C) $\frac{14 + 5\sqrt{3}}{14}$
D) $\frac{17 + 5\sqrt{3}}{14}$

29

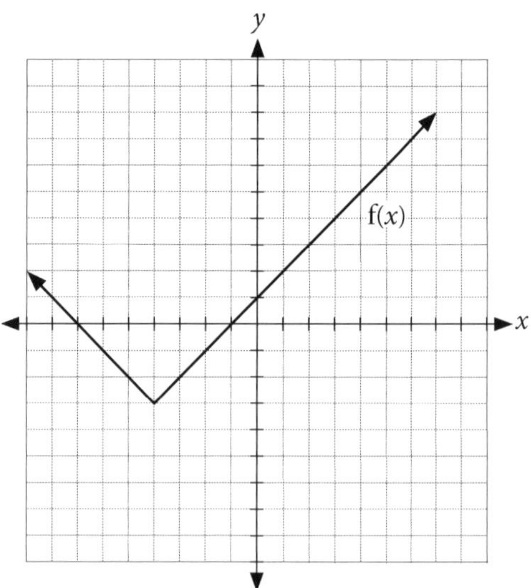

The graph above shows function $f(x)$. Function $g(x)$ is the result of reflecting function $f(x)$ over the y-axis. What is the equation for $g(x)$?

A) $g(x) = |x + 4| - 3$

B) $g(x) = |x - 4| - 3$

C) $g(x) = |x + 4| + 3$

D) $g(x) = |x - 3| - 4$

30

What is the equation of a circle with a center of (5, -2) and a radius of 3?

A) $(x - 5)^2 + (y + 2)^2 = 3$

B) $(x - 5)^2 + (y + 2)^2 = 9$

C) $(x + 5)^2 + (y - 2)^2 = 3$

D) $(x + 5)^2 + (y - 2)^2 = 9$

DIRECTIONS

For questions 31 – 38, solve each problem, enter your answer in the grid, as described below on the answer sheet.

1. Although not required, it is suggested that you write your answer in the boxes at the top of the columns to help you fill in the circles accurately. You will receive credit only if the circles are filled in correctly.
2. Mark no more than one circle in any column.
3. No question has a negative answer.
4. Some problems may have more than one correct answer. In such cases, grid only one answer.
5. **Mixed numbers** such as $3\frac{1}{2}$ must be gridded as 3.5 or $\frac{7}{2}$. (If 3 1 / 2 is entered into the grid, it will be interpreted as $\frac{31}{2}$, not $3\frac{1}{2}$.)
6. **Decimal answers:** If you obtain a decimal answer with more digits than the grid can accommodate, it may be either rounded or truncated, but it must fill the entire grid.

Answer: $\frac{7}{12}$

Answer: 2.5

Write answer in boxes. → 7 / 1 2 ← Fraction line

2 . 5 ← Decimal point

Grid in result.

Acceptable ways to grid $\frac{2}{3}$ are:

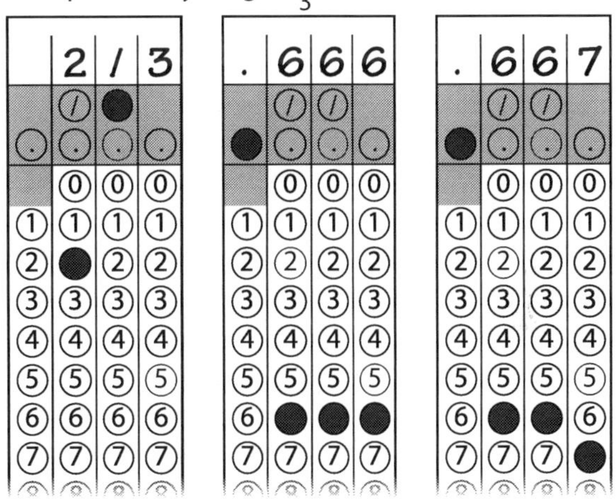

Answer: 201 – either position is correct

2 0 1

2 0 1

NOTE: You may start your answers in any column, space permitting. Columns you don't need to use should be left blank.

31

It is projected that the number of restaurants in a metropolitan area is increasing at a rate of 4.5% annually. The present number of restaurants is 82. To the nearest whole number, how many restaurants will be in the same metropolitan area in 12 years?

32

The following statements about the measures, in degrees, for $\triangle ABC$:

$$m\angle A = 28$$

$$m\angle C = 115$$

In degrees, what is the measure of $\angle B$?

33

The volume of a rectangular prism is 536 cubic centimeters. The height of the prism is 8 centimeters. In square centimeters, what is the area of the base of the prism?

34

The volume of cube A is 8 cubic feet. The length of each dimension of cube B is one foot longer than each dimension of cube A. What is the volume of cube B?

35

Amie owns and operates her own advertising agency. The business generated $435,000 in revenue last year. This year, she set a goal of increasing her revenue by 15%. If she falls $10,000 short of that goal, by what percent, rounded to the nearest tenth, did her revenue grow?

36

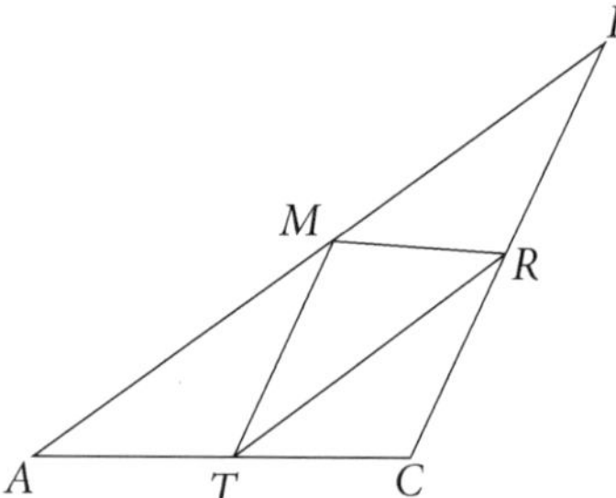

In the figure above, M, R, and T are midpoints of the sides of $\triangle ABC$. If $AB = 18$, $AC = 14$, and $BC = 10$, what is the perimeter of quadrilateral $AMRC$?

Questions 37 and 38 refer to the following information.

The owners of a concert hall have found that the amount of revenue, R, generated by a concert can be represented by the formula, $R = -33t^2 + 360t$ where t represents the price of the ticket. The production costs, C, of the concert is represented by the function, $C = 700 + 5t$.

37

What is the highest ticket price, to the nearest dollar, they can charge in order to earn a positive profit on the event? (Profit is equal to revenue minus expenses.)

38

What is the ticket price, to the nearest cent, that will generate the highest profit?

STOP

If you finish before time is called, you may check your work on this section only. Do not turn to any other section.

Tutor Ted®

SAT® Practice Essay #2

ESSAY BOOK

DIRECTIONS

The essay gives you an opportunity to show how effectively you can read and comprehend a passage and write an essay analyzing the passage. In your essay, you should demonstrate that you have read the passage carefully, present a clear and logical analysis, and use language precisely.

Your essay must be written on the lines provided in your answer booklet; except for the Planning Page of the answer booklet, you will receive no other paper on which to write. You will have enough space if you write on every line, avoid wide margins, and keep your handwriting to a reasonable size. Remember that people who are not familiar with your handwriting will read what you write. Try to write or print so that what you are writing is legible to those readers.

You have 50 minutes to read the passage and write an essay in response to the prompt provided inside this booklet.

REMINDERS:

— Do not write your essay in this booklet. Only what you write on the lined pages of your answer booklet will be evaluated.

— An off-topic essay will not be evaluated.

This cover is representative of what you'll see on test day.

As you read the passage below, consider how Charles Eisenstein uses

- evidence, such as facts or examples, to support claims.
- reasoning to develop ideas and to connect claims and evidence.
- stylistic or persuasive elements, such as word choice or appeals to emotion, to add power to the ideas expressed.

Adapted from Charles Eisenstein, "Disorderly Conduct." CC BY 4.0 2014 by https://charleseisenstein.net.

1 Last weekend I decided I would get the kids outdoors for a little time in nature. The Susquehanna River was frozen over, with the most remarkable ice formations. Even though the water is not deep in this part of the river, ice somehow piled up several feet.

2 It didn't take long before four police cars and two fire trucks showed up. I was yelled at in front of my children, told I could be arrested for endangering the safety of a minor, and cited for disorderly conduct.

3 This small incident reveals a lot about our society. First is the presumption that legally constituted authority should decide what is an acceptable level of safety for oneself and one's family. I suppose going out onto the ice was more dangerous than staying indoors or on the sidewalk, but I deemed it in my children's best interest to be outdoors in this amazing ice world.

4 Secondly, I sensed that what really disturbed the police was not that they actually believed we were in danger of falling through the ice. I'm telling you, that ice was thick. I think what disturbed them was the violation of normality that our little adventure represented. It makes people uncomfortable to see someone flaunting social norms.

5 A third thing I found noteworthy was the routine, automatic attempt to shame and humiliate me. How they behaved was written into their job description, which draws from a whole worldview – which has deep religious and philosophical roots – in which punishment and reward are the main motivators of human behavior. If you want someone to stop doing something, you apply a legal or psychological penalty. Obviously, legal and psychological go closely hand in hand: the essential feature of incarceration is prolonged humiliation, the stripping away of dignity.

6 A fourth observation, that is more personal than social: despite my conviction that I had done nothing wrong, it was hard to resist the feelings of shame that welled up as twenty men and women, decked out in the regalia of authority, surrounded me unified in their belief that I was foolish and irresponsible. We are social animals, our identity a product of our relationships. We learn to see ourselves through how others see us. Even as I strove to maintain my equilibrium, a part of me felt ashamed; it wanted me to abase myself and beg forgiveness, that I might be accepted by the group.

7 While the power of shame, judgment, and social approval to induce conformity is great, and may seem to bear a strong pro-social effect when, for example, it becomes unacceptable to voice racist or homophobic opinions, I am afraid that these tools have important limitations. For one, while they induce conformity, they don't address the root of hateful opinions or antisocial behavior. The racist or homophobe is likely to carry the hate and express it in some other, more subtle way. Secondly, the threat of shame can drive people to defensive, self-justifying positions. In my case, one effect of the shaming was that I became inwardly defensive and absolutely closed to the possibility that maybe I had been reckless or irresponsible. It would be much, much easier to admit I'd been reckless if someone had said, with thoughtful concern, "Hey brother, that ice is thinner than it looks."

8 Is it possible to base a society on dignity rather than humiliation? If that is a truth—if we believe in the fundamental dignity of all people—then the problem is not only that we use the tools of shame, humiliation, and punishment for the wrong ends; the means itself is wrong, and it is inseparable from the end of domination and control.

9 A justice system that were healing rather than punitive in nature would focus not on the principle of obeying the rules, but on providing the opportunity for contrition for the actual crime itself. This is contrary to the mentality of punishment, which is, "I will make you be sorry": instead it holds that given the opportunity, remorse will arise naturally. That implies a trust in other human beings that is the essence of valuing their dignity, and it would turn the established order upside-down.

Write an essay in which you explain how Charles Eisenstein builds an argument to persuade his audience that the principles underlying social harmony in America are misguided. In your essay, analyze how Eisenstein uses one or more of the features listed in the box above (or features of your own choice) to strengthen the logic and persuasiveness of his argument. Be sure that your analysis focuses on the most relevant features of the passage.

Your essay should not explain whether you agree with Eisenstein's claims, but rather explain how Eisenstein builds an argument to persuade his audience.

Practice Test 2

ANSWERS

READING

1	C	27	C
2	B	28	B
3	B	29	D
4	A	30	C
5	C	31	A
6	D	32	C
7	A	33	A
8	D	34	A
9	A	35	B
10	C	36	B
11	A	37	D
12	A	38	B
13	D	39	C
14	B	40	D
15	A	41	D
16	C	42	C
17	D	43	A
18	C	44	B
19	B	45	B
20	B	46	A
21	B	47	A
22	D	48	D
23	D	49	D
24	D	50	D
25	B	51	C
26	A	52	B

WRITING & LANGUAGE

1	A	23	C
2	B	24	B
3	B	25	D
4	D	26	B
5	B	27	D
6	C	28	A
7	A	29	C
8	B	30	B
9	B	31	A
10	D	32	C
11	C	33	C
12	C	34	B
13	B	35	C
14	D	36	C
15	C	37	B
16	B	38	A
17	C	39	D
18	D	40	D
19	A	41	B
20	A	42	B
21	D	43	A
22	B	44	A

MATH

1	C
2	C
3	D
4	A
5	B
6	D
7	C
8	D
9	A
10	B
11	C
12	C
13	A
14	D
15	C
16	60
17	165
18	48
19	3
20	80

MATH

1	D
2	A
3	C
4	C
5	C
6	B
7	B
8	A
9	C
10	B
11	B
12	C
13	B
14	D
15	C
16	A
17	A
18	C
19	D
20	B
21	C
22	B
23	C
24	A
25	C
26	C
27	D
28	A
29	B
30	B
31	90
32	37
33	67
34	27
35	12.7
36	35
37	8
38	5.38

PRACTICE TEST 2: SOLUTIONS

Practice Test 2 SOLUTIONS

SECTION 1: READING

PASSAGE: LADIES' PARADISE

1) **C**
You've just read the entire passage, underlining and taking caveman notes as you went. Main idea questions are easy money! A and B are inaccurate and D is a bait-and-switch. The answer looks correct until it mentions that the colleagues believed that Robineau's colleagues were already theirs.

2) **B**
Vocabulary is easy money! Context clues imply that the salesmen are reacting to Robineau's reappearance. "Hostility" is too extreme and "approach" and "posture" are more literal synonyms of "attitude" that don't work here.

3) **B**
Hutin underhandedly attempting to remove a senior employee would be considered neither "admirable" nor "overbearing." While Hutin may have acted spitefully, "insubordinate" definitely fits best here as Hutin is blatantly self-serving and defiant of authority.

4) **A**
We can eliminate B and D because the tone is neither "critical" nor "eerie." C is also incorrect as the tone could be considered "aggressive," but Robineau's are not angry at him for his absence; they're angry at him for his return.

5) **C**
C best fits here as the salesmen continuously show built-up annoyance and frustration towards Robineau, not jealousy. They are neither intimidated by nor nervous around Robineau.

6) **D**
All of the above provide evidence but only D shows the extent to which Robineau has displayed unprofessional behavior as the salesmen share twenty anecdotes. The continuousness of Robineau's overbearing manner leads to "exasperated" salesmen.

7) **A**
Vocabulary is easy money! The context provides anecdotes concerning Robineau's behavior so "demeanor" is the best fit.

8) **D**
Hutin, Vinçard, and Favier lack major differences throughout the passage as they all align themselves against the return of Robineau.

9) **A**
The author writes, "...everyone in the department, from the newcomer dreaming of becoming a salesman to the senior salesman coveting Robineau's job, had only one fixed idea - to dislodge their comrade senior to them in order to move up a grade..." This sentence shows the consistent outlook across the whole department.

10) **C**
B and D are clearly inaccurate as Robineau does not steal from the company and there is no sense of wonder about him. A lacks evidence that the salesmen also display overbearing manners and treat customers poorly.

PASSAGE: WHY WOMEN SHOULD VOTE

11) **A**
You've just read the entire passage so main idea questions are easy money! Addams argues that women desire the right to vote in order to more fully and capably attend to her duties. She argues they would accept this political responsibility, stating, "one cannot imagine that they would shirk simply because the action ran counter to old traditions."

12) **A**
A most closely answers Question 11 as it asserts that if women are to execute their duties and preserve their homes

in their entirety, they must extend their responsibilities beyond the home by contributing to political decisions which naturally affect them.

13) D
Vocabulary questions are easy money. Grab 'em first! Context clues show that women need to "discharge their duties." "Execute" fits best.

14) B
Addams argues that women require the right to vote in order to fully accomplish their natural duties, which include the education of children. Education decisions are being made by the Board of Education, where women must acquire the power to vote in order to influence school curricula and fulfill their duties as women.

15) A
Knowing your geography is helpful here. The third paragraph discusses how the education of children is a woman's duty but, in recent times, only those who vote make the decisions.

16) C
The passage critiques the fact that women do not yet vote, arguing for a change in the political institutions' attitudes and policies. A and B would not be considered the *main* obstacles to women's suffrage.

17) D
Addams calls for a change in our political institutions as the primary focus of her argument.

18) C
Easy money. In context, "accord a vote" most nearly means "grant" a vote.

19) B
A is close but inaccurate as Addams does not address a stereotype about women and all new traditions. Addams never demonizes or criticizes women, so C and D are also out. In pursuing the right for women to vote, Addams debunks the theory that well-educated women would still choose not to vote due to tradition.

20) B
A is inaccurate and C misses the main idea of the paragraph. Addams asserts that women are not taking anything away from men. D is the main idea of the second paragraph!

PASSAGE: LIMITED EVIDENCE ON THE EFFECTIVENESS OF INTERVENTIONS TO REDUCE LIVESTOCK PREDATION BY LARGE CARNIVORES

21) B
Main idea questions are easy money—a great place to start. A is tempting but B captures the greater purpose of the passage as a whole, calling for more collaborative research to effectively combat carnivore depredation.

22) D
Vocabulary—more easy money! If carnivore species became extinct, livestock depredation would not continue, or just pause, it would stop entirely. "Draw to a close" is not the right tone for the passage.

23) D
A, B, and C flood the author with emotion which doesn't match the tone of the passage. The author is instead dissatisfied with the research so far, and confident a new solution can be determined.

24) D
D displays a confident tone towards future research, implying a dissatisfaction with current approaches towards reducing carnivore depredation.

25) B
We can easily eliminate D and C as the second paragraph does not "scathe" and is not a summary of existing research. It also does not a highlight one "main issue" with the established research, but instead offers "brief insight."

26) A
Be a search engine for Small Picture questions! "Fladry" is discussed in the third

2

paragraph to have been effective against wolves, but not coyotes.

27) C

Another easy money vocabulary question—attack these first! Legal protection of carnivores would *prevent* their unregulated killing so "prohibits" is your best fit.

28) B

This is one of those questions you might remember reading somewhere. Hopefully your caveman notes lead you to the penultimate paragraph which states, "In this regard, complete carnivore removal could be considered effective at eliminating livestock depredation."

29) D

D directly states that removing carnivores would effectively eliminate livestock depredation.

30) C

In the final paragraph, the author concludes, "Attempts to increase the involvement of these actors, contributing together to evidence-based approaches, may be one way to alter the odds in a favorable direction," so she would most likely agree with C. D is never mentioned and the author directly refutes A and B as research should focus on long-term solutions beyond just the local level.

PASSAGE: "FRACKING BANS DO MORE HARM THAN GOOD" AND "FRACKING TEXAS, RECYCLING 'FLOWBACK,' & WATER CONTAMINATION"

31) A

After reading Passage 1 and before reading Passage 2, answer any questions regarding that passage specifically as its content is fresh in your head. D is not relevant to Passage 1.

32) C

The context implies that scientific literature lacks evidence of fracking's pollution or health risks, so "support" most nearly means "substantiation," or evidence that proves something to be true. B and C are too literal, and A doesn't fit the context. Remember, vocabulary questions are easy money—start with these!

33) A

One more Passage 1 question to answer before moving on to Passage 2. The fifth paragraph does not serve to justify disturbances, nor does it outright demonize the coal industry, so B and C are out. D is the opposite as the author supports natural gas. A is the correct answer as the author provides direct comparisons to coal.

34) A

Questions looking for the main idea or primary purpose can often be answered by looking at the intro. The author of Passage 2 discusses the heavy contamination of water used during fracking. D mentions water waste but the author's primary concern is not regulation.

35) B

While A and D technically work, B best fits the tone of Passage 2. Easy money.

36) B

Questions asking you to find specific values on a graph are easy money as well. You know exactly where to look so you can answer these quickly. Locate each answer choice on the graph. The line's steepest slope occurred between 2008 and 2009.

37) D

In the final paragraph 2, the author mentions the concern of rising air pollution due to the release of methane during fracking operations.

38) B

Passage 1 focuses on the many benefits of switching to natural gas, outlining the numerous improvements from coal production. The author would most likely consider the author of Passage 2's fracking concerns as minor considering what those concerns would be regarding coal production.

39) B
The author of Passage 1 agrees that shale production should still be regulated, but clearly considers the side effects of fracking to be minor and manageable.

40) D
After answering the previous two questions, this one feels natural. Passage 1 promotes regulation but would never consider ceasing fracking production.

41) D
Regulation is not the authors' primary concern so A is incorrect. B is only relevant to Passage 2 and C is only relevant to Passage 1. Both passages explore the environmental, economic, etc. cost of fracking.

PASSAGE: MAKING FRIENDS IN VIOLENT NEIGHBORHOODS

42) C
The passage explores research on how children make friends, so C fits best. The other answer choices may be true but do not qualify as the "main purpose" of the passage.

43) A
"Assume" means to take on or adopt. While "embrace" technically works in the sentence, it fits neither the context nor the tone of the passage. Be sure to skim the questions for vocabulary questions if you're running low on time—these are quick to answer so a great way to gather points!

44) B
The author explains that little research has been done on how neighborhood violence affects how children form friendships. Therefore the author justifies the necessity of this study in the first two paragraphs.

45) B
B is clearly noted in the first paragraph. Always read with a pencil in your hand, underlining key information as you go. This strategy will help immensely with Small Picture questions as you'll know exactly where to look in the passage.

46) A
The evidence for Question 45 is located in the first paragraph, likely underlined if you read actively with a pencil in your hand!

47) A
According to the graph, rates of homicide for black male teens ages 15-19 is 46.9 and white male teens of the same age is 5.9. If you round 5.9 to 6 and multiply by 8, you'll get 48 so A is the right answer. D is incorrect because black males are about eight times *more* likely than black females (6.4) to be killed by guns, not less.

48) D
In paragraph 3, the author states, "many children adopt not one but multiple strategies, resulting in a heterogeneous stance toward friendship formation."

49) D
The last sentence of the passage concludes that friendship formation is strategic malleable, and heterogeneous so D provides evidence for the answer to Question 48.

50) D
Easy money vocabulary! In the passage, children turn to kin to "buffer them from violence," or protect them, so D works best.

51) C
The passage as a whole discusses the importance of friends in violent neighborhoods as they stick up for each other and deescalate the threat of violence, providing mutual benefits. Friends are not "role-defined," nor are friendships "short-lived," as children and adults form kin networks throughout their lives so A and D are out. B is also incorrect as friendships are not specific to handling violent situations as the author indicates that friends help manage peer relations and social status as well.

52) B
B correctly interprets data on the graph. Rates of homicide among black children 1-4 are 5.8 (black males) and 5.0 (black females). The rate of homicide for white male teens ages 15-19 is 5.9. These values are about the same.

2

SECTION 2: WRITING AND LANGUAGE

PASSAGE: THE ART OF THE EAST SIDE GALLERY

1) A
What *is* the information that follows? It's all about how borders were closing and a wall was going up. Answer choice A refers back to the first clause in the sentence by creating a clear contrast between "ideological" barriers and "concrete" ones.

2) B
Pay attention to punctuation you cannot change. Here, we cannot change the comma after the word "east," so anything that creates an independent clause following that comma will be creating a comma splice. See ya, A! C would require you to eliminate the comma you cannot eliminate (and it's still a mess even if you do that), and D is just no bueno.

3) B
B both makes the subject of this sentence- The Berlin Wall- the star of the show and provides a clear and direct transition from the previous sentence.

4) D
What is the only condition under which longer answer choices routinely beat shorter ones? When the longer option *clarifies* something the shorter ones leave unclear.

5) B
If you read the entire sentence (and you should have), you should have noticed that "the day the wall was erected until" its tearing down indicate that all of this is in the past tense. "Remained" is the only exclusively past tense verb among the answer choices.

6) C
Parallelism at work! Which answer is the matchiest match? C!

7) A
Okay, first of all, C and D have nothing do to with timeline *at all.* A beats B because we're talking about the aftermath of one specific event- the fall of the Wall- not the runup to another.

8) B
This sentence epitomizes what colons do best: get right to the point.

9) B
These transition/connector words are about the relationship between thoughts. The previous sentence describes works of art conveying critical or cynical ideas, but the following sentence is all about artists reflecting on the positive. Do those thoughts agree or contrast? They contrast! So a contrast word like "however" is our winner. If you chose D, you're not wrong, but the contrast word "although" always begins a dependent clause that will indicate contrast within the two clauses of the sentence itself. (Ex: Although we were initially upset that our flight was delayed, we made the most of it by playing games in the airport all night.)

10) D
This is a difficult diction question that requires black belt knowledge of word connotation. We're looking for a word that essentially means "has," which seems to walk us right to the doorstep, bouquet in hand, of "possesses, "right? And "boasts" can mean the same thing as "brags," so doesn't strategy tell us they both have to be wrong?! I know. It's a doozy. However, the word "boasts" can also mean "to have, own, or enjoy," and we don't really use "possesses" to describe paintings on a wall. (Would you say, "that underpass possesses a lot of graffiti"? Probably not.)

11) C
Forget what you've been told about restating the thesis in order to conclude a passage. The SAT hates redundancy in all forms, and we're playing its game now. We already know this based on other information in the passage, so the correct answer here is C.

PASSAGE 2: TRAVEL IN THE AGE OF THE SHARING ECONOMY

12) C
The other verbs in this sentence act as clues that the verb we are looking for should be similarly past tense, which should eliminate choices B and D. The phrase "would have looked" indicates that we want the past perfect "had gone" rather than the past tense "went."

13) B
To answer the question, "how many reasons are we talking about" depends on the construction of each answer choice. Since "collaborative consumption" is another way to describe "the sharing economy," we are looking for a singular "reason" connected to a singular verb. Only answer choice B fits the bill.

14) D
Shorter is better, am I right?

15) C
"Where people around the world invite strangers into their homes at no charge whatsoever" is, grammatically speaking, an inessential adjective clause further describing "Couchsurfing," so we need to punctuate it either by inserting two commas or two dashes.

16) B
These ideas are different enough that they really want to be separate sentences (bye -bye A!), and the phrase "in addition" is the most logical introduction to the second sentence.

17) C
The first sentence of this paragraph makes a pretty clean break with the last sentence of the previous paragraph, so any transition word that creates a logical link with the previous sentence is going to be wrong. That pretty much eliminates every answer choice but C. C works because it's stating an obvious fact that is expounded upon in the rest of the paragraph.

18) D
This paragraph deals exclusively with the financial benefits of the sharing economy, so it's too early to introduce the idea of "cultural exchange." You can also answer this question by realizing that the second sentence directly responds to the first. That's some Grade A flow of thought right there! We wouldn't want to mess it up by inserting *any* sentence between these sentences regardless of relevance.

19) A
The key to this question is the singular subject "traveler." Do we throw around "theys" and "theirs" pretty casually when referring to singular subjects in speech? Yes. However, the SAT wants you to know that, grammatically speaking, the correct pronoun to describe a singular human subject is "he or she" or "his or her."

20) A
This is a tricky one, with B perhaps the only real stinker (we've moved on from money stuff, bro! Let it go!). The reason A edges out the other choices is the phrase "greater immersion" in sentence 2. That indicates that the greatest benefit is feeling *inside* rather than *outside,* right? C tries to lure you in with the word "immersive," but its focus on language learning alone is too narrow, and D doesn't quite express the kind of insider experience we are looking for. Answer choice A gets right to the heart of this idea.

21) D
Diction! "Effect" both means what we need it to mean and has that dry, academic tone the SAT just can't get enough of.

22) B
It's almost easier to answer this question by asking- where should sentence 2 go? Remember how question #20 hinged upon the main idea of sentence 2? A sentence so important to the rest of the paragraph sure sounds like it should become the topic sentence, doesn't it? If you switch sentences 1 and 2, sentence 2 now introduces the main idea of the paragraph and sentence 1 provides a logical follow-up.

PASSAGE 3: THERE'S NO SUCH THING AS A "LITTLE WHITE LIE"

23) C
Don't overthink this one. It's just a simple little independent clause followed by a comma and coordinating conjunction, followed by a dependent clause.

24) B
Look at the other verbs in the sentence! They are all present tense, so this should be too. That leaves us with B and D, and B correctly uses the possessive "their."

25) D
Only D correctly acknowledges that "in fact" acts as the beginning of a second independent clause. How do we punctuation two independent clauses? Either with a semicolon or a period.

26) B
Remember this question! Nearly all questions about redundancy look exactly like this: 3 choices with extraneous words and one, one-word answer (the correct answer) that cuts out all the fat. What does "beneficial" mean? It means helpful or good. Therefore, if we've already said "beneficial," we don't need to include other words that mean the exact same thing.

27) D
Keep it academic, folks!

28) A
This question is about both chronology and opposition. If you keep reading, you will see the word "however" followed by the key phrase "as subjects were asked to lie more frequently." This indicates that there's a contrast between how subjects' brains reacted *initially* and later after more lying.

29) C
The sentences on either side of this proposed addition both describe a specific study. Why on Earth would we want to interrupt that delicious flow of thought with some more info about the amygdala?

30) B
Can we all agree that C and D are just very bad? Great. Now think about A and B in the context of the sentence as a whole. B is the more active, structurally sound choice. (Hint: if you're every truly stuck choosing between a present/past tense verb and an –ing verb, it's going to be the present/past tense verb almost every time.)

31) A
Every clue in this sentence tells us that we are looking for a present tense, singular verb.

32) C
What kind of relationship does the previous sentence have to this one? They are expressing contradictory ideas (telling the truth is energetically easy, while lying requires effort); therefore, we are looking for a transition word that conveys contrast.

33) C
The key phrase in this question stem is "specific examples." Guess what? If an answer choice doesn't provide *specific examples,* I can eliminate it without a second thought! (See ya B and D!) The claim is that the energy expended by lying causes physical stress. Only C provides specific examples of the consequences of this kind of stress on the body.

PASSAGE 4: PRESERVING LINGUISTIC DIVERSITY

34) B
Let's first eliminate any answers that do not include the possessive "their." Then it's all about verb tense. The passage suggests that the uses both were and continue to be restricted, so we need the verb/s to indicate both tenses.

35) C
As an appositive, this clause should further the thought presented in the previous clause. The previous clause is all about what linguists and anthropologists are *not*

worried about, and only C provides a logical explanation for that statement.

36) C
The key to this question is the phrase "not only." Idiomatically, we must follow "not only" with the phrase "but also," much as we match "either" with "or" and "neither" with "nor." If you know that, you'll get these questions right every time!

37) B
The key words in this question stem are "accurate" and "relevant." C and D are perhaps accurate but not relevant, and A is not supported by the graph.

38) A
Once we realize that you're looking for a simple, present tense verb, this question comes down to singular/plural. What is the noun in question? It's the singular "situation," therefore "situation results" is correct.

39) D
This one can be a little tricky, so use your ears. The sentence feels incomplete without some version of the word "believe," doesn't it? That helps eliminate C. A sounds odd, especially after the comma, and B is a comma splice (meaning you would need to punctuate it with a semicolon or period). That leaves us with D: simple, short, SAT-approved.

40) D
Even if colons *still* freak you out, the rest of the choices here are pretty weird. The information after the colon is a direct explanation of the "reversal" mentioned earlier in the sentence, so a colon is the perfect piece of punctuation.

41) B
Because "language" is singular, there can be only one way. (It's Daoism! The true path to enlightenment!) Just kidding, it's B.

42) B
What is sentence 8 about? It's about how a certain culture's language communicates direction "without relation to the speaker." What is the most direct contrast to that idea? B: a language that where direction *is* relative to the speaker.

43) A
Remember, a conclusion has *two* jobs: to flow clearly from the previous thought AND to tie back to the main idea of the passage. B, C, and D all include information that is irrelevant to the central point of the passage.

44) A
Upon first glance, this sentence can seem redundant. Why add this sentence at all, especially since the first sentence already asks a question that is answered by the passage? However, sentence 2 reads: "let's start with the case for preservation." That must mean there's *another* argument the paragraph will address after the case for preservation. That argument must be the case for "diversity," and thus the sentence should be placed after sentence 1.

SECTION 3: MATH - NO CALCULATOR

1) C
This problem combines both linear equation AND quadratic function knowledge. YAYYYY!!! Since the equation has x to the first power, it must be a line. When we rearrange this one into the $y = mx + b$, we get $y = 5x - 2$, so our slope is 5 and y-intercept is -2.

2) C
What does it mean to have no solutions? When it comes to graphing, it means that two equations will never touch. How is it that two lines, in this case, will never touch? If they are parallel and have different y-intercepts. How do we know that two lines are parallel? They'll have the same slope. In this case, that slope is $\frac{1}{2}$ and the answer is C.

3) D
Nothing fancy here: you just want to plug

in the values. Hopefully you realize that you'll want the bigger value c on top, and the smaller value on bottom. That leaves you with B and D as possible answers. Try those out; you'll get a greater value with D, so that's the winner.

4) A

Two-part question. First, you need to represent the x-intercepts in the function. To get to x-intercepts of -3, 1, and 4, you need factors of $(x + 3)$, $(x - 1)$, and $(x - 4)$. That leaves us with A and C as our two possible answers. Next, let's make use of that other fun fact, that the y-intercept is 24. You'll find a y-intercept when $x = 0$. Plug $x = 0$ into the two remaining answers. A will give you 24 as the result, making it the correct answer!

5) B

What is a rational number? It's one that can be represented as a fraction with integers in both the numerator and denominator. It might be easier to think of what is NOT a rational number: any square root that is not an integer, and any non-repeating number, like e or π. Once you know those two fun facts, it's easy to pick B as the one with all rationals.

6) D

Perpendicular lines have slopes that are negative reciprocals of each other, like 4 and $-\frac{1}{4}$, or in this case, $\frac{2}{3}$ and $-\frac{3}{2}$. Once you know that fact, this question's easy!

7) C

How do you get from m^5 to m^{10}? Think about your properties of exponents. You want to multiply 5 by 2, right? That means you need to raise that side of the equation to the power of 2. You can do that—you just need to do it to the other side of the equation too. So $(m^5)^2 = 8^2$ turns into what we want: $m^{10} = 64$.

8) D

Who loves math vocabulary? Nobody? OK. This one is about the meaning (or significance) of the term "isosceles right triangle." That's a right triangle with two equal sides, which is a right triangle with two equal ANGLES... which is a 45-45-90 triangle. Once you know that's what we're talking about, you can flip back to the reference information at the beginning of the section to know that if the hypotenuse is $s\sqrt{2}$, the legs are s. In this case, the hypotenuse is $36\sqrt{2}$, so the legs are 36.

9) A

This question is tricky in the phrasing. It's meant to be. Write the equation as best you can. You should have the factors $(x + 5)(x + 3)(x - 3)$. The question asks for d, the constant at the end of the polynomial. You can multiply those factors out manually to find d, or you can know that the constant will be the product of the three constants in those factors: $5 \times 3 \times -3 = -45$.

10) B

A tricky little thing in this question that the variables change from one answer to the next. The number line doesn't tell us what variable (w, x, y, or z) it represents, so it doesn't really matter what the letter is.... it only matters that we represent the values correctly. I would start from the number line. Say to yourself, what I want is x (or whatever letter) to be greater than or equal to -3. (By the way, it's got to be greater than or equal to because the little dot is filled in on the -3.) Simplify the answer choices carefully, flipping the inequality sign whenever you multiply or divide by a negative, and you'll find that it is B!

11) C

My favorite way to solve this one is to think about the squares of 11 and 12, which are 121 and 144 respectively. If you want a square root to be between 11 and 12, then the number you are square-rooting has got to be between 121 and 144! Only one of those here, 135, so that must be the right answer.

12) C

The hardest part here is understanding the definition of one-to-one. That is a real math term, and you might even know it already.

If you do, good for you! If not, what it's basically saying is that you'll only ever get one y-value for every x-value, and one x-value for every y-value. That ALSO means that your function needs to pass both the vertical line test and the horizontal line test. The vertical line test means that if you scanned the graph with a vertical line, it would never cross the vertical line more than once. Same definition with the horizontal line test. Which graph would not pass the horizontal line test? The parabola, C.

13) A

I would recommend you try to write this equation yourself based on the graph. You've got a vertex of (-1, -8). From that point, when the graph moves one unit in the x-direction, the y-value goes up 2. That means your a value at the beginning must be 2. From there, you can write the equation in vertex form: $y = 2(x + 1)^2 - 8$. FOIL that out, combine like terms, and you'll wind up with A.

14) D

Recursive formulas are defined in terms of the preceding terms in the sequence. Here, we're starting with a first term of 3 (because t sub 1 = 3). We get to the next term (t sub n) by doubling the preceding term (t sub $n - 1$) and adding 1. Do that three times starting from 3, and you'll get 7, 15, and 31 as the next three terms.

15) C

Ah, a fairly simple factoring problem. That is very welcome at this stage of the test! Pull a 3 out, so you're at $3(x^2 - 4x - 5)$. Factor within the parentheses, and you'll end up at the answer, $3(x + 1)(x - 5)$.

16) 60

Are you looking for these real-world systems of equations problems on EVERY SAT MATH SECTION at this point? If not, start. The two equations should be $p + c = 140$ and $0.1p + 0.5c = 46.00$. One equation for the count, and one equation for the cost. Then it's solve-time, using your favorite method here. I used elimination here, by doubling the second equation then subtracting it from the first one. You could also substitute. Whatever floats your boat! And whatever you get, run it back through the equations to make sure it makes both equations work.

17) 165

Let's turn radians into degrees! Remember that π radians equals 180 degrees. Make that a fraction, in this case $\frac{180 \text{ degrees}}{\pi \text{ radians}}$. Multiply $\frac{11\pi}{12}$ by that and you'll have your answer.

18) 48

Simple little geometry question here—you just have to remember the formula for parallelogram area: $A = bh$, where the height is perpendicular to the base. The formula gives us those numbers, $b = 8$ and $h = 6$, so the area is 48.

19) 3

What do you notice in this table of values? Did you see that there are three separate x-intercepts—the points where $y = 0$? That's the really important thing. Those x-intercepts are also roots. This polynomial, therefore, has at least three real roots, which means it must be at least a third-degree polynomial. Since the highest power of the polynomial, a, must be less than 4, we're left with only one possibility: that the highest power of the function is 3.

20) 80

Remember the formula for inverse proportion? It's $y = \frac{k}{x}$, where k is a constant. In this case, it's $R = \frac{k}{A}$, since those are the values we're living with. All you do once you have that formula is solve for k using $R = 4$ and $A = 100$. $k = 400$. Then plug in $k = 400$ and $A = 5$ and solve for R. $R = 80$.

2

SECTION 4: MATH - CALCULATOR

1) D

Here's a problem where we just need to set up the equations—we don't need to solve them. Suppose that the vice president's age is x. That would make the president's age $x + 3$, since the prez is three years older. Now, the product (the result when you multiply) of their ages is 3,190. To solve, you would multiply x and $(x + 3)$ to get 3,190. We don't even have to solve; we just have to point to the right equation set-up, which is D.

2) A

This question is more about common sense than it is about statistics. Sure, knowing what all these terms mean would probably make you feel more comfortable and certain in your approach. But consider the wording of the question, "deviates most from the mean." To deviate means "to diverge from the usual standards." Basically, the question is really asking us, "which value is furthest away from 8?" That's definitely 10. In statistics terms, 10 is 4 standard deviations away from the mean, but we don't really need to know that—it's simply the data point that is furthest away from the mean.

3) C

What do solutions look like? They are points of intersection with the x-axis. On this question, those are located at -2, 0, and 3. Boom. Easy as knowing the definition of "solution."

4) C

Yay proportion! Addie climbs at the same rate as Jerome, so you can ignore the name change. Set up a proportion:

$\frac{3.5 \text{ hours}}{2100 \text{ feet}} = \frac{x \text{ hours}}{3000 \text{ feet}}$. Cross multiply, and you'll get that $x = 5$.

5) C

Slightly more complicated than the last problem. I would start by finding Jerome's typical climbing rate in feet/hr. He climbs 2100 feet in 3.5 hours. Use your calculator to reduce that and you'll see that his typical rate is 600 feet/hr. When his rate goes down, it'll turn into $600 - 50 = 550$ feet/hr. OK, we're ready to solve. Up to 5000 feet he'll be at his typical rate, then for the last 1000 he'll be at the new rate. $\frac{5000}{600} + \frac{1000}{550} = 10.1515$ etc., which rounds down to 10, the right answer.

6) B

Exponent property question *and* an imaginary number question. When we have the same base multiplied by itself, we can add the exponents, so $i^7 \times i^5 = i^{12}$. Now, what does i^{12} equal? Every set of four consecutive powers of i repeat, like this: $i^1 = i$, $i^2 = -1$, $i^3 = -i$, $i^4 = 1$. That means that every 4th term of the sequence—the 4th, the 8th, the 12th, etc—will equal positive 1. The 12th term is one of those, so it too will equal 1.

7) B

I recommend you try the answers on a question like this. Remember, you are not taking a test that rewards you for showing your work. Just pop these bad boys into the original equation to see if they work. Only 1 does in this case, and that makes B the right answer!

8) A

Classic table question...you just need to read carefully and identify the right value. You want the folks who DO play basketball but DO NOT watch it. That's 3 people. Now put them over the total number of students who took the survey. Boom, $\frac{3}{100}$. By the way, I made up these numbers, but I feel like that's about right, that very few people play basketball without watching it. Also, random unimportant fact, for the record: I watch basketball but do not play it, except under very unusual circumstances. I'm not so good at basketball.

9) C

Another situation when we need to write (but not solve) an equation. Well, an inequality in this case. Start with the flat cost, aka the starting point, aka the y-intercept: \$9.49 for the one large photo. Now buy as many wallet-size photos as you can. They cost \$0.55, so in total they'll cost $0.55x$ for x copies. Add those together, and make sure they don't go OVER \$20. They can EQUAL \$20, they just can't exceed it. That means we want C instead of D.

10) B

How well do you know your exponent properties? Remember that negative exponents flip a number down into the denominator. In other words 3^{-2} equals $\frac{1}{3^2}$. So we start with $\frac{\frac{1}{9}}{\frac{1}{8}}$. Simplify that (by multiplying top and bottom by 8) and you'll be left with $\frac{8}{9}$, the right answer.

11) B

Another real world proportion question. $\frac{8 \text{ hours}}{52 \text{ deliveries}} = \frac{6 \text{ hours}}{x \text{ deliveries}}$. Cross multiply and solve. $x = 39$.

12) C

The most important thing on this question is to keep track of the fact that you want the point that does NOT solve the system. You want the rule-breaker, the rebel. Here, that's (5, -2). That y-value of -2 is not greater than 1. Do you think (5, -2) cares? Not one bit. (5, -2) puts on its black leather jacket, hops on its motorcycle and rides off into the sunset.

13) B

I actually wrote the numbers 1-9 down on my page. Sometimes a little busy work really helps you get some good work done! On the first drawing, you have a $\frac{4}{9}$ probability of success, since we have four even "winners": 2, 4, 6, and 8. On the second drawing, you no longer have the slip that you drew, so now there are 3 winners left out of 8 possibilities, so $\frac{3}{8}$ on the second drawing. To find the probability of multiple things ALL happening, multiply their probabilities: $\frac{4}{9} \times \frac{3}{8} = \frac{12}{72} = \frac{1}{6}$.

14) D

Here's the best way to solve this one: on your calculator. This is the calculator section—let's use that bad boy. I recommend graphing all four equations. Set your window pretty big: up to 100 in the x direction and 400 in the y-direction. Press 'trace.' Pick a value, like 85, and type it in. Which answer gets you closest? D, right? Type the other values in the table on that equation. They're all pretty close, so it's definitely the right answer.

15) C

Unit conversion question. My process here is to go first to milliliters per hour, then per day. Multiply 100 milliliters by 6 to get the per hour rate, then by 24 to get the per day rate. Boom. 14,400 ml per day. Tutor Ted out. Drop the mic.

16) A

What are our rules for sampling? Rule number one, you do not talk about sampling. Wait... that's something else. Rule number one is that your sample needs to be taken at random, NOT by convenience. Answer A includes the word 'random.' This is us trying to throw you a bone.

17) A

Pretty simple—you just need to evaluate these guys and compare. A will give you the biggest value, 9.

18) C

This is about your comfort level with stem-and-leaf plots. Stem-and-leaf plots pull a digit that several points have in common out and put it in front. The smallest three values in this set, for instance are 68, 69, and 69. The 6 repeats for that entire row. The mode will be the value that occurs the most often. You can probably tell that that's going to be 72 since we've got so many 2s after the 7.

19) D
More "fun with data retrieval." Can't computers do this for us now? On this question, put the number of users under 20 (1,636) over the total number of users (12,443... use your calculator!) and find the decimal value.

20) B
The old "given that" trick. Can't fool us, SAT! "Given that" means "including only" to us. We want to include only the folks who are 21 or older. The numerator will be (3,693 + 491 + 6) and the denominator will be (6,617 + 3,693 + 491 + 6). Do the division (on your calculator!) and get an answer of 0.3877, which rounds to 0.39.

21) C
Gotta know what it means for a function to intercept the x-axis. For us on this problem, it means the function must have roots at $(x - c)$ and $(x - d)$. FOIL those two binomials carefully, factor out a $-x$ from the two middle terms and you'll get the answer.

22) B
Ah, cross multiplication. I love thee. Just cross multiply these fractions and you'll have the right answer, B!

23) C
Now we're going to plug some values into the formula and solve. You can either use the original formula from the given information OR the formula we just created in question 22. Either way, plug everything into the proper place and solve. Using the fractional formula, you should have $\frac{50 \text{ lbs}}{29 \text{ inches}} = \frac{30 \text{ lbs}}{x \text{ inches}}$. Use that to get that Object B should be 17.4 inches from the fulcrum.

24) A
Can I let you in on the easiest (yet still somehow legal) way to solve this thing? With a program. I use FACTOR7, written by Wei-Yun Mak. What a program! You can literally punch in the coefficients of a polynomial and it will factor it for you. To do this the manual way, divide the thing by $(x + 1)$, either by long division or synthetic division, then factor what's left. That's not too hard—it just takes more time and brainpower than using the calculator.

25) C
I would use my calculator on this problem too. When it makes our work faster and more accurate, why not? Am I right? Couple of shortcuts here too: you KNOW that the leading coefficient has to be negative. Why? Because the function is pointing downward. That means it's either C or D. Then, it has to be C. D would have additional x-intercepts at -1 an 1, which we don't have. So it's C. Graph it on the calculator (expanding the window a bit) to confirm that it looks like the sketch.

26) C
This one is all about looking for closed and open dots. Answer C is the one that finally gets it right: we've got a closed dot on (3, 20) and another one at (5, 30). That means those points are in the set, and that choice C is right.

27) D
Use either your "math common sense" or your graphing calculator. We're looking for the one that, as x gets bigger and bigger, y gets closer and closer to 0. On the graph, "approaching 0" means getting nearer and nearer to the x-axis. Answer D is the only one that does that.

28) A
The way to reduce these guys is always to multiply top-and-bottom by the conjugate, which in this case is $\sqrt{3} + 5$. Do that, FOIL carefully, combine like terms, and finally reduce by a factor of 2, and you'll arrive at B. It ain't pretty, but it's right.

29) B

Start by drawing $g(x)$, the reflection of $f(x)$ over the y-axis. You want the vertex of that graph, which will be (4, -3). Take that and apply our rules of transformation to the absolute value graph. Thus, we will wind up at $g(x) = |x - 4| - 3$.

30) B

Just about knowing that formula for the equation of a circle. Remember that on TI calculator, it is stored in your APPS menu under the app called CONICS. The formula is $(x - h)^2 + (y - k)^2 = r^2$, where (h, k) is the center of the circle and r is the radius. Plug what we know in this situation into that equation and you'll get B quite readily.

31) 90

Two ways to do this one: either write a fancy formula ($y = 82 \times 1.045^x$, where y is the number of restaurants and x is the number of years later—then plug in $x = 2$), or find the step-by-step values, i.e. multiply 82 by 1.045 once, then multiply THAT value by 1.045. Either way, you'll get 89.54 when you do, which rounds to 90.

32) 37

Just a fancy way of asking if you know that the angles in a triangle add up to 180. You do know that, so you smartly subtract 28 and 115 from 180 to get 37—the right answer.

33) 67

You may know the formula for the volume of a rectangular box is $V = lwh$. If you don't, it's in the Reference Information at the beginning of the section. Woo! If we KNOW the volume and the height, all we need to do is divide that volume by that height. We'll be left with width times height, which is the area of the base... the value we're trying to find in this problem.

34) 27

Cubes are rectangular boxes too, just special ones where all three dimensions are identical. The side of cube A must be 2, since $2 \times 2 \times 2 = 8$. That means B measures $2 + 1 = 3$ on each side. Its volume then will be $3 \times 3 \times 3 = 27$.

35) 12.7

Just a step-by-step "real world" problem. Start by increasing the \$435,000 by 15 percent—the fastest way is to multiply it by 1.15. You'll get \$500,250. Then subtract \$10,000 from that to get \$490,250. Last, to compute percent change, we need to put the amount of change over the original. That's $\frac{490{,}520 - 435{,}000}{435{,}000} \times 100$. You'll get 12.7 when you round that to the nearest tenth. You go, Amie!

36) 35

SAT's favorite geometry topic: similar triangles. Play with the figure, marking up the sides you know. The hardest one to find is probably MR. Since the figure is broken up by midpoints, the small version of the triangle (BMR) has sides that are half as big as the bigger triangle (BAC). So side MR is half the length of side AC. It's 7, and our perimeter will be $9 + 7 + 5 + 14 = 35$.

37) 8

I am using my calculator on this one! I graphed both equations. They will earn a profit when that revenue parabola is ABOVE (or greater than) that cost line. Graph the two equations and trace to find the highest x-value where the parabola is higher. The biggest integer value where that is true is $x = 8$.

38) 5.38

Here I would recommend writing a formula that combines revenue and costs—in other words, a profit formula. It's pretty simple: $-33t^2 + 360t - (700 + 5t)$. Notice how I put that whole second formula in parentheses! I then graphed the equation and used the "calc" tools (located above "trace" on the TI calculators) to find the maximum. Then I rounded carefully! One pitfall to avoid here: the maximum of the revenue curve is NOT the maximum of the profit curve. That's why you need to create that profit formula—to find that specific maximum.

SAT Practice Test 3

Multiple Choice Answer Sheet

TEST 1: READING

1 Ⓐ Ⓑ Ⓒ Ⓓ	9 Ⓐ Ⓑ Ⓒ Ⓓ	17 Ⓐ Ⓑ Ⓒ Ⓓ	25 Ⓐ Ⓑ Ⓒ Ⓓ	33 Ⓐ Ⓑ Ⓒ Ⓓ	41 Ⓐ Ⓑ Ⓒ Ⓓ	49 Ⓐ Ⓑ Ⓒ Ⓓ
2 Ⓐ Ⓑ Ⓒ Ⓓ	10 Ⓐ Ⓑ Ⓒ Ⓓ	18 Ⓐ Ⓑ Ⓒ Ⓓ	26 Ⓐ Ⓑ Ⓒ Ⓓ	34 Ⓐ Ⓑ Ⓒ Ⓓ	42 Ⓐ Ⓑ Ⓒ Ⓓ	50 Ⓐ Ⓑ Ⓒ Ⓓ
3 Ⓐ Ⓑ Ⓒ Ⓓ	11 Ⓐ Ⓑ Ⓒ Ⓓ	19 Ⓐ Ⓑ Ⓒ Ⓓ	27 Ⓐ Ⓑ Ⓒ Ⓓ	35 Ⓐ Ⓑ Ⓒ Ⓓ	43 Ⓐ Ⓑ Ⓒ Ⓓ	51 Ⓐ Ⓑ Ⓒ Ⓓ
4 Ⓐ Ⓑ Ⓒ Ⓓ	12 Ⓐ Ⓑ Ⓒ Ⓓ	20 Ⓐ Ⓑ Ⓒ Ⓓ	28 Ⓐ Ⓑ Ⓒ Ⓓ	36 Ⓐ Ⓑ Ⓒ Ⓓ	44 Ⓐ Ⓑ Ⓒ Ⓓ	52 Ⓐ Ⓑ Ⓒ Ⓓ
5 Ⓐ Ⓑ Ⓒ Ⓓ	13 Ⓐ Ⓑ Ⓒ Ⓓ	21 Ⓐ Ⓑ Ⓒ Ⓓ	29 Ⓐ Ⓑ Ⓒ Ⓓ	37 Ⓐ Ⓑ Ⓒ Ⓓ	45 Ⓐ Ⓑ Ⓒ Ⓓ	
6 Ⓐ Ⓑ Ⓒ Ⓓ	14 Ⓐ Ⓑ Ⓒ Ⓓ	22 Ⓐ Ⓑ Ⓒ Ⓓ	30 Ⓐ Ⓑ Ⓒ Ⓓ	38 Ⓐ Ⓑ Ⓒ Ⓓ	46 Ⓐ Ⓑ Ⓒ Ⓓ	
7 Ⓐ Ⓑ Ⓒ Ⓓ	15 Ⓐ Ⓑ Ⓒ Ⓓ	23 Ⓐ Ⓑ Ⓒ Ⓓ	31 Ⓐ Ⓑ Ⓒ Ⓓ	39 Ⓐ Ⓑ Ⓒ Ⓓ	47 Ⓐ Ⓑ Ⓒ Ⓓ	
8 Ⓐ Ⓑ Ⓒ Ⓓ	16 Ⓐ Ⓑ Ⓒ Ⓓ	24 Ⓐ Ⓑ Ⓒ Ⓓ	32 Ⓐ Ⓑ Ⓒ Ⓓ	40 Ⓐ Ⓑ Ⓒ Ⓓ	48 Ⓐ Ⓑ Ⓒ Ⓓ	

TEST 2: WRITING AND LANGUAGE

1 Ⓐ Ⓑ Ⓒ Ⓓ	8 Ⓐ Ⓑ Ⓒ Ⓓ	15 Ⓐ Ⓑ Ⓒ Ⓓ	22 Ⓐ Ⓑ Ⓒ Ⓓ	29 Ⓐ Ⓑ Ⓒ Ⓓ	36 Ⓐ Ⓑ Ⓒ Ⓓ	43 Ⓐ Ⓑ Ⓒ Ⓓ
2 Ⓐ Ⓑ Ⓒ Ⓓ	9 Ⓐ Ⓑ Ⓒ Ⓓ	16 Ⓐ Ⓑ Ⓒ Ⓓ	23 Ⓐ Ⓑ Ⓒ Ⓓ	30 Ⓐ Ⓑ Ⓒ Ⓓ	37 Ⓐ Ⓑ Ⓒ Ⓓ	44 Ⓐ Ⓑ Ⓒ Ⓓ
3 Ⓐ Ⓑ Ⓒ Ⓓ	10 Ⓐ Ⓑ Ⓒ Ⓓ	17 Ⓐ Ⓑ Ⓒ Ⓓ	24 Ⓐ Ⓑ Ⓒ Ⓓ	31 Ⓐ Ⓑ Ⓒ Ⓓ	38 Ⓐ Ⓑ Ⓒ Ⓓ	
4 Ⓐ Ⓑ Ⓒ Ⓓ	11 Ⓐ Ⓑ Ⓒ Ⓓ	18 Ⓐ Ⓑ Ⓒ Ⓓ	25 Ⓐ Ⓑ Ⓒ Ⓓ	32 Ⓐ Ⓑ Ⓒ Ⓓ	39 Ⓐ Ⓑ Ⓒ Ⓓ	
5 Ⓐ Ⓑ Ⓒ Ⓓ	12 Ⓐ Ⓑ Ⓒ Ⓓ	19 Ⓐ Ⓑ Ⓒ Ⓓ	26 Ⓐ Ⓑ Ⓒ Ⓓ	33 Ⓐ Ⓑ Ⓒ Ⓓ	40 Ⓐ Ⓑ Ⓒ Ⓓ	
6 Ⓐ Ⓑ Ⓒ Ⓓ	13 Ⓐ Ⓑ Ⓒ Ⓓ	20 Ⓐ Ⓑ Ⓒ Ⓓ	27 Ⓐ Ⓑ Ⓒ Ⓓ	34 Ⓐ Ⓑ Ⓒ Ⓓ	41 Ⓐ Ⓑ Ⓒ Ⓓ	
7 Ⓐ Ⓑ Ⓒ Ⓓ	14 Ⓐ Ⓑ Ⓒ Ⓓ	21 Ⓐ Ⓑ Ⓒ Ⓓ	28 Ⓐ Ⓑ Ⓒ Ⓓ	35 Ⓐ Ⓑ Ⓒ Ⓓ	42 Ⓐ Ⓑ Ⓒ Ⓓ	

TEST 3: MATHEMATICS - NO CALCULATOR

		16	17	18	19	20
1 Ⓐ Ⓑ Ⓒ Ⓓ	9 Ⓐ Ⓑ Ⓒ Ⓓ	☐☐☐☐	☐☐☐☐	☐☐☐☐	☐☐☐☐	☐☐☐☐
2 Ⓐ Ⓑ Ⓒ Ⓓ	10 Ⓐ Ⓑ Ⓒ Ⓓ	/ ⓘⓘⓘⓘ	/ ⓘⓘⓘⓘ	/ ⓘⓘⓘⓘ	/ ⓘⓘⓘⓘ	/ ⓘⓘⓘⓘ
3 Ⓐ Ⓑ Ⓒ Ⓓ	11 Ⓐ Ⓑ Ⓒ Ⓓ	. ○○○○	. ○○○○	. ○○○○	. ○○○○	. ○○○○
4 Ⓐ Ⓑ Ⓒ Ⓓ	12 Ⓐ Ⓑ Ⓒ Ⓓ	0 ⓪⓪⓪⓪	0 ⓪⓪⓪⓪	0 ⓪⓪⓪⓪	0 ⓪⓪⓪⓪	0 ⓪⓪⓪⓪
5 Ⓐ Ⓑ Ⓒ Ⓓ	13 Ⓐ Ⓑ Ⓒ Ⓓ	1 ①①①①	1 ①①①①	1 ①①①①	1 ①①①①	1 ①①①①
6 Ⓐ Ⓑ Ⓒ Ⓓ	14 Ⓐ Ⓑ Ⓒ Ⓓ	2 ②②②②	2 ②②②②	2 ②②②②	2 ②②②②	2 ②②②②
7 Ⓐ Ⓑ Ⓒ Ⓓ	15 Ⓐ Ⓑ Ⓒ Ⓓ	3 ③③③③	3 ③③③③	3 ③③③③	3 ③③③③	3 ③③③③
8 Ⓐ Ⓑ Ⓒ Ⓓ		4 ④④④④	4 ④④④④	4 ④④④④	4 ④④④④	4 ④④④④
		5 ⑤⑤⑤⑤	5 ⑤⑤⑤⑤	5 ⑤⑤⑤⑤	5 ⑤⑤⑤⑤	5 ⑤⑤⑤⑤
		6 ⑥⑥⑥⑥	6 ⑥⑥⑥⑥	6 ⑥⑥⑥⑥	6 ⑥⑥⑥⑥	6 ⑥⑥⑥⑥
		7 ⑦⑦⑦⑦	7 ⑦⑦⑦⑦	7 ⑦⑦⑦⑦	7 ⑦⑦⑦⑦	7 ⑦⑦⑦⑦
		8 ⑧⑧⑧⑧	8 ⑧⑧⑧⑧	8 ⑧⑧⑧⑧	8 ⑧⑧⑧⑧	8 ⑧⑧⑧⑧
		9 ⑨⑨⑨⑨	9 ⑨⑨⑨⑨	9 ⑨⑨⑨⑨	9 ⑨⑨⑨⑨	9 ⑨⑨⑨⑨

TEST 4: MATHEMATICS - CALCULATOR ALLOWED

						31
1 Ⓐ Ⓑ Ⓒ Ⓓ	6 Ⓐ Ⓑ Ⓒ Ⓓ	11 Ⓐ Ⓑ Ⓒ Ⓓ	16 Ⓐ Ⓑ Ⓒ Ⓓ	21 Ⓐ Ⓑ Ⓒ Ⓓ	26 Ⓐ Ⓑ Ⓒ Ⓓ	☐☐☐☐
2 Ⓐ Ⓑ Ⓒ Ⓓ	7 Ⓐ Ⓑ Ⓒ Ⓓ	12 Ⓐ Ⓑ Ⓒ Ⓓ	17 Ⓐ Ⓑ Ⓒ Ⓓ	22 Ⓐ Ⓑ Ⓒ Ⓓ	27 Ⓐ Ⓑ Ⓒ Ⓓ	/ ⓘⓘⓘⓘ
3 Ⓐ Ⓑ Ⓒ Ⓓ	8 Ⓐ Ⓑ Ⓒ Ⓓ	13 Ⓐ Ⓑ Ⓒ Ⓓ	18 Ⓐ Ⓑ Ⓒ Ⓓ	23 Ⓐ Ⓑ Ⓒ Ⓓ	28 Ⓐ Ⓑ Ⓒ Ⓓ	. ○○○○
4 Ⓐ Ⓑ Ⓒ Ⓓ	9 Ⓐ Ⓑ Ⓒ Ⓓ	14 Ⓐ Ⓑ Ⓒ Ⓓ	19 Ⓐ Ⓑ Ⓒ Ⓓ	24 Ⓐ Ⓑ Ⓒ Ⓓ	29 Ⓐ Ⓑ Ⓒ Ⓓ	0 ⓪⓪⓪⓪
5 Ⓐ Ⓑ Ⓒ Ⓓ	10 Ⓐ Ⓑ Ⓒ Ⓓ	15 Ⓐ Ⓑ Ⓒ Ⓓ	20 Ⓐ Ⓑ Ⓒ Ⓓ	25 Ⓐ Ⓑ Ⓒ Ⓓ	30 Ⓐ Ⓑ Ⓒ Ⓓ	1 ①①①①
						2 ②②②②
						3 ③③③③
						4 ④④④④
						5 ⑤⑤⑤⑤
						6 ⑥⑥⑥⑥
						7 ⑦⑦⑦⑦
						8 ⑧⑧⑧⑧
						9 ⑨⑨⑨⑨

CONTINUE

SAT Practice Test 3

Multiple Choice Answer Sheet

TEST 4: MATHEMATICS - CALCULATOR ALLOWED *(continued)*

	32	33	34	35	36	37	38
/	(/)(/)(/)(/)	(/)(/)(/)(/)	(/)(/)(/)(/)	(/)(/)(/)(/)	(/)(/)(/)(/)	(/)(/)(/)(/)	(/)(/)(/)(/)
.	(.)(.)(.)(.)	(.)(.)(.)(.)	(.)(.)(.)(.)	(.)(.)(.)(.)	(.)(.)(.)(.)	(.)(.)(.)(.)	(.)(.)(.)(.)
0	(0)(0)(0)(0)	(0)(0)(0)(0)	(0)(0)(0)(0)	(0)(0)(0)(0)	(0)(0)(0)(0)	(0)(0)(0)(0)	(0)(0)(0)(0)
1	(1)(1)(1)(1)	(1)(1)(1)(1)	(1)(1)(1)(1)	(1)(1)(1)(1)	(1)(1)(1)(1)	(1)(1)(1)(1)	(1)(1)(1)(1)
2	(2)(2)(2)(2)	(2)(2)(2)(2)	(2)(2)(2)(2)	(2)(2)(2)(2)	(2)(2)(2)(2)	(2)(2)(2)(2)	(2)(2)(2)(2)
3	(3)(3)(3)(3)	(3)(3)(3)(3)	(3)(3)(3)(3)	(3)(3)(3)(3)	(3)(3)(3)(3)	(3)(3)(3)(3)	(3)(3)(3)(3)
4	(4)(4)(4)(4)	(4)(4)(4)(4)	(4)(4)(4)(4)	(4)(4)(4)(4)	(4)(4)(4)(4)	(4)(4)(4)(4)	(4)(4)(4)(4)
5	(5)(5)(5)(5)	(5)(5)(5)(5)	(5)(5)(5)(5)	(5)(5)(5)(5)	(5)(5)(5)(5)	(5)(5)(5)(5)	(5)(5)(5)(5)
6	(6)(6)(6)(6)	(6)(6)(6)(6)	(6)(6)(6)(6)	(6)(6)(6)(6)	(6)(6)(6)(6)	(6)(6)(6)(6)	(6)(6)(6)(6)
7	(7)(7)(7)(7)	(7)(7)(7)(7)	(7)(7)(7)(7)	(7)(7)(7)(7)	(7)(7)(7)(7)	(7)(7)(7)(7)	(7)(7)(7)(7)
8	(8)(8)(8)(8)	(8)(8)(8)(8)	(8)(8)(8)(8)	(8)(8)(8)(8)	(8)(8)(8)(8)	(8)(8)(8)(8)	(8)(8)(8)(8)
9	(9)(9)(9)(9)	(9)(9)(9)(9)	(9)(9)(9)(9)	(9)(9)(9)(9)	(9)(9)(9)(9)	(9)(9)(9)(9)	(9)(9)(9)(9)

TEST 5: ESSAY - OPTIONAL

If you are writing the essay, you may use the space below to plan and outline your work. Be sure to write the essay itself on the lined pages that follow.

SAT

SAT Practice Test 3

Essay Answer Sheet

BEGIN YOUR ESSAY HERE.

You may continue on the next page.

SAT Practice Test 3

Essay Answer Sheet

DO NOT WRITE OUTSIDE THE BOX.

You may continue on the next page.

SAT Practice Test 3

Essay Answer Sheet

BEGIN YOUR ESSAY HERE.

You may continue on the next page.

DO NOT WRITE OUTSIDE THE BOX.

SAT® Practice Test #3

IMPORTANT REMINDERS

1. A No. 2 pencil is required for the test. Do not use a mechanical pencil or pen.

2. Sharing any questions with anyone is a violation of Test Security and Fairness policies and may result in your scores being canceled.

This cover is representative of what you'll see on test day.

Reading Test

65 MINUTES, 52 QUESTIONS

Turn to Section 1 of your answer sheet to answer the questions in this section.

DIRECTIONS

Each passage or pair of passages below is followed by a number of questions. After reading each passage or pair, choose the best answer to each question based on what is stated or implied in the passage or passages and in any accompanying graphics (such as a table or graph).

Questions 1-10 are based on the following passage.

This passage is adapted from Daniel Defoe, "Robinson Crusoe," originally published in 1719. Alone on an island, narrator Robinson Crusoe has just discovered a single print of a man's foot in the sand with no other around.

Sometimes I fancied it must be the devil, and reason joined in with me in this supposition, for how should any other thing in human shape come into the place? Where was the vessel that brought them? What marks were there of any other footstep? And how was it possible a man should come there? But then, to think that Satan should take human shape upon him in such a place, where there could be no manner of occasion for it, but to leave the print of his foot behind him, and that even for no purpose too, for he could not be sure I should see it - this was an amusement the other way. I considered that the devil might have found out abundance of other ways to have terrified me than this of the single print of a foot; that as I lived quite on the other side of the island, he would never have been so simple as to leave a mark in a place where it was ten thousand to one whether I should ever see it or not, and in the sand too, which the first surge of the sea, upon a high wind, would have defaced entirely. All this seemed inconsistent with the thing itself and with all the notions we usually entertain of the subtlety of the devil.

Abundance of such things as these assisted to argue me out of all apprehensions of its being the devil; and I presently concluded then that it must be some more dangerous creature - that it must be some of the savages of the mainland opposite who had wandered out to sea in their canoes, and either driven by the currents or by contrary winds, had made the island, and had been on shore, but were gone away again to sea; being as loath, perhaps, to have stayed in this desolate island as I would have been to have had them.

How strange is the life of man! and by what secret different springs are the affections hurried about, as different circumstances present! Today we love what tomorrow we hate; today we seek what tomorrow we shun; today we desire what tomorrow we fear, nay, even tremble at the apprehensions of. This was exemplified in me, at this time, in the most lively manner imaginable; for I, whose only affliction was that I seemed banished from human society, that I was alone, circumscribed by the boundless ocean, cut off from mankind, and condemned to what I call silent life; that to have seen one of my own species would have seemed to me a raising me from death to life, and the greatest blessing that Heaven itself, next to the supreme blessing of salvation, could bestow; I say, that I should now tremble at the very apprehensions of seeing a man, and was ready to sink into the ground at but the shadow or silent appearance of a man having set his foot in the island.

In the middle of these cogitations, apprehensions, and reflections, it came into my thoughts one day that all this might be a mere chimera of my own, and that this foot might be the print of my own foot, when I came on shore from my boat. I considered also that I could by no means tell for certain where I had trod, and where I had not; and that if, at last, this was only the print of my own foot, I had played the part of those fools who try to make stories of spectres and

apparitions, and then are frightened at them more than anybody.

1

Which choice best summarizes the passage?

A) A man stranded on an island deliberates the origins of a confounding discovery.
B) A man marooned on an island learns he is not alone and his thoughts spiral.
C) Finding a single footprint by the shore, a man worries that dreams of nights' past may not have been dreams after all.
D) A man finds the devil's footprint on a remote island and fears the repercussions of being in an abandoned place.

2

As used in line 16, "simple" most nearly means

A) effortless.
B) honest.
C) foolish.
D) backward.

3

The passage most clearly implies that Robinson suffers from

A) paranoia.
B) loneliness.
C) fear.
D) dementia.

4

Which choice provides the best evidence for the answer to the previous question?

A) Lines 19-21 ("All...devil")
B) Lines 36-39 ("Today...of")
C) Lines 53-57 ("In...boat")
D) Lines 57-63 ("I...anybody")

5

In the first paragraph, the narrator paints the devil as

A) mischievous.
B) sadistic.
C) fiendish.
D) playful.

6

As used in line 58, "tell" most nearly means

A) describe.
B) discern.
C) reveal.
D) voice.

7

In the last paragraph, Robinson concludes

A) his worry is of his own creation.
B) the footprint in the sand is his own.
C) the footprint is a mirage.
D) he must be more deliberate in tracking his own movements.

8

The main purpose of the third paragraph (lines 34-52) is to

A) discuss the hypocrisy of people generally longing to be with others yet shunning the opportunity when it arises.
B) better understand the inner-workings of the narrator's psyche with relation to his current position.
C) recognize the lack of control and immense danger posed by a threatening unknown invader.
D) exclaim how much the narrator wishes to be reunited with society.

9

The author's use of questions at the beginning of the first paragraph serves to

A) introduce the narrator as a god-fearing man.
B) quicken the pace and heighten the sense of imminent danger.
C) introduce the narrator's state of mind to the audience.
D) expose the narrator's thought process under pressure.

10

Over the course of the passage, the tone shifts from

A) hopeless to determined.
B) terrified to vindicated.
C) obsessive to indifferent.
D) neurotic to sympathetic.

Questions 11-20 are based on the following passage.

This passage is adapted from Frederick Douglas's address to the Ladies' Anti-Slavery Society in 1852.

The simple story of it is that, 76 years ago, the people of this country were British subjects. But, your fathers, they went so far in their excitement as to pronounce the measures of government unjust, unreasonable, and oppressive, and altogether such as ought not to be quietly submitted to. There was a time when to pronounce against England, and in favor of the cause of the colonies, tried men's souls. They who did so were accounted in their day, plotters of mischief, agitators and rebels, dangerous men. To side with the right, against the wrong, with the weak against the strong, and with the oppressed against the oppressor! here lies the merit, and the one which, of all others, seems unfashionable in our day.

Your fathers have lived, died, and have done their work, and have done much of it well. You live and must die, and you must do your work. This truth is not a doubtful one. There are illustrations of it near and remote, ancient and modern. It was fashionable, hundreds of years ago, for the children of Jacob to boast, we have "Abraham to our father," when they had long lost Abraham's faith and spirit. That people contented themselves under the shadow of Abraham's great name, while they repudiated the deeds which made his name great. Need I remind you that a similar thing is being done all over this country today? Need I tell you that the Jews are not the only people who built the tombs of the prophets, and garnished the sepulchres of the righteous? Washington could not die till he had broken the chains of his slaves. Yet his monument is built up by the price of human blood.

Fellow-citizens, pardon me, allow me to ask, why am I called upon to speak here today? What have I, or those I represent, to do with your national independence? Your high independence only reveals the immeasurable distance between us. The blessings in which you, this day, rejoice, are not enjoyed in common. The rich inheritance of justice, liberty, prosperity, and independence, bequeathed by your fathers, is shared by you, not by me. The sunlight that brought life and healing to you, has brought stripes and death to me. This Fourth July is yours, not mine. You may rejoice, I must mourn. To drag a man in fetters into the grand illuminated temple of liberty, and call upon him to join you in joyous anthems, were inhuman mockery and sacrilegious irony. Do you mean, citizens, to mock me, by asking me to speak today?

I hear the mournful wail of millions whose chains, heavy and grievous yesterday, are, today, rendered more intolerable by the jubilee shouts that reach them. If I do forget, if I do not faithfully remember those bleeding children of sorrow this day, "may my right hand forget her cunning, and may my tongue cleave to the roof of my mouth!" To forget them, to pass lightly over their wrongs, and to chime in with the popular theme, would be treason most scandalous and shocking, and would make me a reproach before God and the world. America is false to the past, false to the present, and solemnly binds herself to be false to the future. Standing with God and the crushed and bleeding slave on this occasion, I will, in the name of humanity which is outraged, in the name of liberty which is fettered, in the name of the constitution and the Bible, which are disregarded and trampled upon, dare to call in question and to denounce, with all the emphasis I can command, everything that serves to perpetuate slavery — the great sin and shame of America!

11

The main purpose of this passage is to

A) expose the hypocrisy of asking a black man to speak on independence when the enslavement of black people still thrived.
B) denounce slavery and all who profit from it.
C) reject the idea that a black speaker can shape the minds of his white counterparts with regards to slavery when they still profit greatly from it.
D) compare the struggles of American revolutionaries opposing British tyranny to slaves facing a harsher treatment.

12

As used in line 9, "accounted" most nearly means

A) described.
B) reckoned.
C) labeled.
D) defamed.

13

The orator's feelings towards his audience can best be described as

A) incredulous.
B) disgusted.
C) incensed.
D) cynical.

14

Which choice provides the best evidence for the answer to the previous question?

A) Lines 33-35 ("What…Independence")
B) Lines 35-36 ("Your…us")
C) Line 42 ("This…mine")
D) Lines 46-47 ("Do…today?")

15

The orator most likely uses the phrase "built up by the price of human blood" (line 31) to

A) firmly invoke a commonly known fact to evoke sympathy—that slaves died building Washington's monument—to transition to his argument.
B) aggressively initiate his true argument while actively remind his audience of the ongoing impact of slavery, because of which human lives are interchangeable and valueless.
C) vividly highlight the duplicitous justification of venerating idols who fought for freedom, setting up his argument to come.
D) adamantly demand his audience picture the metaphor and act on anti-slavery legislature.

16

As used in line 49, "rendered" most nearly means

A) decreed.
B) judged.
C) considered.
D) depicted.

17

Which of the following statements is best supported by lines 22-25 ("That people…great")?

A) The orator pleads with his audience to learn from history's mistakes to end oppression.
B) Unaware of inherent contradictions in practice, the public perpetuates hypocritical attitudes towards standards for American citizenship.
C) History continues to be built on the backs of the oppressed by regimes who turn a blind eye.
D) Jewish persecution throughout history mirrors the horrors experienced by slaves in America.

18

The orator's motivation for using the phrase "treason most scandalous and shocking" (line 56) was to

A) vehemently denounce singing America's praise until the country changes its views on slavery.
B) revert to his comparison of revolutionaries resisting British oppression made earlier to solidify his argument.
C) draw a staunch divide between himself as an American and himself as a member of the black community, pledging allegiance to one before the other.
D) clearly separate actions he deems justifiable to celebrate as a nation versus those only celebrated by the white community.

19

Which choice provides the best evidence for the answer to the previous question?

A) Lines33-35 ("What...independence")
B) Lines 43-46 ("To...irony")
C) Lines 48-50 ("I...them")
D) Lines 60-67 ("Standing...America")

20

Which choice best describes the passage's shift in tone?

A) Acquiescent to admonitory.
B) Complimentary to critical.
C) Passive to aggressive.
D) Tranquil to disturbed.

Questions 21-30 are based on the following passage and supplementary material.

This passage is adapted from Devah Pager, "Are Firms That Discriminate More Likely to Go Out of Business?" ©2016 by Pager via Harvard University and Sociological Science.

Economic theory has long maintained that employers pay a price for engaging in racial discrimination. According to Gary Becker's seminal work on this topic and the rich literature that followed, racial preferences unrelated to productivity are costly and, in a competitive market, should drive discriminatory employers out of business. Though a dominant theoretical proposition in the field of economics, this argument has been subjected to surprisingly little empirical scrutiny. This study offers a unique window into the relationship between discrimination and firm survival.

This study builds on the findings of an experimental audit study of racial discrimination in employment conducted in New York City in 2004. Teams of young men were hired to play the role of job seekers. These young men were carefully selected and matched on the basis of their age, physical appearance, and interpersonal skills, and were assigned matched fictitious resumes that reflected identical levels of education and work experience. Teams of three men—including a black, white, and Latino applicant—applied in person for jobs at 170 businesses over the course of 12 months. The results of this study indicated substantial amounts of hiring discrimination. Whites received callbacks or job offers in 31 percent of all cases, Latinos in 25 percent of all cases, and blacks in just 15 percent of cases. The rates of positive responses for whites and Latinos were not significantly different from one another, but both were significantly different from that of blacks. That Latinos and whites received offers of callbacks at 1.7 to 2 times the rate of equally qualified blacks suggests that direct racial discrimination continues to represent an important source of inequality in contemporary labor markets.

Four years later, the financial crisis of 2008 represented a significant shock to the labor market of New York City, as to the rest of the country. During this time, a record number of businesses folded. Given the significant weeding that took place, this represents an ideal time to examine the survival of firms from the earlier study. In particular, the financial crisis created two conditions that bring the relationship of interest into sharp relief: first, economic downturns heighten the costs of inefficient practices. Second, the sheer number of business closures that took place during this period offers increased statistical power with which to detect patterns. For each of these reasons, the recent recession offers an opportune moment during which to examine the relationship between discrimination and firm survival.

We found that 17% of nondiscriminatory establishments had failed by 2010, relative to 36% of those that did discriminate. The likelihood of going out of business for an employer who discriminated thus appears more than twice that of its non-discriminating counterpart. Overall, then, there appears to be a strong and significant association between discrimination and firm survival. Though sample sizes in this study are quite small, the disparities in survival rates among those who did and did not show evidence of discrimination suggest a robust relationship between the two.

An obvious characteristic that may affect both the likelihood of discrimination and the likelihood of business failure is establishment size. The mean size of establishments in our sample that remained in business between 2004 and 2010 was 33 employees compared to a mean size of 24 among those who closed down during that period. And yet, despite this substantial mean difference, establishment size does not appear to mediate the relationship between discrimination and business failure. Like establishment size, we see a clear bivariate relationship between establishment assets and survival. Those still in business in 2010 had mean sales assets of 4.4 million in 2004, relative to 3.7 million among those who were missing by 2010. This relationship is not statistically significant and does little to mediate the relationship between our measure of discrimination and firm survival.

According to Becker's original formulation, discrimination is costly to employers because it prioritizes characteristics of workers that are irrelevant to productivity. In a competitive context, these employers should be at a disadvantage. Is this, then, what's driving the association we observe here? It is possible, for example, that the kinds of employers who discriminate against racial minorities are also those who make poor choices in other areas of business management. Employers who use intuition, describing their hiring philosophy as a reliance on a "gut feeling"—rather than evidence, or more systematic forms of decision-making—may also be led astray in their capital investments, their financial management, and numerous other domains. We cannot, therefore, conclude that it is directly because of the costs of discrimination that employers in our sample appear more likely to have been driven out of business. Rather, whether because of discrimination or other associated decision-making, we can more confidently conclude that the kinds of employers who discriminate are those more likely to go out of business.

The following graph details the business failure rate of companies with discriminatory hiring practices.

Percent of Employers no Longer in Business in 2010 by Evidence of Discrimination in 2004

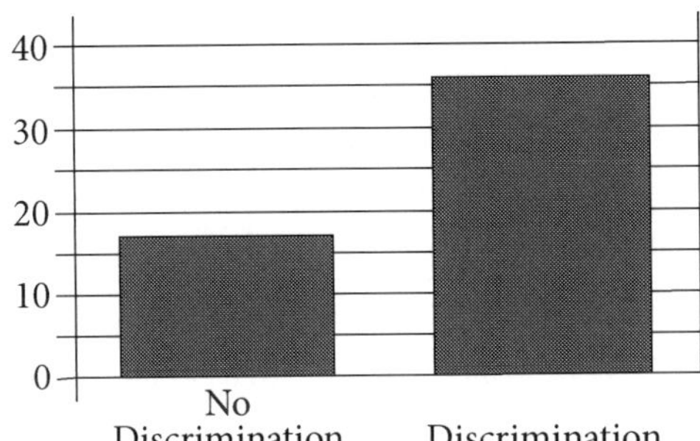

21

The final conclusion reached in this passage is that

A) businesses that discriminate are much more likely to close because discrimination indicates a higher likelihood of decision-making flaws.
B) businesses that do not discriminate are much more likely to stay open because they demonstrate productive and efficient decision-making.
C) businesses that discriminate will go out of business because studies prove diversity among staff drives productivity and divergent thinking.
D) businesses that discriminate on the basis of race generate less profit, averaging $700,000 a year less than other businesses.

22

As used in line 40, "weeding" most nearly means

A) removing.
B) clearing.
C) closing.
D) cleansing.

23

With regards to the success of the author's study, the 2008 financial crisis proved

A) invaluable.
B) devastating.
C) preventable.
D) counterproductive.

24

According to Becker's research, businesses' hiring practices should prioritize

A) racial diversity above all else to enhance the diversity of thought amongst the workforce, leading to unique and creative solutions.
B) talent acquisition above all else to ensure the business is naturally more competitive in financial markets than other firms.
C) whites and Latinos because they are hired at almost a 2:1 ratio to black job applicants.
D) productivity above all else to provide the best chance of success in competitive markets.

25

The main function of the final paragraph is to

A) explore the many possible reasons for a business' potential collapse.
B) reinforce the study's thesis, solidifying the main reason for business closures after 2008.
C) denounce the practice of discriminatory hiring on moral, ethical, and economic grounds.
D) question the validity of Becker's proposed disadvantages regarding discrimination in hiring, suggesting other reasons could play a much larger role in a company's failure.

26

The author discusses the relationship between establishment assets and survival in order to

A) suggest that companies with more capital in 2004 were more likely to still be in business in 2010 because money keeps companies afloat.
B) propose that companies with more employees in 2004 were more likely to remain in business in 2010.
C) imply that the size of a company might indirectly influence racially motivated hiring practices, thus either aiding or devastating the company's future.
D) insinuate that his correlation between racially discriminatory practices and survival may not be perfect, that other factors have influence in businesses' survival, as well.

27

As used in line 90, "intuition" is seen as

A) an excuse made to justify discriminatory hiring practices.
B) the reason that companies fail in crucial decision-making situations and leads to their downfalls.
C) the opposite of evidence-based decision-making and is therefore irrelevant to productive hiring processes.
D) an important factor that separates successful employers who can afford to take a chance on a new hire from failing businesses.

28

Based on the passage, the author was able to study the correlation between racial discrimination in hiring and business survival due to

A) previously established data in New York City and the opportunity to examine the data in conjunction with data taken after a financial crisis.
B) the data provided after the 2008 financial crisis' effect on business closure rates by ReferenceUSA.
C) specific businesses known to discriminate offering retrospective accounts through Becker of how their prejudice led to a plethora of other poor and biased decision-making, ultimately dooming their business.
D) a previous study done around the country by others and the 2008 financial crisis that provided information for building on the previous study.

29

Which choice provides the best evidence for the answer to the previous question?

A) Lines 3-7 ("According…business")
B) Lines 39-42 ("Given…study")
C) Lines 66-70 ("The…period")
D) Lines 86-90 ("It…management")

30

Data in the graph most strongly support which of the following statements?

A) Business with discriminatory hiring practices may make intuitive decisions that adversely affect the business's stability.
B) The financial crisis of 2008 caused a record number of businesses to close.
C) The financial crisis of 2008 disproportionately affected businesses with discriminatory hiring practices.
D) Evidence-based decision making doubles the chances of survival for a business.

Questions 31-41 are based on the following passages and supplementary material.

Passage 1 is adapted from Divine Nkyonyam Akumo, et al., "Social and Economic Issues—Genetically Modified Food," *Food Industry*. ©2013 by Akumo, Reidel, and Semtanska. Passage 2 is adapted from Ademola Adenle, "Response to Issues on GM Agriculture in Africa: Are transgenic crops safe?" ©2011 by Adenle for BioMed Central Research Notes.

Passage 1

Food choice is influenced by a large number of factors, including social and cultural factors. One method for trying to understand the impact of these factors is through the study of attitudes. One such extension is the inclusion of measures of moral concern, which have been found to be important both for the choice of genetically modified (GM) foods and also for foods to be eaten by others.

Many children in the US and Europe have developed life-threatening allergies to peanuts and other foods. There is a possibility that introducing a gene into a plant may create a new allergen or cause an allergic reaction in susceptible individuals. There is a growing concern that introducing foreign genes into food plants may have an unexpected and negative impact on human health. Another concern is that individuals do not always have clear-cut attitudes, but rather can be ambivalent about food and healthy eating. It is important, therefore, to have measures for this ambivalence, and an understanding of how it might impact behavior. One measure of how far we have traveled down that road is that it hardly matters anymore whether objections to GMOs are based on alleged environmental risks of cultivating GM crops or alleged toxicological hazards of eating them. Given that millions of people throughout the world are already benefiting from pharmaceuticals made by GM organisms, this is bizarre.

Among the next generation of GM plants are those that are engineered to produce elevated levels of nutritional molecules such as vitamins, omega-3 fatty acids, and amino acids. Based upon the U.S. current regulatory scheme, the plants and their products may enter our food supply without any required safety testing. The potential risks of this type of GM plants are discussed in the context of human health, and it is argued that there should be extensive safety testing of plants designed to produce biologically active molecules before they are commercially grown and consumed.

Passage 2

Agriculture plays a significant role in the economy of African countries in terms of gross domestic product (GDP), promoting international trade, industrial development and creation of job opportunities. Therefore, there is an urgent need to improve agricultural production. The potential benefits of genetically modified (GM) crops toward alleviating poverty and hunger, improving agricultural productivity, health, and food security, and creating a friendly environment cannot be overemphasized. Of 15.4 million farmers that planted GM crops in 2010, over 90% are resource-poor farmers in developing countries, including three African countries (Burkina Faso, South Africa and Egypt), benefited from the adoption of GM crops. For example, almost 100,000 farmers in Burkina Faso cultivated GM cotton on 260,000 hectares* in 2010 with 126% increase from 115,000 hectares planted in 2009. In terms of contribution to the economy of Burkina Faso, it was estimated that a benefit of over US$100 million per year could be generated based on almost 30% increase in yield. Additionally, close to a 50% reduction in insecticides sprays may be realized, thereby saving fossil fuels and lowering greenhouse gases emission, hence fighting against climate change.

The adoption of GM technology is at its initial stages in Africa and is currently faced with several constraints such as lack of infrastructure, inadequate human resource capacity, poor education, biosafety regulation, intellectual property rights, and many others. A concerted effort from developed countries including international organizations must be put in place to ensure that Africa benefits from this new technology. African governments must also be involved in solving these problems themselves and should come up with coherent strategy to adopt modern biotechnology including educating the public, farmers and government institutions, the media, and private companies. Part of the strategy must include adoption of common policies and a regional platform through which African governments can engage in dialogue and develop a common biotechnology regulatory approach. Africa might pay a huge price in many years to come if the continent continues to depend on outsiders before making decisions that determine their future. Europeans are well fed and may not necessarily require GM technology to boost their crop productions, but African farmers need fast technology that can solve part of their agricultural problems.

*a metric unit of square measure, equal to ~2.5 acres or 10,000 square meters.

The following graph details US rates of food insecurity from 1998-2012. Food insecurity is the state of being without reliable access to a sufficient quantity of affordable, nutritious food.

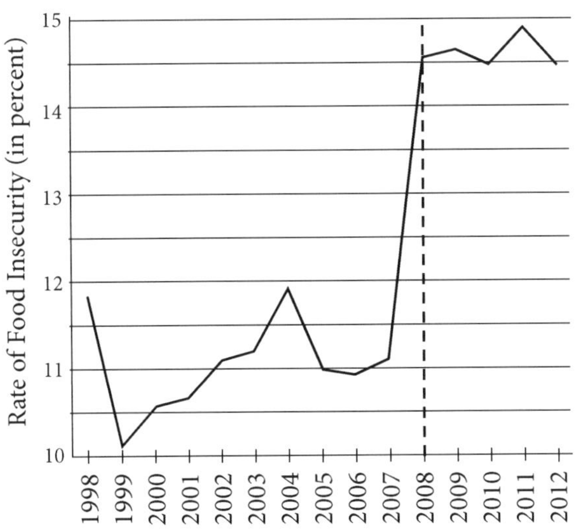

Source: Huffington Post via USDA.

31

The main purpose of Passage 1 is to

A) advise agriculturalists to use caution in the use of GMO in food until GMOs' economic effect is fully researched.

B) stress that GMOs should be subject to strict regulations before they are to be generally accepted, regardless of their benefits.

C) acknowledge the benefits of GMOs around the world but completely condemn their use in America.

D) discuss the proposition of GMOs as the root cause of harmful allergens and other health-related issues.

32

As used in line 33, "scheme" most nearly means

A) plan.

B) pattern.

C) arrangement.

D) system.

33

The authors of Passage 1 begin the second paragraph (lines 9-28) by discussing food-related allergies in order to

A) discuss the susceptibility of many Americans to deadly allergies.

B) spread awareness of little-known facts about peanuts.

C) establish a case for caution when using synthetic food products.

D) warn against the dangers of meddling with nature's genetics.

34

According to the information in the graph, between 1998 and 2012, the United States experienced the highest percentage of food security in

A) 1999.

B) 2004.

C) 2008.

D) 2011.

35

In Passage 2, the author includes lines 65-70 ("The... others") in order to

A) demand African leadership make stronger efforts to stomp out these constraints before biotechnology can be fully adopted.

B) establish the difficulties that hinder spreading the cultivation of GMOs to underdeveloped countries, especially those in Africa.

C) call on developed countries, like those in Europe, to step up their role in establishing common policies with regards to the use of GMOs.

D) acknowledge how well African countries like Egypt, South Africa, and Burkina Faso adopted GMO cultivation despite the listed constraints.

36

As used in line 59, "benefit" most nearly means

A) profit.
B) advantage.
C) subsidy.
D) value.

37

The author of Passage 2 would most likely respond to the argument presented in Passage 1 by

A) explaining that unlike America, Africa has a greater need for agricultural aid, like GMOs, and less time to wait for regulations to be legislated.
B) arguing that America's agricultural profits, as countries' in Africa have, would grow immensely with the wider use of GMOs.
C) proposing that the environmental benefits of GMOs, notwithstanding the agricultural benefits, outweigh any negative side effects they may have.
D) disagreeing that widespread use of GMOs without strict regulation is harmful, as African countries have also yet to establish common policies.

38

Which choice provides the best evidence for the answer to the previous question?

A) Lines 45-49 ("The...overemphasized")
B) Lines 57-61 ("In...yield")
C) Lines 61-64 ("Additionally...change")
D) Lines 85-88 ("Europeans...problems")

39

Which statement is best supported by the data presented in the graph?

A) In 2001, more than 12% of Americans were food insecure.
B) Food insecurity was not a national issue until 2008.
C) The 2008 US financial crisis likely caused the nearly 4% rise in food insecurity.
D) The introduction of GMO crops in 1999 stabilized food insecurity for the next decade.

40

Which choice best describes the relationship between the two passages?

A) Passage 1 denies the validity of the argument presented in Passage 2.
B) Passage 1 and Passage 2 each raise culture-specific concerns regarding the same idea.
C) Passage 2 agrees with the cautious approach discussed in Passage 1.
D) Passage 2 argues directly against the conclusions raised in Passage 1.

41

The main purpose of both passages is to

A) expose the dangers of biotechnology in different societies.
B) compare cultural differences between schools of thought on GMOs.
C) alleviate tension between arguing schools of thought on GMOs.
D) examine GMOs differing societal significances amongst nations.

Questions 42-52 are based on the following passage.

This passage is adapted from Thomas Ichim, et al., "The King is Dead, Long Live the King: Entering A New Era of Stem Cell Research and Clinical Development." ©2011 by the Journal of Translation Medicine.

Started in the early 2000s, a publicity campaign by embryonic stem cell advocates managed to equate the public image of all stem cell research as involving embryonic stem cells. A debate quickly ensued that polarized the pro-choice and pro-life communities with statements made equating to, "if you don't support embryonic stem cells, you are not supporting cures for terrible disease," or conversely, accusations that, "stem cell researchers are baby killers." While public attention was captivated by this debate, and various state governments created billion dollar funds to support embryonic stem cell research, a fundamentally important medical and financial fact was being ignored: embryonic stem cells are extremely immature. To generate adult organ, tissues, or cells, the embryonic stem cell must "fast forward" the process of years of maturation in a matter of weeks in order to create financially valuable products. The second fundamental point is the propensity of embryonic stem cells to form tumors called teratomas. Thus while everyone was arguing about the ethics of embryonic stem cell research, the medical and economic realities were ignored: specifically, it costs too much to create clinical products from these cells. However, the promise of curing incurable diseases with embryonic stem cells seems to have fixated public attention, creating high valuations for companies in this space.

Since 2006, investigators in academia and industry have been developing induced pluripotent stem cells as an alternative to embryonic stem cells as starting material for stem cell therapy. Induced pluripotent stem cells* can be produced from most adult cells and as a result using induced pluripotent stem cells avoids the emotional polarization associated with embryonic stem cells. However, they share many of the inherent problems associated with embryonic stem cells, such as teratoma formation, difficulty in inducing cell maturation, and high costs associated with their clinical application.

Parallel to efforts in embryonic and induced pluripotent stem cell research and development, scientists and physicians in the field of adult stem cells realized that the natural role of adult stem cells in the body is to promote healing, or in other words, to act like endogenous "repair cells." After a heart attack or stroke, the body activates its own adult stem cells in order to try to heal the damaged tissue. In contrast to embryonic stem cells, which are extremely expensive and potentially dangerous, adult stem cells are inexpensive and have an excellent safety record when used in humans.

The same day that Geron** announced its exit from this field, the adult stem cell company Mesoblast announced results of a double-blind clinical study showing significant benefit in heart failure patients receiving adult stem cells. This was one of many studies showing that adult stem cells are practical, patient-applicable, therapeutics that are very close to being available for incorporation into the practice of medicine. Major pharmaceutical companies have already placed their bets on adult stem cells. Thus, the field of stem cells is entering a new era: an era in which companies will be judged on clinical and financial practicality, not hype and manipulation of public emotion.

*Induced pluripotent stem cells are stem cells that can be taken directly from adult cells that can give rise to every other cell type in the body, such as neurons, heart, pancreatic, and liver cells.

**The biotechnology company Geron was the leader of embryonic stem cell research and therapy that ended work on embryonic stem cell research and therapy in November 2011.

42

The main purpose of the passage is to

A) demonstrate the author's knowledge of a budding biotechnology industry.
B) convince the reader of the downfalls of embryonic stem cell research.
C) track the recent history of stem cell research to understand its progress and future.
D) highlight the dangers related to stem cell research that usually go undiscussed.

43

As used in line 14, "immature" most nearly means

A) juvenile.
B) undersized.
C) weak.
D) underdeveloped.

44

The author most clearly views the arguments made in the first paragraph regarding embryonic stem cell research as

A) sensitive.
B) distracting.
C) inappropriate.
D) excessive.

45

Which choice provides the best evidence for the answer to the previous question?

A) Lines 1-4 ("Started…cells")
B) Lines 4-9 ("A…killers")
C) Lines 20-24 ("Thus…cells")
D) Lines 24-27 ("However…space")

46

As described in the passage, the attention of stem cell research efforts focused on

A) embryonic stem cells, followed by induced pluripotent stem cells, followed by adult stem cells.
B) embryonic stem cells, followed by teratoma stem cells, followed by induced pluripotent stem cells.
C) embryonic stem cells, followed by induced pluripotent and adult stem cells simultaneously.
D) embryonic stem cells, induced pluripotent stem cells, and adult stem cells simultaneously.

47

The author describes adult stem cells as

A) cost-efficient and benign.
B) immature yet expensive.
C) dangerous but cheap.
D) safe and insufficiently researched.

48

Which choice provides the best evidence to the answer of the previous question?

A) Lines 9-14 ("While…immature")
B) Lines 35-39 ("However…application")
C) Lines 40-45 ("Parallel…cells")
D) Lines 47-51 ("In…humans")

49

As used in line 40, the word "parallel" most nearly means

A) counterpart.
B) similar.
C) matching.
D) equal.

50

In the final paragraph, lines 61-65 ("Thus…emotion"), the author makes a clear connection to which of the following excerpts?

A) Lines 4-9 ("A…killers")
B) Lines 20-24 ("Thus…cells")
C) Lines 35-39 ("However…application")
D) Lines 52-56 ("The…cells")

51

Which of the following choices most clearly relays the author's feelings in line 24-27 ("However…space")?

A) These highly valued companies draw more of the attention needed to the field of stem cell research.
B) These highly valued companies are problematic because they divert resources from proven safe and cost-effective research.
C) These highly valued companies will require unanimous public support in order to maintain profitability.
D) Too many of these highly valued companies will create an economic bubble that could devastate important research upon popping.

52

The passage indicates that the author's attitude towards the future of stem cell research can best be described as

A) frustrated.
B) apathetic.
C) amazed.
D) optimistic.

STOP

If you finish before time is called, you may check your work on this section only. Do not turn to any other section.

Writing and Language Test

35 MINUTES, 44 QUESTIONS

Turn to Section 2 of your answer sheet to answer the questions in this section.

DIRECTIONS

Each passage below is accompanied by a number of questions. For some questions, you will consider how the passage might be revised to improve the expression of ideas. For other questions, you will consider how the passage might be edited to correct errors in sentence structure, usage, or punctuation. A passage or a question may be accompanied by one or more graphics (such as a table or graph) that you will consider as you make revising and editing decisions.

Some questions will direct you to an underlined portion of a passage. Other questions will direct you to a location in a passage or ask you to think about the passage as a whole.

After reading each passage, choose the answer to each question that most effectively improves the quality of writing in the passage or that makes the passage conform to the conventions of standard written English. Many questions include a "NO CHANGE" option. Choose that option if you think the best choice is to leave the relevant portion of the passage as it is.

The Rise of Yoga in the United States

Yoga—derived from the Sanskrit word for "divine union"—is one of the oldest disciplines in the known world. Even though we know that yoga originated in India over 5000 years ago, much remains unknown about just how the practice developed. Its history in the United States, [1] specifically, is both more recent and better documented.

While the practice was first introduced to Americans in the 19th Century, yoga began its ascent from fringe to mainstream in the [2] 1970s, a time of increased attention to both physical fitness and spirituality that happened to coincide with the loosening of laws restricting Asian

1

A) NO CHANGE
B) moreover,
C) however,
D) fortunately,

2

A) NO CHANGE
B) 1970s; which was a time
C) 1970s. A time
D) 1970s, it was a time

immigration. [3] First practiced by those already affiliated with "new age" lifestyles, yoga's reach [4] expands steadily as more people begin to associate its practice not only with physical and spiritual fitness but also with everyday stress reduction in a fast-paced world.

Today, American yoga is a $27 billion dollar industry serving over 36 million practitioners. Though certain demographics still dominate the "who" and the "where" of its practice, Americans are doing yoga in studios, schools, and even prisons.

However, as with the translation of any idea across culture and time, [5] some readings of the original texts will be incorrect. Some critics decry the consumerism that seems to have overtaken the industry. From designer yoga

3

At this point, the writer is considering adding the following sentence.

In fact, Indian immigrants in the United States--now numbering nearly 1.6 million--are the third largest immigrant group after Mexicans and Filipinos.

Should the writer make this addition here?

A) Yes, because it lends factual support to the claim being made.
B) Yes, because it provides a surprising detail that might pique the reader's interest.
C) No, because it blurs the paragraph's focus by introducing a detail that is tangential.
D) No, because it distracts from the paragraph's emphasis on Indian-Americans' contributions to yoga.

4

A) NO CHANGE
B) steadily expands
C) expand steadily
D) has steadily expanded

5

Which choice most effectively supports the central claim of the paragraph?

A) NO CHANGE
B) questions of authenticity have arisen.
C) doubts exist regarding whether Eastern philosophy can translate to Western societies.
D) there are bound to be multiple, competing interpretations.

pants to yoga selfies on social media, it's easy to see that a practice meant to help one transcend the ego has, **6** <u>on one hand,</u> become a very vanity-driven pursuit. Others lament not what is included in mainstream yoga practice but what isn't. Traditional yoga includes the physical **7** <u>"asanas" or poses</u> as just one of eight facets, yet it seems much modern yoga has been reduced to the practice of physical asanas alone. These critics believe that teaching physical poses without knowledge of the greater philosophical framework at best misses the point of yoga and, at worst, **8** <u>corrupts and negatively cheapens its meaning.</u>

Those who would rebut these criticisms, however, point out that change is inherent in any translation. A practice is essentially useless if it cannot speak the language of those who might benefit from it, and that means adapting to the time and place in which it is introduced. These non-purists believe that there is a difference between diversification and corruption, for what good is an ancient philosophy if it cannot help **9** <u>modern people navigate modern life.</u> They

6

A) NO CHANGE
B) consequently,
C) not surprisingly,
D) in some ways,

7

A) NO CHANGE
B) "asanas" or, poses,
C) "asanas," or poses,
D) "asanas" or poses,

8

A) NO CHANGE
B) corrupts and cheapens its meaning.
C) corrupts its meaning negatively, thereby cheapening it.
D) corrupts thereby cheapening its meaning negatively.

9

A) NO CHANGE
B) modern people and how they can navigate modern life?
C) modern people navigate modern life?
D) modern people navigate life.

point to the ways in which American yoga is still

10 building as evidence. As yoga itself teaches, it would be a mistake to confuse stillness with stasis because life, even in

11 its quietest moments, is always in motion.

10

A) NO CHANGE
B) activating
C) evolving
D) advancing

11

A) NO CHANGE
B) it's
C) their
D) those

The Shared Benefits of Paid Family Leave

The benefits to parent and child of spending quality bonding time after the birth or adoption of a new baby are **12** currently being studied. Bonding increases the emotional connectivity that **13** lead to a host of advantages to babies, including increased weights and healthier immune systems. **14** Also parents benefit as well. Mothers, for example, tend to breast feed for longer periods, and extended breastfeeding can lower a woman's risk for certain cancers.

Because bonding is so crucial in the very beginning, most countries mandate some kind of paid time off from work for new parents. Estonia—at the most generous end of the **15** spectrum, allows for up to 87 weeks of paid leave. Countries from Bulgaria to Japan offer around a year, while the average amount for workers in most industrialized countries is around 17 weeks. **16** On the other end of the spectrum, of all 185 countries in the world, only two provide no paid leave whatsoever to new parents: Papua New Guinea and The United States. Employers can choose to offer paid leave as an incentive designed to attract top talent, but as of 2016 only 12% of American workers have access to such leave.

12

Which choice best establishes the argument that follows?

A) NO CHANGE
B) now in doubt.
C) increasingly important.
D) well-established.

13

A) NO CHANGE
B) leads
C) have led
D) has led

14

A) NO CHANGE
B) Additionally, parents benefit also.
C) Parents, additionally, also benefit.
D) Parents benefit as well.

15

A) NO CHANGE
B) spectrum
C) spectrum--
D) spectrum:

16

A) NO CHANGE
B) When it comes to family leave,
C) To no one's surprise,
D) Similarly,

Why is the U.S. such an exception? Much of the current reality has to do with the perception that PFL (paid family leave) will disrupt productivity and hurt profits. Luckily, since 2002, five states have passed paid leave laws, and economists now have over a decade's worth of data tracking their effects for both employers and workers. When California passed the first PFL law in 2002, employers voiced vehement opposition prior to implementation, fearing the practice would **17** harm business negatively at the beginning. However, surveys conducted by the Center for Economic Policy Research in 2009 and 2010 of employers and workers in both high and low-wage jobs across a diverse group of **18** industries, revealed that paid leave was good for both groups. Employers overwhelmingly rated the program's effect on productivity, profitability, and morale as either positive or neutral. They also reported an increase in worker retention, leading to a decrease in the costs associated with training new employees. **19** Obviously, employees who took advantage of the program were more satisfied with the length of their leave and much likelier to return to the same job compared to those who did not.

The program's implementation has not been **20** perfect, however. California's first decade of PFL shows not only a lack of the kind negative consequences to businesses

17

A) NO CHANGE
B) hurt business.
C) negatively impact business in a harmful way.
D) be detrimental to business that they believed before the bill was passed.

18

A) NO CHANGE
B) industries. Revealing
C) industries revealed
D) industries--revealed

19

A) NO CHANGE
B) Nevertheless,
C) Around the same time,
D) DELETE the underlined portion and begin the sentence with a capital letter.

20

A) NO CHANGE
B) perfect, however,
C) perfect. However
D) perfect; however,

that employers had feared but also a net positive gain **21** <u>in many areas despite minor reductions in productivity.</u> When all parties seem to benefit with very little downside, **22** <u>everyone should be over the moon</u>.

Study of Employers as regarding implementation of CA Paid Family Leave

	Positive	Neutral	Negative
Productivity	59%	30%	11%
Profitability	51%	40%	9%
Morale	87%	12%	1%

21

Which choice best completes the thought within this sentence?

A) NO CHANGE
B) in the areas of productivity, profitability, and morale.
C) with increases in profitability exceeding 90%.
D) in every category in which company health can be calculated.

22

The writer wants to include information with the data that is consistent with the conclusion of the passage. Which choice most effectively accomplishes this goal?

A) NO CHANGE
B) no one should come out ahead of the other.
C) society as a whole wins as well.
D) paid family leave is a necessary evil.

Everyday Applications of Nuclear Energy

Although the concept of the atom has been around for centuries, it was not until the 1930s that humans first became **23** capable of harnessing the powerful energy **24** exploding when atoms split and using this energy toward human ends.

Advances in our understanding of nuclear energy and its applications **25** coincided simultaneously with the onset of a war that would touch every corner of the globe. Thus nuclear technology was first and almost exclusively used in the race to create the "atomic bomb." **26** Soon thereafter, however, scientists began to utilize nuclear energy in a host

23

A) NO CHANGE
B) capable to harness
C) capable of a harness
D) capable to harnessing

24

A) NO CHANGE
B) evicted
C) released
D) dispersed

25

A) NO CHANGE
B) coincided with the beginning of the onset
C) initially coincided with the onset
D) coincided with the onset

26

At this point, the writer is considering adding the following sentence.

> President Truman's rationale for using the A-bomb on the Japanese was that the action would prevent the necessity of a land invasion.

Should the writer make this addition here?

A) Yes, because it provides needed historical context for the point the writer is trying to convey.
B) Yes, because it provides a logical transition between the previous and following sentence.
C) No, because it provides information that contradicts the main idea of the passage.
D) No, because it blurs the paragraph's focus and interrupts the logical flow of thought.

of new, more peaceful enterprises, 27 though the risk of disaster should something go wrong remains equally high. Most people today can probably name a few ways in which they interact with nuclear technology; however, many might be surprised to know the many ways in which nuclear technology is revolutionizing 28 environmental science, agriculture, and medicine.

27

Which choice most effectively sets up the examples provided in the following paragraph?

A) NO CHANGE
B) despite the protestations of those who believe nuclear energy to be dangerous in any form.
C) many of which make our daily lives possible in ways in which we are completely unaware.
D) shifting the entire industry away from weapons manufacturing.

28

A) NO CHANGE
B) environmental, science, agriculture, and medicine.
C) environmental science, agriculture and, medicine.
D) environmental science agriculture, and medicine.

[1] Take, for example, something everyone interacts with on a daily basis: water. [2] In a world of an **29** <u>increased</u> population and changing climate, it is more important than ever to ensure that human populations have adequate sources of water. [3] Through advances in nuclear technology, scientists can now use a technique called isotope hydrology to accurately trace and measure underground water resources. [4] This aids in the **30** <u>management of existing supplies, in identifying new sources of water, and the conservation of both.</u> [5] In agriculture, too, nuclear technology is helping to promote the stability of our sources of food. [6] **31** <u>For example,</u> gamma irradiation is increasingly being used to produce new genetic lines of staple crops like wheat and sorghum that are more resistant to pests and harsh environmental conditions. [7] Nuclear technology is also used in food preservation on Earth and beyond: on their trips to space, astronauts **32** <u>had eaten</u> food preserved by irradiation. **33**

Because it is a fundamental building block of the universe, atomic energy is all around us. Now nuclear technology is too.

29

A) NO CHANGE
B) increasing
C) increasing in
D) increase in

30

A) NO CHANGE
B) management of existing supplies, the identification of new sources of water, and the conservation of both.
C) managing of existing supplies, identifying of new sources of water, and the conservation of both.
D) managing of existing supplies, the identification of new sources of water, and to conserve both.

31

A) NO CHANGE
B) Therefore,
C) Meanwhile,
D) Not only that,

32

A) NO CHANGE
B) ate
C) has eaten
D) eat

33

To make this paragraph most logical, sentence 1 should be placed

A) where it is now.
B) after sentence 2.
C) after sentence 3.
D) after sentence 4.

The Piltdown Man Hoax

The turn of the 20th century saw a flourishing interest in archeology. As tools were developed to unearth and study the artifacts of human history, 34 more—both professionals and hobbyists—began digging up the past. One such amateur was the English lawyer Charles Dawson, who in 1912 "discovered" Piltdown Man: an object whose trajectory would take it from celebrated evidence of evolution to evidence only of 35 its finders ability to perpetrate a massive hoax.

[1] Piltdown Man, so called for the area in which Dawson claimed to have found the artifact, was a humanoid skull. [2] 36 Having both human and ape-like qualities, Piltdown Man seemed, as Dawson claimed, to be the much-sought "missing link" connecting modern humans to their primate ancestors. [3] Though there were skeptics from the beginning, the finding was largely embraced; after all, archeological proof of the "missing link" added further credibility to Darwin's controversial Theory of Evolution. [4] Everything about Piltdown Man 37 has been refuted by newer archeological evidence. [5] Piltdown Man's structure seemed to confirm the hypothesis that humans' large modern brains evolved before their omnivorous diets. [6] And since Englishmen viewed themselves as culturally and

34

A) NO CHANGE
B) more and more—both professional and hobbyist people—
C) more people—professional and hobbyist
D) more people—both the professional and hobbyists—

35

A) NO CHANGE
B) it's finder's
C) it's finders'
D) its finder's

36

The writer wants to add specific details that convey support for Dawson's claim. Which choice best accomplishes this goal?

A) NO CHANGE
B) Because of its large cranium and protruding, ape-like jaw,
C) Though it was not in fact real,
D) Thought at the time to be at least 500,000 years old,

37

Which choice best establishes the idea central to the rest of the paragraph?

A) NO CHANGE
B) satisfied the scientific and cultural beliefs of the English scientific establishment at the time.
C) matched archeological records of human evolution at the time.
D) played into the nationalistic biases of English scientists.

racially superior to other incarnations, it simply made sense that the earliest humans would be found in Britain. **38**

39 Conclusive evidence of Piltdown Man's true identity, and thus its revelation as a hoax, was found in 1953. This is not surprising given the strength of these beliefs. However, it was in that year that anthropologist Joseph Weiner and geologist Kenneth Oakley revealed the truth: Piltdown Man was no 500,000 year-old missing link at all but a human skull with an orangutan jaw and chimpanzee teeth **40** no less then 100,000 years old. **41** By rights, the specimen was exactly what its critics had said it was all along: a hybrid fused together by perhaps skilled but not honest hands.

The question of whose hands those were has never been conclusively answered. Dawson died decades before

38

To make this paragraph most logical, sentence 4 should be placed

A) where it is now.
B) after sentence 1.
C) after sentence 2.
D) after sentence 6.

39

Which choice most effectively combines the sentences at the underlined point?

A) Piltdown Man, not surprisingly given the strength of these beliefs, was a hoax revealed by evidence of its true identity conclusively in 1953.
B) In 1953 Piltown Man's true identity was revealed as a hoax, not surprisingly given the strength of these beliefs, conclusively through evidence.
C) Conclusive evidence of Piltdown Man's true identity, perhaps not surprisingly, given the strength of these beliefs, was found in 1953, revealing it as a hoax.
D) That conclusive evidence of Piltdown Man's true identity, and thus its revelation as a hoax, was not found until 1953 is not surprising given the strength of these beliefs.

40

A) NO CHANGE
B) fewer then
C) no more than
D) much more then

41

A) NO CHANGE
B) Fortunately,
C) Essentially,
D) Consequently,

CONTINUE

the hoax was confirmed, and **42** speculation about who the true engineer could have been included multiple names, including the creator of Sherlock Holmes, author Arthur Conan Doyle. However, the bulk of the evidence points to Dawson himself. For one, **43** it seems like this forgery was either his first or his last but merely his most famous. **44** An analysis of his collection uncovered 38 fake specimens, prompting one critic to describe Piltdown Man not as a "one-off hoax," but, "more the culmination of a life's work." The results of another review published in 2016 come even closer to proving Dawson's involvement, but perhaps the mystery will remain as great as the hoax.

42

A) NO CHANGE
B) forecasting upon
C) sneaking suspicion into
D) shots in the dark about

43

A) NO CHANGE
B) it does not seem like this forgery was either his first or
C) it does not seem like this forgery neither was his first nor
D) it seems like neither this forgery was his first or

44

A) NO CHANGE
B) A scrutinization
C) A dissection
D) An encounter

STOP

If you finish before time is called, you may check your work on this section only. Do not turn to any other section.

Math Test – No Calculator

25 MINUTES, 20 QUESTIONS

Turn to Section 3 of your answer sheet to answer the questions in this section.

DIRECTIONS

For questions 1-15, solve each problem, choose the best answer from the choices provided, and fill in the corresponding circle on your answer sheet. **For questions 16-20,** solve the problem and enter your answer in the grid on the answer sheet. Please refer to the directions before question 16 on how to enter your answers in the grid. You may use any available space in your test booklet for scratch work.

NOTES

1. The use of a calculator **is not permitted**.
2. All variables and expressions used represent real numbers unless otherwise indicated.
3. Figures provided in this test are drawn to scale unless otherwise indicated.
4. All figures lie in a plane unless otherwise indicated.
5. Unless otherwise indicated, the domain of a given function *f* is the set of all real numbers *x* for which *f*(*x*) is a real number.

REFERENCE

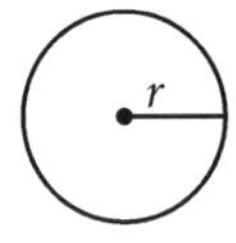

$A = \pi r^2$

$C = 2\pi r$

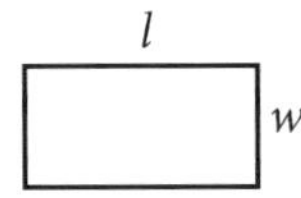

$A = lw$

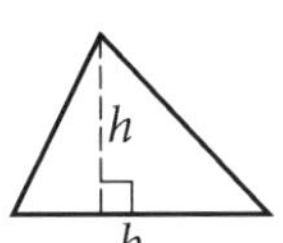

$A = \frac{1}{2}bh$

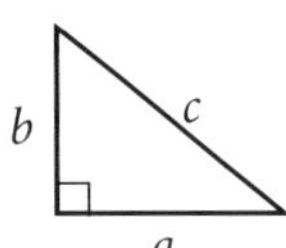

$c^2 = a^2 + b^2$

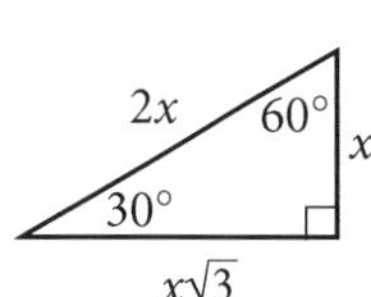

Special Right Triangles

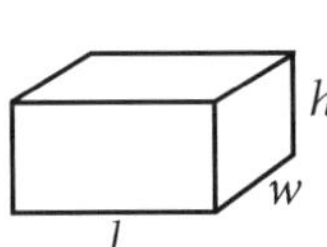

$V = lwh$

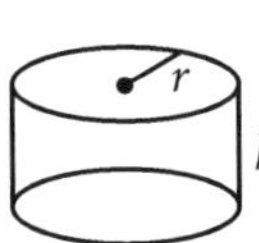

$V = \pi r^2 h$

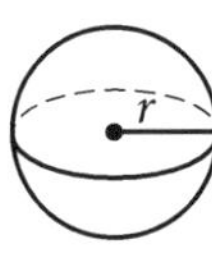

$V = \frac{4}{3}\pi r^3$

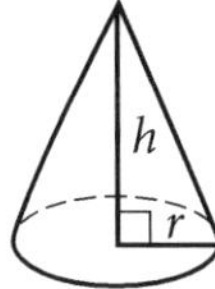

$V = \frac{1}{3}\pi r^2 h$

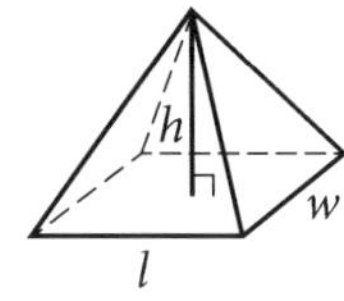

$V = \frac{1}{3}lwh$

The number of degrees of arc in a circle is 360.
The number of radians of arc in a circle is 2π.
The sum of the measures in degrees of the angles of a triangle is 180.

1

Jayme started bicycling 3 miles each day, every day of the week, for a week. For every day of the second week, he biked 4 miles each day. For every day of the third week, he biked 5 miles each day. Assuming this pattern continued for n weeks, which of the following expressions represents the number of miles he biked during the nth week?

A) $n + 1$
B) $n + 3$
C) $7n + 2$
D) $7(n + 2)$

2

If $-5x + 4 = 14$, what is the value of $6x - 1$?

A) 13
B) 11
C) 13
D) -11

3

$$\sqrt[4]{w^2}$$

Which expression is equal to the above expression, for all values of w?

A) $\sqrt{w}$
B) $\sqrt[3]{w}$
C) $\sqrt[4]{w}$
D) $\sqrt[6]{w}$

4

There are 35 violin players in an orchestra. This represents 25% of the total number of members of the orchestra. Which of the following equations could be used to find the total number of members, x, of the orchestra?

A) $0.75x = 35$
B) $0.25x = 35$
C) $x + 35 = 100$
D) $25x + x = 100$

5

Vanessa created a painting with 7 orioles and 9 goldfinches on it. What is the ratio of the number of orioles to the total number of birds in the painting?

A) $\frac{7}{9}$
B) $\frac{9}{7}$
C) $\frac{7}{16}$
D) $\frac{9}{16}$

6

The graph of a system of linear equations results in two lines that are collinear. Which of the following systems meets this criteria?

A) $\begin{cases} y = 2x + 5 \\ y = 2x - 6 \end{cases}$

B) $\begin{cases} y = \frac{1}{3}x + 5 \\ y = -\frac{1}{3}x + 5 \end{cases}$

C) $\begin{cases} 2x + 6y = 38 \\ 2x - 3y = -7 \end{cases}$

D) $\begin{cases} -2x + 8y = 30 \\ 3x - 12y = -45 \end{cases}$

7

Function f is a third degree polynomial. Which of the following equations could be the equation for the function?

A) $f(x) = (x + 2)^2(x - 5)^3$
B) $f(x) = (x - 7)^2(x + 3)^2$
C) $f(x) = x(x + 6)(x - 1)^2$
D) $f(x) = x(x + 5)^2$

8

$$y = \frac{r}{s}x - 5$$

The equation above is the equation of a line, $r \neq 0$, and $s \neq 0$. If the point (12, 3) is on the line, what is the value of $\frac{r}{s}$?

A) $\frac{2}{3}$
B) $\frac{3}{2}$
C) $\frac{3}{4}$
D) $\frac{17}{3}$

9

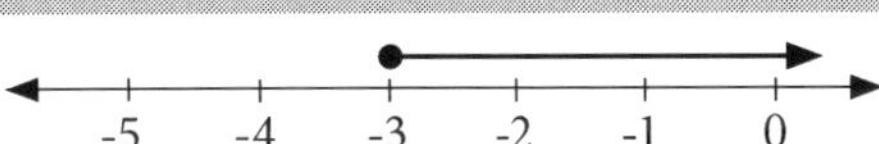

The graph above represents the solutions to which of the following inequalities?

A) $-2w \geq -6$
B) $2 + y \leq -1$
C) $6z > 18$
D) $-\frac{x}{3} < 1$

10

A parabola has x-intercepts at -5 and -1. If $f(-3) = -8$, what is the equation for function $f(x)$?

A) $f(x) = x^2 + 6x + 5$
B) $f(x) = x^2 - 6x + 5$
C) $f(x) = 2x^2 + 12x + 10$
D) $f(x) = 2x^2 - 12x + 10$

11

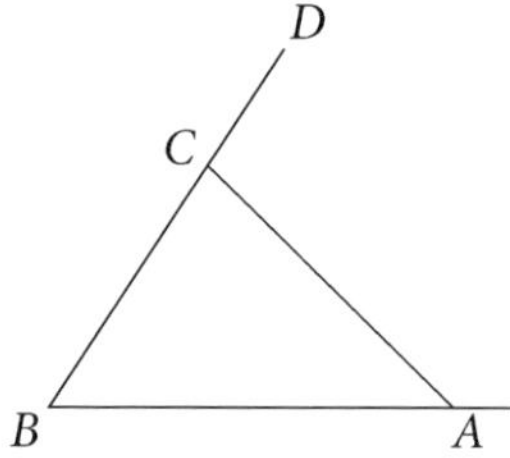

Note: Figure not drawn to scale.

In the figure above, the measure of $\angle DCA$ is $104°$ and the measure of $\angle B$ is $60°$. What is the measure of $\angle BAC$?

A) 30°
B) 44°
C) 46°
D) 76°

12

$$y = x^2 - 6x + 31$$

If the equation above is graphed in the xy-plane, the result is a parabola. What is the vertex of the parabola?

A) (0, 4)
B) (2, 20)
C) (3, 22)
D) (4, 20)

13

$$f(x) = 14x^2 - 11x + 2$$

$$g(x) = 2x - 3$$

Use the functions defined above, what is the result of dividing function $f(x)$ by function $g(x)$?

A) $7x + 5$
B) $7x - 5$
C) $7x + 5 + \frac{17}{2x - 3}$
D) $7x - 5 - \frac{13}{2x - 3}$

14

$$2x^2 + 7 = 4x$$

What are the solutions to the equation above?

A) $1 \pm i\sqrt{10}$
B) $-1 \pm i\sqrt{10}$
C) $1 \pm \frac{i\sqrt{10}}{2}$
D) $-1 \pm \frac{i\sqrt{10}}{2}$

15

A farmer built a storage container for his corn in the shape of a cylinder. It had a radius of 5 ft. and a height of h feet. He built a second cylindrical storage container of the same height, but with a radius of 10 ft. How does the volume of the second container compare to the volume of the first container?

A) It is 2 times as large.
B) It is 4 times as large.
C) It is 5 times as large.
D) It is 8 times as large.

DIRECTIONS

For questions 16 – 20, solve each problem, enter your answer in the grid, as described below on the answer sheet.

1. Although not required, it is suggested that you write your answer in the boxes at the top of the columns to help you fill in the circles accurately. You will receive credit only if the circles are filled in correctly.
2. Mark no more than one circle in any column.
3. No question has a negative answer.
4. Some problems may have more than one correct answer. In such cases, grid only one answer.
5. **Mixed numbers** such as $3\frac{1}{2}$ must be gridded as 3.5 or $\frac{7}{2}$. (If 3 1 / 2 is entered into the grid, it will be interpreted as $\frac{31}{2}$, not $3\frac{1}{2}$.)
6. **Decimal answers:** If you obtain a decimal answer with more digits than the grid can accommodate, it may be either rounded or truncated, but it must fill the entire grid.

Answer: $\frac{7}{12}$ — Write answer in boxes: 7 / 1 2 — Fraction line — Grid in result.

Answer: 2.5 — 2 . 5 — Decimal point

Acceptable ways to grid $\frac{2}{3}$ are: 2 / 3, .666, .667

Answer: 201 – either position is correct

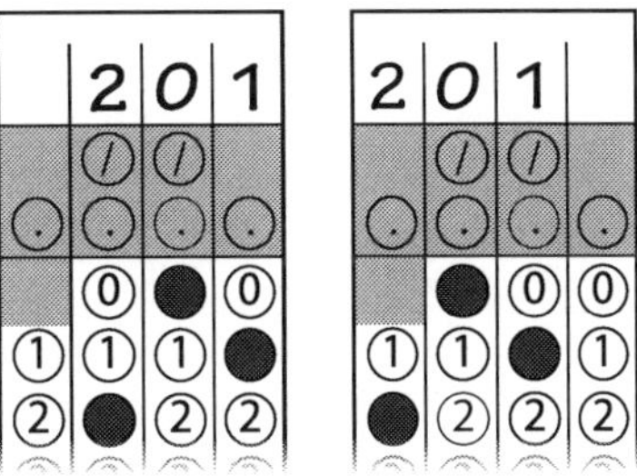

NOTE: You may start your answers in any column, space permitting. Columns you don't need to use should be left blank.

16

When you multiply a polynomial of degree 3 by a polynomial of degree 4, what is the degree of the product?

17

$$\left(\sqrt[4]{x}\right)^3$$

If the above expression is rewritten in the form of x to a power, what is the exponent?

18

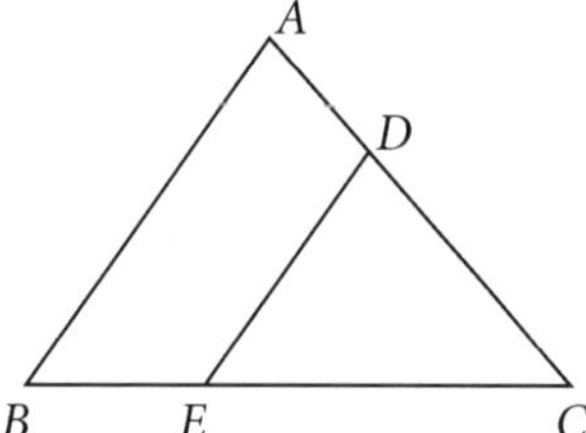

In the figure above, $\triangle ABC \sim \triangle DEC$, the length of $\overline{AB}$ is 18, the length of $\overline{EC}$ is 16, and the length of $\overline{BC}$ is 24. What is the length of $\overline{DE}$?

19

$$25x + 43y = 860$$

If the equation above is graphed on the xy-plane, what is the y-intercept?

20

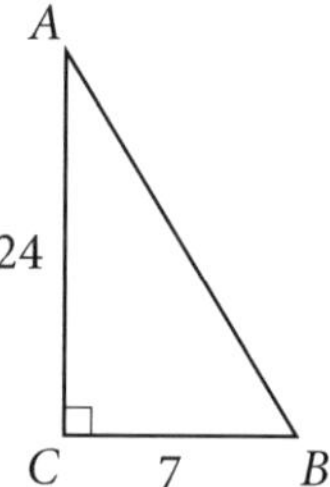

For $\triangle ABC$, which is shown above, what is the value of $\cos(B)$?

STOP

If you finish before time is called, you may check your work on this section only. Do not turn to any other section.

Math Test – Calculator

55 MINUTES, 38 QUESTIONS

Turn to Section 4 of your answer sheet to answer the questions in this section.

DIRECTIONS

For questions 1-30, solve each problem, choose the best answer from the choices provided, and fill in the corresponding circle on your answer sheet. **For questions 31-38,** solve the problem and enter your answer in the grid on the answer sheet. Please refer to the directions before question 16 on how to enter your answers in the grid. You may use any available space in your test booklet for scratch work.

NOTES

1. The use of a calculator **is not permitted**.
2. All variables and expressions used represent real numbers unless otherwise indicated.
3. Figures provided in this test are drawn to scale unless otherwise indicated.
4. All figures lie in a plane unless otherwise indicated.
5. Unless otherwise indicated, the domain of a given function f is the set of all real numbers x for which $f(x)$ is a real number.

REFERENCE

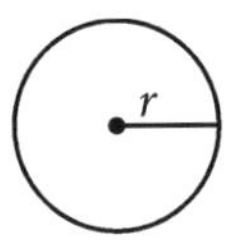

$A = \pi r^2$
$C = 2\pi r$

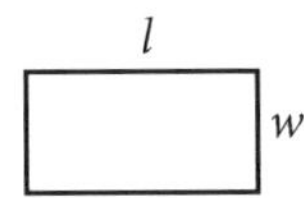

$A = lw$

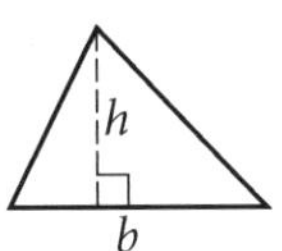

$A = \frac{1}{2}bh$

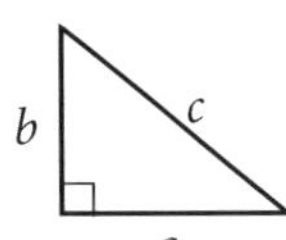

$c^2 = a^2 + b^2$

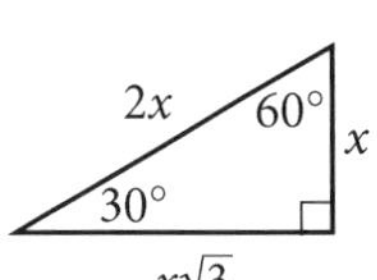

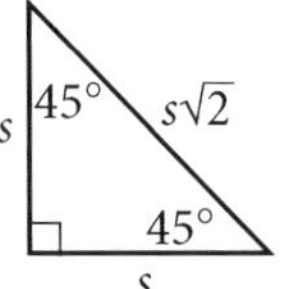

Special Right Triangles

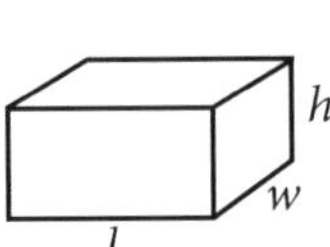

$V = lwh$

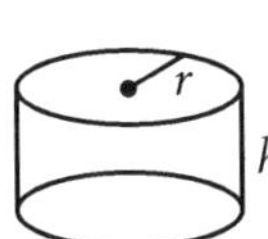

$V = \pi r^2 h$

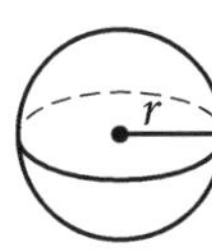

$V = \frac{4}{3}\pi r^3$

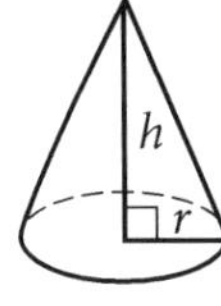

$V = \frac{1}{3}\pi r^2 h$

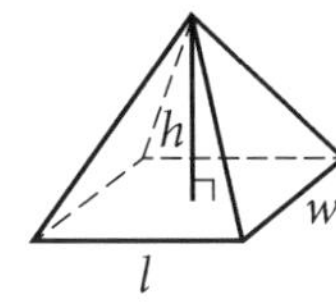

$V = \frac{1}{3}lwh$

The number of degrees of arc in a circle is 360.
The number of radians of arc in a circle is 2π.
The sum of the measures in degrees of the angles of a triangle is 180.

1

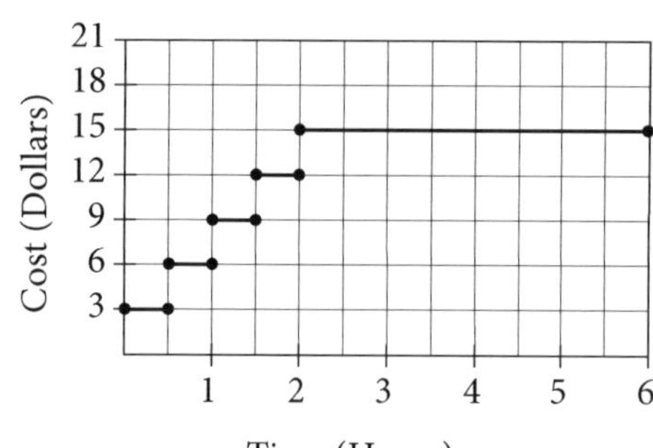

The graph above shows the cost of parking a car in a city parking garage. Using this graph, what would be the cost for parking a car for 1.5 hours?

A) \$6
B) \$9
C) \$12
D) \$15

2

Shona is playing a game where she must flip a coin three times. If she gets heads on all three flips, she will win a prize. What is the probability that Shona will win the prize?

A) $\frac{1}{8}$
B) $\frac{1}{4}$
C) $\frac{3}{8}$
D) $\frac{5}{8}$

3

As a fundraiser, a club is making and selling calendars created with photographs. The club sells the calendars for \$4 each. The equation $y = 4x$ represents the income, y, received for selling x calendars. The club has expenses of \$2 for making each calendar, plus a total of \$20 for expenses related to creating the photos. The equation, $y = 2x + 20$, can be used to represent the total expense for creating x calendars. A graph of both of these equations appears below.

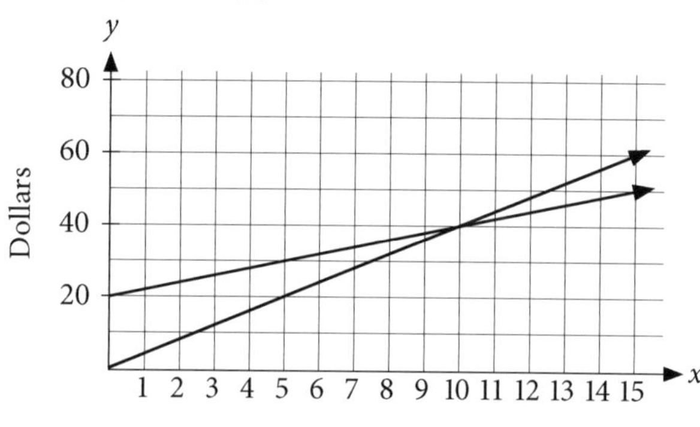

What does the point (10, 40) on the graph represent?

A) the break-even point for the fundraiser
B) a profit of \$40 when they sell 10 calendars
C) the minimum amount of money the club can make
D) the maximum amount of money the club can make

4

A system of equations has infinite solutions. One equation of the system is $-2x + 8y = 5$. Which of the following equations cannot be the equation of the second line?

A) $-4x + 16y = 10$
B) $-2x + 24y = 15$
C) $8x - 32y = -20$
D) $6x - 24y = -15$

5

The owner of a small company took his employees out to a holiday dinner. He paid the bill and added a 15% tip of $50.40. How much was the bill before the tip?

A) $252
B) $300
C) $336
D) $756

6

If $2n + 2 = 14$, what is the value of $2n - 2$?

A) 6
B) 7
C) 8
D) 10

7

$$\frac{m}{11} = \frac{17}{374}$$

What is the value of m in the proportion above?

A) 0.5
B) 2.2
C) 187
D) 242

8

Ethan deposited $1,200 into a savings account. The account had an annual interest rate of 5%. After 7 years, what was the value of Ethan's savings account, to the nearest whole dollar?

A) $1,260
B) $1,426
C) $1,688
D) $1,696

9

Gail has a business making and selling bracelets. She can make 1 bracelet every 35 minutes. Gail has an order for 150 bracelets. Approximately how many 8-hour days will she need to make all the bracelets for the order?

A) 11
B) 27
C) 65
D) 88

Questions 10 and 11 refer to the following information.

When the sun emits a solar flare, the blast wave travels through space at a rate of 3×10^6 km/hr.

10

How many kilometers would the solar flare travel in one minute?

A) 5,000
B) 50,000
C) 250,000
D) 500,000

11

If 1 kilometer = 0.62 miles, what is the rate of travel of the blast wave, in miles per hour?

A) 31,000 mph
B) 310,000 mph
C) 1,860,000 mph
D) 4,838,710 mph

12

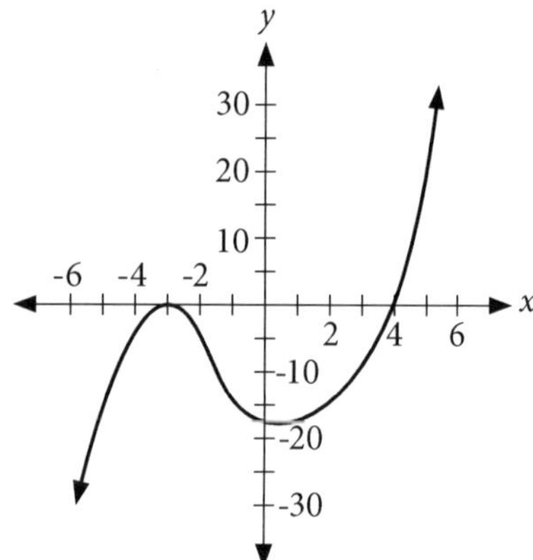

Above is a sketch of function f, which is a polynomial of degree 3, and $f(5) = 32$.

Which of the equations for function f is correct?

A) $f(x) = \frac{1}{2}x(x + 3)(x - 4)$
B) $f(x) = 4x(x + 3)(x - 4)$
C) $f(x) = (x - 3)(x - 3)(x + 4)$
D) $f(x) = \frac{1}{2}(x + 3)(x + 3)(x - 4)$

13

$$V = \sqrt{a^4 b^{\frac{1}{3}}}$$

Using the above equation, which expression is equal to b?

A) $\frac{V^6}{a^{12}}$
B) $\frac{V^5}{a^7}$
C) $\frac{V^2}{a^4}$
D) $\frac{V}{a^2}$

14

54, 18, 6, 2 …

What is the formula for the nth term of the sequence above?

A) $a_n = 6\left(\frac{1}{3}\right)^n$
B) $a_n = 6\left(\frac{1}{3}\right)^{n-1}$
C) $a_n = 54\left(\frac{1}{3}\right)^n$
D) $a_n = 54\left(\frac{1}{3}\right)^{n-1}$

15

Palm Springs Air Temperature

	X			
	X	X		
	X	X		
	X	X		
X	X	X	X	X
100°	101°	102°	103°	104°

Temperature (°F)

The line plot above gives the recorded maximum temperature for 12 days in May for Palm Springs, California. To the nearest tenth of a degree, what are the mean, median, and mode for this data?

A) Mean = 101.7, Median = 101.5, Mode = 101
B) Mean = 101.7, Median = 101, Mode = 101.5
C) Mean = 102, Median = 101.5, Mode = 102
D) Mean = 100, Median = 102, Mode = 101

16

$$x^2 + y^2 - 2x + 6y + 3 = 0$$

The equation above is the equation of a circle. Which form of this equation correctly reveals the center of the circle and its radius?

A) $(x - 1)^2 + (y + 3)^2 = (\sqrt{7})^2$
B) $(x + 1)^2 + (y + 3)^2 = (\sqrt{7})^2$
C) $(x + 1)^2 + (y + 3)^2 = 7$
D) $(x - 1)^2 + (y + 3)^2 = 7$

Questions 17 and 18 refer to the following information.

National Park	Visitors in 2015	Visitors in 2016
Great Smoky Mountains	10,712,674	12,312,786
Grand Canyon	5,520,736	5,969,811
Yosemite	4,150,217	5,028,868
Rocky Mountain	4,155,916	4,517,585
Zion	3,648,846	4,295,128

The table above shows the five U.S. National Parks that were visited by the most people in 2016.

17

According to the information in the table, which park experienced the greatest increase in the number of visitors from 2015 to 2016?

A) Great Smoky Mountains
B) Grand Canyon
C) Yosemite
D) Zion

18

Based on the information in the table, which park showed the least growth in the number of visitors as measured by percent increase from 2015 to 2016?

A) Great Smoky Mountains
B) Grand Canyon
C) Rocky Mountain
D) Zion

19

A tennis court is 36 feet wide and 78 feet long. Jayme is making a model of the tennis court using a ratio of 1 in. to 18 in. What are the dimensions of Jayme's model?

A) 2 in. x 4 in.

B) 12 in. x 14 in.

C) 24 in. x 52 in.

D) 30 in. x 52 in.

20

A political polling agency recently asked 1,000 randomly selected likely voters about the governor of the state. In response to the first question, "Do you approve of the job that the governor is doing?," 56 percent responded yes, with a 3 percent margin of error. In response to the second question, "Would you vote for the governor if an election were held today?," 58 percent responded yes, also with a 3 percent margin of error. Based on the results of the poll, which of the following must be true?

I. Of all the likely voters in the state, 56 percent approve of the governor's job performance.

II. If an election were held today, the governor would likely be re-elected.

III. More people in the state would vote for the governor than approve of the governor's job performance.

A) I only

B) II only

C) II and III only

D) I, II, and III

21

Pedro has a business, and the business has 100 clients. The number of clients has been growing exponentially at a rate of 15% per year. Andrew has a business that has 350 clients and the number of clients has been declining at a rate of 6 per year. After how many years will the number of clients that each business has be approximately the same?

A) 2

B) 4

C) 5

D) 8

22

What is the prime factorization of 504?

A) $2^3 \cdot 3 \cdot 7^2$

B) $2^3 \cdot 3^3 \cdot 7$

C) $2^2 \cdot 3^2 \cdot 7$

D) $2^3 \cdot 3^2 \cdot 7$

23

If $\sin^2(32°) + \cos^2(M) = 1$, what is the value of M?

A) 32°

B) 58°

C) 68°

D) 72°

24

Best Foods is making a cereal with 7 parts bran flakes for every 3 parts raisins. To the nearest tenth of an ounce, what is the amount of bran flakes are needed for each 12 ounce box of cereal?

A) 3.6
B) 4.2
C) 7.2
D) 8.4

25

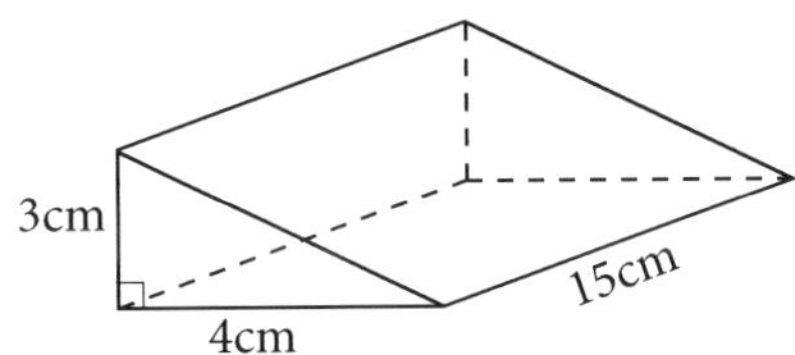

Note: Figure not drawn to scale.

What is the surface area, in square centimeters, of the triangular prism shown above?

A) 180 sq. cm.
B) 192 sq. cm.
C) 201 sq. cm.
D) 216 sq. cm.

26

The axis of symmetry for a parabola has the equation, $x = -2$. Which of the following could be the equation for the parabola?

A) $y = x^2 - 4x + 1$
B) $y = x^2 - 2x + 3$
C) $y = 2x^2 + 8x - 3$
D) $y = 2x^2 + 4x - 7$

27

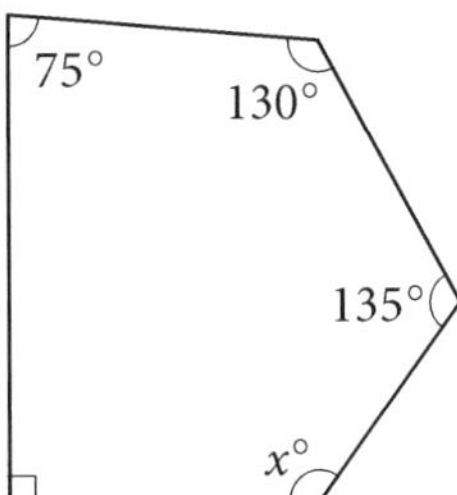

The pentagon shown above has the measures of some angles given. What is the measure of the angle denoted by $x°$?

A) 100°
B) 110°
C) 125°
D) 135°

28

$$\frac{x^2 - 2x^2 - 13x - 10}{x - 5}$$

What is the quotient for the division problem above?

A) $x^2 + 3x - 2$
B) $x^2 + 3x + 2$
C) $x^2 - 3x - 2$
D) $x^2 - 3x + 2$

29

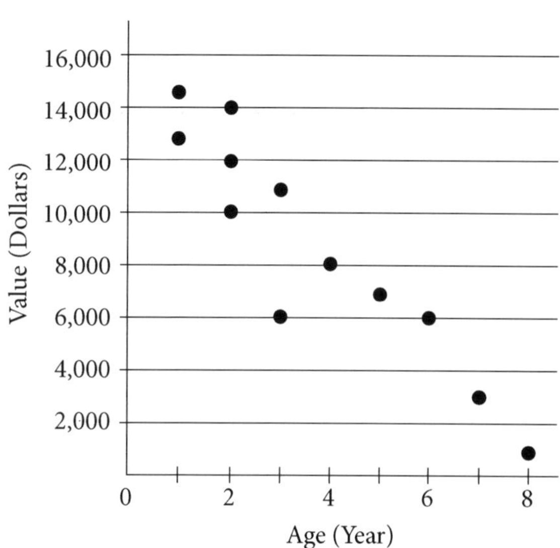

The scatterplot above shows data regarding the value of several midsize pre-owned cars. Each plotted point gives the value, v, of the car after x years of being owned and driven by someone. Which of the following equations shows the best relationship between v and x?

A) $v = -500x + 14{,}000$

B) $v = -800x + 10{,}000$

C) $v = -1{,}000x + 16{,}000$

D) $v = -1{,}700x + 15{,}000$

30

$$4^{x^2 + 4x} = 2^{-6}$$

What is the solution set for the equation above?

A) $\{1, 3\}$

B) $\{-1, 3\}$

C) $\{1, -3\}$

D) $\{-1, -3\}$

DIRECTIONS

For questions 31 – 38, solve each problem, enter your answer in the grid, as described below on the answer sheet.

1. Although not required, it is suggested that you write your answer in the boxes at the top of the columns to help you fill in the circles accurately. You will receive credit only if the circles are filled in correctly.
2. Mark no more than one circle in any column.
3. No question has a negative answer.
4. Some problems may have more than one correct answer. In such cases, grid only one answer.
5. **Mixed numbers** such as $3\frac{1}{2}$ must be gridded as 3.5 or $\frac{7}{2}$. (If 3 1 / 2 is entered into the grid, it will be interpreted as $\frac{31}{2}$, not $3\frac{1}{2}$.)
6. **Decimal answers:** If you obtain a decimal answer with more digits than the grid can accommodate, it may be either rounded or truncated, but it must fill the entire grid.

Answer: $\frac{7}{12}$

Answer: 2.5

Write answer in boxes. →

← Fraction line

← Decimal point

Grid in result.

Acceptable ways to grid $\frac{2}{3}$ are:

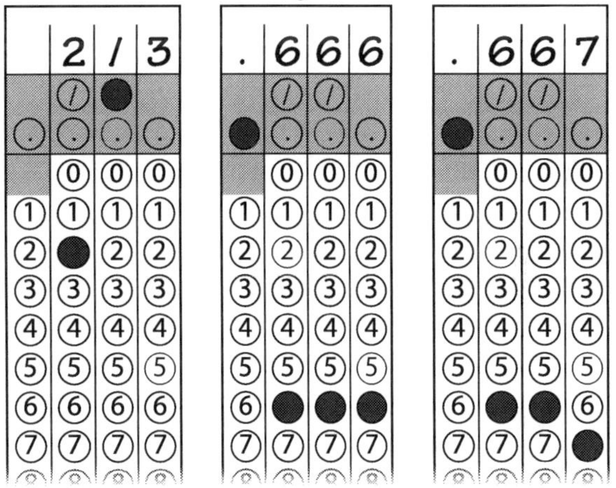

Answer: 201 – either position is correct

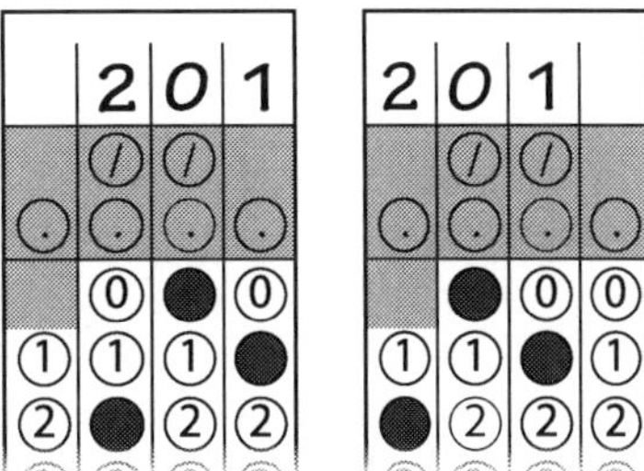

NOTE: You may start your answers in any column, space permitting. Columns you don't need to use should be left blank.

31

For the inequality, $-4y \leq -85$, what is the smallest integer that y can be equal to?

32

Number of Visitors at Track Meet

Alabama	144	Maine	212
California	141	Oregon	305
Delaware	201	Pennsylvania	270
Florida	197	Texas	250
Georgia	224	Wyoming	307

At a national youth track meet, Frederick collected data from people in the stands. The table above shows the number of visitors from ten states. What is the median of the data?

33

A number squared plus 3 times the number is 11,340. There are two numbers that satisfy this requirement. One is positive and one is negative. What is the positive number?

34

What is the number of degrees equal to $\frac{7\pi}{6}$ radians?

35

Carla collected data from 200 students about their favorite sport. She is making a circle graph to display the data. The group that chose soccer was 22% of the population she interviewed. How many degrees will the central angle need to be to represent those students who chose soccer as their favorite sport?

36

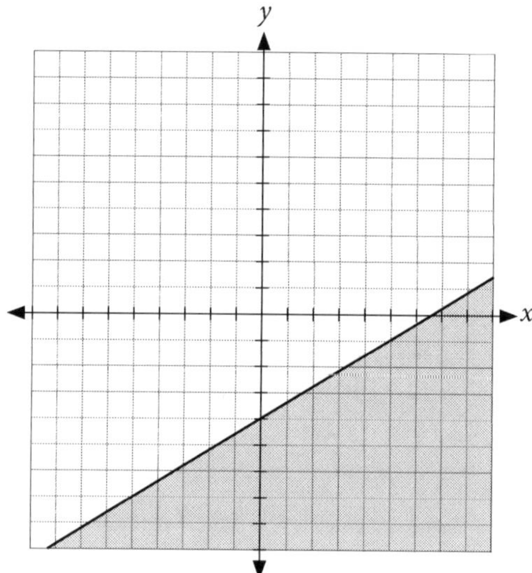

The equation for the graph above is $y < ax - 4$. What is the value of a?

Questions 37 and 38 refer to the following information.

An employee earns $7.00 an hour for the first 35 hours worked in a week, and $10.50 an hour for any hours over 35.

37

How much will the employee earn if he works 41 hours in a given week?

38

The same employee earned $465.50 the next week. How many hours did he work that week?

STOP

If you finish before time is called, you may check your work on this section only.
Do not turn to any other section.

Tutor Ted

SAT® Practice Essay #3

ESSAY BOOK

DIRECTIONS

The essay gives you an opportunity to show how effectively you can read and comprehend a passage and write an essay analyzing the passage. In your essay, you should demonstrate that you have read the passage carefully, present a clear and logical analysis, and use language precisely.

Your essay must be written on the lines provided in your answer booklet; except for the Planning Page of the answer booklet, you will receive no other paper on which to write. You will have enough space if you write on every line, avoid wide margins, and keep your handwriting to a reasonable size. Remember that people who are not familiar with your handwriting will read what you write. Try to write or print so that what you are writing is legible to those readers.

You have <u>50 minutes</u> to read the passage and write an essay in response to the prompt provided inside this booklet.

REMINDERS:

— **Do not write your essay in this booklet. Only what you write on the lined pages of your answer booklet will be evaluated.**

— **An off-topic essay will not be evaluated.**

This cover is representative of what you'll see on test day.

As you read the passage below, consider how Rebecca Sutton uses

- evidence, such as facts or examples, to support claims.
- reasoning to develop ideas and to connect claims and evidence.
- stylistic or persuasive elements, such as word choice or appeals to emotion, to add power to the ideas expressed.

Adapted from Rebecca Sutton, "Creative Approaches to Problem-Solving." © 2017, https://www.arts.gov.

1 Located in the state's eastern Appalachian region, Hindman, Kentucky, has seen its share of hardship in recent decades. The collapse of the coal industry left behind rampant unemployment, and the nation's opiate epidemic has hit Appalachia particularly hard—in 2015, Kentucky had the third-highest rate of overdose- related deaths. Between these two issues, "there's hardly a family in Knott County that has not been affected," Jessica Evans said.

2 But as director of Hindman's Appalachian Artisan Center, Evans has seen how the arts can provide a way forward for the town's 750 residents, the community, and the region as a whole. Here, in a building where stacks of wood wait to be turned into dulcimers[1], where sparks fly from the blacksmith's belt grinder, and where colorful canvases line the walls, artists are creating a balm for Hindman's struggles.

3 The organization was founded in 2001 through former Governor Paul Patton's Community Development Initiative, which also established the nearby Kentucky School of Craft. The two organizations drew on the region's rich cultural heritage, which has been shaped by generations of basketmakers, potters, blacksmiths, and luthiers[2]. By training artists at the school, and then offering them further professional development, studio space, and platforms to promote their work at the Appalachian Artisan Center, it was hoped that a new economy based on the arts and cultural tourism would emerge.

4 And bit by bit, it has. This momentum has been propelled in part by the Kentucky Arts Council and the National Endowment for the Arts. More than half of the Artisan Center's income comes from grants, and in 2016, the Kentucky Arts Council and the National Endowment for the Arts provided a total of $79,000. Operational grants from the Kentucky Arts Council have "had a hand in everything," said Evans, while the council's marketing platforms and invitations to statewide events such as Kentucky Crafted have helped vault the Artisan Center out of Appalachia and onto the state's main stage.

5 On the national level, the NEA has awarded $170,000 to the center through various grant programs since 2011, which have funded residencies, apprenticeships, and the expansion of the center's luthiery school. The school, which is managed by master luthier Doug Naselroad, is a central piece of the Artisan Center's activities, and will eventually include a program to help trained luthiers find work through the Troublesome Creek Stringed Instrument Company.

6 It is clear that these investments by the NEA and Kentucky Arts Council have paid off. As its facilities and programs have grown, the Artisan Center has given people "the ability to provide for their families or supplement their income with their own craft and their own handwork," said Evans. It has also started to put Hindman on the map as a tourist destination: in 2015, the Appalachian Artisan Center drew 10,000 visitors, and artists saw a 67 percent growth in retail sales, with customers hailing from 21 different states.

7 But economic momentum is just one facet of the Artisan Center's impact—equally meaningful has been the deeper social and emotional change. "I truly believe that one of the things that the Artisan Center can offer people is hope for their own future—the gift of a larger life," said Evans. "There are a lot of people for whom the Artisan Center is the reason that they get out of bed and come to town." She has seen people recovering from addiction "latch on to crafts as a way to better themselves as an alternative to any of the other choices they could be making." One paramedic who participates in the center's blacksmithing apprentice program has said the rhythmic pounding helps mitigate the high-stress atmosphere of his job, where he sees overdoses on a daily basis.

8 Indeed, returning to the region's creative roots has been a source of healing for the community at large, as it has refocused residents' collective sense of identity from one of hardship to one of artistic innovation, cultural tradition, and local talent. "When they take that identity and share the story of it not only within the community but beyond, it becomes a symbol and something that makes them proud of their region," said Mark Brown, director of folk and traditional arts at the Kentucky Arts Council.

[1] A stringed musical instrument played with a hammer
[2] A maker of stringed instruments such as violins and guitars

Write an essay in which you explain how Rebecca Sutton builds an argument to persuade her audience that engaging in creative arts and crafts can help heal communities affected by economic loss. In your essay, analyze how Sutton uses one or more of the features listed in the box above (or features of your own choice) to strengthen the logic and persuasiveness of her argument. Be sure that your analysis focuses on the most relevant features of the passage.

Your essay should not explain whether you agree with Johnson's claims, but rather explain how Johnson builds an argument to persuade his audience.

Practice Test 3

ANSWERS

READING

#	Answer	#	Answer
1	A	27	C
2	C	28	A
3	A	29	B
4	D	30	C
5	A	31	B
6	B	32	D
7	A	33	C
8	B	34	A
9	B	35	B
10	D	36	A
11	A	37	A
12	D	38	D
13	A	39	C
14	D	40	B
15	C	41	D
16	C	42	C
17	C	43	D
18	C	44	B
19	D	45	C
20	A	46	D
21	A	47	A
22	C	48	D
23	A	49	B
24	D	50	A
25	A	51	B
26	D	52	D

WRITING & LANGUAGE

#	Answer	#	Answer
1	C	23	A
2	A	24	C
3	C	25	D
4	D	26	D
5	B	27	C
6	D	28	A
7	C	29	B
8	B	30	B
9	C	31	A
10	C	32	D
11	A	33	A
12	D	34	A
13	B	35	D
14	D	36	B
15	C	37	B
16	A	38	A
17	B	39	D
18	C	40	C
19	D	41	C
20	D	42	A
21	B	43	B
22	C	44	A

MATH (No Calculator)

#	Answer
1	D
2	C
3	A
4	B
5	C
6	D
7	D
8	A
9	D
10	C
11	B
12	C
13	C
14	C
15	B
16	7
17	¾, 0.25
18	12
19	20
20	7/25, 0.28

MATH (Calculator)

#	Answer
1	B
2	A
3	A
4	B
5	C
6	D
7	A
8	C
9	A
10	B
11	C
12	D
13	A
14	D
15	A
16	A
17	C
18	B
19	C
20	B
21	D
22	D
23	B
24	D
25	B
26	C
27	B
28	B
29	D
30	D
31	22
32	218
33	105
34	210
35	79.2
36	3/5, 0.6
37	308
38	56

PRACTICE TEST 3: SOLUTIONS

Practice Test 3 SOLUTIONS

SECTION 1: READING

PASSAGE: ROBINSON CRUSOE

1) A
Let's do some elimination here. B assumes there is someone else on the island when we learn in the final paragraph that the footprint could have just been Crusoe's own. Crusoe never mentions dreams so C is out, and that the footprint belongs to the devil is just one of his theories so D is incorrect as well. A is right—the confounding discovery is the footprint, and Crusoe spends the passage thinking (deliberating) about where it came from (or originated).

2) C
Crusoe remarks that if the devil were playing tricks on him, he wouldn't leave a single footprint in the sand with no guarantee of Crusoe actually seeing it, implying he would find a much more effective way of terrifying him. In this context, "simple" most nearly means "foolish." Easy money as you know exactly where to find the answer!

3) A
While fear and loneliness present tempting options, the passage best supports paranoia. After imagining the footprint belonged to the devil or another creature on the island, Crusoe eventually realizes the footprint is likely just his own from when he first stepped off his boat as he has no recollection of where he trod.

4) D
The evidence for the answer to Question 3 is in the final paragraph, when Crusoe comes to the realization that he is playing the "part of those fools who try to make stories of spectres and apparitions, and then are frightened at them more than anybody," an apt description of paranoia.

5) A
"Sadistic" and "fiendish" both mean extremely cruel; the passage never describes the devil in this way. Crusoe states, "I considered that the devil might have found out abundance of other ways to have terrified me than this of the single print of a foot," painting the devil as one who indulges in playing tricks only to terrify. "Playful" is too soft, whereas "mischievous" suitably describes the devil's intention to cause trouble.

6) B
In the final paragraph, Crusoe admits he could not identify, or "discern," his previous path when he first set foot on the island.

7) A
In this passage, we never find out for certain whether the footprint is indeed his own or a mirage. He never states an intention to track his movements. We do know, however, that Crusoe concedes that he acted paranoically, so A is the answer.

8) B
The question asks for the main purpose, not necessarily the main idea. In the third paragraph, Crusoe ponders the fickle nature of man, confessing that he feared the presence of another despite thinking it should have been a welcome miracle. Therefore, B best describes the author's purpose for the third paragraph.

9) B
By using questions, the author technically shows Crusoe's stressed state of mind, but more importantly, he immerses the reader in the urgency and imminent danger of the situation, so B best describes this usage.

10) D
The desperate questions asked at the start of the passage create a sense of stress and urgency. As Crusoe considers possible sources of the footprint, ultimately concluding it is likely his own, this neurotic tone shifts to sympathetic as he reflects on his own foolishness.

PASSAGE: FREDERICK DOUGLAS ADDRESS

11) A
Douglas notes the hypocrisy of speaking as a black man on America's day of independence when slavery still exists by stating, "The blessings in which you, this day, rejoice, are not enjoyed in common... Do you mean, citizens, to mock me, by asking me to speak today?" While Douglas denounces slavery, the speech specifically exposes this hypocrisy, so A is the answer. Main idea questions are always great to answer first while the passage is fresh in your mind.

12) D
Douglas likens the treatment of those who fight against slavery with those who fought for American independence. They were considered rebels and dangerous men, so "accounted" most nearly means "defamed." Easy money—go for vocabulary questions first!

13) A
One could technically describe Douglas' feelings as any of the answer choices; however, "incredulous" best fits his feelings towards his audience during this specific speech he was asked to give on Independence Day. He wonders if his audience mocks him, speaking as a black man while slavery still thrives.

14) D
Douglas' incredulity shows through his questions to his audience, wondering what he and his people have to do with their national independence, so D is correct.

15) C
It is a commonly held theory that the Washington Monument was built by slaves. The duplicitous nature of this construction provides an apt analogy for Douglas' next point: celebrating independence contingent on race.

16) C
The context describes the irony of celebrating American freedom despite the existence of slavery. Enslaved conditions feel even more intolerable when juxtaposed with raucous festivities, so "considered" best fits.

17) C
B appears correct, but Douglas does not consider people unaware of inherent contradictions. Instead, he exposes their choice to take the path of the least resistance and turn a blind eye to the oppressed.

18) C
While everyone celebrates independence from Britain on the 4th of July, Douglas opposes this custom "to chime in with the popular theme." To do so would be treasonous to not only his enslaved black community, but also to what America supposedly stands for.

19) D
The hypocrisy of celebrating independence of only some is treasonous as Douglas urges his audience to stand for the true ideals of America "in the name of humanity which is outraged, in the name of liberty which is fettered, in the name of the constitution and the Bible..."

20) A
Douglas would never be described as a "passive" or "tranquil" speaker, nor was his tone ever "complimentary." Douglas at first reluctantly accepts his duty to speak about America's independence, but then admonishes those who celebrate a conditional independence, so A best describes the passage's shift in tone.

PASSAGE: ARE FIRMS THAT DISCRIMINATE MORE LIKELY TO GO OUT OF BUSINESS?

21) A
A great question to answer first when the passage is fresh in your mind—easy money! C is a trap answer as while the study indicates that discriminatory businesses have a higher likelihood of going out of business, they are not destined to definitely go out of business. While B could technically be

true, it is not discussed in the passage, nor is not discriminating a reliable indicator of productivity and efficiency.

22) C
The sentence using the word "weeding" immediately follows, "During this time, a record number of businesses folded." Therefore, "weeding" refers to the closing of these businesses.

23) A
In the third paragraph, the author describes the financial crisis as an "opportune moment during which to examine the relationship between discrimination and firm survival," so "invaluable" is the right choice.

24) D
Talent acquisition is never directly discussed. While racial diversity is important, the focus is on hiring productively by not discriminating against qualified candidates based on race.

25) A
In the final paragraph, the author asserts that businesses which discriminate likely demonstrate poor decision-making in all areas, citing this among other reasons so many discriminatory businesses collapsed during the financial crisis. A thus more aptly answers the question than simply "reinforcing the study's thesis."

26) D
In the fifth paragraph, the author discusses other factors which influence businesses' survival, conceding that the correlation between discrimination and business survival does not imply causation. The focus of the paragraph is not to discuss reasons why businesses stay afloat, but to disclose the study's inherent flaws.

27) C
The author equates racially discriminatory hiring practices with "gut feeling" decision-making. Employers who fail to prioritize credentials and interview performance over preconceived biases do not make evidence-based decisions.

28) A
In the second paragraph, the author cites an experimental audit study done in New York City in 2004. In the third paragraph, she describes the financial crisis of 2008 as an opportunity to examine the survival of the firms from the previous study, so A best answers this question.

29) B
The third paragraph depicts the 2008 financial crisis as an opportunity to examine the survival of the businesses researched in the 2004 NYC study.

30) C
Wordy questions are typically best to answer last if you're running low on time as your time is better spent on questions you can answer quickly. The graph shows that all businesses were prone to closing during the financial crisis, but those with unproductive business practices were less likely to survive. A, B, and D all draw seemingly logical conclusions that are not explicitly justified by the graph.

PASSAGE: "SOCIAL AND ECONOMIC ISSUES—GENETICALLY MODIFIED FOOD" AND "RESPONSE TO ISSUES ON GM AGRICULTURE IN AFRICA: ARE TRANSGENIC CROPS SAFE?"

31) B
Be sure to answer all the questions regarding Passage 1 before moving onto Passage 2! In the final paragraph of Passage 1, the authors express concern over the rapid introduction of GMOs into our food and pharmaceutical supply without safety testing. Regardless of their benefits, GMOs must be regulated.

32) D
The authors argue that current US regulation allows for untested GM products to be commercially grown and consumed. This "scheme" most nearly means "system."

33) C
Peanut allergies are a result of introducing a gene into a plant, exemplifying the dangers

of GMOs and why they should be extensively regulated.

34) A
Graph questions are typically easy money as you know exactly where to look in order to answer the question rapidly—answer these first if you're short on time! The rate of food insecurity was lowest in 1999.

35) B
The author of Passage 2 lists several constraints on adopting GM technology that underdeveloped countries typically face, hindering the spread of GMO cultivation.

36) A
Gaining "over US$100 million per year" indicates that "benefit" most nearly means "profit." Easy money!

37) A
Passage 1 argues for increased regulation due to the potential hazards of consuming GMOs. Passage 2 stresses the importance of adopting technology to solve Africa's agricultural problems. The author of Passage 2 would most likely argue that widespread poverty and hunger are urgent problems that can't wait for regulation legislation, which could possibly take years.

38) D
The author contends that Europe doesn't have a food shortage and can therefore afford the luxury of safety regulation; fast technology and food security are more important to Africa.

39) C
A and D are inaccurate descriptions of the graph. B is a subjective statement as there is no clear point when food security became a "national issue." The steep 4% rise between 2007 and 2008 could be attributed to the financial crisis, so the answer is C.

40) B
Passage 1 focuses on the need for GMO regulation in the US and Europe due to health risks. Passage 2 focuses on the need for immediate GMO technology in order to combat poverty and food insecurity in Africa, regardless of regulation legislation. The issues regarding GMO regulation in both passages are very culture-specific.

41) D
The passages don't necessarily disagree on factual information or "schools of thought" regarding GMOs, but rather on the significance of their implementation in vastly different nations.

PASSAGE: STEM CELL RESEARCH

42) C
While downfalls and dangers are discussed, the main purpose of the passage is to explore the existing findings of stem cell research. The passage then ends with a note on the future of stem cell research and its "incorporation into the practice of medicine," therefore C best reflects this.

43) D
The author makes the point that embryonic stem cells must mature, or develop, for weeks to become adult tissues, organs, or cells, so "immature" most nearly means "underdeveloped." Tackle easy money vocabulary questions first if you're short on time!

44) B
The author's views are evidenced when he states, "while everyone was arguing about the ethics of embryonic stem cell research, the medical and economic realities were ignored." "Distracting" best fits this description.

45) C
Question 44 mentions the first paragraph, so scan that paragraph for your evidence. C best supports the author's views on the arguments regarding embryonic stem cell research.

46) D
The passage discusses all three branches of stem cell research in no particular

chronological order. In fact, the author mentions, "In parallel to efforts in embryonic and induced pluripotent stem cell research and development, scientists and physicians in the field of adult stem cells," implying the research was simultaneous.

47) A
B best describes embryonic stem cells, C mixes stem cell types as adult stem cells are inexpensive but embryonic stem cells are dangerous, and D describes the safety of adult stem cells, but the author wouldn't label them insufficiently researched. The author would argue that adult stem cells are "cost-efficient and benign."

48) D
D contrasts adult stem cells to embryonic stem cells by stating that they are "inexpensive and have an excellent safety record," or "cost-efficient and benign."

49) B
The sentence likens research of embryonic and induced pluripotent stem cells to that of adult stem cells, so "similar" most nearly means "parallel" in this context.

50) A
The author exemplifies "hype and manipulation of public emotion" with statements like, "if you don't support embryonic stem cells, you are not supporting cures for terrible disease" and "stem cell researchers are baby killers," so A is the answer.

51) B
The author states that companies are highly valued as people are distracted by the "promise of curing incurable diseases," diverting funds from research methods proven to be safe and cost-efficient.

52) D
The author's attitude is best encapsulated in his hopeful final paragraph, ushering in a new era in the field of stem cells, "in which companies will be judged on clinical and financial practicality," an "optimistic" sentiment.

SECTION 2: WRITING AND LANGUAGE

PASSAGE: THE RISE OF YOGA IN THE UNITED STATES

1) C
This sentence includes a contrast, namely that the ancient history is largely "unknown" while the more recent history in the U.S. is "better documented." Therefore, we need a contrast word like "however" to connect the thoughts.

2) A
Two independent clauses need to be to be connected with either a semicolon, colon, or period, while an independent clause followed by a dependent one can be combined with a comma. Answer choice A is the only option that follows these punctuation rules correctly.

3) C
While this piece of information may be accurate, it interrupts the paragraph's focus on yoga with extraneous information about immigration to the United States.

4) D
Based on the other verbs in the sentence, we need the past perfect "has expanded" to convey that the expansion began in the past and continues into present day.

5) B
The rest of the paragraph discusses the debate about whether yoga has remained true to its roots. In other words, critics are "questioning the authenticity" of our western interpretation of yoga.

6) D
We can eliminate A because "one hand" always precedes "on the other hand," which is nowhere to be found in the passage. B is wrong because the outcome of becoming a vanity-driven pursuit is not a direct consequence of the first part of the sentence.

C is wrong because we don't know enough to say that this outcome is not surprising. The more general (and kind of boring) "in some ways" reflects the moderate tone of the sentence.

7) **C**
Thought it clarifies the definition of "asanas" and is therefore essential to the *meaning of the sentence, "or poses" is grammatically inessential because the sentence would be structurally sound without it. Therefore, it's an appositive and should be set aside with two commas.*

8) **B**
Based on standard usage, "cheap" can have a positive or negative connation, but to "cheapen" is always negative. Therefore, the words "negative" and "negatively" are redundant and should be eliminated.

9) **C**
This sentence is posed as a question, so we can eliminate answer choices A and D. Between the remaining choices, C is the more concise and therefore the correct answer.

10) **C**
This question requires us to consider how we use these words, which should help eliminate A and B. C is the best choice between the remaining answers because "evolve" simply means to change while "advance" means to change in a way that makes things better. The following sentence makes clear that we are just talking about change v. no change, not necessarily change that we would describe as progress.

11) **A**
The pronoun in question modifies the noun "life," which is singular. "It's" is a contraction for "it is," so the possessive "its" is the correct answer.

PASSAGE: THE SHARED BENEFITS OF PAID FAMILY LEAVE

12) **D**
What is the argument that follows? It's that the benefits of family leave are well-established.

13) **B**
"Emotional connectivity" is a singular noun and the verb "increases" tells us that we are speaking in the present tense. Thus, the singular, present tense "leads" is correct.

14) **D**
"Also," "additionally," and "as well"? They all mean the same thing! D is the only choice without a redundant word or phrase.

15) **C**
On the SAT, dashes almost always come in pairs. Do you see the first dash after "Estonia"? That's a huge clue that we are looking for its long-lost buddy.

16) **A**
This transitional phrase needs to correctly convey the contrast between countries that provide generous family leave with those that do not. "On the other end of the spectrum" does this perfectly.

17) **B**
Harm is inherently negative, yes? Okay, so then answer choices A and C are wrong because they are redundant. D is a hot mess of wordiness, so we're left with B: simple, short, and SAT-approved.

18) **C**
A is tempting because it looks like an appositive clause, but take it out of the sentence and what happens? The sentence is no longer a complete sentence. B is incorrect because the verb "revealing" makes the newly-created second sentence grammatically incorrect, and D is just weird. Once again, the SAT votes for the choice with no punctuation at all.

19) D
When given the chance to DELETE, take it! It's not always the correct answer, but as the SAT prefers shorter, simpler answer choices, it's never a bad bet.

20) D
Is the word "however" more closely connected to the first clause or the second? I'd say it's the second (Ex: I am not a scientist. However, even I know that if I jump off my roof I'm more liable to fall than fly.) That means the top two choices here are C and D. The semicolon and the period are interchangeable, so let's look at the comma (or lack thereof) after "however." If you'd insert a comma after "however" at the beginning of a sentence (and generally you would), you'd do so after the same word at the beginning of any independent clause.

21) B
This clause is all about "net positive gain." B most directly and specifically makes this point.

22) C
If what they want is accurate, conventional, and academic, C is the only answer choice that is consistent both with the main idea and tone of the passage.

PASSAGE: EVERYDAY APPLICATIONS OF NUCLEAR ENERGY

23) A
Idiomatically, the phrase "capable of" is correct. Between A and C, only A correctly includes the verb "harnessing."

24) C
Only "released" combines the correct verb tense with the meaning we are looking for.

25) D
"Coincided" and "simultaneously" mean the same thing as do "beginning" and "onset." Only D removes all redundant words from the phrase.

26) D
The sentence in question, while interesting, is irrelevant to the topic at hand and interrupts the flow of thought.

27) C
The rest of this paragraph deals with the ways in which we might not recognize the impact of nuclear energy in our daily lives. C provides the most direct introduction to this discussion.

28) A
Let's use commas to punctuate a list!

29) B
"Increasing" needs to match "changing," but what the word "in" is trying to accomplish in answer choice C is anybody's guess.

30) B
This question is testing your knowledge of the rules of parallelism when creating a list.

31) A
Sentence 6 provides an example of the idea expressed in sentence 5.

32) D
Look at the tense of the other verb "is" in the sentence. Almost always, the verb in question should match in tense.

33) A
Sentence 1 introduces the idea that water is important. We can't talk about water in depth before we've introduced it as an issue, can we? Nope, so this sentence should stay right where it is.

PASSAGE: THE PILTDOWN MAN HOAX

34) A
More *what?* Great question. This sentence is unclear unless we specify that it's more *people*. Between C and D, only D sets off the grammatically inessential clause as required.

35) D
We have two possessives in a row here. First, the object has a finder, requiring us to use the singular possessive "its." But the finder

himself possesses an ability. He is a singular finder, so the singular possessive "finder's" is the correct choice.

36) B
The key phrases in this question stem are "specific detail" and "support for Dawson's claim." Dawson's claim is that he found the "missing link" between humans and apes, and since C and D have nothing to do with the idea of a missing link, we can get rid of 'em. Answer choice A supports this claim but is far less specific than B.

37) B
Sentence 5 is about the scientific beliefs of the English scientific establishment at the time, and sentence 6 is about the cultural beliefs of this same group of people. B most directly sets up both sentences and is therefore the best choice.

38) A
If you answered the previous question correctly, this question almost answers itself. If you missed the last one, you could use this question to reverse engineer your answer to the previous question, almost as you can on the reading test for the questions that ask, "which choice provides the best evidence for the answer the previous question?"

39) D
This is one of those questions on the SAT where you just have to choose the least crappy answer. No one loves D. NO ONE. However, the other choices- through varying combinations of awkward wording and bad punctuation- are worse.

40) C
Let's fight the "than v. then" battle first, shall we? (By the way, have you noticed that every time we do this "then" is wrong? That's not a coincidence.) A and C have us deciding between "no less than" and "no more than." If the point is that this object wasn't nearly as old as its owner proclaimed, it could not have been "more than" 100,000 years old.

41) C
Once again, we've got to think about the meaning of these words in relation to the sentences they connect. "Essentially" is the only option that means what we need it to mean.

42) A
Keep it academic, baby! Answer choices B, C, and D are all too wordy and informal to be the answer the SAT wants.

43) B
The phrase "but merely his most famous" tells us that this hoax was "neither his first nor his last". "Neither" and "nor" are sworn blood brothers, and nothing can tear them asunder.

44) A
This is one more example of the SAT's attempt to sneak some vocab into the Writing and Language Test. The dictionary defines the word analysis as a "detailed examination of the elements or structure of something, typically as a basis for discussion or interpretation." That's what we want, isn't it? While the other three answer choices come close to this definition, none hits it so squarely on the head as "analysis."

SECTION 3: MATH - NO CALCULATOR

1) D
Make a table of values to get started here. Week 1 is 3 miles a day, week 2 is 4 miles, week 3 is 5, etc. You can see a relationship there: the mileage per day is always two bigger than the week number. So the mileage in week n must be $n + 2$ per day. To find the total mileage for the week, simply multiply that by 7: $7(n + 2)$.

2) C
You know algebra, so do your thing. Carefully solve for x. You should get -2. Then plug that value back into $6x - 1$. Mind your negative signs and you'll get $6(-2) - 1 = -13$.

3

3) A

I recommend rewriting this as "x to the 2nd power raised to the $\frac{1}{4}$ power." That's what roots are, fractional exponents. Once you have $(x^2)^{\frac{1}{4}}$, you can use your exponent properties to simplify to $x^{\frac{2}{4}} = x^{\frac{1}{2}}$. And $x^{\frac{1}{2}}$ is another way of expressing a square root, so $\sqrt{x}$ is the answer.

4) B

Think through this equation in a narrative sort of way. Here's what I mean: you want your brain to say, "OK, if I multiply the total number of orchestra members by 0.25, I should get 35, the number of violinists." That sentence IS the equation. When you can say it, you can write the equation: $0.25x = 35$.

5) C

Just a careful reading question. Make sure you get the right bird, and make sure you give the answer the SAT wants! Orioles over total, so $\frac{7}{16}$.

6) D

What does collinear mean? It means "sharing the same line." Essentially, they've got to be the same equation to make that happen. Get rid of the ones you know are NOT the same line. Answer A, for instance... those are parallel lines, not the same line. Answer B is wrong because the two lines have different slopes. Answer C, if you simplify it or move it around, will reveal that the lines have different slopes and are therefore different. We're left with D, which does not LOOK like the equations are the same...but do a little algebraic manipulation and you'll see that they are. Multiply the top equation by -3 and the bottom one by 2. Boom! Same equation! Collinearity! Which is not a word.

7) D

I love questions that LOOK more complex than they are. Here, you just want to count the x's. You don't even need or want to simplify these fully. The highest power of x in the first equation is going to be 5, because we'll have an x^2 times an x^3. Highest power in B is 4, highest power in C is also 4...leaving D as the one with a highest power of 3.

8) A

My favorite trick on this question is to realize that you can treat $\frac{r}{s}$ as one value rather than two values. Just solve for it as a whole. Here's what I mean. Start by plugging in 12 for x and 3 for y. Now you've got $3 = \frac{r}{s}(12) - 5$. Simplify. $8 = 12\left(\frac{r}{s}\right)$. $\frac{2}{3} = \frac{r}{s}$. Done. Don't need to find r, or s. You CAN'T find them, in fact, but we don't need to, because we already have what we want.

9) D

Make life easy on yourself! Notice that in the diagram the dot is empty, not filled in. That means we want to include the endpoint, which means we want a > or <, not a ≥ or ≤. Now simplify C and D, the two answers left after we apply that clue. C gives you $z > 3$. D gives you $x > -3$ (don't forget to flip the sign when you multiply by -3). Must be D!

10) C

Start from the roots. We know that $(x + 5)$ and $(x + 1)$ must be roots of this function. Now FOIL those together. When you plug $x = -3$ into that function $(x^2 + 6x + 5)$, do you get -8? Nope, you get -4. We need to double that, by adding a factor of 2 out front. Answer C is that option—the same function, just twice as big.

11) B

That angle DCA is an exterior angle...find the interior angle by subtracting 104 degrees from 180. Now we know two interior angles, 76 and 60, which leaves 44 degrees for our last angle in the triangle.

12) C

Complete The Square! Complete The Square! Say it with me this time! Yeah, we really do need to complete the square. If we had our calculators, we could just graph it and find the minimum. Alas. Step one of the CTS process is to create a perfect square: $x^2 - 6x + 9 + 31 - 9$. Notice the -9 at the end? I have to subtract that because I added it on earlier.

Just playing around with the expression without changing its value. Next, factor and simplify: $(x - 3)^2 + 22$. That's it. We have our parabola in vertex form, and the vertex is $(3, 22)$.

13) C

Bad news: you want to do polynomial long division on this bad boy. And since polynomial long division is much easier to show than to describe, here's how you would do it:

$$\begin{array}{r} 7x + 5 + \frac{17}{2x-3} \\ 2x - 3 \overline{\smash{)}\,14x^2 - 11x + 2} \\ -(14x^2 - 21x) \\ \hline 10x + 2 \\ 10x - 15 \\ \hline 17 \end{array}$$

14) C

Another problem that really needs a visual solution, this time using the quadratic equation. Just move all the terms to one side, then use that quadratic formula and simplify carefully. Watch:

$$2x^2 - 4x + 7 = 0$$

$$a = 2$$
$$b = -4$$
$$c = 7$$

$$x = \frac{-(-4) \pm \sqrt{(-4)^2 - 4(2)(7)}}{2(2)}$$

$$= \frac{4 \pm \sqrt{-40}}{4}$$

$$= 1 \pm \frac{i\sqrt{4}\sqrt{10}}{4}$$

$$= 1 \pm \frac{i\sqrt{10}}{2}$$

15) B

Wordy question that can be solved in a couple of ways. The long way is to look up the formula for the volume of a cylinder in the reference information. Plug in a value for h, calculate volume of the first storage container, then double the radius, calculate the NEW volume, and compare the two values you found. The new cylinder should have four times the volume. The OTHER way to do it is to think about the formula. The height stays the same and the only change that gets made is that the radius doubles. In the formula, the radius gets squared. If you multiply that value by 2 then square it, the effect will be that the volume is now $4x$ as great. You get more bang for your buck when you change the radius because of the fact that it gets squared in the formula.

16) 7

Exponent properties. Think about multiplying x^3 by x^4. What do you get? x^7. That's the answer to the question—the highest power will be 7.

17) 3/4, 0.25

Exponent and root properties. This is the same as $(x^3)^{\frac{1}{4}}$. Multiply those exponents together and you'll get $x^{\frac{3}{4}}$, so $\frac{3}{4}$ is the answer to the question.

18) 12

Ah, similar triangles, with their equal angles and proportional sides. Set up a little proportion here. $\frac{AB}{DE} = \frac{BC}{EC}$. $\frac{18}{x} = \frac{24}{16}$. Cross multiply, and $x = 12$.

19) 20

Fun with linear equations. Move this thing around until you're in $y = mx + b$ format. Your b value will be equal to $\frac{860}{43}$, which is 20.

20) $\frac{7}{25}$, 0.28

Helpful to know the "Pythagorean triple" 7-24-25. If you don't know it, you could find it manually. But who has time for that? Anyway, once you know the hypotenuse is 25, you use your Soh-Cah-Toa knowledge and put the adjacent leg, 7, over the hypotenuse, 25. Voila! $\frac{7}{25}$.

3

SECTION 4: MATH – CALCULATOR

1) B

These step graphs are kinda strange, aren't they? To get a price for 1.5 hours, find that bar between 1 and 2 and read the y-value. It's \$9, right? Well, that's the answer.

2) A

When multiple things have to happen for you to win a game, you can find the probability of winning the WHOLE game by multiplying together the probability of each individual outcome. Here's a less wordy way of saying that: you need to get heads three times in a row. The probability of getting heads on a single flip is $\frac{1}{2}$. The probability of doing it three times in a row is $\frac{1}{2} \times \frac{1}{2} \times \frac{1}{2} = \frac{1}{8}$.

3) A

Let's interpret equation narratively, shall we? Look at that point (10, 40)—it's where the functions intersect, the function for cost and the function for income. When costs equal income, that is break-even; you've made exactly as much as you've spent. After that, you start to make profit. Hooray profit!

4) B

Systems of equations have infinite solutions when the functions overlap exactly—when they are the same function, essentially. Our job here is to find the one that is NOT the same. A good clue as to why B is the winner is that it has the SAME x-coefficient (-2) as the first equation, but a different y-coefficient. If you rearrange that equation and the first equation into the convenient $y = mx + b$ format, you'll see that they are indeed different. That makes B the right answer. The other three, if you're in the mood for "fun with math," can all be shown to be the exact same as the first equation.

5) C

Let's turn words into numbers. 15% of the bill was \$50.40. In math terms, that's $0.15x = 50.40$, where x is the amount on the bill. Solve for x by dividing both sides by 0.15 and you'll get $x = 336$, the answer!

6) D

The most important thing on this little algebra question is to make sure you deliver what the SAT is asking you to deliver. Know what I mean? You could solve for x if you wanted and get $x = 6$. Notice how that's an answer choice too. It's just not the right answer. Plug that $x = 6$ back into $2x - 2$ to get the right answer, $2(6) - 2 = 10$.

7) A

Who loves cross multiplying? I do! And I might be the only one, but I will stand by my irrationally strong feelings. When you cross multiply here, you'll get $11 \times 17 = 374m$. Use your calculator from there, and you'll find that $m = 0.5$.

8) 8 C

Gotta know your interest formula on this one. It's $A = P(1 + r)^t$, where P is your principal investment, r is the interest rate expressed as a decimal, and t is the number of years. Once you know the formula, the question is awfully easy. The answer will be \$1,688.

9) A

All unit conversion, all the time. I would go about it this way: $150 \text{ bracelets} \times \frac{35 \text{ min}}{1 \text{ bracelet}} \times \frac{1 \text{ hour}}{60 \text{ min}} \times \frac{1 \text{ day}}{8 \text{ hours}} = 10.9375 \text{ days} = \text{about } 11$ days.

10) B

More unit conversion! Multiply 3×10^6 km/hr $\times \frac{1 \text{ hr}}{60 \text{ min}}$ and you'll find yourself with 50,000 km/min.

11) C

And a little more unit conversion because why not. 3×10^6 km/hr $\times \frac{.62 \text{ miles}}{1 \text{ km}} =$ 1,860,000 miles/hr. Please use your calculator!

12) D

There is a shortcut on this question, and that is recognizing that the function has a "double-root" at $x = -3$. I know that because the function had a relative maximum at that point. Put more simply, it bounced off the x-axis at -3, which means it actually had two roots there. That means we need $(x + 3)$ as a factor in the function TWICE. Which choice does? D. Graph it on your calculator to confirm that it's right. It is.

13) A

Use your knowledge of roots and exponents to rewrite this bad boy, first as $V = a^2 \times b^{\frac{1}{6}}$. Divide both sides by a^2, then raise both sides to the 6th power, and you'll be left with $\frac{V^6}{a^{12}} = b$. And that's what we want.

14) D

You could write this formula yourself, or you could try the answer choices out. I think I'd use the latter method on the test. Pick a specific term, say the 2nd one, 18. When you plug in 2 as the n value, you need to get 18 as the term's value. Only choice D will deliver.

15) A

I've got a fun hack on this question that involves your TI graphing calculator. If you have one of those (and if you don't have one of those, get one), press the "stat" button to get to the statistics menu. Press "Edit." Choose L1, and punch in all the values for temperatures in Palm Springs. (For the record, I've been in Palm Springs when it was HOTTER than this...). Press "stat" again, and from the CALC menu, choose "1-Var Stats." Press Calculate. That'll give you the mean (that's the x with the line above it) of 101.6666, and the median of 101.5. And that'll answer the question! Alternately, you could do the work by hand. If you do that, I would start with the mode, which is clearly 101. That gets you down to A and D. Then find the mean. You can probably guess that the mean is bigger than 100, but if you compute then you'll KNOW that it is. Then you'll definitely choose A.

16) A

We are back to completing the square, which, you know what? It's not nearly as bad as it first seemed. Group your x terms and your y terms first, and move the rest over to the right side of the equation: $x^2 - 2x + y^2 + 6y = -3$. Now create your perfect square trinomials by taking half of the coefficient in front of the x and y and squaring it, then adding that value to both sides of the equation: $(x^2 - 2x + 1) + (y^2 + 6y + 9) = -3 + 1 + 9$. Now factor and simplify: $(x - 1)^2 + (y + 3)^2 = 7$. Last thing: since the right side of the circle equation is r^2(radius squared), let's express that side as $(\sqrt{7})^2$. Now we can see the coordinates of the center $(1, -3)$ and the radius $\sqrt{7}$ as plain as day.

17) C

This question is just about staying patient and making sure to answer the question that's being asked. You can either ballpark the differences between 2015 and 2016 and answer based on that estimate, or you can use your calculator to find those differences. I would recommend the latter approach; sure, it takes 15 extra seconds, but it basically guarantees that you're going to get this right. The winner is Yosemite at a difference of 878,651.

18) B

The questions asks for the park that showed the *least* growth as measured by percent change. Do you think the percent change part is going to be important? Me too. Let's start calculating percent changes. We can ignore Yosemite since it's not one of the answer choices (but don't ignore Yosemite in real life—it's amazing!). To find percent change, we *put* the amount of change over the original amount and multiply by 100. Do that carefully for all four parks in the answer choices, and you'll see that, by a narrow margin (8.1% for Grand Canyon, 8.7% for Rocky Mountain), Grand Canyon showed the least amount of growth. Notice that by AMOUNT of growth, Rocky Mountain had the least growth. But that's not the question you had to answer.

19) C

Start by converting feet to inches here. That tennis court is 432 inches wide and 936 inches long. Now convert those values using the ratio. You could set up a proportion, like $\frac{x}{436} = \frac{1}{18}$ and $\frac{x}{936} = \frac{1}{18}$. When you solve those, you'll get $x = 24$ and $x = 52$, the proportions for our mini tennis court (aka a ping pong table).

20) B

Man, you really have to mind the details on these stats questions. Statement I does not HAVE to be true because of the margin of error. 56 percent is a pretty good estimate, but it isn't necessarily the exact value. Statement II is true—we asked likely voters who were randomly selected, and we asked a TON of them. When 58 percent of them said they would vote for the governor today, even with a 3 percent margin of error, the governor has the support of at least 55% of the population. That's a winning formula for getting elected! Statement III does not have to be true, again because of the margin of error. It could be that 59% approve of the job s/he is doing and 55% would vote for him/her. We don't know, which is why statement III does not have to be true.

21) D

Write two equations, one for Pedro and one for Andrew. $P = 100(1.15)^x$, and $A = 350 - 6x$. Now, either set those two equations equal and solve, or graph them and find the point of intersection. The year when they will be closest to the same is 8 either way.

22) D

Do you remember doing factor trees? Basically, you keep pulling out prime factors until you can't pull out any more. Here, that would look like this:

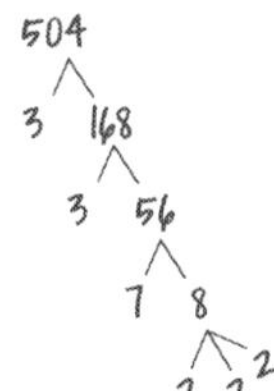

And when you group those factors together, you'd be left with $2^3 \times 3^2 \times 7$.

23) A

Fun with trig identities. Since this little equation is equal to 1, and because $\sin^2$ and $\cos^2$ are involved, well, we know that the angle value must stay the same. That's why M has to equal 32.

24) D

I turned the ratio into a decimal. There are 10 total parts of raisin bran, and 7 of those parts are bran flakes. So $\frac{7}{10}$ of the mixture is bran, or 0.7. Multiply that decimal value by the total amount, 12 oz., and get the answer: 8.4 oz.

25) B

You want to find the dimensions of each face and carefully add them together. You've got two triangular faces that have base and height of 3 and 4, so that's $2 \times \left(\frac{1}{2} \times 3 \times 4\right) = 12$. Then you have three separate rectangular faces that measure 3×15, 4×15, and 5×15. Multiply those together, add them up, add on the 12, and you'll get the total surface area of 192.

26) C

You've got a few different ways to do this. The easiest would be to graph them on your calculator and look for the one with a vertex at $x = -2$. Another way would be to complete the square...four times. OK, I don't mind completing the square, but I don't like it enough to do it FOUR TIMES on one problem. The best way to do it mathematically would be to use the $-\frac{b}{2a}$ trick... the fact that the x-coordinate of the vertex of a parabola is always at $-\frac{b}{2a}$. In answer choice C, that would be $\frac{8}{(-2 \times 2)} = -2$, which is just what we want.

27) B

You'll need to know how to find the number of degrees in an n-sided polygon. You can divide a shape into triangles and then multiply the number of triangles by 180. Or you can memorize the formula $(n - 2) \times 180$. Or you can remember that every polygon's exterior angles add up to 360. However you do it, the number of degrees in a pentagon will be 540. Subtract the angles we know to get to the one we don't, which you'll find to be 110 degrees.

28) B

Sweet—we can do synthetic division on this one. FYI, you can only use synthetic division when the lead coefficient, the one in front of the x you're dividing by, is 1. And it is here, so let's go. Here's what it looks like:

5	1	-2	-13	-10
		3	15	10
	1	3	2	0

$x^2 + 3x + 2$

And those numbers at the bottom are the coefficients of the right answer.

29) D

Draw a "line of best fit" here. That's a line (not a squiggle... an actual straight line) that drives down the middle of the points as best as possible. Now pick a point that's close to the line, like, say, (4, 8000). Now plug that value into the answer choices to see which formula fits that point the best. If more than one seem like they work, try another point, like (7, 3,000). Once you test that point, you'll see that D is the best fit for the data in the graph.

30) D

Our favorite trick for exponent problems is to change the bases so that the match. We'll do that here, then set the exponents. THEN, it turns into a quadratic. They are making us work here. Watch and see:

$$4^{x^2 + 4x} = 2^{-6}$$

$$(2^2)^{x^2 + 4x} = 2^{-6}$$

$$2^{2x^2 + 8x} = 2^{-6}$$

$$2x^2 + 8x = -6$$

$$2x^2 + 8x + 6 = 0$$

$$2(x^2 + 4x + 3) = 0$$

$$2(x + 3)(x + 1) = 0$$

$$\boxed{x = -3, -1}$$

31) 22

Don't be afraid of inequalities; just simplify them the same way you simplify equations. Only exception is that when you multiply or divide by a negative, you flip the way the inequality sign is pointing. That happens here, and we end up with $y \geq 21.25$. If y has to be an integer, then 22 is the least value it can be.

32) 218

Put these guys in order from least to greatest before you find the median. When you do, you'll have TWO middle terms, 212 and 224. The median is the average of those two: $\frac{212 + 224}{2} = 218$.

33) 105

Turn this sentence into an equation, which quickly turns into a quadratic equation: $x^2 + 3x = 11,340$. Use your favorite technique to solve from there. Mine is to use a quadratic program on the calculator, which very quickly tells me that $x = -108$ and 105. Since we want the positive one, the answer is 105.

34) 210

To convert radians to degrees, multiply by the unit $\frac{180 \text{ degrees}}{\pi \text{ radians}}$. Do that here and you'll end up with what you want: 210 degrees.

35) 79.2

Pie charts are always a matter of finding what part of 360 degrees you want to devote to a sector. Here, you can either set up a proportion: $\frac{22\%}{100\%} = \frac{x \text{ degrees}}{360 \text{ degrees}}$. Or you can find 22% of 360. Either way, you'll get exactly 79.2, which is exactly the right answer.

36) $\frac{3}{5}$, 0.6

What is a in this equation? The slope, right? I highly recommend you find the slope based on what are called "lattice points"—points that clearly and cross a clear point of intersection on the grid. Here, two of those are (-5, -7) and (0, -4). Find the slope between those two: $\frac{-4-(-7)}{0-(-5)} = \frac{3}{5}$.

37) 308

Split the payment between regular time and bonus time. The employee will make $35 \times \$7$ for the first 35 hours, then 6×10.50 for the extra 6 hours. That adds up to $308.

38) 56

This employee really brought it last week! From that total of $465.50, subtract the regular time pay of $35 \times \$7$. That leaves $220.50 in bonus payment. Divide that by the bonus rate of $10.50 to find that the worker put in 21 hours on top of the regular 35. Last step: add the 21 to the 35 to find that the worker put in a total of 56 hours last week.

Tutor Ted®

SAT Practice Test 4

Multiple Choice Answer Sheet

SAT

TEST 1: READING

1 ⒶⒷⒸⒹ	9 ⒶⒷⒸⒹ	17 ⒶⒷⒸⒹ	25 ⒶⒷⒸⒹ	33 ⒶⒷⒸⒹ	41 ⒶⒷⒸⒹ	49 ⒶⒷⒸⒹ
2 ⒶⒷⒸⒹ	10 ⒶⒷⒸⒹ	18 ⒶⒷⒸⒹ	26 ⒶⒷⒸⒹ	34 ⒶⒷⒸⒹ	42 ⒶⒷⒸⒹ	50 ⒶⒷⒸⒹ
3 ⒶⒷⒸⒹ	11 ⒶⒷⒸⒹ	19 ⒶⒷⒸⒹ	27 ⒶⒷⒸⒹ	35 ⒶⒷⒸⒹ	43 ⒶⒷⒸⒹ	51 ⒶⒷⒸⒹ
4 ⒶⒷⒸⒹ	12 ⒶⒷⒸⒹ	20 ⒶⒷⒸⒹ	28 ⒶⒷⒸⒹ	36 ⒶⒷⒸⒹ	44 ⒶⒷⒸⒹ	52 ⒶⒷⒸⒹ
5 ⒶⒷⒸⒹ	13 ⒶⒷⒸⒹ	21 ⒶⒷⒸⒹ	29 ⒶⒷⒸⒹ	37 ⒶⒷⒸⒹ	45 ⒶⒷⒸⒹ	
6 ⒶⒷⒸⒹ	14 ⒶⒷⒸⒹ	22 ⒶⒷⒸⒹ	30 ⒶⒷⒸⒹ	38 ⒶⒷⒸⒹ	46 ⒶⒷⒸⒹ	
7 ⒶⒷⒸⒹ	15 ⒶⒷⒸⒹ	23 ⒶⒷⒸⒹ	31 ⒶⒷⒸⒹ	39 ⒶⒷⒸⒹ	47 ⒶⒷⒸⒹ	
8 ⒶⒷⒸⒹ	16 ⒶⒷⒸⒹ	24 ⒶⒷⒸⒹ	32 ⒶⒷⒸⒹ	40 ⒶⒷⒸⒹ	48 ⒶⒷⒸⒹ	

TEST 2: WRITING AND LANGUAGE

1 ⒶⒷⒸⒹ	8 ⒶⒷⒸⒹ	15 ⒶⒷⒸⒹ	22 ⒶⒷⒸⒹ	29 ⒶⒷⒸⒹ	36 ⒶⒷⒸⒹ	43 ⒶⒷⒸⒹ
2 ⒶⒷⒸⒹ	9 ⒶⒷⒸⒹ	16 ⒶⒷⒸⒹ	23 ⒶⒷⒸⒹ	30 ⒶⒷⒸⒹ	37 ⒶⒷⒸⒹ	44 ⒶⒷⒸⒹ
3 ⒶⒷⒸⒹ	10 ⒶⒷⒸⒹ	17 ⒶⒷⒸⒹ	24 ⒶⒷⒸⒹ	31 ⒶⒷⒸⒹ	38 ⒶⒷⒸⒹ	
4 ⒶⒷⒸⒹ	11 ⒶⒷⒸⒹ	18 ⒶⒷⒸⒹ	25 ⒶⒷⒸⒹ	32 ⒶⒷⒸⒹ	39 ⒶⒷⒸⒹ	
5 ⒶⒷⒸⒹ	12 ⒶⒷⒸⒹ	19 ⒶⒷⒸⒹ	26 ⒶⒷⒸⒹ	33 ⒶⒷⒸⒹ	40 ⒶⒷⒸⒹ	
6 ⒶⒷⒸⒹ	13 ⒶⒷⒸⒹ	20 ⒶⒷⒸⒹ	27 ⒶⒷⒸⒹ	34 ⒶⒷⒸⒹ	41 ⒶⒷⒸⒹ	
7 ⒶⒷⒸⒹ	14 ⒶⒷⒸⒹ	21 ⒶⒷⒸⒹ	28 ⒶⒷⒸⒹ	35 ⒶⒷⒸⒹ	42 ⒶⒷⒸⒹ	

TEST 3: MATHEMATICS - NO CALCULATOR

1 ⒶⒷⒸⒹ	9 ⒶⒷⒸⒹ	16 □□□□	17 □□□□	18 □□□□	19 □□□□	20 □□□□
2 ⒶⒷⒸⒹ	10 ⒶⒷⒸⒹ	/ ⊘⊘⊘⊘	/ ⊘⊘⊘⊘	/ ⊘⊘⊘⊘	/ ⊘⊘⊘⊘	/ ⊘⊘⊘⊘
3 ⒶⒷⒸⒹ	11 ⒶⒷⒸⒹ	. ⊙⊙⊙⊙	. ⊙⊙⊙⊙	. ⊙⊙⊙⊙	. ⊙⊙⊙⊙	. ⊙⊙⊙⊙
4 ⒶⒷⒸⒹ	12 ⒶⒷⒸⒹ	0 ⓪⓪⓪⓪	0 ⓪⓪⓪⓪	0 ⓪⓪⓪⓪	0 ⓪⓪⓪⓪	0 ⓪⓪⓪⓪
5 ⒶⒷⒸⒹ	13 ⒶⒷⒸⒹ	1 ①①①①	1 ①①①①	1 ①①①①	1 ①①①①	1 ①①①①
6 ⒶⒷⒸⒹ	14 ⒶⒷⒸⒹ	2 ②②②②	2 ②②②②	2 ②②②②	2 ②②②②	2 ②②②②
7 ⒶⒷⒸⒹ	15 ⒶⒷⒸⒹ	3 ③③③③	3 ③③③③	3 ③③③③	3 ③③③③	3 ③③③③
8 ⒶⒷⒸⒹ		4 ④④④④	4 ④④④④	4 ④④④④	4 ④④④④	4 ④④④④
		5 ⑤⑤⑤⑤	5 ⑤⑤⑤⑤	5 ⑤⑤⑤⑤	5 ⑤⑤⑤⑤	5 ⑤⑤⑤⑤
		6 ⑥⑥⑥⑥	6 ⑥⑥⑥⑥	6 ⑥⑥⑥⑥	6 ⑥⑥⑥⑥	6 ⑥⑥⑥⑥
		7 ⑦⑦⑦⑦	7 ⑦⑦⑦⑦	7 ⑦⑦⑦⑦	7 ⑦⑦⑦⑦	7 ⑦⑦⑦⑦
		8 ⑧⑧⑧⑧	8 ⑧⑧⑧⑧	8 ⑧⑧⑧⑧	8 ⑧⑧⑧⑧	8 ⑧⑧⑧⑧
		9 ⑨⑨⑨⑨	9 ⑨⑨⑨⑨	9 ⑨⑨⑨⑨	9 ⑨⑨⑨⑨	9 ⑨⑨⑨⑨

TEST 4: MATHEMATICS - CALCULATOR ALLOWED

1 ⒶⒷⒸⒹ	6 ⒶⒷⒸⒹ	11 ⒶⒷⒸⒹ	16 ⒶⒷⒸⒹ	21 ⒶⒷⒸⒹ	26 ⒶⒷⒸⒹ	31 □□□□
2 ⒶⒷⒸⒹ	7 ⒶⒷⒸⒹ	12 ⒶⒷⒸⒹ	17 ⒶⒷⒸⒹ	22 ⒶⒷⒸⒹ	27 ⒶⒷⒸⒹ	/ ⊘⊘⊘⊘
3 ⒶⒷⒸⒹ	8 ⒶⒷⒸⒹ	13 ⒶⒷⒸⒹ	18 ⒶⒷⒸⒹ	23 ⒶⒷⒸⒹ	28 ⒶⒷⒸⒹ	. ⊙⊙⊙⊙
4 ⒶⒷⒸⒹ	9 ⒶⒷⒸⒹ	14 ⒶⒷⒸⒹ	19 ⒶⒷⒸⒹ	24 ⒶⒷⒸⒹ	29 ⒶⒷⒸⒹ	0 ⓪⓪⓪⓪
5 ⒶⒷⒸⒹ	10 ⒶⒷⒸⒹ	15 ⒶⒷⒸⒹ	20 ⒶⒷⒸⒹ	25 ⒶⒷⒸⒹ	30 ⒶⒷⒸⒹ	1 ①①①①
						2 ②②②②
						3 ③③③③
						4 ④④④④
						5 ⑤⑤⑤⑤
						6 ⑥⑥⑥⑥
						7 ⑦⑦⑦⑦
						8 ⑧⑧⑧⑧
						9 ⑨⑨⑨⑨

CONTINUE

SAT Practice Test 4

Multiple Choice Answer Sheet

TEST 4: MATHEMATICS - CALCULATOR ALLOWED *(continued)*

	32	33	34	35	36	37	38
/	(/)(/)(/)(/)	(/)(/)(/)(/)	(/)(/)(/)(/)	(/)(/)(/)(/)	(/)(/)(/)(/)	(/)(/)(/)(/)	(/)(/)(/)(/)
.	(.)(.)(.)(.)	(.)(.)(.)(.)	(.)(.)(.)(.)	(.)(.)(.)(.)	(.)(.)(.)(.)	(.)(.)(.)(.)	(.)(.)(.)(.)
0	(0)(0)(0)(0)	(0)(0)(0)(0)	(0)(0)(0)(0)	(0)(0)(0)(0)	(0)(0)(0)(0)	(0)(0)(0)(0)	(0)(0)(0)(0)
1	(1)(1)(1)(1)	(1)(1)(1)(1)	(1)(1)(1)(1)	(1)(1)(1)(1)	(1)(1)(1)(1)	(1)(1)(1)(1)	(1)(1)(1)(1)
2	(2)(2)(2)(2)	(2)(2)(2)(2)	(2)(2)(2)(2)	(2)(2)(2)(2)	(2)(2)(2)(2)	(2)(2)(2)(2)	(2)(2)(2)(2)
3	(3)(3)(3)(3)	(3)(3)(3)(3)	(3)(3)(3)(3)	(3)(3)(3)(3)	(3)(3)(3)(3)	(3)(3)(3)(3)	(3)(3)(3)(3)
4	(4)(4)(4)(4)	(4)(4)(4)(4)	(4)(4)(4)(4)	(4)(4)(4)(4)	(4)(4)(4)(4)	(4)(4)(4)(4)	(4)(4)(4)(4)
5	(5)(5)(5)(5)	(5)(5)(5)(5)	(5)(5)(5)(5)	(5)(5)(5)(5)	(5)(5)(5)(5)	(5)(5)(5)(5)	(5)(5)(5)(5)
6	(6)(6)(6)(6)	(6)(6)(6)(6)	(6)(6)(6)(6)	(6)(6)(6)(6)	(6)(6)(6)(6)	(6)(6)(6)(6)	(6)(6)(6)(6)
7	(7)(7)(7)(7)	(7)(7)(7)(7)	(7)(7)(7)(7)	(7)(7)(7)(7)	(7)(7)(7)(7)	(7)(7)(7)(7)	(7)(7)(7)(7)
8	(8)(8)(8)(8)	(8)(8)(8)(8)	(8)(8)(8)(8)	(8)(8)(8)(8)	(8)(8)(8)(8)	(8)(8)(8)(8)	(8)(8)(8)(8)
9	(9)(9)(9)(9)	(9)(9)(9)(9)	(9)(9)(9)(9)	(9)(9)(9)(9)	(9)(9)(9)(9)	(9)(9)(9)(9)	(9)(9)(9)(9)

TEST 5: ESSAY - OPTIONAL

If you are writing the essay, you may use the space below to plan and outline your work. Be sure to write the essay itself on the lined pages that follow.

SAT

SAT Practice Test 4
Essay Answer Sheet

BEGIN YOUR ESSAY HERE.

You may continue on the next page.

SAT Practice Test 4

Essay Answer Sheet

DO NOT WRITE OUTSIDE THE BOX.

You may continue on the next page.

SAT Practice Test 4

Essay Answer Sheet

BEGIN YOUR ESSAY HERE.

You may continue on the next page.

SAT Practice Test 4

Essay Answer Sheet

DO NOT WRITE OUTSIDE THE BOX.

SAT® Practice Test #4

IMPORTANT REMINDERS

1. A No. 2 pencil is required for the test. Do not use a mechanical pencil or pen.

2. Sharing any questions with anyone is a violation of Test Security and Fairness policies and may result in your scores being canceled.

This cover is representative of what you'll see on test day.

Reading Test

65 MINUTES, 52 QUESTIONS

Turn to Section 1 of your answer sheet to answer the questions in this section.

DIRECTIONS

Each passage or pair of passages below is followed by a number of questions. After reading each passage or pair, choose the best answer to each question based on what is stated or implied in the passage or passages and in any accompanying graphics (such as a table or graph).

Questions 1-10 are based on the following passage.

This passage is adapted from Bram Stoker, *Dracula*, originally published in 1897.

Dr. Seward's Diary

20 August.—The case of Renfield grows even more interesting. He has now so far quieted that there are spells of cessation from his passion. For the first week after his attack he was perpetually violent. Then one night, just as the moon rose, he grew quiet, and kept murmuring to himself: "Now I can wait; now I can wait." The attendant came to tell me, so I ran down at once to have a look at him. He was still in the strait-waistcoat and in the padded room, but the suffused look had gone from his face, and his eyes had something of their old pleading—I might almost say, "cringing"—softness. I was satisfied with his present condition, and directed him to be relieved. The attendants hesitated, but finally carried out my wishes without protest. It was a strange thing that the patient had humour enough to see their distrust, for, coming close to me, he said in a whisper, all the while looking furtively at them:—

"They think I could hurt you! Fancy me hurting you! The fools!"

It was soothing, somehow, to the feelings to find myself dissociated even in the mind of this poor madman from the others; but all the same I do not follow his thought. Am I to take it that I have anything in common with him, so that we are, as it were, to stand together; or has he to gain from me some good so stupendous that my well-being is needful to him? I must find out later on. Tonight he will not speak. He will only say: "I don't take any stock in cats. I have more to think of now, and I can wait; I can wait."

After a while I left him. The attendant tells me that he was quiet until just before dawn, and that then he began to get uneasy, and at length violent, until at last he fell into a paroxysm which exhausted him so that he swooned into a sort of coma.

Three nights has the same thing happened—violent all day then quiet from moonrise to sunrise. I wish I could get some clue to the cause. It would almost seem as if there was some influence which came and went. Happy thought! We shall tonight play sane wits against mad ones. He escaped before without our help; tonight he shall escape with it. We shall give him a chance, and have the men ready to follow in case they are required.

23 August.—"The unexpected always happens." How well Disraeli knew life. Our bird when he found the cage open would not fly, so all our subtle arrangements were for nought. At any rate, we have proved one thing; that the spells of quietness last a reasonable time. We shall in future be able to ease his bonds for a few hours each day. I have given orders to the night attendant merely to shut him in the padded room, when once he is quiet, until an hour before sunrise. The poor soul's body will enjoy the relief even if his mind cannot appreciate it. Hark! The unexpected again! I am called; the patient has once more escaped.

CONTINUE

1

Which choice best summarizes the passage?

A) A doctor journals ongoing interactions with a patient.
B) A psychologist complains of his assistants' incompetence.
C) A rare disease plagues a doctor of high influence's friend, Disraeli.
D) Confined in a mental health facility, a patient continually attempts escape.

2

As used in line 13, "relieved" most nearly means

A) calmed.
B) comforted.
C) released.
D) dismissed.

3

Unbeknownst to the narrator, the "influence which came and went" (line 38-39) is most likely connected to

A) the passing of time, night and day.
B) the patient's fluctuating straightjacket tightness.
C) the arrival and departure of beloved cats.
D) internal emotional turmoil within the patient.

4

Lines 21-24 ("It…thought") serve to paint the narrator as

A) relieved.
B) distant.
C) nonchalant.
D) arrogant.

5

The author includes lines 19-20 ("It…fools") in order to

A) suggest the doctor's physical strength.
B) display the patient's lack of control.
C) humanize the relationship between doctor and patient.
D) acknowledge the potential of the patient's behavior.

6

Which choice provides the best evidence for the answer to the previous question?

A) Lines 3-4 ("For…violent")
B) Lines 12-13 ("I…relieved")
C) Lines 13-15 ("The…protest")
D) Line 28 ("Tonight…speak")

7

As used in line 48, "spells" most nearly means

A) allures.
B) formulas.
C) charms.
D) intervals.

8

At the passage's end, the narrator's attitude toward the patient can best be described as increasingly

A) sympathetic.
B) playful.
C) irritated.
D) inquisitive.

9

Which choice provides the best evidence for the answer to the previous question?

A) Lines 42-43 ("We...required")
B) Lines 47-48 ("At...time")
C) Lines 52-54 ("The...it")
D) Lines 54-55 ("I...escaped")

10

The purpose of the final paragraph is to

A) foreshadow trouble, by way of the anecdote about the bird.
B) document Renfield's progress as time passes.
C) suggest the impossibility of curing the patient.
D) express the narrator's disbelief in the porous facility.

Questions 11-20 are based on the following passage and supplementary material.

This passage is adapted from Orlando Acosta, Ph.D. and Alejandro Chaparro, "Genetically Modified Food Crops and Public Health." ©2008 by Acta Biológica Colombiana, Universidad Nacional de Colombia.

Improving food crops to provide better nutrition for humans and livestock has been a major long-term aim of traditional breeding programs. Biofortification (an approach consisting of bred food crops producing high bio-available nutrient concentrations in some of their edible tissues) has been presented as a promising alternative for fighting malnutrition in poor countries. Iron, vitamin A, zinc, and iodine deficiencies are of the greatest public health importance as they represent a serious threat to the health and productivity of more than one-half of the world's population, women and children being most exposed to such micronutrient deficiencies. Vitamin A deficiency (VAD) is one of the leading causes of micronutrient malnutrition in less industrialized countries, annually causing about half a million children to become partially or totally blind, and claiming 3,000 lives every day. The World Health Organization (WHO) estimated that 254 million children were vitamin A deficient in 1995 and around 2.8 million children aged less than five were afflicted by xerophthalmia, a severe manifestation of VAD. About 45% of the children affected by VAD and xerophthalmia and the pregnant women having low or deficient vitamin A live in South and Southeast Asia where rice is a staple crop. Micronutrient intervention by fortifying staple foods has been found to be a major factor in reducing micronutrient deficiencies in developed countries.

Although breeding-based solutions to micronutrient deficiencies initially need substantial investment for their development, micronutrient-improved varieties can be grown and consumed during the years ahead without incurring greater additional cost. Transgenic technology has recently been used for producing genetically modified (GM) rice that produces high pro-vitamin A concentration, this being an example of direct benefit to the consumer by increasing micronutrient content in the crop edible parts. Staple mineral- and vitamin-dense foods represent a low-cost, sustainable strategy for reducing the percentage of micronutrient malnutrition. The most current Golden Rice, a variety of rice engineered to produce β-carotene (pro-vitamin A), has been further improved to produce 23 times more total carotenoids than previous versions.

GM crop critics commonly ignore the fact that conventionally bred varieties contain proteins and metabolites, which are eventually harmful for humans. Indeed, several conventional crop varieties have been removed from the market due to the severe toxic effects produced on humans. In the case of allergy to food, about 68% of children and 2-3% of the adult population present allergic reactions to food. Most food allergies are induced by peanuts, milk, eggs, tree nuts, and fish and crustaceans, although more than 160 foods and food-related substances have been identified as allergic reaction inducers. All known food crop allergens are contained in conventionally modified crops. By contrast to GM crops, conventional crops have not been routinely tested for toxic or allergic effects on consumers prior to their commercial release, disregarding that traditionally bred food may contain natural toxins, anti-nutrients, and carcinogenic compounds.

Biofortification of currently accepted food crops, together with transgenic technology and conventional breeding, could offer a sustainable alternative to malnutrition affecting many millions of people (mainly children) around the world. Biofortification through GM crops represents a potential complement to current supplement and fortification programs and campaigns. Rather than causing new food safety problems, food crops developed until now have shown their potential for improving the nutritional quality of food and feed. Developing more nutritious food by using transgenic technology may contribute towards reducing the number of undernourished people in the world; however, policies and strategies aimed at increasing the income of people living below the poverty line must also be developed. A growing world population critically needs the effective contribution of science and technology for increasing the global food supply. Non-scientific disputes concerning GM crops could result in serious consequences for agricultural policy, food security, and world trade.

The following graph details US rates of planted genetically engineered crops between 1996-2003.

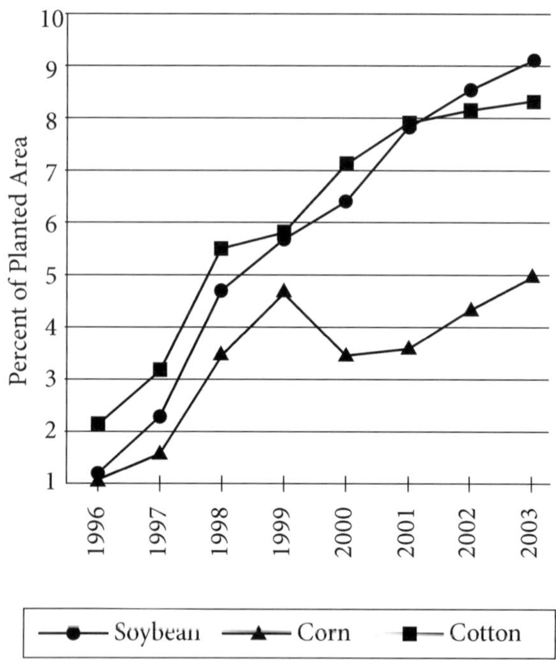

Herbicide resistant crops in US.
Source: Colorado State University

11

The main purpose of this passage is to

A) present the dangers of malnutrition and VAD faced around the world.

B) challenge the stigma of cultivating genetically modified foods.

C) offer a cost-effective, scientific strategy to combat malnutrition.

D) offer an alternative food source to traditionally harvested crops.

12

As used in line 3, "aim" most nearly means

A) design.

B) goal.

C) wish.

D) grail.

13

The main purpose of the third paragraph is to

A) counter critiques of GM food based on its strict testing.

B) argue for the replacement of conventional crops by GM foods.

C) caution against conventional crops' use due to high allergen concentrations.

D) suggest those prone to allergies stay away from GM foods.

14

Data in the graph indicate that the genetically modified crop which experienced the largest growth in production over two years was

A) cotton from 1997 to 1999.

B) soybean from 1997 to 1999.

C) corn from 2001 to 2003.

D) cotton from 1999 to 2001.

15

In the first paragraph, lines 13-25 ("Vitamin…crop") best serve to

A) criticize India's reliance on food that lacks basic nutritional value.

B) analyze the social impact of VAD on the undernourished.

C) introduce the WHO's problem of getting resources to South and Southeast Asia.

D) establish a connection between malnutrition and VAD.

16

In lines 45-47 ("GM…humans"), the authors address critics of the GM food movement to

A) provide evidence of a counter-argument.
B) undermine the research of their argument.
C) examine the shortcomings of their argument.
D) attack their argument as unscientific.

17

The authors' tone in the third paragraph can best be described as

A) accusatory.
B) critical.
C) defensive.
D) insensitive.

18

In the passage, the authors' chief intention is to

A) provide a purely scientific narrative regarding GM food.
B) present the dangers in conventionally grown food.
C) argue against GM food's acceptance worldwide.
D) suggest GM food should be the world's primary nutrient source.

19

Which choice provides the best evidence for the answer to the previous question?

A) Lines 25-28 ("Micronutrient…countries")
B) Lines 52-56 ("Most…inducers")
C) Lines 58-63 ("By…compounds")
D) Lines 81-84 ("Non-scientific…trade")

20

Which statement is best supported by the data presented in the graph?

A) Farmers' recent reliance on cotton and soybean has caused decreased production of corn from 2000 to 2003.
B) From 2000 to 2003, the majority of soybeans and cotton planted by farmers in the USA consisted of genetically engineered plans.
C) Since 1996, farmers invested more of their fields in cotton but had to switch some plots to soybean due to a shortage of seed in 2001.
D) Prices of soybean, cotton, and corn plummeted in 1999, causing the highest spike in production of all three plants.

Questions 21-30 are based on the following passage and supplementary material.

This passage is adapted from Jaime Jiménez, "How Third World Countries Can Take Advantage of Globalization - A Mexican Experience in Learning and Research," a chapter of Zlatan Delic's *Globalization and Responsibility.* CC BY 3.0 license 2012.

The world is experiencing an enormous acceleration in the interchange of goods and services due in great part to globalization in general and the globalization of the economy in particular. As we progress into the 21st century, it becomes clear that people's advancement is strongly tied to the way we acquire and apply knowledge. Countries with advanced technology have a competitive advantage over those whose technology is lagging behind. Since the end of the 20th century, it became fashionable to assert that society as a whole was approaching a new era, the era of knowledge. Every human activity would be permeated by the knowledge used, either currently available worldwide or produced within some organizational bounds. Indeed, the most important factor for the progress of the world's inhabitants is neither capital nor labor force but the knowledge they put into their products and services. However, not all the progress related to the explosion of the information and communication technologies has been of disadvantage for Mexico and other countries south of the US.

A number of university professors in Mexico not involved in "mainstream" science took advantage of some features of globalization to help non-conventional students get PhDs in science. By putting into practice an innovative way of learning, researchers aimed to prepare new scientists and concurrently solve specific research problems detected by the students in their own geographic regions. Convinced that the education imparted in universities was not conducive to student learning, they created the Innovation and Educational Development Center (CIDE) in the 1980s. The CIDE model is an eclectic amalgam of several advanced proposals that emerged from innovative, new, and alternative education models: open education, teaching at a distance, and problem-based learning.

This method considers the students' heterogeneity of conditions, which makes it necessary to design nonuniform programs adapted to the special circumstances of the individual. The model guarantees the democratization of education, providing the student equal access and individualized attention, thus liberating education from the dogma of traditional pedagogy. The student is able to go through an individual process and design his/her own learning, reaching intellectual independence by consistently exercising critical judgment.

CIDE continues to seek to form regional scientific communities. A community is formed on the basis that members share an interest in scientific development and put all their efforts toward attaining that objective. In the words of one of their founders: "We are, above all, interested in generating brains already involved in a professional activity (business, farm, teaching, agriculture, laboratory analysis, etc.)." In the process of research, students interact with scientists at the frontier of knowledge thus creating themselves their own network that includes national scientists. It is clear that these communities do not emerge from universities, even when they are involved in research, since they exhibit different objectives.

By the year 2004, 77 individuals have graduated from CIDE with Masters and Doctorate degrees. This is not, nor does it pretend to be, the solution to the problems of high level human resources formation for the country; however, it is a viable alternative for professionals who need to reach a higher academic degree but cannot undertake traditional graduate programs. Globalization does not necessarily mean a widening of the gap between the industrialized countries and the countries in the process of advancement. There are opportunities for less-developed countries to take advantage of the global explosion of information, communication technologies, and networking possibilities at a relatively low cost. In synthesis, CIDE's experience demonstrates that it is possible to reach desired objectives with a system whose parts enjoy ample flexibility, without the need for a costly physical and human infrastructure.

The following graph details US rates of inflation for college tuition/fees, medical costs, and the cost of living from 1978-2008.

Inflation of Tuition and Fees (Private 4-Year Colleges), Medical Costs, and Cost of Living, 1978-2008

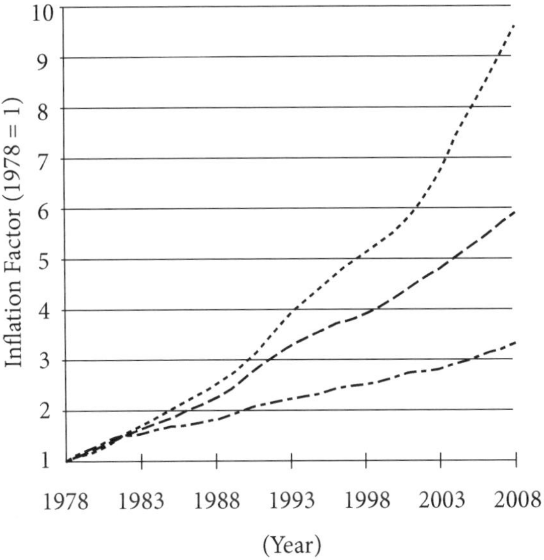

Source: Wikimedia Commons via John Uebersax, 2009.

21

Which choice best summarizes the passage?

A) The author critiques developed countries' biased view of technological advances in Mexico.

B) The author discusses an alternative effort to engage in global knowledge development.

C) The author analyzes the ever-rising cost of earning a scientific degree in higher education.

D) Mexico's novel approach to solving regional issues through education is highlighted and emulated.

22

As used in line 38, "conditions" most nearly means

A) habitats.

B) theories.

C) climate.

D) background.

23

The primary goal of the CIDE is to

A) provide graduate education to students who would likely not receive one otherwise.

B) eliminate a knowledge gap between the Mexican and American economies.

C) create a solution to a high level human relations problem.

D) provide graduate education opportunities on a flexible schedule.

24

Which choice provides the best evidence for the answer to the previous question?

A) Lines 22-25 ("A number...in science")

B) Lines 48-49 ("CIDE...communities")

C) Lines 62-63 ("By the year...degrees")

D) Lines 63-66 ("This is not...country")

25

The author's attitude toward CIDE can best be described as

A) defensive.

B) reserved.

C) arrogant.

D) appreciative.

CONTINUE

26

Based on the graph, the cost of living in the US between 1978 and 2003 underwent inflation

A) at a rate double that of college tuition.

B) at approximately half the rate of college tuition.

C) at a rate approximately double that of medical costs.

D) at approximately half the rate of medical costs.

27

The main purpose of the third paragraph is to

A) describe CIDE's approach to higher education.

B) draw a comparison between two educational programs.

C) justify the value of CIDE's program.

D) address shortcomings of traditional education programs.

28

One stated advantage of CIDE's approach to graduation education is that it provides students with

A) state-of-the-art research facilities.

B) networking opportunities with professionals.

C) access to an internationally renowned faculty of professors.

D) a tuition forgiveness program upon graduation.

29

Which choice provides the best evidence to the answer of the previous question?

A) Lines 25-29 ("By...regions")

B) Lines 40-44 ("The...pedagogy")

C) Lines 55-58 ("In...scientists")

D) Lines 72-75 ("There...cost")

30

Data in the graph provide most direct support for which idea in the passage?

A) A contemporary challenge of providing advanced education is its cost.

B) If recent trends continue, college tuition inflation will more than quadruple the inflation factor of the cost of living by 2028.

C) Students who would benefit from an alternative approach to education often face higher costs than those who do not.

D) College and graduate education is a luxury out of the reach of most students.

Questions 31-41 are based on the following passage.

Passage 1 is adapted from Alexander Hamilton, *Report on a National Bank,* originally published in 1790. Passage 2 is adapted from Thomas Jefferson *Opinion on the Constitutionality of a National Bank,* originally published in 1791.

Passage 1

The Secretary respectfully reports: a National Bank is an Institution of primary importance to the prosperous administration of the Finances, and would be of the greatest utility in the operations connected with the support of the Public Credit. It is evident that the money, which a merchant keeps in his chest, waiting for a favorable opportunity to employ it, produces nothing 'till that opportunity arrives. But if instead of locking it up in this manner, he either deposits it in a Bank, or invests it in the Stock of a Bank, it yields a profit during the interval. His money thus deposited or invested, is a fund upon which himself and others can borrow to a much larger amount. It is a well-established fact that Banks in good credit can circulate a far greater sum than the actual quantum of their capital in Gold and Silver.

The same circumstances illustrate the truth of the position, that it is one of the properties of Banks to increase the active capital of a country. The money of one individual, while he is waiting for an opportunity to employ it, by being either deposited in the Bank for safe keeping, or invested in its Stock, is in a condition to administer to the wants of others, without being put out of his own reach. This yields an extra profit, arising from what is paid for the use of his money by others when he could not himself make use of it; and keeps the money itself in a state of incessant activity. This additional employment given to money, and the faculty of a bank to lend and circulate a greater sum than the amount of its stock in coin, are to all the purposes of trade and industry an absolute increase of capital. Purchases and undertakings, in general, can be carried on by any given sum of bank paper or credit, as effectually as by an equal sum of gold and silver. And thus by contributing to enlarge the mass of industrious and commercial enterprise, banks become nurseries of national wealth.

There is nothing in the Acts of Congress, which imply an exclusive right in the institution, to which they relate, except during the term of the war. There is therefore nothing, if the public good requires it, which prevents the establishment of another. This is a strong argument for a new institution.

Passage 2

I consider the foundation of the Constitution as laid on this ground: "All powers not delegated to the United States, by the Constitution, nor prohibited by it to the States, are reserved to the States or to the people." To take a single step beyond the boundaries thus specially drawn around the powers of Congress is to take possession of a boundless field of power, no longer susceptible of any definition. The incorporation of a bank, and the powers assumed by this bill, have not been delegated to the United States by the Constitution. They are not among the powers specially enumerated, for these are: 1) A power to lay taxes for the purpose of paying the debts of the United States; no debt is paid by this bill, nor any tax laid. Were it a bill to raise money, its origination in the Senate would condemn it by the Constitution. 2) To "regulate commerce with foreign nations, and among the States, and with the Indian tribes." To erect a bank, and to regulate commerce, are very different acts.

It would reduce the whole instrument to a single phrase that of instituting a Congress with power to do whatever would be for the good of the United States; and, as they would be the sole judges of the good or evil, it would be also a power to do whatever evil they please. It may be said that a bank whose bills would have a currency all over the States, would be more convenient than one whose currency is limited to a single State. So it would be still more convenient that there should be a bank, whose bills should have a currency all over the world. But it does not follow from this superior conveniency, that there exists anywhere a power to establish such a bank; or that the world may not go on very well without it. The present is the case of a right remaining exclusively with the States, and consequently one of those intended by the Constitution to be placed under its protection.

31

As used in line 8, "employ" most nearly means

A) hire.
B) occupy.
C) involve.
D) utilize.

32

The author of Passage 1 indicates that printing more money than can be backed with gold and silver will

A) generate confidence in buyers and sellers.
B) stimulate the economy.
C) pacify inflationary fears.
D) benefit only the wealthy.

33

Which choice provides the best evidence for the answer to the previous question?

A) Lines 14-16 ("It…Silver")
B) Lines 19-24 ("The…reach")
C) Lines 28-32 ("This…capital")
D) Lines 38-40 ("There…war")

34

The author of Passage 1 refers to the Acts of Congress in order to

A) address those who consider a National Bank unconstitutional.
B) suggest that the Acts of Congress are discretional.
C) reveal his disapproval of the US Constitution.
D) express his support for the Federalists.

35

As used in Passage 2, line 51, "definition" most nearly means

A) meaning.
B) explanation.
C) parameters.
D) clarity.

36

The author of Passage 2 indicates that allowing the Congress to do whatever is good for the United States could have which negative effect?

A) Congress would no longer abide by the written Constitution.
B) Congress would change legislation too frequently.
C) Congress would have the power to do whatever evil they please.
D) Congress would become easily manipulated.

37

The central claim of Passage 2 is that

A) a National Bank would destroy the American economy.
B) the Constitution must be upheld in order to protect States' rights.
C) powers enumerated in the Constitution are discretionary.
D) national currency would be more convenient than currency limited to a single State.

38

As used in line 63, "instrument" refers to

A) the National Bank.
B) the United States.
C) Congress.
D) the Constitution.

39

Which statement best describes the relationship between the passages?

A) Passage 2 cautions against the central claim advanced in Passage 1.
B) Passage 2 disputes the practicality of the proposal put forth in Passage 1.
C) Passage 2 questions the validity of the prediction discussed in Passage 1.
D) Passage 2 illustrates the phenomenon described in more general terms in Passage 1.

40

The author of Passage 1 would most likely respond to the discussion of which powers are specifically enumerated to the United States in lines 44-53, Passage 2, by claiming that

A) as the United States evolves, so should its Constitution.
B) if something promotes the general welfare, it can bypass the Constitution.
C) the regulation of commerce can only be achieved by a National Bank.
D) a National Bank would not hinder the development of state banks.

41

Which choice provides the best evidence for the answer to the previous question?

A) Lines 1-5 ("The...Credit")
B) Lines 32-34 ("Purchases...silver")
C) Lines 38-40 ("There...war")
D) Lines 40-42 ("There...another")

Questions 42-52 are based on the following passage.

This passage is adapted from Juergen Krause and Gailene Tobin, "Discovery, Development, and Regulation of Natural Products," a chapter of Marianna Kulka's *Using Old Solutions to New Problems – Natural Drug Discovery in the 21st* Century. ©2013 by Krause and Tobin.

Since ancient times, civilizations used plants and plant extracts to ameliorate diseases and foster healing. Early historic examples for medical treatments from natural sources include the discovery of the beneficial effects of foxglove for treating some manifestations of heart disease in the 18th century, the use of the bark of the willow and cinchona trees in treating fever, and the effectiveness of poppy extracts in the treatment of dysenteries. By 1829, scientists discovered that the compound salicin, in willow trees, was responsible for pain relief. Continuing into the 20th century, 244 prototypic chemical structures (over 80% came from animal, plant, microbial, or mineral origin) have been used as templates to produce medicines up to 1995, but relatively few new scaffolds have appeared since. About half of the marketed agents in today's drug arsenal derive from biological sources with the large majority based on terrestrial natural product scaffolds.

The field of natural products drug discovery, despite the success stories of penicillin and others, also had aspects that made it less attractive. In the traditional approach, drug targets were exposed to crude extracts, and in case of evidence of pharmacological activity, the extract was fractionated and the active compound isolated and identified. This method was slow, labor-intensive, inefficient, and provided no guarantee that a lead from the screening process would be chemically workable or even patentable.

However, the recently renewed interest in natural drugs is determined by the urgent need to find and develop effective means to fight infections caused by viruses, like HIV (Human Immunodeficiency Virus) and so called "superbugs" (bacteria with multiple resistance against antibiotics). Of the 175 anti-cancer agents developed and approved from 1940 until 2010 in Western countries and Japan, 85 compounds, representing 48.6%, were natural products or directly derived from natural products. HIV-1 is the cause of Acquired Immune Deficiency Syndrome (AIDS), a major human viral disease with over 34 million people infected worldwide as of 2012 and approximately 1.7 million dying per year. Failure of anti-HIV therapy is observed due to the emergence of drug resistance and the significant side effect profile of existing therapies. Hence, the quest for novel prospective drug candidates with fewer side effects and increased efficacy against various HIV strains also relies on natural products. Naturally derived anti-HIV compounds have been found to be the most promising for treating HIV infections, with the potential to overcome drug-resistance of mutated HIV strains. Only a few of the many natural products that have been reported to exhibit anti-HIV activities have reached clinical trials and none of them made it on the list of conventional antiretroviral drugs.

Natural products, although a valuable and precious resource, also come with their fair share of challenges in a variety of aspects. One of the major issues concerning the use of natural products is the difficulty associated with obtaining sufficient amounts of material pure enough for discovery and development activities. If a compound is derived from a plant growing only in small quantities or remote locations, or from a marine organism residing in great depth or difficult to access regions, resupply becomes a problem. To meet the increasing demand for raw material, to conserve wild resources, and to reduce the potential variability in the active ingredient content in medicinal plants from different collection areas, it is important to implement more controlled cultivation programs to ensure quality and to protect resources.

As of today, only a very small fraction of bioactive structures of potential therapeutic relevance from plants, microbes, and marine organisms have been chemically analyzed or examined. The discovery of valuable therapeutic agents from natural sources continues in the 21st century by reaching into new and untapped terrestrial and marine source organisms as the chemical novelty associated with natural products is higher than that of structures from any other source. There is growing awareness of the limited structural diversity in existing compound collections as well as the extreme chemical diversity, high biological potency, and potential to frequently discover drug-like characteristics in natural products. Therefore, they constitute a valuable platform for the development of new therapeutics for a variety of indications, yet may still not contain enough versatility to yield suitable treatments for all heritable human diseases.

42

The main purpose of this passage is to

A) entreat legislators to permit further exploration of natural products to find a cure for HIV and "superbugs."
B) explain natural products' relevance and challenges with regard to disease prevention and treatment.
C) justify the dangers of abandoning HIV research, as the disease affects 34 million people and kill 1.7 million people a year.
D) provide the history of natural drug development and explain why it will be difficult to continue in the future.

43

As used in line 2, "foster" most nearly means

A) promote.
B) raise.
C) adopt.
D) neglect.

44

The main function of the second paragraph is to

A) establish the need for innovation.
B) explain the traditional approach to plant extraction.
C) describe penicillin's success story.
D) introduce the method of isolation and identification.

45

As used in line 19, "field" most nearly means

A) reach.
B) calling.
C) bounds.
D) domain.

46

The authors believe that the process of learning to make new drugs from natural products is

A) frustrating but worthwhile.
B) practical and simple.
C) ongoing and valuable.
D) optimistic but unrealistic.

47

Which choice provides the best evidence for the answer to the previous question?

A) Lines 19-21 ("The...attractive")
B) Lines 45-47 ("Hence...products")
C) Lines 72-75 ("As...examined")
D) Lines 75-80 ("The...source")

48

According to the passage, the resurgent interest in natural medicine was caused by

A) the need to impede formerly untreatable viruses and mutant diseases.
B) the increasingly profitable pharmaceutical industry.
C) Japan's use of 85 medicinal compounds made from natural products.
D) competition with Japan's recent breakthrough in medicinal research.

49

Naturally derived products have thus far struggled to combat HIV on a large scale due to

A) failures to be listed as conventional antiretroviral drugs.
B) their lack of reproducibility in production.
C) variations in active ingredients occurring during production.
D) few even exhibiting anti-HIV activities.

50

The lines 85-89 ("Therefore...diseases") best serve to

A) address the realistic challenges ahead.
B) succinctly summarize the passage's argument.
C) discuss potential shortcomings of future research.
D) lament the immeasurability of human frailty.

51

According to the passage, the biggest challenge facing the production of natural medicine is

A) funding.
B) pollution.
C) supply.
D) patentability.

52

Which choice provides the best evidence for the answer to the previous question?

A) Line 25-28 ("This...patentable")
B) Line 51-55 ("Only...drugs")
C) Line 57-62 ("One...activities")
D) Line 81-85 ("There...products")

STOP

If you finish before time is called, you may check your work on this section only.
Do not turn to any other section.

Writing and Language Test

35 MINUTES, 44 QUESTIONS

Turn to Section 2 of your answer sheet to answer the questions in this section.

DIRECTIONS

Each passage below is accompanied by a number of questions. For some questions, you will consider how the passage might be revised to improve the expression of ideas. For other questions, you will consider how the passage might be edited to correct errors in sentence structure, usage, or punctuation. A passage or a question may be accompanied by one or more graphics (such as a table or graph) that you will consider as you make revising and editing decisions.

Some questions will direct you to an underlined portion of a passage. Other questions will direct you to a location in a passage or ask you to think about the passage as a whole.

After reading each passage, choose the answer to each question that most effectively improves the quality of writing in the passage or that makes the passage conform to the conventions of standard written English. Many questions include a "NO CHANGE" option. Choose that option if you think the best choice is to leave the relevant portion of the passage as it is.

Tatau: Polynesia's Mark on the World

The word "tattoo" is the most well known Polynesian word in the world. While the practice of the permanent marking of the body is [1] a worldwide phenomenon not unique to this region, "tatau," as it is traditionally spelled, lies at the heart of Polynesian history and culture. Samoa, in particular, has a legacy of tatau that stretches unbroken for over 2000 years. Here, tattoo is a way for both women and men of every social stratum to express identity and can indicate everything from [2] status, sexual maturity, genealogy, and occupation.

1

A) NO CHANGE
B) not uniquely found in this region
C) not unique to this region
D) found worldwide and thus is not unique

2

A) NO CHANGE
B) status, and sexual maturity, to geneology, and occupation.
C) status and sexual maturity, to geneology and occupation.
D) status and sexual maturity to geneology and occupation.

CONTINUE

Tatau design is greatly influenced by the environment of the South Pacific. Not surprisingly, those who look to the sea for sustenance also do so for inspiration, and images like ocean waves and shark teeth are ubiquitous in Samoan tatau. Sea animals, too, are prominent. Turtles signify [3] healing and living long, while stingrays, which [4] can cleverly hide from sharks by burying themselves in the sand, are associated with protection and stealth. Human figures, called "enata," can be drawn both singularly and as part of a [5] pattern; one popular design depicts a row of enata holding hands, indicating a group of ancestors guarding over [6] there descendants. The placement of these images on the body is also important. In Samoan tradition, [7] Rangi (Heaven) and Papa (Earth) are the ancestors of humans,

3

A) NO CHANGE
B) health and living long
C) healing and to live a long life
D) health and longevity

4

Which choice most effectively explains the symbolism of the stingray?

A) NO CHANGE
B) are as graceful as they are venomous,
C) have far shorter lifespans than do turtles,
D) are found in large numbers in the waters of Polynesia,

5

Which choice most effectively combines the sentences at the underlined portion?

A) NO CHANGE
B) pattern, one
C) pattern; one,
D) pattern: with one

6

A) NO CHANGE
B) its
C) it's
D) they're

7

A) NO CHANGE
B) humans are descendants of Rangi (Heaven) and Papa (Earth),
C) humans have Rangi (Heaven) and Papa (Earth) as ancestors,
D) Rangi (Heaven) and Papa (Earth) decended from humans,

CONTINUE

8 who were once united. The body is seen as a link between the two, and tatau are placed on different parts of the body accordingly. The head is seen as the contact point to Rangi, and thus tatau on the upper body represent spirituality, knowledge and wisdom. The lower body, on the other hand, is more earthly, so tatau here **9** are largely viewed as taboo.

[1] The experience of getting tattooed **10** is a privilege reserved only for warriors, as undergoing it is seen as a test of strength, endurance, and respect for the culture. [2] The physical pain, for Samoans, pales in comparison to the shame of remaining one of the unadorned, for Pala'ai—or "Cowards"—are seen as forever incomplete. [3] In traditional Samoan society, the full men's tattoo covers the body from mid-torso to knee. [4] The process can take up to three months, with work done each day until the man receiving the tattoo can not stand the pain any longer. [5] Within six months the distinctive designs appear on the skin, but the healing process can take up to a year, with family members or friends helping the newly tattooed man with acts as simple as walking if it becomes too painful. **11**

8

A) NO CHANGE
B) whom were once united.
C) to whom were once united.
D) which were once united.

9

Which choice provides information that is most consistent in style and content with the information presented in the previous sentence?

A) NO CHANGE
B) represent the body's life energy, strength, and sexuality.
C) are also richly symbolic.
D) often depict animals and other natural elements.

10

Which choice provides the most effective transition from the previous paragraph in a way consistent with the information presented in the rest of the passage?

A) NO CHANGE
B) is a rite of passage for boys but not girls,
C) carries just as much cultural symbolism as do the designs themselves,
D) is seen as parallel to the experience of childbirth,

11

To make this paragraph most logical, sentence 2 should be placed

A) where it is now.
B) after sentence 3.
C) after sentence 4.
D) after sentence 5.

Global Markets and the Rise of High Frequency Trading

[1] Globalization is by now an established reality, and nowhere is that more clear than in the scope and power of global financial markets. [2] Technological innovation **12** have catalyzed the reciprocity that make the world's money ever more interconnected, specifically the rise of High Frequency Trading. [3] Humans program the computers, but after that the process is entirely automated. [4] Also known as Algorithmic or "algo" trading, HFT is a type of trading in which large volumes of shares are bought and sold automatically at high speed. [5] **13** Their uses are growing ever more frequent in markets from the U.S. to India, and because the interconnectedness of the global financial system raises the stakes for any trading **14** system—it is crucial to take care to maximize the benefits of HFT while mitigating the risks such a driverless system can create. **15**

Algo trading's advantages are **16** numerous. Why else would companies have adopted it so enthusiastically in the last few decades? Any system that accounts for 70% of all

12

A) NO CHANGE
B) has been catalysts for
C) has been a catalyst for
D) have been catalysts in

13

A) NO CHANGE
B) Due to use
C) Uses of it are
D) Because its use is

14

A) NO CHANGE
B) system, it
C) system; it
D) system. It

15

To make this paragraph most logical, sentence 3 should be placed

A) where it is now.
B) after sentence 1.
C) after sentence 4.
D) after sentence 5.

16

Which choice most effectively combines the sentences at the underlined portion?

A) numerous; so why
B) numerous—why
C) numerous: so, why
D) numerous why

trades made in U.S. markets must have benefits. The most obvious advantage to HFT, of course, is speed. 17 The fastest computers are called "supercomputers," and their performance is measured in floating-point operations per second. The increased volume that comes with this kind of speed, consequently, allows algorithmic programs to spread risk around, thereby minimizing the effect of potential losses. Algo trading also eliminates the part human emotion can play in trading; computers programmed to stick to the plan can't hesitate after a particularly difficult loss or act 18 rashly in an effort to eke out a little more profit. This kind of systematic discipline can be especially useful in times of greater market volatility.

19 Coincidentally, however, the greatest risks to a financial system dominated by automated trading come from some of these very same advantages, and it is these risks that concern governments and financial institutions worldwide. Simply put: automated systems 20 are not

17

Which choice provides the best supporting example for the main idea of the paragraph?

A) NO CHANGE
B) As of 2015, there are supercomputers that can perform up to quadrillions of operations per second.
C) Due to this, some traders criticize these automated programs as having an unfair advantage over their human counterparts.
D) Computers can make millions of transactions in a matter of seconds, with better connectivity and processing speeds than human traders.

18

Which choice best fits with the tone of the rest of the passage?

A) NO CHANGE
B) wildly
C) apace
D) helter-skelter

19

A) NO CHANGE
B) Ironically,
C) Unfortunately,
D) Subsequently,

20

A) NO CHANGE
B) have no immunity with error.
C) are not immune to err.
D) err without immunization.

immune to error. Computers are **21** vulnerable: to mechanical failure, Internet loss and hacking. Some algorithms that look good on paper end up performing disastrously in the real world. Humans, of course, make errors as well, but the very speed and volume that give algorithmic programs an edge increase exponentially the damage a single error can cause. Combine that with the strong inter-linkages between markets, and it's easy to see how a crash in one could send shock waves throughout the whole global economy. **22**

High Frequency Trading will perhaps become only more entrenched in the years to come. It is this very fact that should make governments and financial institutions work tirelessly to ensure there are safeguards protecting the citizens of the world from financial Armageddon.

21

A) NO CHANGE
B) vulnerable to mechanical failure, Internet loss and, hacking.
C) vulnerable to mechanical failure, Internet loss, and hacking.
D) vulnerable—to mechanical failure internet loss, and hacking.

22

At this point, the writer is considering adding the following graph.

May 10, 2006 Stock Market "Flash Crash"

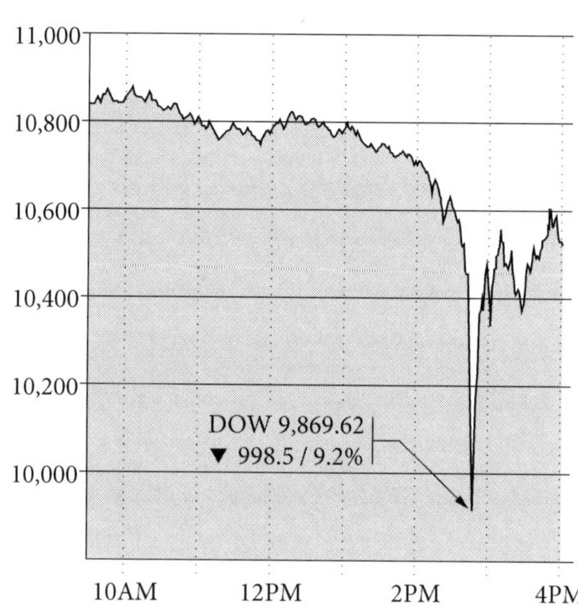

Should the writer make this addition here?

A) Yes, because the statistical information in the graph lends credibility to the writer's prediction.
B) Yes, because it provides objective evidence for the scenario the writer is attempting to depict.
C) No, because the information is irrelevant to the main idea of the paragraph.
D) No, because the information is already included elsewhere in the passage.

Conserving Water in a Changing Climate: Lessons from California

From 2012 to 2016, California experienced its driest period in 1200 years. Such an extended period of drought in the U.S.'s most populous state produced a water crisis heretofore unseen in its scope and impact on both urban and rural populations, raising concerns from the agricultural and power industries to environmentalists [23] worried about the collapse of certain ecological systems.

Drought can have catastrophic [24] consequences, (both direct and indirect) for the environment and those who live in it, and this period of extreme dryness in California was no different. Farms had to cut back on irrigation, thus reducing crop yield. A lack of water elongated and exacerbated California's wildfire season, [25] that caused millions of dollars in damage to homes and businesses. Municipalities had to find creative ways to ensure that residents have reliable sources of water for everything from drinking to bathing to washing clothes and maintaining urban landscapes. So in 2013, California instituted a law combining both voluntary and mandatory conservation measures intended to [26] eliminate the disastrous effects of its most protracted drought in modern history.

[27] Despite measures designed to curb water wasting at industry and city levels, private citizens were asked to limit personal usage. These practices, though not new to areas in which water has always been scarce, can be seen as a blueprint for other areas in which climate change threatens to make water scarcity the new normal. During

23

A) NO CHANGE
B) overreacting
C) in dire straits
D) ambivalent

24

A) NO CHANGE
B) consequences (both direct and indirect)
C) consequences—(both direct and indirect)—
D) consequences both direct and indirect,

25

A) NO CHANGE
B) causing
C) which causes
D) it caused

26

Which choice best maintains the style and tone of the passage?

A) NO CHANGE
B) mitigate
C) lighten up
D) shackle

27

A) NO CHANGE
B) In lieu of
C) Due to
D) In addition to

the height of the drought, Californians were asked to reduce usage in ways that, while saving water and money, did not fundamentally inhibit quality of life. They turned off the tap while brushing teeth, **28** declining to wash clothes or dishes unless the machines were full, and shortened the time of personal showers. They cut back on washing cars and, in some cities, were paid to either let lawns go brown **29** or replace grass with drought resistant landscaping. Municipalities gave rebates for homeowners who installed efficient showerheads, low-flush toilets, and faucet aerators which **30** cost on average a mere $4-6.

These restrictions resulted in a reduction of water consumption **31** by approximately one-third by mid-2015, and due to the combination of these measures and increased rainfall during the winter of 2017, California has seen its water resources **32** in restoration to more then three quarters of its pre-drought levels. A new law

28

A) NO CHANGE
B) having declined
C) declined
D) they declined

29

A) NO CHANGE
B) and
C) nor
D) yet

30

The writer wants to add specific information that is consistent with the list of water-saving devices. Which choice most effectively accomplishes this goal?

A) NO CHANGE
B) are low-cost retrofits for kitchens and bathrooms.
C) alter how much water comes out of the tap.
D) reduce water usage by delivering a mixture of water and air.

31

The writer wants to support the paragraph's main idea with accurate, relevant information from the graph. Which choice most effectively accomplishes this goal?

A) NO CHANGE
B) which steadily increased over the period of mandatory restriction,
C) in both urban and rural areas throughout the state,
D) that exceeded the state-mandated 25% throughout 2015,

32

A) NO CHANGE
B) restored to more than
C) in restoration to more than
D) restored to more then

signed by Gov. Jerry Brown in 2016 relaxed some of the most stringent restrictions, giving more autonomy to local water boards as to how water is allocated. However, since climate change presents a continuing danger not unique to California, [33] much more drastic conservation measures will likely have to be taken in the future.

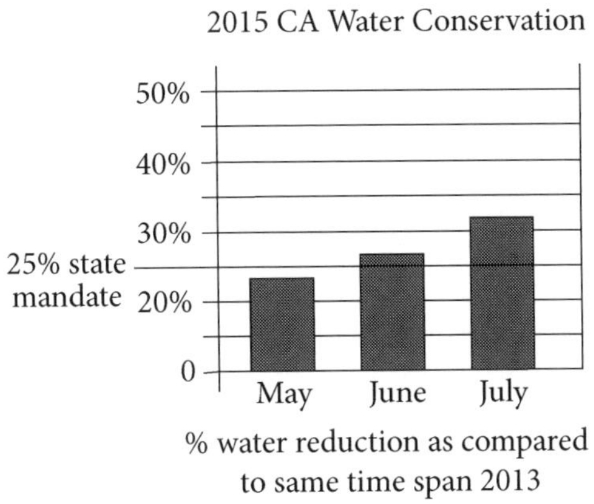

2015 CA Water Conservation

% water reduction as compared to same time span 2013

33

Which choice provides the most effective conclusion to the passage?

A) NO CHANGE

B) the state is also working on improving its ability to fight wildfires and protect species vulnerable to a warming world.

C) the lessons regarding sustainable water conservation gleaned by the "California Experiment" are of import worldwide.

D) it is important to note that areas under more immediate threat have been finding ways to conserve water far longer.

The Mars Mission and the Human Psyche

Scientists planning the first manned mission to Mars hope this unprecedented feat can achieve many things, including a deeper understanding of the planet's history, the possible discovery of life, and the feasibility of human colonization. However, before any such mission can be undertaken, one question must first be answered: how will the astronauts involved in such an undertaking fare **34** physically and, perhaps, even more importantly, psychologically? In the attempt to resolve such basic questions, space programs around the world have been attempting to re-create the conditions of such a mission by sequestering possible participants for anywhere from four to seventeen months **35** by themselves on Earth.

The most recent experiment, named HI-SEAS (the Hawaii Space Exploration Analog and Simulation) and conducted from 2015-1016, involved six participants spending an entire year atop an isolated slope of the Mauna Loa volcano on the island of Hawaii. Living in a 1200 square-foot solar powered dome, these scientists—experts in fields from medicine to engineering to astrobiology—were chosen not only **36** for their expertise but also for their perceived psychological stamina, **37** and knowing how long and arduous the journey alone **38** was **39** requires the attempt of that person to be psychologically resilient.

34

A) NO CHANGE
B) physically and perhaps even more importantly
C) physically, and perhaps even more importantly
D) and, perhaps even more importantly,

35

A) NO CHANGE
B) alone
C) in isolation
D) DELETE the underlined portion.

36

A) NO CHANGE
B) for being experts but
C) because they were experts but also
D) for expertise but

37

A) NO CHANGE
B) for
C) so
D) yet

38

A) NO CHANGE
B) is
C) would have been
D) will be

39

A) NO CHANGE
B) require anyone attempting it to be
C) require everyone attempting be
D) requires that any person who attempts it be

40 <u>The reasons for this necessary resiliency are both humane, and practical</u>. No one, of course, wants to send human beings into a situation in which they are likely to suffer maladies **41** <u>ranging from depression to psychotic break</u>, but it is also paramount to the success of the mission that all participants are able to do their jobs in a way that promotes team performance and cohesion. In other words, when the stakes are this high, you need all team members performing at their best.

42 <u>The American Space Program is not the only one to have attempted such a simulation.</u> An experiment performed in Russia on a group of cosmonauts tracked

40

A) NO CHANGE
B) The reasons for this necessary resilience are both humane, and, practical.
C) The reasons for this necessary resilience are both humane and practical.
D) The reasons for this necessary resilience: are both humane and practical.

41

Which choice provides the most precise depiction of the kinds of "maladies" travelers to Mars might experience?

A) NO CHANGE
B) as a result of living in such close quarters with his or her fellow travelers,
C) due to isolation, homesickness, and the physical constraints of the living environment,
D) detrimental to their health,

42

Which choice provides the most effective transition from the previous paragraph?

A) NO CHANGE
B) Previous studies have made clear just how closely related physical and psychological health can be.
C) Conditions on Earth are not always as easy to replicate in space as humans would like.
D) Sleep habits are perhaps the single greatest predictor of success.

how even small changes in circadian rhythms **43** can drastically impact performance. Of the six cosmonauts involved in this study, four suffered deleterious health effects related to disturbed sleep cycles. One cosmonaut, who suffered chronic sleep deprivation, **44** single-handedly accounted for a majority of mistakes made on a computer test used to measure concentration and alertness. While the test posed no real-world threat, one can easily see how these mistakes could seriously endanger his fellow space travelers on an actual mission.

The results of the HI-SEAS experiment have not yet been released, but we can already glean some insights from interviews with the scientists "on board." As the German physicist and HI-SEAS participant Christiane Heinicke reported, "emergencies play a surprising role in helping people get along."

43

At this point, the writer is considering adding the following.

—those clocks that regulate our sleep cycles—

Should the writer make this addition here?

A) Yes, because it helps clarify a technical term important to the writer's point.
B) Yes, because it introduces the idea that sleep is important to psychological health, a point previous paragraphs have not addressed.
C) No, because it shifts the paragraph's focus away from the Russian experiment.
D) No, because it restates what has already been said in the sentence.

44

Which choice most effectively reinforces the main idea of the paragraph?

A) NO CHANGE
B) was only able to communicate with family and friends over an email system that included a 20-minute delay.
C) saw his activity levels plummet in the first three months, a phenomenon which continued over the year.
D) suffered the kind of bone and muscle wasting associated with sedentary life in reduced gravity.

STOP

If you finish before time is called, you may check your work on this section only. Do not turn to any other section.

Math Test – No Calculator

25 MINUTES, 20 QUESTIONS

Turn to Section 3 of your answer sheet to answer the questions in this section.

DIRECTIONS

For questions 1-15, solve each problem, choose the best answer from the choices provided, and fill in the corresponding circle on your answer sheet. **For questions 16-20,** solve the problem and enter your answer in the grid on the answer sheet. Please refer to the directions before question 16 on how to enter your answers in the grid. You may use any available space in your test booklet for scratch work.

NOTES

1. The use of a calculator **is not permitted**.
2. All variables and expressions used represent real numbers unless otherwise indicated.
3. Figures provided in this test are drawn to scale unless otherwise indicated.
4. All figures lie in a plane unless otherwise indicated.
5. Unless otherwise indicated, the domain of a given function f is the set of all real numbers x for which $f(x)$ is a real number.

REFERENCE

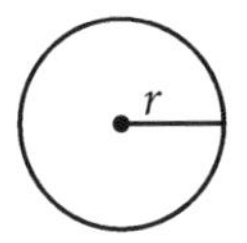

$A = \pi r^2$
$C = 2\pi r$

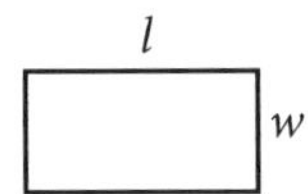

$A = lw$

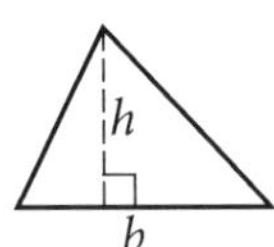

$A = \frac{1}{2}bh$

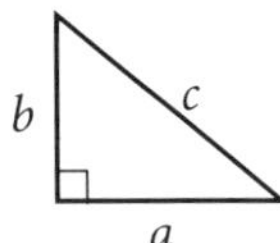

$c^2 = a^2 + b^2$

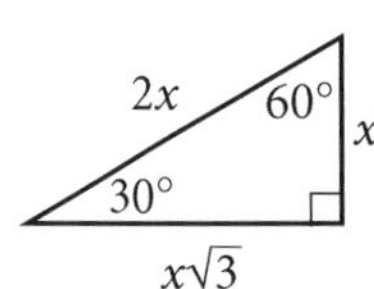

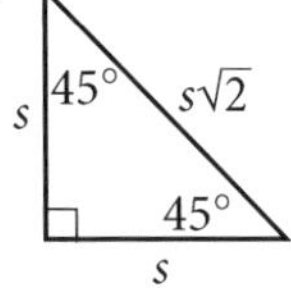

Special Right Triangles

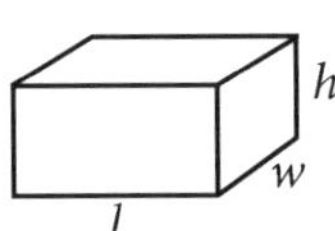

$V = lwh$

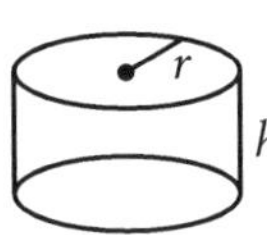

$V = \pi r^2 h$

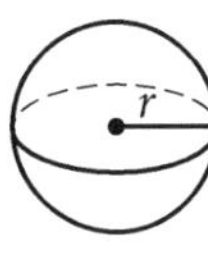

$V = \frac{4}{3}\pi r^3$

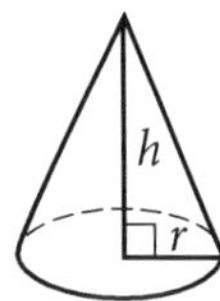

$V = \frac{1}{3}\pi r^2 h$

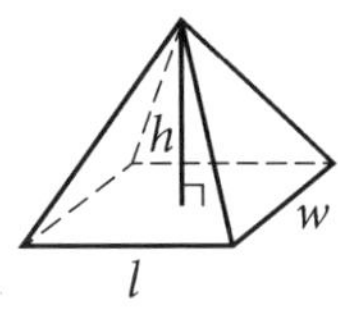

$V = \frac{1}{3}lwh$

The number of degrees of arc in a circle is 360.
The number of radians of arc in a circle is 2π.
The sum of the measures in degrees of the angles of a triangle is 180.

1

If $\sqrt{x - 4} = 7$, what is the value of x?

A) 11
B) 18
C) 45
D) 53

2

x	0	5	10	15	20
$f(x)$	1	-3	-7	-11	-15

The table above shows 5 coordinate pairs for function What is the equation for the function $f(x)$?

A) $f(x) = x - 4$
B) $f(x) = \frac{4}{5}x + 1$
C) $f(x) = 5x - 1$
D) $f(x) = -\frac{4}{5}x + 1$

3

$$2x + 5y = 20$$
$$4x + 10y = C$$

The system of equations given above has an infinite number of solutions. Which statement about the value of C is correct?

A) C must be 20.
B) C must be 40.
C) C can be anything but 20.
D) C can be anything but 40.

4

If $f(x) = 2x + 7$, what is the equation for $f^{-1}(x)$?

A) $f^{-1}(x) = \frac{x - 7}{2}$
B) $f^{-1}(x) = \frac{x}{2} - 7$
C) $f^{-1}(x)= 2x - 7$
D) $f^{-1}(x) = -2x - 7$

5

What is the factored form of $a^2 - b^2$?

A) (2a)($2b$)
B) $(a - b)(a - b)$
C) $(a + b)(a + b)$
D) $(a + b)(a - b)$

6

On a graph, the inverse of a function is the reflection of the original graph over the line $y = x$. Which of the following graphs has an inverse that is a function?

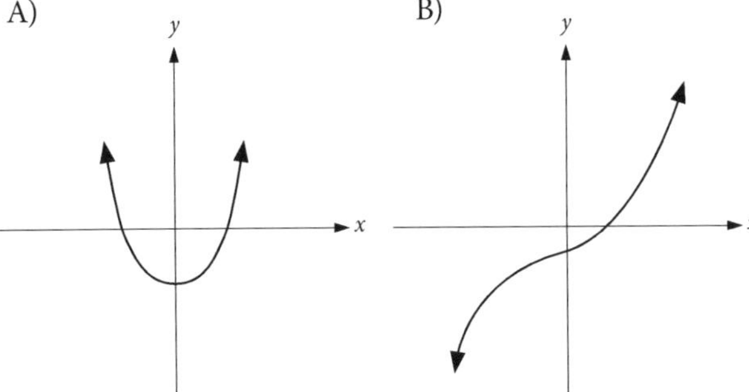

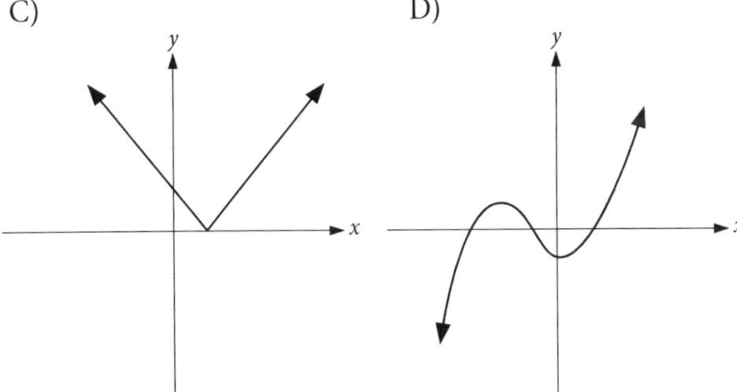

7

Carlos is working on a sculpture made of wood. He has a wooden rod, 72 inches long, that needs to be cut so that one piece is 6 inches longer than the other piece. Which of the following equations can be used to find the length of each piece?

A) $x + 6 = 72$
B) $x + 6x = 72$
C) $x + (x + 6) = 72$
D) $(6 - x) + x = 72$

8

$$3y = 2x + 18$$

The graph of the function $g(x)$ is a line that is perpendicular to the graph of the equation shown above. Additionally, the graph of $g(x)$ has the same y-intercept as the graph of the equation above. Which of the following is the correct definition for function $g(x)$?

A) $g(x) = \frac{3}{2}x + 6$
B) $g(x) = -\frac{3}{2}x + 6$
C) $g(x) = \frac{3}{2}x + 18$
D) $g(x) = -\frac{3}{2}x + 18$

9

$$g(x) = x^4 + 3x^3 - 6x^2 - 6x + 8$$

When $g(x)$ is divided by $x + 4$, the remainder is 0. Which of the following statements about $g(x)$ is true?

A) $g(4) = 0$
B) $g(0) = 4$
C) $g(-4) = 0$
D) $g(0) = -4$

10

$$x - 4 = \sqrt{2x}$$

When Isabella solved the equation shown above, she found that $x = 2$ and $x = 8$. Since the equation is a square root equation, Isabella checked for extraneous solutions. Which statement about these two solutions is correct?

A) Both 2 and 8 are solutions.
B) Neither 2 nor 8 are solutions.
C) 2 is a solution, but 8 is not.
D) 8 is a solution, but 2 is not.

11

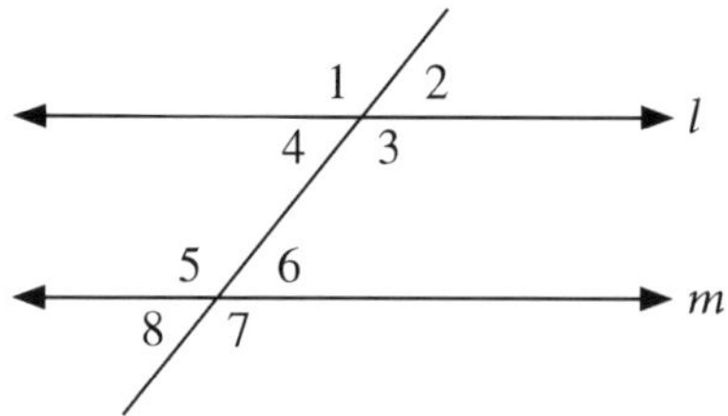

In the diagram above, $l \parallel m$. Which list contains all the angles that are congruent to $\angle 4$?

A) $\angle 1, \angle 5$

B) $\angle 2, \angle 6$

C) $\angle 2, \angle 6, \angle 8$

D) $\angle 1, \angle 5, \angle 8$

12

Which of the following equations can be used to find three consecutive integers with a sum of 90?

A) $n + 3 = 90$

B) $n + n + n = 90$

C) $n + (n + 1) + (n + 2) = 90$

D) $n + (2n + 1) + (3n + 2) = 90$

13

$$f(x) = x^2 - 3$$
$$g(x) = x - 1$$

Given the two functions defined above, which of the following lists all the values of x for which $f(x) = g(x)$?

A) 1, 2

B) -1, 2

C) 1, -2

D) -1, -2

14

What is the result of multiplying $3 + 2i$ and $3 - 2i$?

A) 5

B) 9

C) 13

D) 15

15

$$y = x^2 - 2x + 3$$

The graph of the above equation is a parabola. What is the vertex of the parabola?

A) (1, 2)

B) (-2, 3)

C) (3, -2)

D) (2, -3)

DIRECTIONS

For questions 16 – 20, solve each problem, enter your answer in the grid, as described below on the answer sheet.

1. Although not required, it is suggested that you write your answer in the boxes at the top of the columns to help you fill in the circles accurately. You will receive credit only if the circles are filled in correctly.
2. Mark no more than one circle in any column.
3. No question has a negative answer.
4. Some problems may have more than one correct answer. In such cases, grid only one answer.
5. **Mixed numbers** such as $3\frac{1}{2}$ must be gridded as 3.5 or $\frac{7}{2}$. (If 3 1 / 2 is entered into the grid, it will be interpreted as $\frac{31}{2}$, not $3\frac{1}{2}$.)
6. **Decimal answers:** If you obtain a decimal answer with more digits than the grid can accommodate, it may be either rounded or truncated, but it must fill the entire grid.

Answer: $\frac{7}{12}$

Write → answer in boxes.

7 / 1 2

← Fraction line

Grid in result.

Answer: 2.5

2 . 5

← Decimal point

Acceptable ways to grid $\frac{2}{3}$ are:

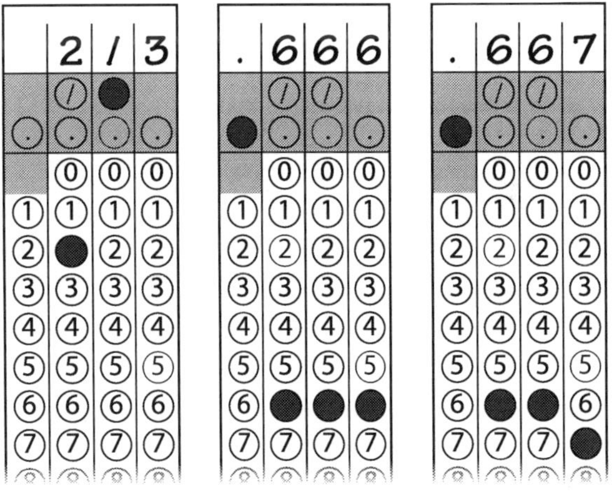

Answer: 201 – either position is correct

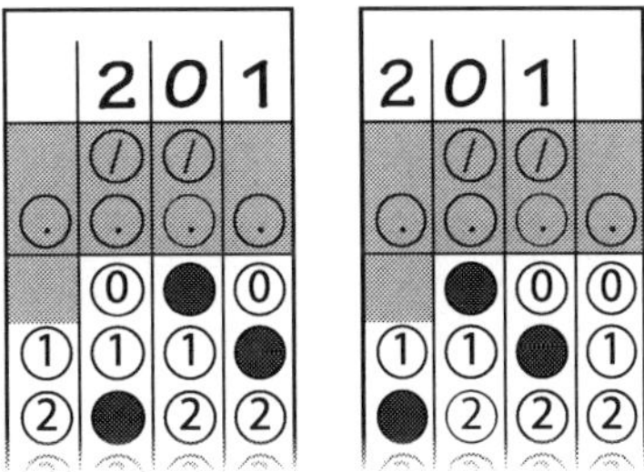

NOTE: You may start your answers in any column, space permitting. Columns you don't need to use should be left blank.

16

$$y = x^2 + 3$$
$$y = x^2 - 3$$

How many ordered pairs (x, y) satisfy the system of equations shown above?

17

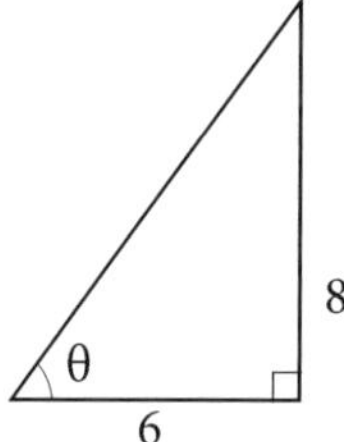

In the triangle above, what is the value of $\sin(\theta)$?

18

$$x^2 = 4x + 21$$

What positive value of x is a solution to the above equation?

19

$$\begin{cases} 7x - 12y = -26 \\ -5x + 6y = 16 \end{cases}$$

What is the y-value of the solution for the system of equations above?

20

A refrigerator makes an electric field of 60 volts per meter (V/m). This field is 4 V/m less than four times the field made by a vacuum cleaner. What is the strength of the field a vacuum cleaner makes?

STOP

If you finish before time is called, you may check your work on this section only. Do not turn to any other section.

Math Test – Calculator

55 MINUTES, 38 QUESTIONS

Turn to Section 4 of your answer sheet to answer the questions in this section.

DIRECTIONS

For questions 1-30, solve each problem, choose the best answer from the choices provided, and fill in the corresponding circle on your answer sheet. **For questions 31-38,** solve the problem and enter your answer in the grid on the answer sheet. Please refer to the directions before question 16 on how to enter your answers in the grid. You may use any available space in your test booklet for scratch work.

NOTES

1. The use of a calculator **is not permitted**.
2. All variables and expressions used represent real numbers unless otherwise indicated.
3. Figures provided in this test are drawn to scale unless otherwise indicated.
4. All figures lie in a plane unless otherwise indicated.
5. Unless otherwise indicated, the domain of a given function f is the set of all real numbers x for which $f(x)$ is a real number.

REFERENCE

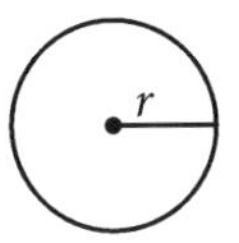

$A = \pi r^2$
$C = 2\pi r$

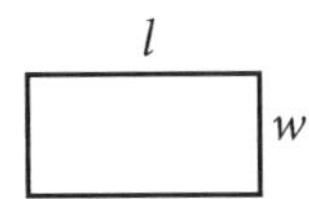

$A = lw$

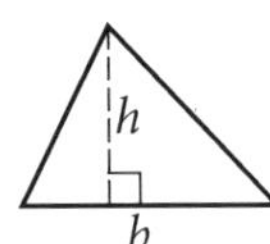

$A = \frac{1}{2}bh$

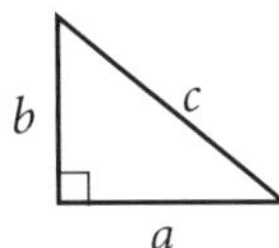

$c^2 = a^2 + b^2$

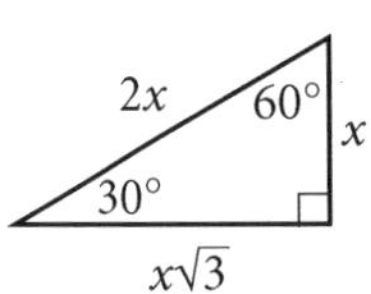

Special Right Triangles

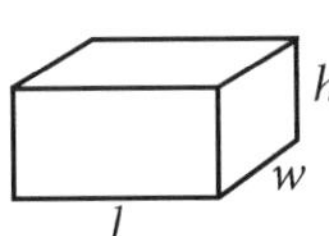

$V = lwh$

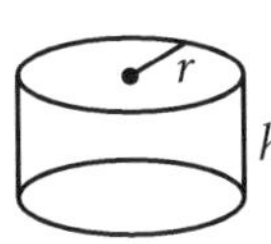

$V = \pi r^2 h$

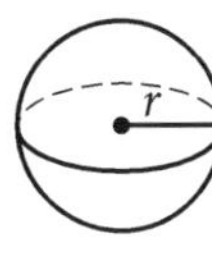

$V = \frac{4}{3}\pi r^3$

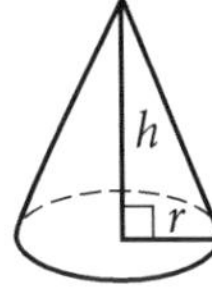

$V = \frac{1}{3}\pi r^2 h$

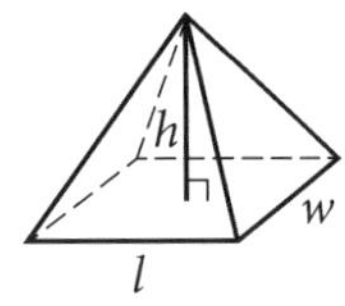

$V = \frac{1}{3}lwh$

The number of degrees of arc in a circle is 360.
The number of radians of arc in a circle is 2π.
The sum of the measures in degrees of the angles of a triangle is 180.

4

1

Ted received a bill of $355 for his car repair. The cost for parts was $215. The cost of labor was $35 per hour. How many hours did the repair take?

A) 3
B) 4
C) 5
D) 6

2

Julia owns a gift shop. She sold 10 t-shirts in July. Some of the t-shirts were sold for $12.95 each, and $15.99 each for the rest. Not including tax, she received $138.62 from the sale of the t-shirts. Which of the following equations can be used to find the number of t-shirts sold at each price?

A) $12.95x + 15.99(10 - x) = 138.62$
B) $12.95x + 15.99x = 138.62$
C) $12.95 + 15.99 + x = 10$
D) $15.99x = 138.62$

3

Jan has a shop and she wraps gifts for her customers. She has 200 yards of ribbon. On average it take 2.5 feet of ribbon to wrap each gift. How many gifts can Jan wrap with the supply of ribbon that she has?

A) 80
B) 160
C) 240
D) 500

4

A factory packaged 150 boxes of light bulbs. A sample of 8 of the boxes were checked for defects. It was found that the number of defective light bulbs in those 8 boxes were as follows: 5, 3, 5, 1, 2, 9, 4, 3. Based on this data, what is a good estimate of the total number of defective light bulbs in all 150 boxes?

A) 128
B) 150
C) 300
D) 600

5

Anchor Bank has a savings account that pays an annual rate of 4%. A client had made a deposit and left the money in the saving account for 2 years. The value of the account at the end of the 2 years, was $2,163.20. How much did the client deposit into the account, to the nearest dollar?

A) $1,993.60
B) $2,000.00
C) $2,089.10
D) $2,100.00

6

Afton is writing a term paper. He wants to include a table that has 5 columns and is 5 inches wide. He needs the first column to be 2.75 inches wide, and the remaining columns to be equal in width. What equation can Afton use to find the width, a, of each of the 4 columns?

A) $3a + 2.75 = 5$
B) $3a + 5 = 2.75$
C) $4a + 2.75 = 5$
D) $4a + 5 = 2.75$

7

Frequency Table

Number of Siblings	0	1	2	3	4	5
Number of Students	2	10	8	4	0	1

The frequency table above summarizes a survey taken of 25 students in a statistics class. Each student reported the number of sibling he/she has. What is the median number of siblings reported?

A) 1
B) 1.72
C) 2
D) 2.5

8

Point $R(6, 4)$ is on line m, which has a slope of $-\frac{2}{3}$. Which of the following points is also on line m?

A) (8, 1)
B) (8, 7)
C) (9, 2)
D) (9, 6)

9

Area of Study	Class				
	Freshman	Sophomore	Junior	Senior	Totals
Natural Sciences	50	35	33	29	147
Social Science	20	25	28	24	97
Humanities	40	40	39	37	156
Totals	110	100	100	90	400

The table above gives areas of study for 400 students presently enrolled at a small college. If a sophomore is selected at random, what is the probability that his or her area of studies is the humanities?

A) $\frac{1}{10}$
B) $\frac{2}{5}$
C) $\frac{10}{39}$
D) $\frac{1}{4}$

Questions 10 and 11 refer to the following information.

Capacity of tank (gallons)	100	500	1,000	2,000
Cost to build tank (dollars)	$200	$580	$920	$1,460

The table above gives the cost, in dollars, to build a storage tank that has a given capacity, in gallons.

10

Use x to represent the number of gallons of the storage tank and y to represent the cost of building the tank. Which of the following equations best relates x and y?

A) $y = 9.4x$
B) $y = 9.4\sqrt{x}$
C) $y = 9.4x^{\frac{3}{4}}$
D) $y = 9.4x^{\frac{2}{3}}$

11

Using the relationship between capacity and cost, how much would it cost to build a 30,000 gallon storage tank?

A) $1,955
B) $9,076
C) $21,427
D) $60,000

12

$$f(x) = x^3 + 4x^2 - 7x - 10$$

Use the above equation for function $f(x)$. Which list gives all the x-intercepts of the graph of function?

A) -1, 2
B) -5, -1
C) 1, 2, 5
D) -5, -1, 2

13

Which of the following functions represents exponential decay?

A) $f(x) = 280(0.375)^x$
B) $f(x) = 52(1.004)^x$
C) $f(x) = 124(1.5)^x$
D) $f(x) = 0.82(2)^x$

14

The coordinates of $\triangle ABC$ are $A(1,1)$, $B(2,3)$, and $C(3,1)$. $\triangle A'B'C'$ is the result of a reflection of $\triangle ABC$ over the y-axis. Which statement about $\triangle A'B'C'$ is true?

A) $\triangle A'B'C'$ is a right triangle.
B) $\triangle A'B'C'$ is an equilateral triangle.
C) $\triangle A'B'C'$ is a scalene triangle.
D) $\triangle A'B'C'$ is similar to $\triangle ABC$.

15

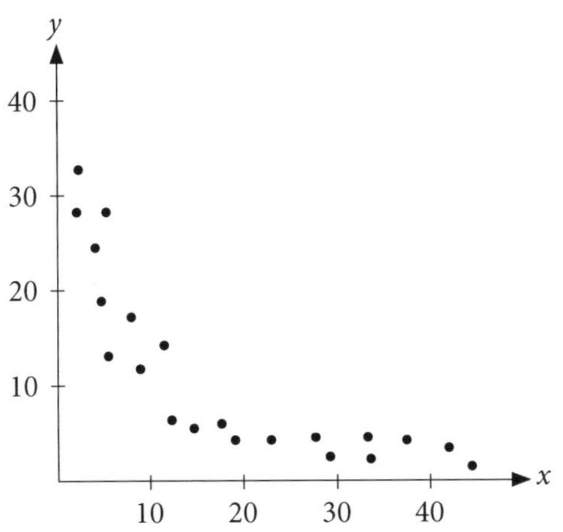

Use the scatterplot shown above for this problem. The equation, $y = ab^x$, can be used to model the data in the scatterplot. What must be true about the value of b?

A) $0 \leq b < 0$
B) $0 < b < 1$
C) $1 < b < \infty$
D) $-1 < b < 0$

Questions 16 and 17 refer to the following information.

An engineer designing a curved road must make the curve's radius large enough so that car passengers are not pulled to one side as they round the curve at the posted speed limit. The minimum radius, r, (in feet) that should be used is given by $r = \frac{1}{3}s^2$ where s is the expected speed of traffic (in miles per hour).

16

If the expected speed around a curve is 30 miles per hour, what should the minimum radius of the curve be?

A) 20 feet
B) 30 feet
C) 200 feet
D) 300 feet

17

How fast, to the nearest whole number, can a car comfortably round a curve with a radius of 400 feet?

A) 12 mph
B) 15 mph
C) 35 mph
D) 38 mph

18

$$S = \pi r^2 + \pi rl$$

A park in Minneapolis has a sculpture garden that has several geometric figures. A cone shaped sculpture is in need of painting on all of its surfaces. In order to determine how much paint to buy, the city engineer computed the surface area of the cone. He measured the diameter to be 14 yd and the slant height to be 25 yd. In the formula above, the variable r represents the radius of the base of the cone and the variable l represents the slant height of the cone. In square yards, what is the approximate surface area of the cone shaped sculpture?

A) 572 sq. yd.
B) 594 sq. yd.
C) 704 sq. yd.
D) 1, 166 sq. yd.

19

$$2x^2 + x = 5$$

To the nearest thousandth, what are the solutions to the above equation?

A) 1.351 and -1.851
B) 1.311 and -1.811
C) 1.079 and -0.579
D) 0.579 and -1.079

20

$$C = 62(1.05)^t$$

The equation above can be used to find the cost, in dollars, of a new pair of running shoes t years from now. To find the cost of a pair of running shoes 9 months ago, what value should be used for t?

A) 0.75
B) -0.75
C) 9
D) -9

Questions 21 and 22 refer to the following information.

The table below gives the average number of attendees at a small concert venue for each month during the year 2014.

Jan.	Feb.	Mar.	Apr.	May	June
65.9	70.7	75.5	84.5	93.6	103.5

July	Aug.	Sept.	Oct.	Nov.	Dec.
105.9	103.7	98.3	88.1	74.9	66.2

21

What is the mean of the data?

A) 79.1
B) 85.9
C) 86.3
D) 95.2

22

What is the range of this data?

A) 37.5
B) 37.8
C) 39.7
D) 40.0

23

The heights of the girls in grade 12 are normally distributed with a mean of 66 inches and a standard deviation of 2.5 inches. Which of the following statements is true about the heights of the students?

A) No student in this group is shorter than 51 inches tall.
B) The majority of students' heights are between 61 and 71 inches.
C) The average height of the girls will be less than the average height of the boys.
D) The average height of the girls will be greater than the average height of the boys.

24

Consider the graph of $f(x) = \sin(x)$, where x is in degrees and $0 \leq x \leq 360$. Over which interval(s) is the graph of $f(x)$ increasing?

A) $0 \leq x \leq 90$
B) $0 \leq x \leq 180$
C) $0 \leq x \leq 45$ and $135 \leq x \leq 180$
D) $0 \leq x \leq 90$ and $270 \leq x \leq 360$

25

$$\frac{2bc}{b-c}$$

The expression above will be positive for some values of b and c. Which of the following inequalities provides a set of values for b and c that will always make the expression positive?

A) $b < c < 0$
B) $c < b < 0$
C) $b < c < 2$
D) $c < b < 2$

26

$$f(x) = \begin{cases} 5x - 1, & \text{if } x < -2 \\ x - 9, & \text{if } x \geq -2 \end{cases}$$

Using the definition of function $f(x)$ given above, what is the value of $f(-10)$?

A) -51
B) -19
C) 19
D) 49

27

Clothing Prices (dollars)

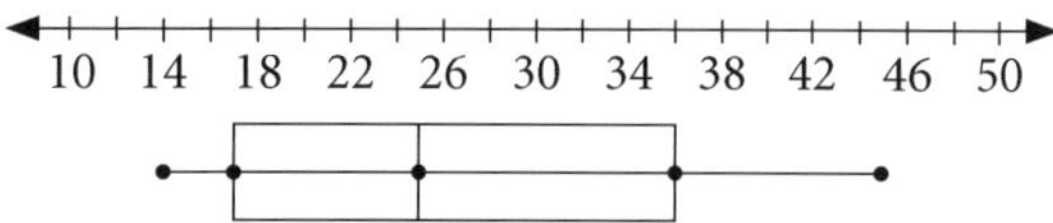

The owner of a clothing store kept track of the price of each item, not including any tax, that was sold on a given day. There were 64 items sold that day. The box-and-whisker plot shown above summarizes the data about the prices. Which of the following statements about the sales for the day is not true?

A) About 16 items sold that day were priced between \$17 and \$25.
B) About 16 items sold that day were priced between \$36 and \$45.
C) About 32 items sold that day were priced between \$17 and \$25.
D) About 32 items sold that day were priced between \$14 and \$25.

28

$$\sqrt{3x+7} = x - 1$$

Which set of numbers has all the solutions for the above equation?

A) {6}
B) {-1}
C) {-1, 6}
D) {-6, 1}

29

Liam has taken 3 tests in his science class, and has an average score of 88 for these tests. He wants to know what score he needs on the next test in order to have an average of exactly 90. Which equation can he use to find the score, x, that he needs?

A) $\frac{3x}{4} = 90$
B) $\frac{x + 264}{4} = 90$
C) $3(88) + x = 90$
D) $3(88) + x = 94$

30

How many of each type of solution for x does the equation below have?

$$-x^2 + 2x = 2$$

A) One real
B) Two real
C) One imaginary
D) Two imaginary

DIRECTIONS

For questions 31 – 38, solve each problem, enter your answer in the grid, as described below on the answer sheet.

1. Although not required, it is suggested that you write your answer in the boxes at the top of the columns to help you fill in the circles accurately. You will receive credit only if the circles are filled in correctly.
2. Mark no more than one circle in any column.
3. No question has a negative answer.
4. Some problems may have more than one correct answer. In such cases, grid only one answer.
5. **Mixed numbers** such as $3\frac{1}{2}$ must be gridded as 3.5 or $\frac{7}{2}$. (If 3 1 / 2 is entered into the grid, it will be interpreted as $\frac{31}{2}$, not $3\frac{1}{2}$.)
6. **Decimal answers:** If you obtain a decimal answer with more digits than the grid can accommodate, it may be either rounded or truncated, but it must fill the entire grid.

Answer: $\frac{7}{12}$

Write answer in boxes. → 7 / 1 2 ← Fraction line

Grid in result.

Answer: 2.5

2 . 5 ← Decimal point

Acceptable ways to grid $\frac{2}{3}$ are:

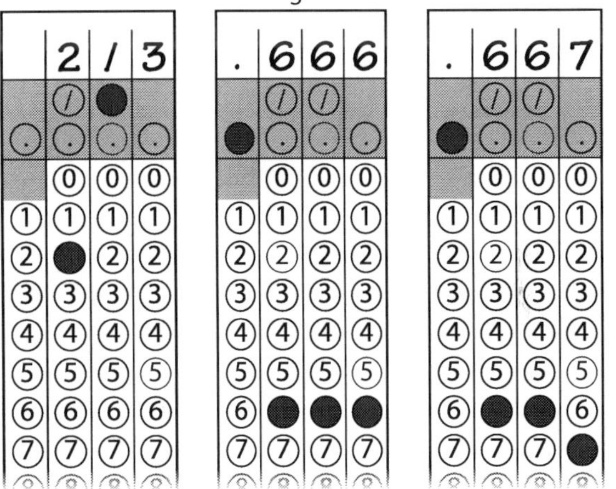

Answer: 201 – either position is correct

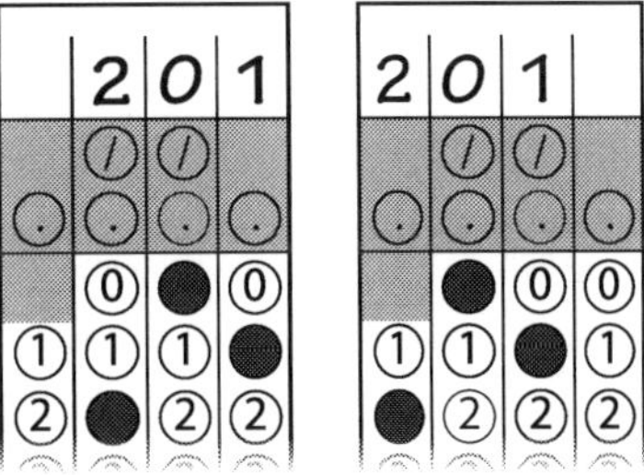

NOTE: You may start your answers in any column, space permitting. Columns you don't need to use should be left blank.

31

A cube has a surface area of 337.5 square feet. What is the length, in feet, of one of its edges?

32

What is the solution of the equation shown below?

$$3(x + 1)^{\frac{1}{5}} + 5 = 11$$

33

What is the fraction form of the decimal $0.02\overline{7}$?

34

$A(-4, 5) \quad B(-7, -2)$

Point A and point B, given above, are on a coordinate grid. What is the length of $\overline{AB}$, to the nearest hundredth?

35

A rectangular pyramid has a base that is a rectangle with a length of 14 ft. and a width of 12 ft. The pyramid has a height of 8 ft. What is the volume, in cubic feet, of the rectangular pyramid?

36

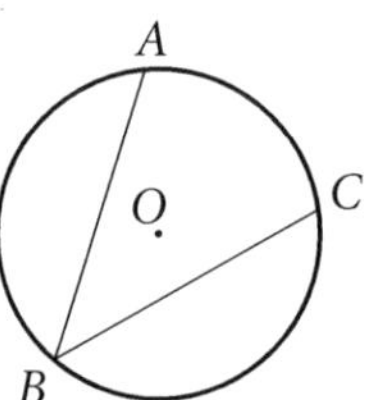

In the diagram above, $\angle ABC$ is inscribed in circle O. Expressed as a fraction, what is the ratio of the measure of $\angle ABC$ to the measure of $\overset{\frown}{AC}$?

Questions 37 and 38 refer to the following information.

Susie is turning 18 in May. Susie's grandmother told Susie that is going to give her a choice for her birthday present. Choice One is a gift of $100. Choice Two is to receive 20 cents on May 1, 40 cents on May 2, 80 cents on May 3, etc. The amount of money would follow this pattern for until (and including) May 9.

37

Susie took Choice 2. In cents, how much more money did Susie receive from her grandmother by choosing Choice 2 instead of Choice 1?

38

$$S_n = a_1\left(\frac{1 - r^n}{1 - r}\right)$$

The formula for the sum of a geometric sequence is above, where S represents the sum total, a_1 represents the initial amount, r represents the ratio by which the original amount is multiplied, and n represents the number of values in the set.

When Susie chooses Option Two, what is the value of the expression inside the parentheses?

STOP

If you finish before time is called, you may check your work on this section only. Do not turn to any other section.

Tutor Ted®

SAT® Practice Essay #4

ESSAY BOOK

DIRECTIONS

The essay gives you an opportunity to show how effectively you can read and comprehend a passage and write an essay analyzing the passage. In your essay, you should demonstrate that you have read the passage carefully, present a clear and logical analysis, and use language precisely.

Your essay must be written on the lines provided in your answer booklet; except for the Planning Page of the answer booklet, you will receive no other paper on which to write. You will have enough space if you write on every line, avoid wide margins, and keep your handwriting to a reasonable size. Remember that people who are not familiar with your handwriting will read what you write. Try to write or print so that what you are writing is legible to those readers.

You have <u>50 minutes</u> to read the passage and write an essay in response to the prompt provided inside this booklet.

REMINDERS:

— Do not write your essay in this booklet. Only what you write on the lined pages of your answer booklet will be evaluated.

— An off-topic essay will not be evaluated.

This cover is representative of what you'll see on test day.

As you read the passage below, consider how W. E. B. Du Bois uses

- evidence, such as facts or examples, to support claims.
- reasoning to develop ideas and to connect claims and evidence.
- stylistic or persuasive elements, such as word choice or appeals to emotion, to add power to the ideas expressed.

Adapted from W. E. B. Du Bois's editorial, "Woman Suffrage." © 1915 by *The Crisis, Vol.* 11.

1 This month 200,000 Negro voters will be called upon to vote on the question of giving the right of suffrage to women. THE CRISIS[1] sincerely trusts that every one of them will vote Yes. But THE CRISIS would not have them go to the polls without having considered every side of the question. Intelligence in voting is the only real support of democracy. For this reason we publish with pleasure Dean Kelly Miller's article against woman suffrage. Meantime, Dean Miller will pardon us for a word in answer to his argument.

2 Briefly put, Mr. Miller believes that the bearing and rearing of the young is a function which makes it practically impossible for women to take any large part in general, industrial and public affairs; that women are weaker than men; that women are adequately protected under man's suffrage; that no adequate results have appeared from woman suffrage and that office-holding by women is "risky."

3 All these arguments sound today ancient. If we turn to easily available statistics we find that instead of the women of this country or of any other country being confined chiefly to childbearing they are as a matter of fact engaged and engaged successfully in practically every pursuit in which men are engaged. The actual work of the world today depends more largely upon women than upon men. Consequently this man-ruled world faces an astonishing dilemma: either Woman the Worker is doing the world's work successfully or not. If she is not doing it well why do we not take from her the necessity of working? If she is doing it well why not treat her as a worker with a voice in the direction of work?

4 The statement that woman is weaker than man is sheer rot: It is the same sort of thing that we hear about "darker races" and "lower classes." Difference, either physical or spiritual, does not argue weakness or inferiority. That the average woman is spiritually different from the average man is undoubtedly just as true as the fact that the average white man differs from the average Negro; but this is no reason for disfranchising the Negro or lynching him. It is inconceivable that any person looking upon the accomplishments of women today in every field of endeavor, realizing their humiliating handicap and the astonishing prejudices which they face and yet seeing despite this that in government, in the professions, in sciences, art and literature and the industries they are leading and dominating forces and growing in power as their emancipation grows,--it is inconceivable that any fair-minded person could for a moment talk about a "weaker" sex.

5 To say that men protect women with their votes is to overlook the flat testimony of the facts. In the first place there are millions of women who have no natural men protectors: the unmarried, the widowed, the deserted and those who have married failures. To put this whole army incontinently out of court and leave them unprotected and without voice in political life is more than unjust, it is a crime.

6 There was a day in the world when it was considered that by marriage a woman lost all her individuality as a human soul and simply became a machine for making men. We have outgrown that idea. A woman is just as much a thinking, feeling, acting person after marriage as before. She has opinions and she has a right to have them and she has a right to express them. It is conceivable, of course, for a country to decide that its unit of representation should be the family and that one person in that family should express its will. But by what possible process of rational thought can it be decided that the person to express that will should always be the male, whether he be genius or drunkard, imbecile or captain of industry? The meaning of the twentieth century is the freeing of the individual soul; the soul longest in slavery and still in the most disgusting and indefensible slavery is the soul of womanhood. God give her increased freedom this November!

[1] The magazine in which this editorial appeared. Du Bois was editor of *The Crisis*.

> Write an essay in which you explain how W. E. B. Du Bois builds an argument to persuade his audience that women should gain the right to vote. In your essay, analyze how Du Bois uses one or more of the features listed in the box above (or features of your own choice) to strengthen the logic and persuasiveness of his argument. Be sure that your analysis focuses on the most relevant features of the passage.
>
> Your essay should not explain whether you agree with Du Bois's claims, but rather explain how Du Bois builds an argument to persuade his audience.

Practice Test 4 ANSWERS

READING

#	Answer	#	Answer
1	A	27	A
2	C	28	B
3	A	29	C
4	D	30	A
5	D	31	D
6	C	32	B
7	D	33	C
8	A	34	A
9	C	35	C
10	B	36	C
11	C	37	B
12	B	38	D
13	A	39	A
14	B	40	B
15	D	41	D
16	C	42	B
17	B	43	D
18	A	44	A
19	D	45	D
20	B	46	C
21	B	47	C
22	D	48	A
23	A	49	A
24	A	50	A
25	D	51	C
26	D	52	C

WRITING & LANGUAGE

#	Answer	#	Answer
1	1 C	23	A
2	D	24	B
3	D	25	B
4	A	26	B
5	A	27	D
6	B	28	C
7	B	29	A
8	A	30	D
9	B	31	A
10	C	32	B
11	D	33	C
12	C	34	D
13	D	35	D
14	B	36	A
15	C	37	B
16	B	38	D
17	D	39	D
18	A	40	C
19	B	41	A
20	A	42	B
21	C	43	A
22	B	44	A

MATH (No Calculator)

#	Answer
1	D
2	D
3	B
4	A
5	D
6	D
7	C
8	B
9	C
10	D
11	D
12	C
13	B
14	C
15	A
16	0
17	.8, 4/5, 8/10
18	7
19	1
20	16

MATH (Calculator)

#	Answer
1	B
2	A
3	C
4	D
5	B
6	C
7	C
8	C
9	B
10	D
11	B
12	D
13	A
14	D
15	B
16	D
17	C
18	C
19	A
20	B
21	B
22	A
23	B
24	D
25	B
26	A
27	C
28	A
29	B
30	D
31	7.5, 15/2
32	31
33	1/36, .027, .028
34	7.62
35	448
36	½, 0.5
37	220
38	511

PRACTICE TEST 4: SOLUTIONS

Practice Test 4 SOLUTIONS

SECTION 1: READING

PASSAGE: DRACULA

1) A
The title of the passage tells us we're reading "Dr. Seward's Diary," followed by the dates of August 20 and August 23. According to the passage, the doctor is chronicling his interactions with a perpetually violent madman who wears a strait-waistcoat in a padded room, so A fits best.

2) C
Be sure to tackle vocabulary questions first—easy money! Stoker writes, "I was satisfied with his present condition," implying the patient is cleared for release. "Dismissed" is a tempting answer choice, but it doesn't fit the context of a patient in an insane asylum as well as "released."

3) A
There is no evidence in the text to support B or C. Earlier in the paragraph, the narrator mentions that three days have passed during which the patient is, "violent all day then quiet from moonrise to sunrise." If an "influence" comes and goes, it is most likely connected to the passing of time.

4) D
The narrator finds it soothing to be "dissociated even in the mind of this poor madman from the others," implying he is unlike the other people Renfield interacts with. This desire to not be associated with everyone else demonstrates the narrator's arrogance.

5) D
The attendants' hesitation to leave the doctor alone and the patient's disclosure of their distrust both showcase the possibility of dangerous behavior. The passage does not focus on the relationship between the two, but rather Dr. Seward's observations of Renfield's behavior. The doctor's physical strength is never mentioned, and the patient in fact exhibits control during these lines.

6) C
The hesitation of the attendants to abandon the doctor establishes that the patient is unpredictable and at risk to behave dangerously.

7) D
The patient has grown quiet, displaying "spells of cessation from his passion," indicating that for periods of time, or "intervals," the patient is subdued. Never leave a vocabulary question unanswered—easy money!

8) A
In the final paragraph, the narrator writes of increasingly sympathetic treatment towards the patient, noting plans to "ease his bonds for a few hours each day."

9) C
Stoker writes, "the poor soul's body will enjoy the relief," expressing sympathy for the madman.

10) B
The final paragraph shows that the doctor has chosen to decrease Renfield's restrictions as a result of perceived improvement. This illustrates the patient's progress since the perpetual violence with which the passage began.

PASSAGE: GENETICALLY MODIFIED FOOD CROPS AND PUBLIC HEALTH

11) C
A is the primary purpose of the first paragraph, not the passage as a whole. B is the purpose of the third paragraph. The authors seek to offer biofortification as a promising and sustainable alternative to malnutrition in poor countries.

12) B
Better nutrition for humans and livestock is

the "aim," or "goal" of improving food crops. While "wish" and "grail" could perhaps technically fit, they do not fit the tone of the passage.

13) A
The third paragraph begins with the fact that GM crop critics often ignore that conventionally bred food crops may have severe toxic effects on humans. The authors further argue that GM crops are "routinely tested for toxic or allergic effects on consumers prior to their commercial release," contrary to conventional crops.

14) B
Use the answer choices by looking up each two-year period on the graph and estimating the growth in production. A is about a 30% growth, B a 35% growth, C a 15% growth, and D a 10% drop.

15) D
The authors present the health risks of vitamin A deficiency, including malnutrition, blindness, or death, further noting that VAD is especially common in South and Southeast Asia. Health and malnutrition are intimately linked with resource availability.

16) C
The authors observe that conventional crops contain toxins and allergens, stating that GM critics "commonly ignore" this fact, a shortcoming of their argument. Neither "attack" nor "undermine" fit the authors' tone in the third paragraph.

17) B
Their tone can best be described as "critical," as the authors objectively analyze and evaluate the known dangers of conventional crop consumption. "Accusatory," "defensive," or "insensitive" would not describe the tone of a scientific publication.

18) A
The authors present the dangers of conventional crops in only the third paragraph, so B is incorrect. C is out as the authors are pro-GM foods. D extrapolates beyond what the authors present in the passage, so the answer is A.

19) D
The authors describe the grave consequences of "non-scientific disputes concerning GM crops" as food security remains an urgent global issue. The authors seek to provide irrefutable scientific evidence in support of biofortification in order to offer a cost-effective strategy to combat malnutrition.

20) B
What does "majority" mean? It means more than 50%. Since more than 50% of soybeans and cotton planted in the years 2000-2003 were genetically engineered, this answer has got to be true. As always, think very literally on these table/graph questions.

PASSAGE: HOW THIRD WORLD COUNTRIES CAN TAKE ADVANTAGE OF GLOBALIZATION

21) B
The author discusses the importance of the globalization of knowledge, especially in disadvantaged countries. He describes CIDE, which is designed to allow students who otherwise lack opportunity to become immersed in science and technology.

22) D
Make sure to read the whole sentence that contains this word so you know the context. The "students' heterogeneity of conditions" is parallel/connected to the phrase "special circumstances of the individual." That word 'conditions' is referring to the circumstances—or background—of CIDE students.

23) A
Make sure you stay "evidence-based" on a question like this. Multiple answers might seem to make good common sense, but only one will be justified by the evidence in the passage. That's A. Stay tuned for the next solution to see why.

24) A
The evidence to justify question 23 is in this

phrase: "A number of university professors in Mexico not involved in "mainstream" science took advantage of some features of globalization to help non-conventional students get PhDs in science." This is the origin story of CIDE. The most helpful part of that phrase is the adjective "non-conventional," which lines up with the phrase "who would likely not receive one otherwise" in the right answer to question 23.

25) D
The two more extreme answers, "defensive" and "arrogant," should be pretty easy to get rid of, given the fairly straightforward and unemotional tone of this essay. Now, is the author "reserved" or "appreciative" towards CIDE? Reserved means "slow to reveal emotions" and appreciative means "showing appreciation or gratitude for." Look at a sentence like the last sentence in the essay to see that the author does have some positive regard for the program. That justifies answer D.

26) C
This is a math question hiding within a reading passage. I know—I don't like it either. It's SAT's world and we just live within it. Do some simple math—and read the answer choices carefully—to see that the rate of inflation for cost of living is about half of the rate for medical costs.

27) A
In the third paragraph, the author explains CIDE's approach of using students' heterogeneous conditions to create individualized programs catered to every student's specific needs. That's their approach.

28) B
In the fourth paragraph, the author states the importance of regional scientific communities in which "students interact with scientists at the frontier of knowledge thus creating themselves their own network that includes national scientists," so the answer is B.

29) C
See previous question—the author discusses networking opportunities within scientific communities in the fourth paragraph, whereas there is no evidence to support any of the other answers to Question 28.

30) A
When a question asks you to use data from the graph to support an idea in the passage, make sure you use both! A trap on these questions is that some answers, like B in this case, might be true based on the graph but not the passage, or vice versa. Here, the fact that can be justified by both the passage and the graph is the fact that traditional education is expensive. You can see that based on the rate of inflation of college education, which is much higher than the inflation of the cost of living in the graph, and you can also read about it at the very end of the passage, which notes that a traditional education requires a "costly" infrastructure.

PASSAGE: *REPORT ON A NATIONAL BANK* AND *OPINION ON THE CONSTITUTIONALITY OF A NATIONAL BANK*

31) D
"It is evident that the money, which a merchant keeps in his chest, waiting for a favorable opportunity to employ it, produces nothing 'till that opportunity arrives." So the money "produces nothing" before it is employed. We want a synonym of "use" to replace "employ." That's "utilize."

32) B
In the second paragraph of Passage 1, Hamilton writes that purchases can be made with bank paper or credit as effectively as with an equal sum of gold or silver. By lending and circulating a greater sum of money, the bank increases capital "to all the purposes of trade and industry," thereby stimulating the economy.

33) C
While A provides evidence of the ability of

a bank to circulate a greater sum of money than is actually backed by gold or silver, it does not mention its effect on the economy. C provides evidence that profit generated from unbacked paper money leads to an "absolute increase of capital."

34) A
In the final paragraph of Passage 1, Hamilton suggests that those opposed to a National Bank have pointed to the Acts of Congress as evidence that the government has no power to create a new institution. He responds that "if the public good requires it," no established law would prevent its establishment.

35) C
Vocabulary questions are quick to answer—tackle them right away if you're pressed for time! Jefferson writes that failing to abide by the rules set by Congress is to "take possession of a boundless field of power, no longer susceptible of any definition." Ignoring the Constitution doesn't leave it devoid of "meaning" or "clarity," but instead renders its "parameters" irrelevant.

36) C
In the second paragraph of Passage 2, Jefferson divulges that "instituting a Congress with power to do whatever would be for the good of the United States... it would be also a power to do whatever evil they please."

37) B
At the beginning of Passage 2, Jefferson maintains that "powers not delegated to the United States, by the Constitution, nor prohibited by it to the States, are reserved to the States or to the people." Therefore, above any economic benefit a National Bank might represent, Jefferson protects States' rights as written in the Constitution. According to Jefferson, the Constitution is not to be interpreted at one's discretion, so C is incorrect. There is no evidence to support A. D is a specific detail in Passage 2, but not the central claim.

38) D
The first paragraph of Passage 2 quotes the Constitution, outlining specific powers delegated to the United States national government. Referring to Hamilton's argument that the Constitution can be bypassed "if the public good requires it," Jefferson goes on to write, "It would reduce the whole instrument to a single phrase..." Therefore, the "instrument" to which Jefferson refers is the Constitution.

39) A
Jefferson doesn't focus on the practicality of having a National Bank, rather the consequences of giving the government that power, so B is incorrect. Jefferson never discusses Hamilton's prediction of a National Bank's vast financial benefits, so C is incorrect as well. Instead, Jefferson addresses the ramifications of conceding power to the national government beyond what is established in the Constitution, hence cautioning against Hamilton's central claim to establish a National Bank, so the answer is A.

40) B
In Passage 2, Jefferson focuses on maintaining only powers specifically given to the national government, fearing that exceptions would lead to a "power to do whatever evil they please." On the other hand, in Passage 1, Hamilton argues that laws can be sidestepped "if the public good requires it," or "if something promotes the general welfare."

41) D
In addressing those who point to the specific laws delineated in the Acts of Congress as reason to not establish a National Bank in the final paragraph of Passage 1, Hamilton claims that nothing should prevent the establishment of a new institution "if the public good requires it."

PASSAGE: DISCOVERY, DEVELOPMENT, AND REGULATION OF NATURAL PRODUCTS

42) B
Tackle main idea questions right after you read the passage so it's fresh in your mind. From the start of the passage, the authors explain the widespread use of natural medical treatments throughout history, highlighting their applicability in disease prevention and cures. For example, in recent years, 48.6% of anti-cancer agents were derived from natural products. In the fourth paragraph, the authors discuss challenges specific to resupplying natural naturally derived compounds. HIV research is not the purpose of the passage as a whole, and the passage concludes with the necessity, not difficulty, of natural drug development, so the answer is B.

43) A
Plants have been used to "ameliorate diseases and foster healing." The passage argues for the benefit of natural remedies, so "foster" most nearly means "promote." Easy money!

44) A
Penicillin's success story is only briefly mentioned so we can eliminate C. Beyond explaining or introducing traditional methods of natural drug discovery, the second paragraph serves to reveal that the method was "slow, labor-intensive, inefficient," establishing the need for innovation, so the answer is A.

45) D
This is a slightly tougher vocab-in-context question! Stick to your guns: read the sentence without "field" in it. Find another word that might fit. Something like "area" or "topic" might work well. The only match—the only word that would fit the passage is answer choice D, "domain."

46) C
This question is a good demonstration of the tendendy of the SAT to give you answer choices that sound just about right... but that aren't specifically justified in the text. Which one is justified? I would use the line references in the next question to help you figure it out. When you read lines 75-80, I think you'll agree that it justifies both adjectives—ongoing and valuable.

47) D
Let's talk about why this evidence works to prove the correct answer to #46. "...continues in the 21st century..." is the "ongoing part. "The discovery of valuable therapeutic agents..." is the "valuable" part. That makes D a winner on this question.

48) A
In the third paragraph, the authors note, "Failure of anti-HIV therapy is observed due to the emergence of drug resistance and the significant side effect profile of existing therapies," leading to a resurgent interest in natural drugs.

49) A
At the end of the third paragraph, the authors maintain that only few natural products have actually reached clinical trials and "none of them made it on the list of conventional antiretroviral drugs."

50) A
The authors conclude the passage not with a summary, but with an assessment of the realistic challenges ahead, noting that natural products may still lack enough versatility to produce "suitable treatments for all heritable human diseases."

51) C
In discussing the challenges associated with naturally derived drugs in the fourth paragraph, the authors observe that compounds derived from rare or remote plants, or from marine organisms which reside in inaccessible regions, create problems for resupply.

52) C
In the fourth paragraph, the authors admit the challenges associated with "obtaining sufficient amounts of material pure enough for discovery and development activities,"

indicating that production of natural medicine is hindered by adequate supply.

SECTION 2: WRITING AND LANGUAGE

PASSAGE: TATAU: POLYNESIA'S MARK ON THE WORLD

1) **C**
Redundancy question. "Not unique" means that it happens other places, so A and D are out. C does B's job in fewer words, and as we well know: shorter is better!

2) **D**
Upon first glance, A looks like a correctly punctuated list. However, notice the word "from" just before our examples? Every "from" must be followed by a "to," so A is out. If you've done enough of these, you'll recognize this an another example of the SAT keeping things short, simple, and free of extraneous commas.

3) **D**
The rules of parallelism eliminate answer choices B and C. Between A and D, D is more concise.

4) **A**
Why would an animal symbolize stealth? Probably because they're stealthy, yes? What's stealthier than the ability to hide from sharks?

5) **A**
Colons are supposed to replace connector words like "with," not precede them (which eliminates D). Now that we've got that out of the way, the clauses on either side of the proposed punctuation are both independent, meaning we can punctuate them with a semicolon, colon, or period. Answer choice C would be grammatically correct without the additional comma, but since it makes no, sense at, all to, pause, there (See? Unnecessary commas interrupt the flow of thought!), the colon is your best bet.

6) **B**
This is one of the SAT's favorite tricks: singular noun (group) followed by a plural noun as the object of a preposition (ancestors) followed by the verb or pronoun in question. I know it sounds crazy, but the pronoun is technically modifying the collective noun "group," and therefore we must use the singular possessive "its." Hey, I don't make the rules; I just tell you how to implement them on the SAT.

7) **B**
Most people get this one down to A and B pretty easily. The key to choosing the correct answer here is to look at the following clause "who were once united." Ask yourself: who was once united? Humans? Or Rangi and Papa? Aha. The answer is Rangi and Papa, so their names need to immediately precede the comma. For this reason, we call A a "misplaced modifier."

8) **A**
Because Rangi and Papa are described in human-like terms, we need some version of "who" or "whom" here. If the "who v. whom" battle is confusing, feel free to go back and reread this lesson in the book; however, a quick shortcut is to remember that "whom" will always follow a preposition (to/from/for/with/by/etc.). The only answer choice that does this is C, and I think we can all agree that C is probably the worst-sounding of the bunch.

9) **B**
The correct answer here should provide the most direct contrast with the idea that the upper body represents "spirituality, knowledge, and wisdom," which are relatively cerebral, disembodied concepts. What's the opposite of the mind/spirit? The body!

10) **C**
If you're reading the whole passage (and you should be), you'll recognize that we've already said that tatau is for everybody, which eliminates A and B. Now let's look at the keys

to the question stem: "effective transition" and "consistent with the information." C builds a bridge to the previous paragraph by referring to the "designs themselves" and completes bridge construction by introducing the "cultural symbolism" of getting tattooed this paragraph will go on to discuss.

11) D
Sentence 2 moves the conversation from the physical experience of getting tattooed to the cultural shame of remaining unadorned. However, we haven't even really gotten into the physical experience yet! Sentences 2-5 all discuss the process itself, and only after we've finished that conversation should we move on to something else.

PASSAGE: GLOBAL MARKETS AND THE RISE OF HIGH FREQUENCY TRADING

12) C
Because "technological innovation" is singular, we must use the singular "has" as well as the singular "a catalyst."

13) D
There are two dependent, introductory clauses before the independent clause in this sentence, so let's make them parallel, yes? "Because its use is" most closely matches "because the interconnectedness" in the second clause.

14) B
Semicolons and periods are grammatically interchangeable, so if they're both right... they're both wrong! All we need here is a comma to connect the two previous dependent clauses to this independent one.

15) C
We can't further describe how HTF works before we even know it's a thing, right? Right. Sentence 4 introduces and defines High Frequency Trading, so it must precede sentence 3. However, since the sentence in question provides a simple supporting detail, it should come after sentence 4 but before the thesis statement (sentence 5).

16) B
For the punctuation averse, this can be a scary group of answer choices. So let's work backwards from worst to best! Yes, the SAT loves eliminating commas, but D is just weird. C is the flip side of the same coin- no punctuation is odd-sounding, but this amount of punctuation is full-on crazy. If you remember that literally the only way you are ever allowed to use a semicolon is to combine two clauses that could stand alone as complete sentences, you know that A is grammatically incorrect.

17) D
The main idea of the paragraph, obviously, is that computers are fast, but that still leaves us with three possible answer choices. However, the point is that all computers (not just supercomputers) are fast, which makes answer choices A and B too narrow in scope.

18) A
Of the options presented, A is definitely the most conventional, academic choice.

19) B
We are looking for a transition word that conveys the contrast within the sentence (as opposed to that between the previous sentence and this one). "Unfortunately" comes close, but "ironically" more directly states that two realities shouldn't be but are simultaneously true.

20) A
A and C are the only real competitors here, so it comes down to the battle or "error" versus "err." Error is a noun while err is a verb (Ex: To err is human.) Generally speaking, we are immune to things (for example, diseases) not actions, so "error" is correct.

21) C
The correct punctuation includes commas separating items in a list.

22) B
What scenario is the writer trying to depict? According to the previous sentence, it's one in which a local crash can send "shock waves

throughout the whole global economy." Does the graph depict the sudden and dramatic decrease in the entire Dow Jones Average during the flash crash? It does.

PASSAGE: CONSERVING WATER IN A CHANGING CLIMATE: LESSONS FROM CALIFORNIA

23) A
B and C are too informal in tone, and "ambivalent," which means "having mixed feelings," doesn't mean what the word we are looking for should mean.

24) B
Using a parenthetical is another way to set off inessential information, essentially taking the place of two commas or two dashes. And since this aside is referring directly to "consequences," we don't want to separate these ideas (with extra punctuation) any more than we already have.

25) B
This one generally comes down to A and B, in which case it might be helpful to review the "that v. which" lesson earlier in the book. Remember the shortcut? "Which" tends to follow a comma while "that" does not. Since you cannot eliminate the comma in this sentence, "that" is probably incorrect.

26) B
This question also generally comes down to A and B, since C is off tonally and D doesn't even come close to meaning what we need it to mean in this sentence. Based on the rest of the passage, do these measures hope to completely get rid of the bad effects of drought or simply make them less bad? The passage never asserts that the problem can be solved entirely; what it does discuss are ways to reduce its negative consequences.

27) D
Not only were conservation measures enacted on an industrial scale but also individual citizens were asked to conserve. Only the choice "in addition" conveys this duality.

28) C
The verb in question is second in a list of three, and thus we need to adhere to the rules of parallelism. People did three things to reduce water usage: "turned off," "declined," and "shortened."

29) A
"Either" and "or" are like those new couples who can't get enough of each other: you'll never see one without the other.

30) D
Remaining consistent with this list is all about showing how these devices save water. C is not terrible but, as per our instructions, D provides the most "specific" information as to how faucet aerators conserve water.

31) A
What, math on the Writing test? Yep. One-third, as you likely know, is 33.333 (et cetera) %, which is supported by the graph. B is too broad because the graph does not span the entire period of mandatory restriction. C is unsupportable because the graph does not differentiate between urban and rural areas. D is definitely meant to be tempting but is wrong because of the inclusion of the word "throughout." Notice how May's conservation level is below 25%? That means that the level was not above 25% for the entirety—or throughout—2015.

32) B
You've got two battles to fight here, so pick the one you find easiest first. "Than" is comparative while "then" relates to time, so we're down to B and C. "Restored" is the active, more succinct option, so that's going to be our winner.

33) C
When in doubt about the main idea of a passage, read its title! The phrase "lessons from California" insinuates that the issues explored in this passage have import beyond the borders of the Golden State. C does the best job of flowing logically from

the ideas presented in the last paragraph AND harkening back to central point of the passage.

PASSAGE: THE MARS MISSION AND THE HUMAN PSYCHE

34) D
You should be able to remove an appositive clause from a sentence without damaging it structural integrity. In this sentence, "and perhaps even more importantly" is a separate thought interspliced into the middle of the sentence, and as such should be punctuated accordingly.

35) D
This is a redundancy question as "to sequester" means "to isolate." However, if you didn't know that, there's still the handy SAT tip that if more than one answer choice is right for the same reason, they both (or all 3) are wrong! In this sentence "by themselves," "alone," and "in isolation" all mean the same thing! Thus, they all must be wrong.

36) A
Not only/but also, baby! These phrases are like swans: they mate for life. In other words, if you use "not only," you're stuck with using "but also" too. The battle between A and C is won by thinking about parallelism. "Expertise" is the best match for "stamina."

37) B
Modern English speakers don't use "for" to describe a cause/effect relationship as much as they do other words like "because" or "since," but it can mean the same thing. Insert the word "since" in the sentence and see how it sounds. Good, right? Then "for" is a perfect, if unusual, candidate.

38) D
When is this journey to Mars happening? In the future.

39) D
The key to this question is the gerund (verb acting as a noun) "knowing" earlier in the sentence, for that is the noun this verb must match in tense and number. "Knowing" is a singular thing, so we would say "knowing requires." Then it gets tough because we've hit an exception to the rule "shorter is better." No one is in love with D, but A is so awkwardly worded that D wins by process of elimination.

40) C
Keep it short. Keep it simple. Keep it C.

41) A
This question stem asks us to choose the most "precise depiction," so let's eliminate B and D because they are too vague. A is slightly better, but C is by far the most precise.

42) B
Answer choice A is tempting because it seems to contrast the American space program with that of another nation, but a slightly deeper dive into sentence 2 reveals that the real focus of this paragraph is the connection between physical and psychological health.

43) A
Without this clarification, readers who are unfamiliar with the term "circadian rhythms" would not understand that we are talking about sleep cycles. The SAT hates extraneous information, but clarity is crucial.

44) A
To find the main idea of a paragraph, re-read the topic sentence. In this paragraph, it's answer choice B on question 42, which introduces the idea that physical and psychological health are interrelated. C and D are only about physical health, and B is not about either physical or psychological health but rather technical limitations.

4

SECTION 3: MATH - NO CALCULATOR

1) D
Core algebra skills here, folks. Square both sides, then add 4. That will get you directly to $x = 53$.

2) D
I would start this one by noticing that the y-intercept is (0, 1). That means our b value must be positive 1, and that means that it's got to be B or D. Last step, find the slope. Using the first two points, the slope would be $\frac{1 - (-3)}{0 - 5} = \frac{4}{-5} = -\frac{4}{5}$. That means D is the winner.

3) B
Systems with an infinite number of solutions consist of the same exact line. Notice how the second equation looks like it's twice as big as the first one. To make them the same equation, you need C to be twice as big as 20 as well. That means C has to be 40.

4) A
That "f to the -1" thing is code for the inverse function. To find an inverse function, replace $f(x)$ with y. Then swap y for x in the equation, then resolve for y. Like so:

$$y = 2x + 7$$
$$x = 2y + 7$$
$$x - 7 = 2y$$
$$y = \frac{x - 7}{2}$$

It's a simple process...you just have to know the math vocabulary.

5) D
Do you remember difference of squares? It's the factoring trick that tells us that $x^2 - y^2 = (x + y)(x - y)$. It works the same way for a and b, so in this case $a^2 - b^2 = (a + b)(a - b)$.

6) B
Two ways to do this. The first is to draw all of the reflections of the graphs to determine which inverse function is still a function. Typically the way to figure that out would be to use the "vertical line test." A function will only ever intersect a vertical line at a maximum of one point at a time. The other way is to know the math fun fact that, for an inverse function to be a function, the original function must pass the HORIZONTAL line test—the same thing as the vertical line test above, just with a horizontal line instead. If you know that, you can quickly identify B as the one that passes the test and therefore has an inverse that is a function.

7) C
Classic word problem into math expression. If one piece is x, then the other one should be $x + 6$, and together they should add up to 72. Boom, C.

8) B
Start by rearranging this function into the more familiar $y = mx + b$ format. You should get $y = \frac{2}{3}x + 6$. A perpendicular line's slope will be the negative reciprocal of $\frac{2}{3}$, so it's got to be $-\frac{3}{2}$. The y-intercept is the same, so the new equation will be $y = -\frac{3}{2}x + 6$.

9) C
Remainder theorem buys you some really easy points if you know it! Look it up in our book if you don't know or can't remember it. It basically IS this problem: if a function is divisible by a factor like $(x + 4)$, then it must have a zero at that point... in this case, at $x = -4$.

10) D
Test the two values. Why doesn't 2 work in this equation? On the left side, we would get -2. On the right, we'd get the square root of 4, which is positive 2. Try it with 8, and you'll find you get the same result on both the left and the right That's why 8 is a solution and 2 is not.

11) C

This problem numbers the angles pretty much the way we did in the geometry chapter. When you number them that way, convenient things happen...including the fact that all of the even-numbered angles will be the same as each other. Since we're trying to match all the angles that are equal to angle 4, the ones we want must be angles 2, 6, and 8. If you forgot that trick, you could also eyeball this question carefully. All the acute angles are the ones that will be equal to angle 4. If you're a visual thinker, go ahead and apply that strategy!

12) C

Consecutive integers are just integers that are right in a row, like 4, 5, and 6, or 99, 100, 101, etc. To find them algebraically, you'd call one of them n, the next one $n + 1$, the one after that $n + 2$, etc. Here, we just need those three, and we need them to add up to 90, so C is the answer!

13) B

Set these two equations equal to each other and solve! You'll quickly be left with the quadratic $x^2 - x - 2 = 0$. It's up to you to decide what approach to take to solve from there. I think the easiest one on this problem is factoring. You'll factor it to $(x - 2)(x + 1) = 0$, which means that $x = 2, -1$, and B is the answer.

14) C

Difference of squares again...this time in reverse. You can just FOIL these guys too—you'll get the same result. If you see the difference of squares thing, though, you'll know that the product has to be $3^2 - (2i)^2 = 9 - 4i^2 = 9 - 4(-1) = 13$.

15) A

And we are completing the square once more. Please see the work below:

$$y = x^2 - 2x + 3$$

$$y = x^2 - 2x + 1 + 3 - 1$$

$$y = (x - 1)^2 + 2$$

vertex: (1, 2)

16) 0

You can do this in a couple of ways. The first one is purely algebraic. Set the two equations equal to each other. You'll have $x^2 + 3 = x^2 - 3$. Subtract the x^2 from both sides, and you'll be left with $3 = -3$. How often is that true? Never. So there are zero ordered pairs that will make this statement true. The other way is to think about the graphs of these two guys. One is a parabola with its vertex at (0, 3). The other is an identically shaped parabola with its vertex at (0, -3). These are like parallel parabolas. They look the same, but they'll never intersect.

17) 0.8, $\frac{4}{5}$, $\frac{8}{10}$

Start with Pythagorean: the hypotenuse has to be 10. Then use your Soh-Cah-Toa know-how. We want the "opposite over the hypotenuse" here. That's $\frac{8}{10}$. Since that fraction fits on the grid, you can answer that. Or you can reduce it to $\frac{4}{5}$. Or you can grid it as a decimal, 0.8. Whatever floats your boat.

18) 7

Are you sick of quadratics yet? I hope not, because there are a ton more of them on the SAT. Move all the terms to one side of the equation, then pick your favorite approach for solving. I'd recommend factoring. $(x - 7)(x + 3) = 0$, $x = 7, -3$. We want the positive one, so $x = 7$.

19) 1

Ah, systems. The best approach on this one, I think, is to double the second equation, then add the equations together. You'll get that $-3x = 6$, and $x = -2$. Plug that back into either (or better yet, both) equations, and you'll find that $y = 1$.

20) 16

Turn this real world situation into a li'l equation. $60 = 4x - 4$. Solve for x, and you'll get $x = 16$.

SECTION 4: MATH - CALCULATOR

1) B

Sneaky little real world algebra question. The set-up is $\$215 + \$35x = \$355$. When you solve that, you get $x = 4$. Yay.

2) A

It's so nice when the SAT lets us write the equation but not have to solve it, right? The right answer here is A. Let's make sense of it: the x would represent the number of t-shirts priced at \$12.95. That means she sold $(10 - x)$ t-shirts at the \$15.99 price, because the total number of t-shirts sold was 10. When you multiply the number of shirts by their prices and add those values together, you'll get the total revenue, \$138.62. That's what A does, and that's why it's right.

3) C

Unit conversion problem. Read carefully to see that the total amount of ribbon is in YARDS and the ribbons are measured in FEET. Here's how you'd do it: 200 yards $\times \frac{3 \text{ feet}}{1 \text{ yard}} \times \frac{1 \text{ ribbon}}{2.5 \text{ feet}} = 240$ ribbons.

4) D

Cool question. It does not tell you to find an average, but that is what we want to do. The average number of defects in those 8 boxes was 4. If there are 4 defects per box, on average, then there should be $4 \times 150 = 600$ defects in total.

5) B

Got to know your interest formula on this bad boy. $A = P(1 + r)^t$. The value we DON'T know here is P, the amount invested. Plug in everything else and divide \$2,163.20 by $(1 + 0.04)^2$ and you'll find that the client invested \$2,000 to start.

6) C

More real world linear algebra. The "starting point" is the first column, which is 2.75 inches wide. Whatever's left after that will comprise the remaining 4 columns. So $4a + 2.75 = 5$ will give us our column width for the rest.

7) C

Wanna know the fastest way to find a median? Know which value you're trying to find. Here's what I mean: in a set of 25 terms, there is a middle one. Where is it? Well, if you subtract that term from the set and divide by 2, you'll realize that there need to be 12 terms that are bigger than the median and 12 that are smaller. That makes it the 13th term when you either count up from the bottom or down from the top. The 13th term here will be in the group that has 2 siblings.

8) C

Two ways to do it: use the point, the slope, and the point-slope formula $(y - y_1) = m(x - x_1)$, where $(x_1, y_1)$is the point you know and m is the slope. Find the equation and plug in the points to see which one is on the line. Or, start from the point you know and move three units right and two units down (or three units left and two units up) to find additional points on the line. Either approach will work; in this case, the second approach will work faster, because we'll land right on the point (9, 2).

9) B

Careful table reading. You only want to select from the sophomores, so that's 100 people in total. Of those, you want the Humanities majors, which is 40 people. Put $\frac{40}{100}$ and reduce to $\frac{2}{5}$ and you'll be so, so happy.

10) D

I recommend you use your calculator aggressively on these two questions (10 and 11). Graph the four equations. Set your window pretty big, so that x can range up to 2,000 (or even 30,000 for the next question) and y can range to at least \$2,000 too. Press trace, then start typing values. If a function does not give you the number you're expecting, or close to it, press up to jump to the next function. Keep trying till you find the best fit for all the data. That's D.

4

11) B
Same deal as question 10—use your calculator and set your window pretty big. You need the right answer to 10 to get 11 right, by the way, which is kind of cruel. When you plug 30,000 for x into answer choice D, you'll get the right answer of about $9,076.

12) D
We are on the calculator section, and we already have that bad boy handy since we just used it on 10 and 11, so why not use it again! Graph this thing, then trace, and type in the values in the answers. Where does it cross the x-axis? At -5, -1, and 2.

13) A
You don't have to DO any math here... you just have to realize that decay refers to something getting smaller or decreasing in quantity. For that to happen in an exponential equation, the thing you are multiplying by has to be less than 1. That's why it's A: because of the 0.375 that we're multiplying by.

14) D
One way to do this question would be to evaluate all the answer choices. The problem with that approach is that it requires you to essentially write four separate geometry proofs in your head. That's not the best use of your time, is it? I would draw the triangle and its reflection, then review the answers to see if any stand out based on what you see. Your new triangle HAS to be similar to the original, because it will have the exact same shape. Triangles with the same shape have the same angles and are therefore similar!

15) B
What's happening in this graph? As x gets bigger, the y-values are getting smaller... but they are staying positive. That means we need to multiply by something that makes them get smaller. Aha! That's a value that's less than 1. Answers A and B both include values between 0 and 1. Here, we want the one that does NOT include 0, because if b were zero, we would not get any positive values for y at all.

16) D
Fun with formulas. On this one, plug in 30mph for s and carefully simplify to find that $r = 300$ feet.

17) C
More fun with formulas...just using the other side this time. Plug in 400 for r, solve, simplify, and round, and you'll get that s is about 35mph.

18) C
Wordy question, simple procedure. JUST BE SURE TO CONVERT THE DIAMETER TO A RADIUS. I would say that mistake is the second-most common careless mistake on the SAT just behind dropping a negative sign. OK, the radius here is 7 yards. Plug that in for r, and plug 25 in for l. Use your calculator big time, and get that the surface area is about 704 sq. yards.

19) A
Dude, use your calculator. Either graph it to find the intercepts, or run a quadratic program. You can do the quadratic formula by hand if you like, but it's slower and less accurate and a lot less fun. Again, if you don't have a graphing calculator, why not? Get one on eBay—they are crazy cheap there. Anyway, the calculator will tell you that the answer is A.

20) B
Interesting practical question about an exponential function. The formula gives us prices in terms of "t years from now." If we want to go back in the past, we can just plug in a negative value. And if we want to calculate for 9 months ago, we've got to know how much of a year that is. $\frac{9\text{ months}}{12\text{ months}} = 0.75$ years. So -0.75 is the t value we want to use.

21) B
Crank this guy by hand by adding all the values together (in your calculator!) and then dividing by 12. Not too hard—just takes a little bit of patience.

22) A

Range...if you know what that means, you know how easy this question is. All we need to do is find the smallest value and subtract it from the biggest value. That's 105.9 – 65.9 = 40. Easy peasy.

23) B

No math...just interpretation of a set of statistical data. We do NOT know that no student is shorter than 51 inches. A girl shorter than that would be atypical but not an impossibility. We also do not have any information other than our cultural biases to compare the heights of the girls to the heights of the boys, so C and D are both out. Answer B is right. Technically, 95% of the students will be within two standard deviations of the mean. You don't NEED to know that, but it'll make you more confident in picking B if you do.

24) D

I would graph it. You may already know this one, but whether you do or not, your calculator can show you the answer. Make sure you're in degree mode (press "mode" at the top of the calculator to find out), graph it, and press "zoom" and "ZTrig" to have a pretty window. Then look for where the graph is going up! That'll be between $0 < x < 90$ and $270 < x < 360$.

25) B

Two ways to do this one: the first one is to think logically/algebraically—i.e., that the numerator and denominator can either both be positive or both be negative, and then trying to create one of those two conditions. The other way is to test values based on the answer choices. I'd recommend the latter option for most students. If the first one works for you, go for it! Otherwise, grab some numbers and try them. For instance, to test answer choice A, plug in $b = -2$ and $c = -1$. You should wind up with $\frac{3}{-1} = -3$. That's negative, so that's out! When you test out answers C and D, make sure to try several sets of values: both positive, both negative, and one of each. Certain sets of numbers WILL work, but others won't, and you need a set of values that will ALWAYS work. That's B.

26) A

This is called a piecewise function, and it's nobody's favorite thing in math. It's not hard, either—you just need to determine which part of the function you should be using. Here, it's the top part because the x-value we're investigating is -10, and that's less than -2. Plug -10 into the top function and you'll get $5(-10) - 1 = -51$.

27) C

This question really requires you to know what this box-and-whisker plot means. Once you do, the question is kind of easy, actually. The dots on the far left and far right represent the minimum and maximum values, respectively. The left edge of the "box" (the little rectangle) represents the first quartile value—the one at the 25th percentile. Likewise, the right edge is the third quartile, or the 75th percentile. The value in the middle is the median. OK! So which statement is not true? The stinker is C. The gap between \$17 and \$25 is the distance between the first quartile and the median. That is $\frac{1}{4}$ of the set. Since there are 64 items in the set, one quarter of them would equal about 16, not 32. C is false, and we're onto the next question.

28) A

When it comes to evaluating sets of solutions, I am a BIG fan of working from the answer choices. It just seems so much more efficient because the answer are all right there. Try these values out. You'll see quickly that only 6 will make this equation true.

29) B

Let's work backwards from answer B, the right answer. We find an average by adding ALL the terms then dividing by the number of terms. So far, Liam has scored $3 \times 88 = 264$ points. He's going to add a fourth as-yet-unknown score, x. Add the points he's scored plus his NEW score, then divide by the new number of tests, 4. That will hopefully get ol' Liam up to that 90 he so desperately needs.

30) D

My favorite approach to this is to use the discriminant—the part of the quadratic formula that's under the radical, $b^2 - 4ac$. When that value is positive, we have two real roots. When it's zero, we have one double root. When it's negative, we have two imaginary roots. Here $4^2 - (1)(2) = -4$, which means we have two imaginary roots.

31) 7.5, 15/2

You find the surface area of a cube like so: $6s^2$. That's because we have 6 identical faces on a cube, each of side length s. Set that equal to 337.5, divide by 6, take the square root, and you'll find that $s = 7.5$.

32) 31

More good ol' careful algebra. Start by subtracting 5 from both sides. Then divide by 3. THEN raise both sides to the 5th power using your calculator. Finally, subtract 1. $x = 31$.

33) $\frac{1}{36}$

There is a very specific (and kind of fun) way to find the fractional value of a repeating decimal. You set the decimal equal to x, then multiply it by a power of 10 to move the decimal place such that you can subtract the portion of the decimal that repeats. Then you do algebra and happiness is the result. Watch and learn:

$$\begin{aligned} .27\overline{7} &= 10x \\ -\ .02\overline{7} &= x \\ \hline .25 &= 9x \end{aligned}$$

$$x = \frac{.25}{9} = \boxed{\frac{1}{36}}$$

Also, this just in... out of curiosity, I just tried a hilariously sloppy approach to this problem and... it worked. Type 0.0277777777777777777 etc. into you calculator. If you type 7 ten or more times, then convert it to a faction ("math" ">FRAC" on TI calculators), the calculator will tell you that it's $\frac{1}{36}$. Hilarious.

34) 7.62

Either use the distance formula (which is not supplied, so if you need it, make SURE you know it) or use a distance program in your calculator. Either way, when you round CAREFULLY, you'll get a distance of 7.62. Yep, 7.61 is wrong. Just barely, but still wrong.

35) 448

Whenever some weird geometry thing pops up, make sure to check your page of Reference Information at the beginning of the section. Sure enough, the formula for the volume of a rectangular pyramid is included. It's $\frac{1}{3}lwh$. All you need to do is plug those three numbers into the formula. You'll get 448 cubic feet.

36) $\frac{1}{2}$, 0.5

Funny question...you may be thinking, "but they didn't give me any numbers!" Well, they didn't have to. Every inscribed angle (that's an angle in a circle with its vertex ON the circle) has a measure that is half the measure of the angle that it cuts. And that's the answer: $\frac{1}{2}$.

37) 220

There are some fancy ways to find the sum of a geometric sequence, including the formula that's given on the next question. I would personally recommend finding the values for these 9 days manually and then adding them. You have to do so carefully, but it does work. And you have that calculating machine there to help you! When you do, you'll find that Susie earned 10,220 cents via Choice Two. That's 220 cents bigger than Choice One (once you convert Choice One from 100 dollars into 10,000 cents).

38) 511

Don't worry about the fanciness of the equation here—all you need to do is drop the values you are using into the equation and report a number back. Our r value is 2, because she gets twice as much each day as the day before. Our n value is 9 because we are repeating the process 9 times (for the 9 days she gets her gift). When you plug those in, you'll find that the fraction in the parentheses equals exactly 511.

SAT Practice Test Approximate Score Curve

How to use this curve:

1) Count up the # of questions you answered correctly on Math (No Calculator PLUS Calculator Allowed), Reading, and Writing and Language. Those **three numbers** are your raw scores.

2) Find your raw score on the table to get your section scores. Your "Evidence-Based Reading and Writing" score is the sum of your Reading and Writing and Language scores.

Raw Score (# of correct answers)	Math Score	Reading Score	Writing and Language Score
58	800		
57	800		
56	790		
55	780		
54	760		
53	750		
52	740	400	
51	730	390	
50	720	390	
49	710	380	
48	700	370	
47	690	370	
46	680	360	
45	670	360	
44	660	350	400
43	650	340	390
42	640	330	380
41	630	330	370
40	620	320	360
39	610	320	350
38	610	310	340
37	600	310	340
36	590	300	330
35	580	300	320
34	570	290	320
33	570	290	310
32	560	280	310
31	550	280	300
30	540	270	290
29	530	270	290
28	530	260	280
27	520	260	280
26	510	250	270
25	510	240	260
24	500	240	260
23	490	230	250
22	480	230	250
21	470	220	240
20	460	220	230
19	450	210	230
18	440	210	220
17	430	200	210
16	420	200	200
15	400	190	200
14	390	180	190
13	380	180	180
12	360	170	180
11	350	170	170
10	340	160	160
9	320	150	160
8	310	150	150
7	290	140	140
6	280	130	130
5	260	120	120
4	250	110	110
3	230	100	110
2	220	100	100
1	210	100	100
0	200	100	100

Tutor Ted®

TED TALKS

A Note from Ted

If you got through these four practice tests, you are better at the SAT than you were before.

Here are some suggestions for how you can continue to improve!

1. Study the areas you want to strengthen.

   One great choice for SAT studying is our online course. It's just me teaching lessons directly to you. That's fun, right? Our online courses are at learn.tutorted.com.

   How about half off on those courses? Since you're already a Tutor Ted student, I made a 50% off coupon code you can use when you sign up. Just type the coupon code BOOKHALFOFF at checkout and you'll pay half the price. :)

2. Take more practice tests.

   The College Board has made some previously administered tests available at this link:

   https://collegereadiness.collegeboard.org/sat/practice/full-length-practice-tests
   (Man that's a long link.)

   I recommend printing your test and completing it on paper rather than on screen!

stay in touch with us! We love to hear from our students. You can find us in all of the usual places on the Internet, or you can email us at sayhello@tutorted.com.

I would say, "good luck," but you're not going to need luck.

TED

67420704R00172

Made in the USA
Columbia, SC
26 July 2019